UNDER FIRE

My Own Story

Captain Simon Hayward

With a foreword by John Gorst MP

W H ALLEN

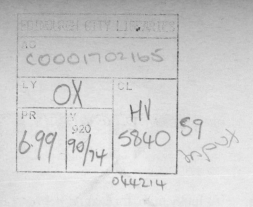
Copyright © Simon Hayward, 1989

Foreword copyright © John Gorst, 1989

Set in Times by Greenaway·Harrison Limited, London
Printed and bound in Great Britain by
Biddles Ltd, Guildford & King's Lynn
for the Publishers, W H Allen & Co Plc,
Sekforde House, 175/179 St John Street, London EC1V 4LL

ISBN   0 352 32588 7

Acknowledgements

I count myself a lucky man, for I could not have better friends. So many people helped me during 1987-1989 that it would be quite impossible to mention all their names. I cannot thank them all enough. So many people wrote to me, many of whom I had never met, that it was impossible to reply to them all. To those who did not receive acknowledgment I would like to take this opportunity to apologise. For all who wrote, my heart-felt thanks.

I would like to offer special thanks to: Sandra Agar, no one could have been a more loyal best friend; Rodney Agar, without whose sterling efforts much of the new evidence would never have come to light; John Gorst, for his tireless efforts on my behalf and for allowing me to use his exhaustive notes without which I would not have been able to complete this work; my brother Justin for his unquestioning support and loyalty; Brigadier James Emson, CBE; Sir David Napley; Christopher Murray; Tom Placht; Mrs Myrtle Matthews; Major General Sir Desmond Langley, KCVO, MBE; Colonel Tony Goodhew, MBE; Lt. Col. James Ellery; Colonel Andrew Parker Bowles, OBE; Major Simon Falkner; David Naylor-Leyland; Julian and Phyllis Earl; Gavin and Patricia Bell; Gwen von Steman; Larry Gilmurray; Christopher Shale; Roy Boulting.

And finally my love and thanks to my mother, who has had to endure more pain and suffering than any of us, who has been to me more than a mother, more than a friend, more than my most loyal support.

For my brother David

Life is eternal. Love is immortal.
Death is a horizon, and the horizon
is no more than the limit of our earthly sight.

Happy the man, and happy he alone,
He who can call today his own:
He who, secure within, can say,
Tomorrow do thy worst, for I have lived today.
Be fair or foul or rain or shine
The joys I have possessed, in spite of fate, are mine.
Not Heaven itself upon the past has power,
But what has been, has been, and I have had my hour.

John Dryden

Foreword

The proper administration of justice, without any favour or bias, is a prerequisite in a genuinely civilised society. One of the hallmarks of an unhealthy or tyrannical society is that its administration of the law is selective or non-existent.

When I became involved with the case of Captain Simon Hayward, I was appalled to find myself caught up not only in the anomalies of an unfamiliar judicial system, but also in the ethos of a state which placed political and bureaucratic expediency before respect for what we would describe as the inalienable rights of the individual, especially his right to a fair and unprejudiced trial.

Sweden is a country with a worldwide reputation for socially progressive legislation. On the social level, Swedish 'progress-iveness' is paternalistic. It is handed down from above and accepted without argument by a docile, conditioned, even grateful electorate. The Swedish people tolerate the edicts of their political masters because those edicts are presented to them in the seductive wrappings of social security and material prosperity. Swedes are so anaesthetised by affluence that they have become unquestioning about issues of personal freedom, liberty and dissent. Indeed, so far as the latter is concerned, serious dissent can sometimes be regarded as a form of social malady requiring enforced periods of correction in a psychia-tric institution until the condition has been remedied.

In arguing with Swedes against the treatment Simon had to endure, one of the noticeable features of their response was a reluctance to answer argument with argument. Invariably their reply, when it was not of complete silence, would be to denigrate the critic. This is behaviour that is all too familiar at the bottom end of the political world: when an opponent is on shaky ground, he attacks the man rather than the argument. But when such a negative ploy arises in a discussion on how justice is being administered, it does untold harm to the esteem in which that country is held abroad.

Criticism of the Swedish judicial system, and of their apathy about human rights issues, should not be taken as a censure on all Swedes. They are as capable of spontaneous acts of sympathetic kindness as the people of any other nation. And Simon pays tribute during the course of his book to many examples of exemplary kindness he received from individuals.

There is no reason why legal systems in different countries should all be the same. Obviously, there can be many perfectly legitimate ways of establishing the truth, and dispensing justice; but people in this country ought to ponder about the manner in which the 'enlightened' Swedes came to find Simon Hayward guilty.

In this book Simon gives an account of Swedish legal practices that may well surprise readers in this country, where we are accustomed to a judiciary that is totally separate from the executive. We are accustomed to juries determining matters of fact at a trial, not politically appointed 'assessors' acting as both judge and jury. We would find it a travesty of justice to give the prosecution the opportunity to denigrate an accused person through the media before his case has been tried, let alone to deny him a right of reply. Indeed, we would regard it as intolerable to hold him, in solitary confinement, and in complete ignorance of what was being alleged in the media.

After reading incomplete accounts of his trial in the press, people have wondered why Simon was not even slightly suspicious when he drove his brother's car in which cannabis had been hidden. When they have read his own account, I believe they will have a better perspective and may see things differently.

Inquiries into the ramifications of a case as that of Simon Hayward would have been complex and difficult for the police of any country. But for the police force of a European country with a population of only 8 million people, lacking in sophistication or experience, and not apparently endowed with a willingness to get to the bottom of an internationally organised crime, this offered too formidable a challenge. It was an undertaking that proved to be beyond them.

Bungled investigations into the assassination of their late Prime Minister had already demonstrated that at a national level they lacked both confidence and competence. Simon describes what he had to endure when a bigoted publicity-seeking provincial prosecutor, assisted by a far-from-scrupulous local police inspector, were faced with unravelling a criminal conspiracy that originated beyond their borders as well as their comprehension. What he describes of his own treatment is disturbing, but he describes his experiences with a commendable restraint and objectivity. His tone is all the more remarkable when one considers the extent to which his career and prospects now lie in ruins, and beyond mere financial compensation.

In addition to covering the events before his arrest, Simon describes the many weeks he spent in solitary confinement. He tells of the disorientating régime to which he was subjected. He explains that its purpose was to undermine his morale so that he would be unable to resist pressures to sign a confession which he knew to be false. He recounts how this process of demoralising him was deliberately reinforced by withholding his mail without explanation, and by capriciously denying visitors access to him.

All these actions clearly raised questions about Sweden not observing its obligations under the European Convention of Human Rights. However, comment on these matters has resulted in predictable protests. Sweden is a sovereign nation. These questions have nothing to do with foreigners. Swedes need no advice on how to conduct their internal affairs.

Unfortunately for Simon, the Swedes handled matters incorrectly even according to their own rules. So now, in order to clear his name, he has only one option. He has to appeal to the European Court of Human Rights, under Article 6 of the Convention, claiming that he did not receive a fair trial. This appeal, which he lodged in June 1988, is now being pursued separately from any retrial he can ask for under Swedish law on the basis of new evidence.

The procedures at Strasbourg, where the European Court has its headquarters, are laborious in the extreme. Redress can take years, and will certainly not be available until long after Simon has completed his sentence.

There ought to be a 'fast track' so that those who are in custody can be dealt with more promptly than those who are at liberty. On the basis of the most recent figures, that would only involve a small minority of appeals, hardly constituting an insurmountable administrative problem if the will to achieve such a reform was there. Unfortunately, the interests of some member governments, particularly those of this country and Sweden, take precedence over justice for the individual; but in the eyes of a Commission of Human Rights the priorities ought to be just the reverse.

Valuable as the European Convention may be in theory, and ultimately in practice as well, it is a serious flaw that its signatories starve the Commission of the funds and resources necessary for it to discharge its duties promptly. Ironically, there are occasions when the European Court has to reprimand member nations for delays in dispensing justice, even though the biggest offender of all is the European Court itself. In Simon's case, the delays at Strasbourg have added yet another wrong to several existing ones.

A major iniquity was perpetrated by the Swedish courts when the prosecution was allowed to lean heavily on very dubious evidence acquired from the United Kingdom. It was only possible to present this evidence which was hearsay on hearsay with the assistance of a Norwegian Interpol police inspector, the British police having declined to vouch for the truth and accuracy of the unverifiable police intelligence upon which the Norwegian's testimony was based. At least part of the blame for this must rest with the two Scotland Yard police officers working for the National Drugs Intelligence Unit. To this day, their conduct has never been officially explained or justified: all we have to go on is Simon's description of his encounters with them which is an understandable mixture of bewilderment and anger.

I have inquired into this episode in as much detail as an MP is ever allowed to go in matters of police work. Despite assurances given to me after extensive internal inquiries, I am still sceptical of the explanations I have been given by senior police officials.

What is clear, however, is that the Home Secretary shared at least some of my misgivings about the way in which these two police officers had conducted themselves in Sweden. In July 1987, he asked the Chief Inspector of Constabulary to consider what new guidance to Chief Officers might be necessary on the subject of providing information to foreign police forces. This June, two years later, he has told me that new advice, bearing directly on the issues which arose out of this case, had recently been issued in order to avoid difficulties in future.

A farcical absurdity during the Swedish court proceedings was the appearance of a Dutch lawyer representing an enigmatic Irishman, known in the Baghwan cult circles of Ibiza as 'Dook'. He had vanished very hurriedly from Ibiza on hearing of Simon's arrest. The prosecution afforded his lawyer the opportunity to plead his non-involvement without him being present in person, and on the bizarre grounds that they had to prove that he had nothing to do with the case.

Eighteen months later, at a trial in Stafford Crown Court, it transpired that this sinister character did have a close connection with the Ibiza-based drug traffickers and the Hayward case. Those proceedings clearly established just how misguided the Swedish authorities had been. Indeed, matters that came to light during that case are to form an important element in Hayward's plea for a retrial.

When the defence exercised their right to ask for a full investigation into events that had occurred outside Sweden, nothing was done and their protests were ignored for months on end. How the authorities, in the shape of Ulf Forsberg, the prosecutor, and Inspector Jan Bihlar, in charge of police investigations, could suppose they possessed the full facts, with no further inquiries being necessary, was never easy to understand. They had uncovered a crime whose origins were in a distant part of Europe. They were dealing with a foreign suspect whose pattern of behaviour they could not, and indeed never came to understand. The main prosecution witness – a Scotsman called Forbes Mitchell – was a leading, if not *the* leading member of the gang they had arrested. He and the consignment of cannabis had come from Ibiza.

Another leading figure in the smuggling conspiracy whom

the Swedish police not only avoided inviting to give evidence at the trial, but also declined even to question, was Mitchell's common-law wife, Prita. Having used a false British passport in order to get into Sweden, she was given clandestine access to Mitchell by the police, even though he was in solitary confinement. This unjustifiable irregularity was to lead to bitter defence complaints at the appeal stage of the proceedings. But it was no wonder once the authorities had been caught out, that they dissembled to their utmost. Their subterfuges were not only injudicious; they also made it difficult for the prosecutor to appear to be acting impartially. Connivance could not be passed off as an oversight. They had virtually had Prita in their custody and the only way they could explain their failure to interrogate her was to deny the truth.

At the trial, Inspector Bihlar asserted that he had never seen Prita; but under the pressure of cross-examination at the appeal a few weeks later, a very different story was to emerge. He admitted that he had in fact met Prita. To put it as mildly as possible, his economical use of the truth, together with his manipulation of other pieces of evidence to which Simon draws attention in various parts of the book, made one fact stick out a mile. As the prosecution could not rely on the unvarnished truth to secure a conviction, evidence had to be so manipulated that the borders between genuine fact and plausible fiction would become indistinguishable.

At the very least, the British people believe that the interests of justice are best served, on those occasions when there is insufficient evidence to convict a suspect, in giving him the benefit of the doubt. For evidence to be fabricated, or for inquiries into what really happened to be suppressed, is completely anathema to our concept of justice.

As he began to appreciate the lengths to which the authorities were prepared to go in order to obtain his conviction, Simon gives his readers a rare glimpse of bitterness bordering on despair as he began to lose hope of ever receiving a fair trial in Sweden.

The death in Ibiza of Simon's sister-in-law, Chantal, aroused no interest among the Swedish investigators. This seemed an astonishing attitude partly because her husband was Simon's elder brother, Christopher Hayward, for whose arrest a warrant had been issued through Interpol; but mainly because of the suspicious circumstances of her death. Before it occurred, threats had been made against her son to the effect that if Christopher spoke out in any way, harm would come to the boy.

The police indifference to this development was doubly surprising when Chantal's mysterious death was followed by her grave being tampered with after her funeral; but none of these events to which the defence attached considerable significance, were thought to be relevant by the prosecution. They undermined an already shaky case. The balanced, even-handed objectivity that the Swedish legal system is supposed to require from the prosecutor was nowhere in evidence.

By the time that Simon's trial and appeal were over, it might have been expected that the authorities would have been satisfied to let matters rest; but they were not. They turned their attentions to a self-confessed Indian drug smuggler. He had come forward with new evidence bearing on Simon's innocence; but the police were determined to silence him. This is another of the new items of evidence which Simon reveals in this book and which forms part of his justification for seeking a retrial.

The important question which is central to Simon's innocence is whether or not he knew drugs were hidden in the car he was driving. I have probed very widely into every aspect of this question, and I have satisfied myself that whoever *did* know that drugs were hidden in Christopher Hayward's Jaguar, Simon was not one of them.

When I first became involved, I had to start by convincing myself that the young Life Guards officer I had encountered on half a dozen occasions three years before his arrest, was indeed innocent. At the outset, I had only an instinctive feeling to go on: that drug smuggling was out of character. I didn't have the advantage of knowing any of his family or friends. All I knew for certain was that he wouldn't be represented by any other Member of Parliament, because he had no permanent residence in the United Kingdom. So I wrote to him in Sweden, offering to help.

In his reply, Simon put me in touch with his former commanding officer, Brigadier James Emson. I found that he was a reliable and perceptive judge of people. He had a direct and straightforward approach, and it was reinforced by an ability to offer shrewd, intuitive judgements which were based on considerable professional experience of interviewing soldiers. He convinced me he would not have been easily taken in or fooled. His opinion, having grilled Simon searchingly in the presence of the Swedish police, was that Simon had not knowingly smuggled drugs into Sweden.

So, a week later, I went to Sweden to satisfy myself that James Emson's judgement and my own gut-feeling were correct. In itself it was important to do so; but I went for two other reasons. I was disturbed by reports that Simon was being kept in solitary confinement in circumstances that were objectionable, regardless of whether they were in formal breach of the European Convention on Human Rights. Secondly, I had grounds also for suspecting that the true reason why the Swedes were holding Simon might be in order to flush out his brother, Christopher. It was my impression that the Swedish police had convinced themselves that Christopher Hayward was behind the smuggling, and that he might give himself up if they kept his brother as a 'hostage'. I had no means of knowing what, if any, part Christopher Hayward might have played in drug trafficking to Sweden. That was irrelevant. What mattered, and what went against the grain, was the idea that an innocent person might be in custody because the Swedes suspected someone else might have been the ringleader.

The possibility was outrageous; and, in fact, I said so briefly to the Prime Minister before I left for Sweden. Later, when I mentioned this to Simon in the presence of the British Consul and the police inspector in charge of the case, it was to lead to libellous allegations which achieved two positive results. The first was to show me, on a matter about which I knew precisely what the true facts were, the extent to which these particular Swedish authorities were willing to say publicly things that were false, and not be prepared to correct them when they knew the true facts. The other was that the newspaper damages I subsequently received paid all the expenses for every visit I later made to Simon's trial and appeal, as well as for two visits that I made to see him in prison in Malmö.

On these visits I had an opportunity to get to know Simon rather better. In the space of four days, I spent 20 hours discussing his case with him, and our talks reinforced my belief in the wrongness of the verdict at his trial. They also strengthened my resolve to help Simon clear his name.

I hope that in pursuit of that objective, this book will play an invaluable part. Meanwhile, however, there remain many questions to which there are still no answers. Where is Christopher Hayward and why did he disappear? In what way was he involved? What was the real part played by the 'Dook' and Mitchell in this whole affair? Why did the Swedes refuse to conduct proper investigations into all aspects of the case? Did they make a deal with Mitchell in order to 'pervert the course of justice'; and did they organise a cover-up to hide it? Was Simon given a fair trial, either as required by the European Convention on Human Rights, or by comparison with standards obtaining in the United Kingdom? And if not, why did the Ministry of Defence ask for his resignation? It was not in accordance with the requirements of Queen's Regulations, even though it may have been thought expedient by some individuals at the higher echelons of the general staff.

In the final analysis, the main questions are when and how Simon will be able to clear his name. It is said that the Swedes are sensitive to foreign opinion and criticism; that comment from abroad is more likely to affect the Swedish government than any campaign waged at home. If that is true, perhaps the publication of this book will act as a spur to the Swedes to give Simon a retrial and a belated vindication.

At the very least, I hope Simon's story will implant a widespread concern about his case here in the United Kingdom. He could never have been convicted in a British court on the false and flimsy evidence produced in Sweden. I have followed his ordeals from the very outset, right up to the present time, and I am convinced of one thing in particular. Justice has not been done. Nor has it been seen to have been done. When that happens, history reminds us that such an issue will not easily fade away: too many people all over the world get indignant about injustice, particularly in this country.

John Gorst
London
19 July 1989

One

'Can you tell me the way to the railway station, please?'

It was nine-thirty in the evening and I had arrived in Linköping, a small provincial town in Sweden, about 200 kilometres south of Stockholm. I was not due to meet Lokesh until ten. It was Friday 13 March 1987. Armed with directions, provided by a striking blonde who spoke good English, I set off to find the station. Five minutes later I was there. The car-park was almost full but I managed to find a space right at the back. I reversed the Jaguar in, switched off and surveyed my surroundings. Although it looked as though it had not snowed for some time, the ground was still quite thickly covered. It was bitterly cold outside.

The station itself was sandwiched between the tracks and a dual-carriageway. It was a two-storey, symmetrical, brick building with a black lead roof. Rather Gallic in style, not unlike a small French Chateau, with a clocktower over its central entrance. Newer single storey extensions had been built on either side, with the car-park off to the right as you approached.

There were a couple of other drivers sitting in their cars, obviously waiting for passengers to arrive. One was talking on a car telephone. Otherwise the place was as quiet as a churchyard.

I was pleased to have arrived. There had been a time when I had thought I would not make it. Three days from Ibiza to Sweden was not bad going but now I was tired, my back ached and I was looking forward to a good meal and bed. Tomorrow I would have another journey, this time by train to Stockholm and then on again to a ski resort. With luck I would get in three days skiing before having to catch a flight back to England.

There was about twenty minutes to go before Lokesh would arrive, if the man was punctual. I settled back to snooze for a few minutes, it would be good to get a few hours proper sleep. Last night had been spent in the car and even Jaguar seats were not conducive to real rest.

I could hear voices. Hell, it was cold. My feet were numb. I started the engine and turned the heater up full. The voices belonged to two teenagers who came chattering along from the station building and into a white Volvo station wagon. Its rear lights came on and I saw a belch of white condensation, exaggerated by the cold, come out from its exhaust pipe.

Good, they're leaving. I moved up to take the vacated place, again reversing in so that I would not miss Lokesh when he arrived. The driver with the telephone was still there and now I could see another man standing at the entrance of what must be a walkway direct onto the platforms. He was wearing a blue bobble woollen hat, glasses, and an orange coloured anorak. He had his hands pushed well down into his pockets and was stamping his feet against the cold. His breath making the customary white clouds. I settled back down into the seat, enjoying the warmth that was now gushing forth from the heater vents.

It was ten-ten. Still no sign of the bloody man. I would give him until half past ten at the latest. I had no intention of hanging around here all night. I would not be at all surprised if he did not appear, I was after all quite used to any plan of Christopher's going badly amiss. He was not the most organised and reliable of people. One needed no better example of this than the fact that here I was in Sweden, when I had left England three weeks previously to go sailing with him off Gibraltar. If the worst came to the worst I suppose I would have to try and get hold of him through Echo, or failing that I could just leave the car at this station, hide the keys somewhere and leave a message for Chris. I did not have the time to hang around and it was his car, and his problem. These thoughts were going lazily through my mind as I dozed fitfully, becoming increasingly impatient.

There was a knock at the window. I looked up, it was Lokesh. Good. I glanced at my watch, ten-twenty, not too bad. I touched a button and the electric window buzzed down.

'Hello.'

'Hi, sorry I'm late but my train from Stockholm was delayed. Have a good drive up?'

'Yes', I replied. 'No problems.' And as I reached across to the passenger door handle, 'Hop in.'

'No, no, I'm going with this guy, you will have to follow us.'

For the first time I noticed the man with the bubble hat loitering rather hesitantly behind Lokesh.

'It's only forty kilometres, but I see you don't have snow tyres so take it easy, the roads are very icy.'

'What is forty kilometres?'

'The house, my house where we are staying.'

'Yes but . . . 'I started to say, but already Lokesh was turning on his heel. With a final . . .

'Don't worry, follow on.'

Bloody Hell! What on earth was going on. I did not want to drive another forty damn kilometres, Chris had said the man lived in Linköping. And why had he arrived by train, and why this other chap, couldn't he have travelled with me? I had started to say that Lokesh could take the Jaguar immediately and I would stay in Linköping, but he was already climbing into an old orange Saab, which by coincidence was parked directly alongside. Well, in for a penny, in for a pound! I had come this far . . . Somebody had just better be prepared to drive me to a station first thing in the morning. It was to prove to be the worst decision of my life!

The Saab moved off and I pulled in behind it. There were traffic lights at the entrance to the station approach road, where it joined the dual-carriageway. The other car just made it, I was caught. I was not feeling in a good mood. I hoped the other chap has the sense to wait. The lights changed. I drove out onto the main road. Up ahead I could see the Saab waiting at the kerbside. That at least was something. Two other cars left the car-park behind me. Busy night.

I have driven extensively on the Continent and have often remarked on the fact that European drivers rarely decrease speed in snowy or icy conditions, being well used to them. The Saab driver, just like the Swiss, was no exception. He was an experienced driver tearing along and I was having difficulty keeping up. We drove along dual-carriageways and around numerous roundabouts. I got stuck behind more lights. The roads became narrower, darker and the street lamps were beginning to peter out. We passed through the normal type of continental suburbs and industrial estates. The traffic was next to non-existent, the occasional oncoming vehicle, and apart from about half a dozen cars directly behind me the road was clear. That was strange in itself. If this was Northern Ireland, where all soldiers are constantly briefed to check their tails, I would have started to become nervous about being followed. But this was not Ireland, it was Sweden and who would want to follow me here? Perhaps the train Lokesh arrived on was a busy one from Stockholm and the cars behind had also collected passengers? It must be that.

The car slid for a few metres. I was getting drowsy. I opened the window and fumbled with a cassette. The fresh air and music would keep me awake. Talking Heads, '*On the Road To Nowhere*' blasted out. I was later to remember this choice and think 'how apt!' For the moment, I just turned the volume down. I had not been paying attention. The Saab had disappeared. 'Blast!' I increased speed and flicked the arm to put the headlights onto high beam. Instead of more light the road ahead went totally black. Shit! I frantically played with the arm, flicking it back and forth. The lights came back on, this time on high beam.

Ah, I could see the Saab ahead. It was turning off to the right into a small side road. I followed suit. Bloody hell! The car behind me had also turned but in the process had almost overshot, sliding all over the place. I slowed to see if it would make it, yes, but only just. The idiot driving should be more careful. Again it looked as though he was following me, but that just could not be so.

The road now was narrow, dark and icy with many curves. I drove along at the best speed I could, which was not all that fast. The Saab was pulling away. I caught it intermittently about three or four bends ahead. Every time it was out of sight I flashed my lights to high beam to see better. The problem was that I was not always rewarded with a clearer view but sometimes with a wall of disconcerting blackness.

These moments saw me furiously flicking the switch to prevent myself from driving off the road into a ditch.

I was approaching a T-junction with another main road. Left to Motala, said the signpost, and right to a place called Zinkgruvan. Where had Lokesh gone? I wished he would slow down: it was alright for a local, but I did not know the roads. There he was, to the right, about three to four hundred metres ahead. The way clear I turned right as well. This surface was also extremely icy, the snow banked up on either side of it. Beyond I could just make out trees and open fields. Obviously a farming district. The road sloped upwards to a crossroads, beyond which I could see buildings. Perhaps we were getting close to journey's end.

One of the following cars overtook. Then another. They must have been waiting for a wider spot in which to pass. And I thought they might have been following me. Stupid!

What happened next was a complete blurr. Looking back I still cannot picture it totally clearly. As if looking through to the end of a long tunnel I saw the two cars that had passed me draw level with the Saab. One then pulled straight in front of it forcing it to a halt, while its companion blocked it in from the rear. I thought I saw a door open. I remember feeling shocked at the sight, perhaps nonplussed would be a better description. There was no time for any more.

A third car pulled alongside the Jaguar and then deliberately drove me off the road. Short of broadsiding him I had no option but to swerve over and stop. I did so: I had no reason to damage Chris's car by going onto the offensive. Another car screeched to a halt alongside me. Scenes of soldiers being murdered in Northern Ireland in just such ambushes now flashed through my mind, but again the realisation that this was friendly Sweden slowed me down. My assailants, whoever they were, did not look like policemen, an obvious possibility, so were they some kind of bandits or terrorists? I instinctively attempted to reverse out but before the car had travelled six inches it struck something solid. As I did so the man in the vehicle beside me had apoplexy, grabbing at something on the seat next to him. I turned to look over my shoulder, yet another car blocking off any chance of retreat. What ever it was, this was a fairly professional operation.

Figures, wearing jeans, bomber jackets – casual, almost scruffy clothes, came tumbling out from every door. No guns, that was something. In seconds the Jaguar was surrounded, one man tried my door handle. It was locked. I could hear rather than see the other doors being tried. I smiled up at a face peering in at me.

'What do you want. Who are you?' I asked as calmly as I could.

'Open this door,' was the reply in English.

'Not until you tell me who you are!'

'Unless you open the door, I will break in.' The man said producing what looked like a small truncheon.

There was little reason in arguing this point. They were going to get me one way or another. I unlocked and opened the door. Immediately hands grabbed me and pulled me from my seat. I started to fight back, clearing a space around me. A breathing space, no more.

'Who the hell are you? What do you want?'

'It's okay, It's okay. We are the Police.' One man shouted, raising both arms in a pacifying manner.

At last my assailants had identified themselves. The Police, well that was okay. I relaxed.

'We are going to search you and then put these handcuffs on you.'

Despite the gravity of the moment I was spun around and spreadeagled up against the side of the Jaguar. Hands were running all over me, searching. It was thorough. Then my arms were locked behind my back.

'Why are you doing this? You are making a mistake. What is this all about?' No reply. I was taken to the car that had forced me off the road and placed in the back. There was a man sitting behind the wheel. He looked me over but said nothing. There was a grip bag on the seat beside him, the constant chatter of a radio set came from within it.

By twisting around, difficult with your hands tied behind your back, I could make out other men rummaging through the Jaguar. All its doors were open, the scene silhouetted by the headlights of the car behind looked rather ethereal. After a few minutes the officer who had put the cuffs on me opened my door.

'We are taking you to a Police Station. One of my men will drive your car.' I was bewildered but I said nothing. There seemed little point. My driver spoke for the first time.

'Do you know why you have been arrested?'

'I have no idea. Suppose you tell me!'

'I have nothing to say to you. You will find out.'

'In that case I too have nothing to say. Not until I see a lawyer in any event,' I replied curtly.

He turned his back on me, staring fixedly out of the windscreen. The conversation was obviously at an end.

An engine started behind me. One of the assault cars accelerated forward, trying to obtain traction on the icy surface. It managed a wheel spin all the way up the incline to where the Saab was still being searched. Partly due to the ice, a great deal to do with its driver's exuberance. A real cowboy, I couldn't help thinking. Doors were being slammed. Final shouted instructions. Motors pulling away. The noises, muffled by the enclosed vehicle I was sitting in, added to the sense of unreality. We drove up to the crossroads where everyone was turning. I caught a glimpse of Lokesh in the back of another car. He looked pale and scared.

'Where are you taking me?'

No reply was forthcoming. I realised that no one had read me my rights. I had not even been shown any ID. I had forgotten to ask. I remember hoping that we were going to a Police Station. They could have been taking me anywhere! The drive was short and fast. With another car in front and the Jaguar behind. My driver was very obviously pleased with himself, and showing off to me in the way he handled his car. So be it. It did not matter to me, just so long as he did not crash. We went back past the T-junction taking the route to Motala. Soon we were passing built-up areas again. The cuffs were uncomfortable, biting into my wrists. They had been put on too tight. The passing scenery was of little interest to me. I tried to analyse my feelings. I was not scared; perhaps apprehensive. After all it was not every day that one was arrested, especially not in an ambush, but I was being cushioned by a detached sense of unreality. I knew that there was nothing to worry about, I had not committed any offence. The mistake would soon be sorted out. Best to stay calm, be polite and explain the situation as soon as I was given the chance. The driver got lost, we had to turn and retrace our steps.

We arrived at a Police Station. I felt safe at last. Down a ramp and parked beside a wall. I was taken out and frog-marched through a door into what was easily recognizable as a reception area. Well lit and spartan. White walls and blue linoleum floor. About ten foot square. Two walls covered in small lockers, presumably for the possessions of anyone arrested. There was a bench and a desk complete with typewriter. A corridor led off from one corner.

I was met by an elderly Police Sergeant, the first uniform I had seen. He had a flabby belly, hair greying, and was about fifty. The cuffs were removed. A stab of pain as circulation was restored. I massaged my wrists, thankful to be able to move my arms again.

'Take your jacket off. Sit down, I want your shoes.'

All this in Swedish. I did not understand a word. I shrugged my shoulders and did nothing. My 'driver' was still with me and at this moment more plain-clothes men came clattering through the door. The sergeant repeated his demand, this time louder and with added menace.

'I do not understand what this man wants me to do.'

More excitable babbling in Swedish, and four faces turned towards me.

'Take your jacket off!' This time in heavily accented English. I did as I was told, handing it to the fat sergeant.

'Sit down. Give me your shoes. Now your watch. Now the belt. Empty your pockets. Come with me!'

I was escorted down the corridor by all four of them. They weren't taking any chances. More white walls and lino floor. We turned a corner. The corridor went on for another thirty metres or so, except now there were rows of metal doors, each with a small inspection hatch at eye level. The cells. The first on the left was opened, I was ushered inside. I expected to be left alone but the three plain-clothes men entered behind me, the sergeant waiting outside, looking in. A look of anticipation on his face. My immediate thought was that they were going to give me a hiding. I prepared myself, clenching my fists. I would get one or two good blows in. All I could hope for against such odds and in such a confined space.

'Take off your clothes.' It was not what I expected.

'What?'

'Take off your clothes. We are going to search you. STRIP!'

I had no option but to obey. I stripped. Handing each of them a piece of clothing as I took it off. They checked thoroughly, running their hands along the seams, turning each item inside out, before dropping it onto the floor. I noticed that they were all wearing surgical gloves, although I had not seen them put them on. Soon enough I was standing naked in front of them. I should have felt self-concious but I didn't. Instead I was getting angry.

'Look, what is this all about?' I shouted.

'Turn around!'

'What?'

'Turn around, NOW!'

I turned around. I stood with my hands on my hips, my back towards them. If I was ordered to bend over they were going to have a fight on their hands. No one, but no one was going to stick their fingers up my bum! If they wanted to conduct an intimate search they would have to get a bloody doctor!

'Good. Right around.' At least that danger was over.

I turned back to face them. They told me to get dressed and left. The cell door clanged shut behind them. I was alone. My new, and hopefully temporary home was pretty nondescript. It was about six foot by ten. Off-white walls, covered in graffiti, the same blue floor. I could just touch the ceiling with the tips of my fingers. There were sturdy pine fittings. A bunk complete with green plastic mattress, a desk and stool. Nothing was moveable, presumably to prevent detainees from using them as weapons. The only light came from a square fitment on the ceiling – there was no corresponding switch on the walls. I was already losing control of even the smallest things. The only switches anywhere were those on what looked like an intercom system. I pushed away. No reply. So much for that. There was a window but it was, of course, heavily barred, with a blind in between the panes of double glazing. Closed, and again no controls.

A thin blanket was folded on the bunk. Fully clothed I lay down and pulled it over me. I suppose I was in a state of shock, confused, bewildered. It had been eleven-thirty when we had arrived at the Police Station and in just over an hour so much had happened. An hour ago I had been free, my own master, and now here I was in a grubby cell. I had no idea why I had been arrested and no one seemed willing to tell me.

As hard as I tried I could come up with no logical explanation for these recent events. There seemed little point in agonizing over them. I would be sure to find out soon enough. I dozed off to sleep.

The sound of keys rattling in the door woke me up. It was the fat sergeant.

'You want know why you arrested?' he asked me in very broken English.

'Yes, I damn well do!'

He gave me a long hard look. Then he smiled, almost a sneer.

'Drugs!'

Two

I was born on 1 August 1955 in Cambridgeshire. At the time my father was in the Royal Air Force. As a teenager he had flown on Bombers in the final stages of the Second World War and due to his love of flying had decided to remain in the Services when hostilities ceased. By the mid-fifties however, he had made up his mind that enough was enough, and resigning his Commission he took a job flying with the fledgling Middle East Airlines.

Consequently, in 1957, the family found itself living in Beirut, the capital of Lebanon, and at that time described as the 'Pearl of the Middle East'. A far cry from the sad war torn city of today.

I was to be the third of five children. Christopher, the eldest, is my senior by five years. He will feature frequently in this tale. Judith, my only sister, is three years older than I, Justin (who has no connection with the pop star of the same name) was born in 1958 and David in 1964. We were to remain in the Middle East, living in Lebanon and Persia, until 1972 when my father died and my mother took the family back to live in London. After an initial two years in Lebanon we moved temporarily to Persia, my father then flying for Iran Airways, before once again returning to Beirut.

I have very few memories of that early period. The arrival of a new baby brother, Justin; he was to become my constant companion through many childhood adventures. Our hurried evacuation in 1958 when religious tensions rose to fever pitch in Lebanon was another. I remember bidding a tearful farewell to my Palestinian nanny, Marmi, leaving her crying on our doorstep (we were unable to take her with us) as we raced for the airport where my father flew us and other expatriate

21

families to London. As a three-year-old I did not understand what was going on, but I do recall complaining bitterly and loudly because the normal hostess did not put in an appearance dispensing sweets to prevent my ears from popping. There had been no time for the usual provisioning before take-off.

When we returned home Marmi was still there, waiting on the doorstep. I naturally enough was convinced that my nanny had loyally remained at her post throughout the period we had been away.

Persia was picturesque if rather chaotic. The country was then quite backward, a long way from the highly modern State it was to become in the seventies under the Shah, using its oil wealth. We lived in a house on the outskirts of Tehran, its large walled garden becoming my little world and sanctuary. There was always something new to explore, something exciting to do within it. From the garden gate I was able to watch in wonder as camel trains slowly plodded past, with much rattling of tinny bells and squeaky shrills from bandy legged urchins. They always left in their wake a distinctive pungent smell that hung in the air long after they had disappeared. They had emerged, at least in my own infantile imagination, from some distant desert. By contrast, silhouetted behind the house were high mountains capped in snow. What better playground for a five-year-old?

Of the second stay in Lebanon I have vivid memories. They were good, happy, carefree days. There can have been few better places in which to grow up. In winter one could ski in the Cedar Mountains during the morning and be waterskiing in the Mediterranean that same afernoon. Justin and I spent many a fine hour playing golf or swimming or exploring the hidden secrets of the ancient Capital. We were always safe, whether in the old Souks near the port or in amongst the modern buildings of West Beirut. The Lebanese had a natural hospitality and affection, especially towards children.

My *Curriculum Vitae* states that I was educated at Wellington College and The Royal Military Academy, Sandhurst. There were of course other schools. My nurseries and kindergartens were local British institutions set up for the expatriate communities. I state the plural because I attended several as we moved around. French schools in Beirut were renowned as being the best, so at the age of ten I was packed off to the Lycée Français du Liban. The experiment however was not a success. In a year I learnt practically no French and my circle of fellow ten-year-olds a good deal of English. I was therefore looked upon by the haughty French as being a thoroughly disruptive influence, and expelled. My parents then had little choice but to decide that it was high time to send me home to boarding school.

I had been to a Prep School called Fonthill for one term when eight years old, during the brief period when my father was based in England between leaving Iran and returning to Lebanon. On this occasion however, in 1966, Eagle House, a small Surrey school of just over one hundred boys was chosen because it was only a mile down the road from Wellington where I was due to go when I was thirteen, and where Christopher was already completing his education.

On the whole I greatly enjoyed Eagle House, acquitting myself passably on the academic front and playing 1st XV Rugby for the school. In the Michaelmas term of 1968 I passed my common entrance exam and in the following Lent made the one mile trip to my new Public School. I'm afraid that I cannot in all honesty say that I enjoyed Wellington. In retrospect I often wonder why I never ran away. Perhaps it was the inbuilt sense of self-discipline that all such establishments instil in a boy, though my reaction was definitely not the school's fault.

Wellington was, and I am sure still is, a fine school with all the facilities one could hope for. It was only that after the freedom of Beirut I felt caged and restless, and I could not wait for my 'A' levels and freedom. (At least freedom is what I thought, with no experience of the big wide World, was waiting for me.)

My initial problem was not one of my own making. It was having to follow in my big brother Christopher's footsteps and live down his reputation. We overlapped by one term. He was an intelligent but highly lazy pupil and after his 'O' levels had become the school rebel and consequently a thorn in the side of most of the Senior Common Room.

When a second Hayward arrived on the scene I was naturally tarred with the same brush. It was a stigma that was to prove difficult to repudiate, especially since my own record was not to be without blemish. My Housemaster, a northerner called David Spawforth, did his best for me, even trying on numerous occasions to make me one of his prefects. He was only to succeed in my final half-term since I would invariably go and do something stupid just at the critical moment, making any such promotion impossible. Indeed I was lucky on one occasion not to be expelled. It was to have been my final coup: a simulated 'assassination' of the Headboy with an airgun – although to describe my plot in such dramatic terms is an exaggeration.

Boys' Houses at Wellington are divided into those situated in the main College building, really more like dormitories, and those more independently spread out amongst the extensive grounds. They are all named after the Iron Duke's Commanders, for instance Blucher, Hardinge, Benson, Picton, Combermere and Murray. The main building is designed around a number of quadrangles, known as Quads, with classrooms at ground level and Houses on the upper floors. My own House was the Murray. Rows of windows, each representing a boy's study, faced each other across these Quads. My plan was to identify my victim's window, which by chance almost faced my own, and then to 'scare the living daylights out of him'.

Two things went wrong. First, I had bargained on the window panes being strong enough to deflect my shots, so ensuring that no lasting damage was to be done. Instead the glass in question was probably generations old and shattered on impact, only adding a fairly lethal shrapnel effect. Second, I chose the wrong window, and targeted two young day boys busy doing their prep, and not my intended 'enemy'. The effect of my fire made them dive for cover under their desks and squeal for help. I was onto the third round when Spawforth came bursting in, having been alerted to the problem by a nervous and highly irate colleague.

As I have said I was not expelled, although how I escaped that fate is beyond me, it was probably by the skin of my teeth. Canings at Wellington were conducted only by the headmaster, known simply as the Master. The then incumbent was a strict disciplinarian although kindly man called Frank Fisher. I was extremely saddened to read of his death recently. Kind he may have been but he knew his stuff when it came to handing out a well deserved beating to an errant teenager.

My father died of cancer on 27 May 1972, during my last eighteen months at Wellington. Like so many he fought the disease every inch of the way with great courage and fortitude, undergoing numerous major operations, but the eventual outcome was inevitable. The problem was one of late diagnosis, the doctor he originally went to in 1969 telling him that the bleeding was merely a bad case of piles, something many pilots suffer from. By the time a London clinic had correctly diagnosed cancer it was too late. The disease had spread.

Watching a man gradually wither away over a three-year period is a painful and harrowing experience, especially when that man is your father. I never truly believed that he would die. Even in early 1972, when he was too weak to climb stairs and spent increasingly long periods in hospital, he was still telling me that he was going to beat the cancer and make a full recovery. It was not to be.

The pain of his death was indescribable, perhaps especially to a sixteen-year-old who relied heavily on the guidance only a fine father could give. Such a loss creates a kind of void, a dark, empty hole that can never be filled. Time, thank God, is a healer and one learns to endure and carry on with life, but the void remains. I still think of him.

My father had not been a rich man but he could have been described as comfortably well off. As children we had wanted for nothing, growing up accustomed to large airy homes, with servants to look after us. However, after his death my mother was not left as secure as she should have been. Bad investments along with enormous hospital fees saw to that. As a consequence, 1973 found the family on fairly hard times.

Adversity, it is said, brings out the best in a person, and she rose to the occasion and showed a strength of character that perhaps became more publicly evident during 1987. No personal accolade of mine would be tribute enough. Finding herself alone in the world with three children to educate she set to work with a will. In London she founded a small estate agency with an American friend that has flourished to this day. Through sheer hard work and diligence she provided a secure home, financial stability and a loving environment. No mean feat and one that her children selfishly did not properly appreciate at the time. She succeeded where many would have given up and failed. I look upon her not only as my mother but a very dear friend.

Wellington College is often described as a military school. It may have been once but I would not have described it as such in my day, or indeed now. It had, maybe even still has, a large Combined Cadet Force (CCF) which all boys were obliged to join, but so do most Public Schools.

As to my own record in the CCF, I rose to the dizzy heights of 'L/Cpl storeman', and when I left Wellington in the summer of 1973 it had never crossed my mind to join the Army. Indeed I can safely say that it was the furthest thing from my mind. I was looking forward to a year off, in which I would travel the world, before setting my mind to a long term career. I had already decided not to go to University. My mother had other ideas. She had seen one son hit the 'Hippy Trail' and was not about to see another go the same way. I was given an ultimatum: 'Choose a career and start on it immediately, or leave home for good.' I was not about to risk calling her bluff (if indeed it was a bluff) so I chose the former option.

Two openings were arranged for me. One with Lloyds, the other with Knight, Frank and Rutley, the London based property company. I settled for the latter thinking that selling houses would at least get me out of the office, and it had the second advantage of preparing me to take over from my mother in the family firm one day. I loathed it. I was treated little better than an office boy, doing the most menial tasks, and to add insult to injury my salary was insufficient to qualify for income tax.

I stuck it out for six months. There had to be more to life.

My salvation came quite by chance. I was invited to a 1973 New Year's Eve party given by an old school friend called Charlie Grant. He was a year older than me and had recently been commissioned into a cavalry regiment, The 16/5

Lancers. He told me that he was thoroughly enjoying himself and was just about to start training as a helicopter pilot on secondment to the Army Air Corps. When I compared my lot to his, he won on every score. I made up my mind then and there to follow his example.

To begin with I made discreet inquiries, filling out what seemed like an endless stream of application forms. The first my family knew of my plans was when I came home one day with the shortest haircut I had had since before leaving Prep. School. My mother was visibly shocked by my sudden decision but I believe secretly pleased and gave me her blessing. One of the forms to be filled in by all prospective candidates seeking commissions in the Army requires that three choices of Regiment are listed in order of priority. Mine were the Army Air Corps, because I wanted to fly, the Household Cavalry because we lived close to their barracks in Knightsbridge and they came to mind, and finally the 16/5 Lancers in homage to Charlie.

My first real contact with the system was an interview at Horse Guards in early February 1974 with a Colonel Lefeuvre, retired officer working in the schools liaison branch. I can remember absolutely nothing about him except that his office was tucked away in the depths of Horse Guards, well away from the machinations of The Household Division and Regular Army. He asked me the type of question that was to become all too familiar.

'Why do you want to join the Army?'

'What school did you go to?'

'What did your father do for a living?' And so on and so forth. Then came the crux of the matter.

'I see you have put down the Household Cavalry as your second choice of Regiment. Well they won't like that you know, they won't like that at all. We will have to change it, won't we?' He looked up at me in an almost menacing sort of way.

'But I want to fly helicopters: that is why I have named the Army Air Corps as my first choice. That is my first reason for wishing to join the Army.'

'Well yes my boy, I quite understand that. Let's see now. Why not join the Household Cavalry, I have an interview arranged with them in a few minutes by the way, and subsequently apply for a secondment to the Air Corps. Much better to be a member of a proper Regiment.'

I acceded, it seemed like a good idea. It was after all what Charlie was doing, and in any case who was I to argue with a Colonel? He appeared pleased with my decision and took me along corridors, upstairs and downstairs until, having lost all sense of direction, we arrived at the Offices of Regimental Headquarters Household Cavalry. I was to be seen by something called the Silver Stick.

I was to learn later that the Household Cavalry comprises three Regiments. The Life Guards, The Blues and Royals, and The Mounted Regiment (well known to tourists in London who watch them mount guard on their fine black horses). Each of these Regiments is commanded by a lieutenant colonel but with a full colonel sitting in overall command based at a small Headquarters in Horse Guards. To make matters even more confusing this man, albeit a full colonel, is known as the Lieutenant Colonel Commanding. On ceremonial occasions he carries a silver topped stick, hence the title 'Silver Stick'.

The Silver Stick in February 1974 was Colonel Desmond Langley. I was to be his ADC seven years later when he became The Major General Commanding The Household Division. On this day he, and his Regimental Adjutant Major Trevor Morris, probed me with the same questions as Lefeuvre, before finally inviting me to lunch at Knightsbridge. It was an enjoyable occasion and when back in his office that afternoon Colonel Langley offered me a Short Service Commission in The Life Guards; I readily accepted. It was only made subject to my first passing a potential officers' course known as the Brigade Squad, held at the Guards' Depot in Pirbright; being accepted by the Regular Commissions Board; and finally successfully attending the Royal Military Academy Sandhurst. It was apparent that I was only on the first rung of a very long ladder. None the less it was with a light step that I left Horse Guards that day.

March and April passed all too quickly. I resigned from Knight, Frank and Rutley and took myself off on holiday. When I arrived at the Guards' Depot in May no one could have been less prepared for what was to come in the next seven weeks than me. I reported to the Guardroom at nine o'clock in the morning carrying a large and heavy suitcase containing all the things I thought I was going to need, but of course did not. Leaving it outside, I entered. My first impression was of the floor; it shone like a mirrored glass with the deepest shine I have ever seen. My second was of a sergeant dressed in an immaculate khaki uniform, the creases in the arms of his tunic looked as though they would have cut newly baked bread, sitting stiffly behind a desk. The shine on his boots matched that of the floor. I approached him across its gleaming surface. At that time I had no fear of sergeants, an omission that was very quickly rectified.

'Excuse me, I'm on the Brigade Squad, I was told to report here for directions. Can you help? Where do I go?'

He continued to stare at me, as if in shock, his face going a strange puce colour. The seconds ticked by. I was beginning to wonder if he had heard me. I cleared my throat, and made to ask once more. His chest suddenly expanded at an alarming rate, as he sucked in a rasping breath.

'Get off my bloody floor!' he bellowed at me. 'Get out! Get out! GET OUT!' I did not have to walk out! I was literally blown from the room by the explosion of his voice. I shot out into the sunlight. He followed quickly on my footsteps.

'You never walk on my floor again,' he roared at me. 'That is lesson number one. DO YOU HEAR?'

'Yes,' I replied somewhat tentatively.

'Yes, Sergeant! Stand to attention! You can stand to attention, CAN'T YOU? You little pillock!'

I stood to attention, as I had been taught in my CCF days. It did not appear to satisfy this monster.

'Oh God, where do they get them from?' He muttered under his breath. A mutter that you could have heard a mile away.

'So you're on the Brigade Squad, are you? Well you just wait there sonny until I get someone to see you. And STAND UP BLOODY STRAIGHT! YOU'RE LEANING OVER LIKE THE TOWER OF BLEEDING PISA. STRAIGHT, DAMN YOU. STRAIGHT!'

He called for a corporal who seemed to materialise from the woodwork and ordered him to march me to my correct destination. I was instructed to pick up my suitcase, and if I had entertained any ideas of taking a leisurely amble to my new home I was to be very disappointed. Suitcase and all I was 'doubled' (military term for run) to it. By the time my escort and I had arrived I was exhausted, and the course had not even begun.

It was an initiation that was to set the standard for the next seven weeks. There were twenty young men in the Squad, all hoping to win a place in one of the Regiments in the Household Division. We were shouted at, cajoled, persuaded and otherwise given orders we could not refuse. I had had what I considered to be an especially short haircut before reporting; it did not matter. We were all given Guards' Depot standard cuts once a week, whether we needed one or not. The first left me with little more than bristle, so you can imagine what I looked like after seven. Our feet hardly touched the ground from the first moment onwards. There was no free time and precious little sleep. The course timetable consisted of: Drill, drill and more drill. Always more drill: Cleaning periods, where we were taught to polish every item of our equipment until it gleamed, especially our heavy, leather-soled ammunition boots; PT, including murderous long races up sheer-sided sand hills; forced marches in full battle order; an assault course that would have made the Royal Marines blanch; weapon training and range periods; even more drill; something called a March and Shoot, which combined a five-mile run in full battle order, the assault course, followed immediately by a platoon shoot on the ranges (points being won on timings and shooting scores). The penultimate test was a week's exercise on the Thetford Training Area.

Seven weeks may not sound long, so let me assure you it was long enough. It was a hard course. It was designed to be. Throughout, every man was assessed, every weakness, every strong point carefully logged. It turned schoolboys into men. I am certain there is no better preparation for the Regular Commissions Board and Sandhurst. In seven weeks potential officers complete the same basic training as a guardsman receives in twenty-nine.

The ultimate test was the Commandant's Inspection, which entailed a march and shoot followed by a drill parade. Once this final hurdle was over the course dispersed, with each man being given a date on which to report to the Regular Commissions Board at Westbury near Salisbury Plain. Mine was immediate, so I drove directly there from Pirbright. The RCB consists of three days of interviews and aptitude and intelligence tests. Candidates are also required to take an active part in discussion periods, give lectures and complete an intricate mini-assault cum assault course. The aptitude test takes the form of command tasks where one man is placed in temporary charge of a team of six, given two lengths of mouldy old rope, a short plank, a broken ladder and an impossibly heavy oil drum, and told to get all men and pieces of equipment across a twenty-five foot ditch (filled with imaginary crocodiles) in four minutes flat and without falling in. The team leader's plans, orders, attitude to his fellow candidates and overall reaction are carefully monitored. On arrival candidates are each given a numbered bib to wear, so the panel would be judging numbers not names, and then split into teams of approximately twelve. Each team is warned that one of its number will be interviewed by the Commanding Officer.

'If you are chosen don't worry and above all don't read anything into it.' I was chosen, I did worry, and I did read the very worst into it. I had been of the belief that I had done reasonably well on every test to date, but as I mentally prepared myself for the oncoming confrontation I reckoned my chances of ever becoming an Army officer had reached rock bottom, especially when I was told, in the subsequent interview, that as a trained Guardsman I had not achieved as many points as might reasonably be expected on the assault course. This was due to getting an ammunition box full of concrete stuck in one of the obstacles. Retrieving it wasted valuable seconds. I need not have worried: the rigours of the Brigade Squad had prepared me well. To my delight I passed. The next step after RCB was Sandhurst. I was told to report there the following September.

The Royal Military Academy Sandhurst used to be run along similar grounds to a university, though with an obvious military slant. Those cadets going for Short Service Commissions went to Mons College in Aldershot. Two years before I was to win a place the curriculum changed. All Officer

Cadets, whether aspiring for Regular or Short Service Commissions would now attend a six-month Standard Military Course at New College in Sandhurst. Mons was closed down. Those successfully completing the SMC and who wanted and had been chosen for Regular Commissions stayed on for a further six months at Old College, to study the more theoretical aspects of military life.

The six month's SMC was intense, though the first month's being along similar lines to the Brigade Squad made life for those who had attended it easy. The remaining five were designed not only as basic training for officer cadets but also to provide each of us with a framework on which to build experience. It was a damned hard six months but overall I thoroughly enjoyed myself, making several lifelong friends. However, I cannot pretend to have passed out with flying colours. In fact as I marched up those famous stone steps in the centre of the Old College Building in March 1975 at the finale of the Sovereign's Parade, marking the ritual commissioning of all successful cadets, following in the footsteps of some of the most famous names in British history I counted myself lucky to be there at all. I knew I was passing out near the bottom of the list. In direct contrast, strangely enough, I was six months later to win first place on my Young Officers Specialist to Arm Course at the Royal Armoured Corps Centre at Bovingdon. Perhaps armoured cars and tanks appealed to me more than did infantry work, which had formed the basis of the SMC at Sandhurst.

I was commissioned into The Life Guards on 7 March 1975. However, before that date and final acceptance I had to pass one last interview. It was to be with Earl Mountbatten of Burma. All Regiments and Corps have Honorary Colonels, usually referred to simply as 'The Colonel'. In 1975 and until his brutal and cowardly murder by the IRA in 1979, Lord Mountbatten was Colonel of The Life Guards and as such had the final word in the acceptance of any new officer. Known to all Life Guards Officers as Colonel Dickie, he lived while in London in a house in Wilton Crescent. I arrived there five minutes before the appointed time and waited hesitantly around the nearest corner. I was about to meet somebody who was a legend in his own time, not to mention one of my lifelong heroes. A man who had fought at the Battle of Jutland as a young boy; who had led a distinguished naval career, having his destroyer *HMS Kelly* literally sunk from beneath his feet in WWII; who had been Supreme Allied Commander in the Far East during the latter stages of the war against the Japanese; and had been the last Viceroy of India leading that great Continent to independence in 1947, to mention but a few of his feats. I was at last to meet him face to face for a private discussion, an opportunity I had never dreamt of. Exactly on schedule I knocked on his front door.

I need not have worried. This great man put me immediately at ease. He was charming and I hardly said a word throughout the half hour we spent together. He did all the talking after asking me one or two of the usual type of questions. He spoke with great affection about The Life Guards, and told me I was lucky to have been accepted by such a wonderful Regiment. He spoke of himself and a few of his experiences as a military man. I sat and listened spellbound. Finally he concluded the interview by telling me that if I turned out to be half as good as his great nephew, The Prince of Wales, then I would make a very fine soldier indeed.

I count it as a very rare privilege to have met Lord Mountbatten. Few men can have led such a varied and fulfilling life. He certainly lived it to the full and in so doing achieved much for his country.

He was, of course, by the time I joined The Life Guards, by no means a young man. He was incredibly strong for his age – indeed he was fit enough to take the Salute, just a few months before his murder, at the Final Rehearsal for the 1979 Queen's Birthday Parade. To do so he had to remain mounted for well over two hours wearing full State Uniform including the heavy helmet and cuirasses, an order of dress that many men less than half his age find exhaustingly uncomfortable.

I joined my Regiment for the first time in West Germany, three weeks after leaving Sandhurst. It was April Fool's Day 1975, a fact that has quietly amused me ever since. Military life is multifarious, unpredictable, diverse, and at times extremely exciting. That has been its great appeal to me, as I'm sure to many others. It certainly could not have been a greater contrast to the existence that Knight, Frank and Rutley offered me. I could not have enjoyed the twelve years leading up to Friday 13 March more.

My father once said to me that he counted himself as being amongst the luckiest men in the world because his career was his hobby. I too would put myself in that category. Being a member of a Regiment is often described as having a second family. The Life Guards has certainly been that to me. Like any family a Regiment expects allegiance but it also returns such qualities in kind, and I am reaping those benefits now when it would have been far easier for The Life Guards to have turned its back on me. The Regimental system is second to none when it comes to taking care of its members.

There can be few other occupations that offer young men such early responsibility. Being placed in charge of, and with full responsibility for, a platoon or troop of soldiers (often very down to earth soldiers) certainly ensures that young officers, many of whom are still teenagers, grow up and mature quickly.

In 1981, when I was ADC to General Desmond Langley, the Household Division Brigade Major summed up to me one morning what I believe all career soldiers must feel. He had just returned to work at Horse Guards after two years abroad. He lived near Sunningdale and commuted to work each day.

'You know Simon,' he told me, 'during the past two years I have been stationed in Hong Kong and I've travelled throughout the Far East. I've seen some incredible sights and done some amazing things. On the station platform this morning I recognised the same faces that I last saw all those months ago; those people must have been catching the same train each morning, day in, day out since then. God, what an existence!'

He could not have been more right. One may never become rich in the Forces: of course one's financial prospects cannot be compared to those of a contemporary working in the business sector, perhaps even one taking the same train as Colonel Heywood each morning; but money is by no means everything.

Despite the 'End of the Empire' and the consequential decrease in Great Britain's overseas commitments, there is still good scope for foreign postings and travel in the Armed Forces. British soldiers are still to be found all over the World, in Cyprus, Canada, Hong Kong, The Oman, Brunei, Belize, The Falkland Islands, Zimbabwe, Mozambique, Kenya, Gibraltar, Germany, Norway, Denmark, and so the list goes on. For my part, I have been fortunate and served in many of them. The Household Cavalry offers its officers and men a myriad of opportunities. The two Service Regiments share a six-year rotational cycle between Windsor, where they are equipped with the Scorpion family of armoured vehicles, and in Germany, where they convert to Challenger Main Battle Tanks. Thus they offer the best of both 'Cavalry' worlds, something no other cavalry regiment can do on a regular basis.

In addition, there is the Mounted Regiment at Hyde Park Barracks, Knightsbridge, where all ranks can serve, normally on a volunteer basis. I spent two highly enjoyable years there as a subaltern. Variety is the spice of life, and there is certainly no greater contrast than that between commanding a squadron of 60-ton tanks on the West German Plain and commanding Divisions of Mounted Cavalry on the Queen's Birthday Parade. On any particular day, Household Cavalrymen will also be found in just about every posting available to the Armed Forces in all parts of the world.

If life in the Army is varied it can also be extremely exciting and it is this scope for sudden unforeseen circumstances that adds to the appeal. One is encouraged to find the amusing side to even the darkest situation, and it is perhaps this innate sense of fun that has made my own service so enjoyable. I quote one 'war story' as an example:

It was August 1976 in Cyprus, only two years after the Turkish invasion and occupation of the northern half of the island, when tension was high and prone to sudden increase that made life interesting. One flashpoint, in the British UN sector, then held by the 3rd Battalion Royal Green Jackets, centred around the Turkish occupied village of Avlona. It sat right on the border of the DMZ which was patrolled and supposedly controlled by the UN Forces. Trouble had been steadily brewing for some weeks as the Turks flexed their muscles in an attempt to consolidate the border and incorporate more farmland into their zone. They had already held several strength-testing skirmishes with the Green Jackets, and a couple of days before I had found myself along with one other Ferret from my troop confronting a very heavily armed Turkish platoon which produced Browning machine guns and anti-tank bazookas in an attempt to scare us off. So far it was stalemate all round, a game of bluff and counter-bluff.

On the day in question my troop was back in the Avlona area, acting in support of the infantry, this time to prevent Turkish farmers, most of whom were soldiers dressed up as farmers, from tilling Greek owned land. The Ferrets were set to work herding tractors back north-ward to their side of the border, whilst the Green Jackets rounded up the pedestrian insurgents. The Ferret is not ideally suited to driving over ploughed fields, as it is notoriously top heavy and capsizes easily (often crushing its commander), nor can it turn in a tight circle. Tractors are, of course, in their element in ploughed fields and can turn on a sixpence. Consequently we had our hands full trying to catch our prey, and short of opening fire on unarmed 'civilians' we more often than not could not prevent the tractors from running circles around us.

My Corporal of Horse had already been forced to ram one particularly tricky customer when my most junior and inexperienced car commander radioed to me saying that he had managed to corner another in a fenced off orange grove. However, the tractor was now ramming him and he required assistance. I raced to the scene, finding callsign 12C blocking the gateway into the grove by parking sideways across it, but surrounded by a small hostile crowd which cheered loudly each time the tractor, finding its only exit barred, reversed at high speed into the side of the little armoured car, putting its ploughing hooks to good use, and causing it to rock precariously onto two wheels.

Closing down all hatches I ordered my driver to forge a path through the crowd and to ram the tractor, at the same time radioing to 12C to back out of the way at the critical moment. It seemed like a good plan except that the tractor, on seeing my approach, gave up pretending to be a battering ram and made a dash for a hitherto unseen second gate. My Ferret was temporarily stuck in the mob, I could hear men clambering on to it and beating on the armour. My driver, Trooper Jenkins, pushed his way through and chased after the tractor, managing to pull alongside and nudging it forcibly away from the gate, buckling one of its large rear wheels in the process.

The problem, when closed down in a Ferret, is that one's field of view becomes extremely limited – in fact the commander is almost blind. I was frustrated therefore, in my attempts to see what was going on and, believing that we were free of the crowd, decided to re-open my turret hatch. It was a mistake. I had bargained on all the 'farmers' jumping off as soon as Jenkins had broken free of the throng and had accelerated after the tractor. I was wrong – at least one had hung on. As I started to open up I caught a fleeting glimpse of a pair of dirtily clad legs before the hatch came crashing back down with great force. Who ever was up there must have sat on it. There was a numbing sensation in my right hand, and I could feel water, or something, flowing down my wrist and over my knees. I looked for the cause, and it was not difficult to find. The end of my two middle fingers had disappeared from just below the second knuckle. The wound was not clean-cut and pieces of bone were jutting out from the stumps. In slamming the hatch my assailant had caught my fingers in its hinge. I looked on in detached fascination; there was no pain, just a steady trickle of blood.

The driver in a Ferret sits directly in front of the commander, almost between his knees. I patted Jenkins on the shoulder, told him to stop, and thrust my hand under his eyes.

'Look! No fingers.'

The poor chap went a whiter shade of pale, a look of astonishment on his face. He brought us to a very abrupt halt. I looked for the tractor but it had escaped, in fact with its buckled wheel it only managed to wobble into a nearby ditch.

About 200 yards away I could see a UN Land-Rover manned by two Australian Policemen. I ordered Jenkins to drive over to it, at the same time telling 12C over the air what had happened and asking him if there was still anyone sitting atop my scout car. He replied that there was not.

Arriving alongside the Land-Rover, I again opened up my hatch, this time with no trouble, and found my fingers to be still lying on top of the turret. I picked them up. It felt strange being able to feel them – and they were surprisingly heavy – but not being able to feel them being felt. The realisation that they were no longer attached to me made my hand throb painfully.

With the grisly titbits in my left hand I jumped to the ground and walked over to a burly Police Sergeant, Jenkins protectively at my side.

'Good afternoon, I seem to have a small problem. Could you help please?' At the same time I reached out and handed him my fingers. He accepted them instinctively before realising what was being proferred.

To his great credit he did not equally instinctively drop the gooey mess on the spot. He looked with amazement at the two 'chipolata sausages' that now lay in the palm of his hand; his eyes flickered from them to my ragged stumps. 'CHRIST ALIVE! Thanks a bloody lot mate!'

After this initial hesitation he quickly sized up the situation and took efficient control, ordering his companion to radio for a helicopter, while he and the trusty Jenkins sat me down against one of the Land-Rover wheels and started to repair the damage, bandaging the fingers back in place. A Wessex helicopter arrived to take me to the British Military Hospital in Dhekalia.

It landed with a clatter, its rotors continuing to turn as it waited for me, something I believe the RAF call 'burning and turning'. The Flight Sergeant load master, who sits in the back attached to the machine by a long umbilical cord, waved me towards him and helped me to climb into the large side door. As soon as I was inside the pilot lifted off, and looking through a porthole I could see my Ferrets, the Australian Land-Rover, the wayward tractors, indeed the entire 'battle' scene diminishing to Dinky Toy size in the distance. A week later the Turks opened fire on UN troops.

I was not the only passenger on board. There was a second man dressed in Finnish UN uniform. Unbuckling his seat belt he came over and sat down beside me. He smiled at me. I smiled back. Strange fellow, I thought. Then taking my hand he started to fiddle with the bandages. I angrily pushed him away, telling him to mind his own business, but he persisted. I quite forcibly shoved him away a second time. The man was wearing no badges of rank nor insignia of any kind, for all I knew he could have been a car mechanic. With my left hand I took a firm twisting grip on one of his shoulders and held him off at arm's length. 'LOOK, will you bloody well keep your hands to yourself!' I shouted into his face.

He was no longer smiling. He looked at me mystified and then folded back a lapel to reveal the international medical sign, a snake curled around the hilt and blade of a sword, pinned to the under side. He repeated the word, 'Doctor, Doctor!'

I now understood but why hadn't he said so in the first place? I released my handful of the would-be good Samaritan's uniform and with extreme reluctance allowed him to start to unravel the bandages. The doctor, although with hindsight I think he was only a medical orderly, obviously spoke not a word of English. He also had no idea of the extent of the damage. As hard as I tried to explain that the ends of two fingers were not attached to the rest of me as they should be, it was equally obvious that the message was not getting through. He continued to smile reassuringly at me as he removed my dressings. Eventually the bandage came off, but so did my fingers. They fell with a *plop, plop* to the floor of the cabin. The doctor's mouth dropped open in horror. I, by this time quite used to the sight, adopted a smug 'I told you so' expression. The Flight Sergeant looked sick.

The pilot chose this exact same moment to make an alteration in course, banking the helicopter sharply to the right and sending my fingers rolling towards the door that had been left partly open. All three of us in the back looked on aghast as they came closer and closer to disappearing for good. Then, as of one mind, we made a simultaneous grab for the odious things, managing to retrieve them in the nick of time. There were embarrassed smiles of relief all round, followed by fits of uncontrollable laughter.

As luck would have it, there was a Guys Hospital surgeon at the BMH in Dhekelia, completing his annual two weeks with the Territorial Army Medical Corps. He sewed my digits back on, although admitting to me later that he had probably put the wrong tip on the wrong stump. No matter. My fingers, albeit slightly shorter and stumpier than their opposite numbers, are now almost as good as new.

I was promoted to Lieutenant in 1977 and to Captain in early 1979 when I was only twenty-three; I was due for Majority in 1987 but the Swedes got in the way. Of all my postings, I have enjoyed none more than those to Northern Ireland. If that sounds strange, so be it. The British Army has become expert at counter-insurgency and internal security operations, learning lessons the hard way through experience in Malaya, Kenya, Borneo, Aden, Oman, and now Northern Ireland. The troubles in that sad Province have made us the leading experts in the anti-terrorist field today. Although the 'troubles' started in 1969 and were in full swing when I joined the Army, I have only been posted to Northern Ireland twice. The first time was not until 1982 when I was attached to the Coldstream Guards as a Company Operations Officer during a four-month emergency tour to South Armagh. The second time came in 1985, on a two year posting to Headquarters Northern Ireland in Lisburn, County Antrim.

After my arrest in Sweden, a great deal of speculation appeared in the media as to the exact nature of this latter appointment. The Ministry of Defence, however, adopts a policy of not revealing details of a soldier's work when on an operational tour. It will neither confirm nor deny any press reports on the subject. The *Private Eye* magazine published an article in July 1987 claiming that I was a member of the SAS Regiment, and another later in the year stating that I had played a leading role in an incident that took place in Strabane in April 1985, in which three heavily armed and dangerous terrorists, intent on murder, were intercepted by the Security Forces and shot dead.

Other newspapers, especially the tabloids, jumped on the bandwagon and before long I was not only in the SAS but working for MI5, the E4A Department of Special Branch and the Intelligence Corps. Some of this publicity was quite complimentary, even calling me a 'Hero', but that does not make it any less inaccurate. The fact is that I have not seen one single article that has come anywhere near the truth, and I sometimes wish that I could be allowed to talk of my rather mundane job to prove the point. That MOD ruling, however, is there for very good reason, to protect people much more important than me. What I can categorically say is that I have never been a member of the SAS Regiment. As for the Strabane contact, I did not even arrive in the Province until June 1985, two months after the incident took place.

Whatever my appointment entailed, I completed my Tour and left Northern Ireland in February 1987, looking forward to a month's leave before taking up a position on the Staff in Whitehall.

Three

In conventional terms, my brother Christopher would be described as a dropout. Since leaving school in 1969 he has never committed himself to any recognised career, preferring instead to roam the world, settling wherever the fancy took him and doing any odd job that came along. A carefree life? Perhaps. A lazy life? Certainly. A waste of a life? That depends on your point of view. However in anyone's book, even his own, he would be described as the 'Black Sheep' of the Hayward family.

The rot – if indeed it is rot – began to set in soon after taking his 'O' levels at fifteen. He is of above-average intelligence but also naturally lazy, always looking for the easy way out. He found he could achieve good results without having to exert himself, thus leaving more time for leisurely pursuits, which included an early discovery of the pleasures of the opposite sex. Nothing wrong with that of course, except that as this appetite grew his academic achievements diminished noticeably. However, he eventually managed acceptable grades in his 'A' level subjects enabling him to win a place at Hamble, the BOAC pilot-training school. It was his wish to follow in our father's footsteps into aviation. He failed to complete the course, outside attractions proving to be too much of a temptation and preventing him from sustaining the necessary levels of concentration.

After being sent down from Hamble he made one final attempt at a conventional career, really to please my father, who was by then a very sick man, by applying for a Commission in the RAF. His heart was not in it, however, and he never made it past the initial interview.

To begin with his conduct hurt my parents bitterly,

especially my father who could never fathom his eldest son's attitude to life. It was not so much that Christopher's behaviour was evil or intentionally damaging to anyone, it was just that they could not understand it. Their son was an intelligent, good-looking boy; he had been lucky enough to receive the very best of educations; the world was at his feet if only he had the gumption to grab the opportunity. In their eyes he was now throwing it all away. It was the age-old problem of children rebelling against their parents, but that did not make it any the less inexcusable or intolerable for them.

Since my father's death, my mother has taken a more philosophical stand towards her eldest son, having long given up trying to change or fully understand him. During the 70s and 80s she saw him rarely, at the most once or twice a year, never receiving letters, and only the occasional telephone call; clearly he had rejected our normal family life.

I fail to see eye to eye with Christopher on many issues; I neither like nor comprehend his general attitude to life; but there again the reverse is also true. My becoming a soldier was a complete anathema to him. In short, we could not be less alike; the proverbial 'chalk and cheese'. If I am painting too derogatory a picture of my brother it is not intentional. The truth is I do not know Christopher all that well and have hardly seen him in the past sixteen years. That was one of my reasons for deciding to sail with him. However, despite any differences he is still my brother and I love him as a brother should, even if I cannot always respect him. The Haywards are nothing if not a close family, that is the way we have been brought up. Christopher has chosen his lifestyle. I have chosen mine. when it boils down to bare principles everyone has that right.

Christopher has not lived at home since 1970. In 1972 he married a Swiss girl, Chantal Heubi. Together they set off on the 'Hippy Trail', drifting through Thailand, Bali and India. They also lived in various parts of Europe before finally settling on Ibiza, one of the Balearic Islands off the east coast of Spain. In 1980 they had a son whom they named Tarik, which I believe is an old Phoenecian name.

As the oldest son, Christopher was left some money by my father but he supplemented his income by doing odd jobs. For instance working as a car mechanic in Switzerland and selling leatherwork to tourists in the Canary Islands. Anything that came to hand and did not require too much effort. In the early eighties he became a disciple of the Indian Guru Bhagwan Shree Rajneesh. The cult, whose members call themselves Sannyassans or Orange People (because they wear orange, or pink clothes), is best known for its Rancho Rajneesh in central Oregon, USA, described as an 'International Meditational University'. There, before it was closed by the American authorities in 1985, the Bhagwan kept forty-seven Rolls-Royces to play with, given to him by his devoted and undoubtedly gullible followers. They flocked to him in their hundreds to work in the 'Peace City' and paid through the nose for the highly dubious pleasure.

Other smaller 'Love Centres' have been set up by this successful conman all over the world. However, following the Oregon closure Mr Bhagwan was deported from America, and he has now returned to India, whence he was originally forced to flee to avoid a $4 million tax bill. I have often wondered at the powers of these Gurus who seem able to hypnotise large numbers of the credulous into not only blind obedience but also into so readily parting with their riches.

How Christopher came under this influence I do not know. I presume it was during his travels in India, or even from the commune on Ibiza, but he took to dressing from head to toe in pink baggy clothes which caused a certain amount of eyebrow-raising on his infrequent visits home. I always thought he looked bloody stupid, all the more so because of his height of 6 feet 3 inches, but I have to admit that it must have taken a good deal of courage to appear in public dressed as he did.

The last time I saw Christopher in England was in London in September 1986. I was in England on a preparatory course for my Staff College Exam and on going home for the weekend I found he was making one of his unexpected and unannounced visits. The occasion also saw an improvement in our relationship. Gone were the pink robes, the asinine soft affectation in his voice, and the expression of openly provocative views. For the first time in years we actually sat down and talked to each other, swapping opinions on a range of subjects, and we never once raised our voices. We were genuinely pleased to see one another and both of us were making an effort to tolerate the other's views. Chris explained that he was enjoying life on Ibiza and was making a comfortable living from chartering his yacht, a forty-five foot catamaran called *True Love*. Indeed he was in London to buy a large car to enable him to collect customers from the airport and, therefore, supply a better service and charge higher fees. During our conversation he invited me to sail with him whenever I next had leave. After the weekend I returned to my course. Chris stayed on in London for another ten days, eventually buying the Jaguar that was to feature so prominently in my own future.

Just prior to Christmas 1986 I was told that my tour in Northern Ireland would come to an end on 12 February the following year, two days after taking my Staff Exam. I wrote to Christopher asking if his invitation was still good and gave him the dates of my prospective leave. I received a reply via home that he was looking forward to seeing me and that he would telephone London nearer to the time to arrange final details, adding that we would have to meet up in Gibraltar where his boat had been wintering.

As it happened I was unable to leave the Province until the 16th, finally flying to Gibraltar from London on the morning of Wednesday 18 February. The plan was to spend two weeks sailing off Gibraltar, possibly going as far as the Canaries, before I flew on to Germany where I intended to buy a car for myself. I should perhaps explain that many servicemen take advantage of the opportunity to purchase cars on the Continent tax free, enabling them to make a considerable saving, even when British import duty is paid. I had not owned a car for two years and now that I had been posted back to London I was going to need one. To this end I withdrew £7,000 from my London bank before leaving for Gibraltar. There had been no time to arrange traveller's cheques so I was forced to take it in cash. This money was to figure prominently, to my detriment, at a later stage in Sweden.

My first impression on arrival in Gibraltar was that it was even smaller than I had expected. The airport, lying between the Rock and the Spanish border, being the only expanse of flat open ground in the entire colony. My second was the comforting one of seeing a British 'Bobby' sweltering in his blue uniform under a Mediterranean Spring sun. On the down side there was no brother to meet me and I had no idea where to find his boat. I need not have worried, however, for after a short wait Christopher arrived in a taxi from Spain, accompanied by a girlfriend. They had flown from Ibiza to Malaga that morning and had completed their journey by road. Christopher and Chantal had separated in 1982, although both continued to live on Ibiza. Tarik living with his mother but still seeing a lot of his father, a solution that appeared to suit all parties. Subsequently Chantal settled down with a Canadian friend and Christopher with a string of different girlfriends.

Christopher is thirty-eight, a tall man, of slim, muscular build and fair hair, and he was then clean-shaven and deeply tanned. He has always led an outdoor life and has the healthy complexion to prove it. Jamille, his girlfriend, is of French Algerian extraction, in her late twenties and as slim as a rake. An attractive girl with lovely long legs, dark oval eyes and a mass of thick black hair, she has a bubbly exuberant character which greatly adds to her appeal.

Together we drove to the marina, a journey of no more than three minutes, but there was bad news awaiting us. Chris had engaged a local boatyard to carry out some minor repairs to *True Love,* but despite having had ample time to complete them, by the time we arrived the work had not even been started. Chris was furious. Indeed it was a blow to all of us because we had hoped to set sail early the following morning. As it was, Jamille and I set to work cleaning the boat out, airing bedding and cabins after their long winter without use, whilst Chris stormed off to find the recalcitrant craftsman. *True Love,* not a first choice as a name but an inherited one, was, perhaps still is, a home-made catamaran built around two Prout hulls, with a box-like cabin perched in between. She could not boast the most graceful nor the most beautiful lines but there was character in her ugliness and she was Christopher's pride and joy. Her layout comprised three double cabins, each with its own tiny saloon and washbasin. There was an expansive main saloon and a large galley. But for all her neatness it was evident even to the most inexperienced eye that she was not the result of a master boatbuilder's endeavours. If she had been I doubt whether Chris would have been able to afford her.

We waited for two days but it became obvious that the necessary repairs were not about to be commenced, let alone completed immediately. There was some spare part or other that needed to be made, or ordered from England. *True Love* would not be ready for the high seas for at least another week to ten days. What to do?

The choice boiled down to three options. I could give up any hope of going sailing and carry on immediately with the remainder of my holiday as planned; but both Chris and I were keen on sailing together and I did not want to miss the opportunity to get to know my brother a little better. The three of us could remain on Gibraltar until all necessary repairs were complete; but having spent two days on the Rock there was nothing else to see and at the time I was not willing to waste my precious leave. The third option was Christopher's suggestion: why not fly to Ibiza, spend a week there and return once everything was ready on *True Love*?

To begin with I was not too keen on the idea. I had been to Ibiza once before for a week in 1984 and I did not much like the place, nor approve of much of what I saw there.

The island is small but heterogeneous. There are three communities living there: the local Spanish, a large force of expatriates and last but by no means least tourists. Each community comprises its own distinct but sometimes overlapping character with, sadly, the indigenous way of life gradually giving way to the new order brought about by tourism of the very worst kind. The only saving grace is that tourism is largely confined to several resorts, leaving other parts of the island relatively unspoilt. It is in these unspoilt areas that the expatriates like Christopher live, often rubbing shoulders with the local people in fairly congenial circumstances.

The newspapers have described the expatriate community on Ibiza as a freewheeling hippy colony, ridden with drug abuse, free sex and every other sordid practice that is associated with the term 'Hippy'. The best objective description I have been able to find is the one quoted in a report submitted in mid 1987 by a private detective sent to the island by my lawyers:

> To describe the circles in which Christopher Hayward and his friends lived as hippy would be an inaccurate portrayal. It would incorrectly conjure up a mental picture of the long-haired, bead-wearing and frequently unwashed and unkempt hippies of the 1960s, so memorable to most people.
>
> In contrast, those on Ibiza appear, in the main, to be from good backgrounds, reasonably or well educated, and of casual but clean appearance. Their accommodation is mostly rented and consists of simple but well maintained houses, sometimes even without electricity. Many are couples with children, who regularly attend the local English school. Most have some means of transport. As to why they have come to reside on Ibiza, most appear to have decided to leave their previous city jobs to 'live in the country'. As a result of its climate, and low cost of living, Ibiza provided an ideal environment where this could be achieved on minimal incomes.
>
> Some undoubtedly have private incomes, from legitimate external sources. However, most appear to work locally in some shape or form, and the regular Ibiza tourist markets are the main source of income for many, where they maintain stalls selling home-made leatherwork, jewellery etc. This is obviously orientated towards the summer months, and they need to earn sufficient during that period to maintain themselves during the winter.

In addition to this type of foreigner there is a large following of the Bhagwan cult on the island, many intermingling with the former but easily recognizable by their pink and orange clothes. During my visit to Ibiza in 1984 Chris was fairly heavily involved with this lot, although he admitted to me in London two years later that he had played along with them in a rather tongue-in-cheek fashion. One of the greatest motivators, he told me, was that the Sannyassans presented a captive market for his chartering business. Being one of the brotherhood meant that visiting pinkos came to his boat before any other for their summer fun. I can think of nothing worse.

It was not so much that I had nothing in common with any of Christopher's friends on Ibiza, nor that I was not accepted by them that made me hesitate before agreeing to go there with him and Jamille on this occasion. There are other aspects of the place that I find particularly unappealing.

A year after my arrest a British journalist was to spend a few weeks on the island trying to find a lead into the drug scene that had been unearthed by my case. Part of his report, which I was shown, read as follows:

'I trawled the Clubs of Ibiza City, a deeply memorable experience, in the company of a French heroin addict and a hooker, seeking information from druggies, transvestites and butch boys in bondage, watching them blow smoke from joints into the impotent faces of the Guardia Civil, who, of course, can do damn all about it these days. Ibiza isn't so much a toilet, as a blocked toilet!' That, I hasten to add, is an aspect of Ibiza that I have never personally witnessed but it does highlight the damage that tourism has done to a once beautiful and unspoilt island.

All in all I did not relish the prospect of spending another week on Ibiza, and very nearly refused Christopher's invitation. However, if we were to go sailing it did appear to be the best option, especially since I had decided to telephone my girlfriend Sandra to ask her if she would join me there. Together we could avoid any unpleasant areas and enjoy ourselves alone.

The final decision not to remain in Gibraltar was made on the Friday night (20 February) so Chris, Jamille and I travelled to Ibiza on the following morning. There is an important point worth mentioning here because it will attain greater relevance later on. That is that I found Chris to be almost broke, indeed I had to pay all his travel costs, including taxi fares and plane tickets. Again on arrival on Ibiza, when we hired a car because my brother's was in for repair, it was I who paid for it.

It is necessary that I should describe the remaining days before my arrest in some detail, because this was to form the basis of my testimony in Court and is crucial to the reader's understanding of the affair.

So Christopher, Jamille and I arrived on Ibiza on the Saturday evening, we hired a car, a red Ford Fiesta, and drove to Christopher's house which lay in the hills above a village called San Juan. The final ten kilometres was on a rugged mountain track, known on the island as a camino, hundreds of which criss-cross the inland areas. This particular one was tortuous and uneven in the extreme, the car moaned and groaned its way over the bumpy surface, much of it a steep incline. There were numerous expensive-sounding scrapes and thuds as we hit large stones or dropped into holes and I found myself secretly thanking God that the car was hired and not my own.

The house, when we finally reached it, was nothing more than a concrete shack. It was a white, one storey rectangular box. I could not see more of the surroundings that first night except for a small scrubby garden. Inside was one large living room, two small bedrooms, a storeroom, a kitchen, and a minute bathroom. There was no electricity and no mains water supply. What little water there was available came from a well in the garden and had to be pumped into a tank on the roof before use. This at least gave the house running water, but it had to be used very sparingly. The furnishings were spartan – a bed in the living room which doubled as a sofa, an old electric cable spool used as a table, carpet and cushions for sitting on. A fireplace and lanterns gave off a crackling, hissing homely atmosphere.

The morning revealed that the 'villa' was perched on the edge of high cliffs, giving a stunning view over wooded ground to the sea. Surrounding it on other sides were ploughed fields and scrubland. Directly to its front was a concrete terrace, the small scrubby garden and an open area where visiting cars parked. Living in such a place may have been simple in the extreme, but the privacy and panoramic views more than compensated for that. I understood what Chris saw in it.

That afternoon Christopher and Jamille drove off to see friends whilst I elected to remain behind to read in the Spring sunshine. They returned later in the evening and we dined that night at a local taverna. During this meal Chris told me that he wanted to sell the Jaguar that he had bought in England the previous September because, he explained, since its purchase he had moved to the mountain villa and the car was too low to climb the camino. He had actually tried once but had been forced to turn back. Consequently he had had to buy a Lada Jeep and now needed the cash that the sale of the Jaguar would bring. It was clear that this conversation was leading up to something. My mother had visited Ibiza a month before Christmas the last year to spend a week with her only grandson and Christopher had asked her then if she would drive his Jaguar back to England to sell for him, but time had been against her and she had refused. He now asked me if I would take it back for him and try to sell it. I was slightly annoyed with this because he knew that I was intending to fly to Germany to buy a car of my own, but he appeared so desperate that I agreed to change my plans. He even suggested that I might buy the Jaguar myself, but it was not the kind of car I wanted, and we also discussed swapping it for a Landrover I had in England but seldom used. The new plan was to drive in the Jaguar to Gibraltar to go sailing and for me to drive on from there to England. Monday 23 February saw an event that almost certainly played a significant role in my case. We got up in mid-morning and drove in to Ibiza City for a late breakfast. The city is not large, is built around a small harbour and dominated by a medieval castle on the hill above. It has undergone extensive modern rebuilding with the appearance of many hideous concrete apartments and office blocks. But there was an attractive main square surrounded by old Colonial-style buildings. It was in this Square that everyone seemed to congregate at a popular café called Montesol, especially during the latter part of the mornings for brunch.

We had intended to have a quick snack before collecting Christopher's Jeep from a garage near the airport and then returning the hired Ford. However, by the time we arrived at the garage we had left it too late and it had closed for lunch. Mediterranean shops close for lunch at the normal time but do not reopen again until four o'clock, and stay open until as late as seven. There was nothing else to do but return to San Juan for a siesta and try again later in the day. It was on our way home that the event I refer to occurred.

At the time it appeared innocent enough. We stopped off for

petrol, and at the adjacent pump was a white Volvo shooting brake. As Christopher waited for the tank to be filled he chatted to the driver of this other car, whom he obviously knew. I was still sitting in the Ford and I could see a woman doing the same in the Volvo. I have no memory of what she looked like except that she had dark hair. When we pulled away I asked who the man had been and Chris replied that he was a friend of his called Lokesh. He also added something about the man being a Swede, or living in Sweden. At the time I paid little attention and I have now forgotten exactly what it was that he said, but I do remember thinking that Lokesh was not a name I had heard before and could well have been of Scandinavian origin. Since he was driving a Volvo, it all seemed to make sense at the time. Lokesh proved to be a Scot by the name of Forbes Cay-Mitchell, and a leading figure in the drugs ring that tricked me – Lokesh was his Bhagwani pseudonym.

Later that afternoon we drove into town once more to collect the Jeep and to return the Ford. Again it is important that I stress that not all the repairs to it had been carried out. There was a problem with the transmission or something that produced a strong vibration when driving at more than 60 mph. It was an easy enough fault to rectify, they said, but the necessary spares were not available on the island and would have to be bought privately in Spain. We handed in the hire car, had dinner in a restaurant in Ibiza City and eventually returned to San Juan for bed.

Tuesday was the day on which Sandra, known to all her friends as Sands, was to arrive. I had telephoned to ask her to come out and join me and she had been able to squeeze a week's holiday, at short notice, from her employer. As on previous days Chris and Jamille took themselves off before lunch, leaving me at the villa to fend for myself, saying as they left that they would be back in time to take me to the airport to collect Sands, whose plane was due in at half past four in the afternoon.

I amused myself by spring-cleaning the house, something that appeared a little overdue, then by sitting on the terrace and polishing off the best part of a bottle of wine, before going for a long walk to explore the surrounding area and to enjoy the views. It was the first time for almost two years that I had been totally alone. My work in Ireland had kept me pretty busy. Alone to relax and to think without some pressing problem to constantly distract me, I found that I was enjoying my solitude – my thoughts were of my immediate future, and my relationship with Sandra. I sat on a large boulder, the sun beating down, glistening off the surface of the sea far below me, the air still and the silence deafening.

Sandra and I had been friends for some eight years but we had only been going out together for the past eighteen months. In that time we had become very close, although my being posted to Northern Ireland had meant that we had spent long periods apart. I was thirty-one and was beginning to wonder if it wasn't time to settle down, get married and raise a family. After all, I reminded myself, by my age my father had already had a wife and three children. My next posting would allow us to see a great deal more of each other and I could not go on expecting Sands to wait forever. I loved her and I felt confident that the feeling was mutual. However, selfishly perhaps, marriage was something I did not want to rush into.

I had seen too many service marriages go wrong and my own family had a poor record in that department. Chris was separated and my sister, Judith, was divorced, as was one of my closest cousins. It was proving to be a nerve-racking decision, which was the main reason why I had come on this holiday alone. I needed time to think for both of our sakes. As it was, I was already not being totally honest with Sands; not a good start if we were going to spend the rest of our lives together, and I felt rather awkward about it. I believed my motives to be honest, but that did not make the situation any better. I had not told Sandra that I was going on leave and, therefore, I was going to have some explaining to do when she arrived that afternoon. I realised that I had taken the easy way out by not telling her, but I had felt it the best thing to do under the circumstances. My reasons had been that I needed time to be alone and to unwind after leaving Ireland. Every moment of leave I had had in the past eighteen months I had spent with Sands and on this occasion I just felt that I had to get away. Also, I had not thought that Sands would enjoy sailing with Christopher, and if I had told her of my intentions she might have tried to change my mind. And lastly, if I had told her that I was going off on holiday alone she would have been quite naturally and justifiably extremely upset, and I had wanted to shield her from that, and to avoid any unnecessary row.

If I had been selfish and deceitful, and I had been, it was only because I could see no other solution without hurting someone I loved. In any event, the problem was now compounded by her imminent arrival. She had told me that her boss had only given her a week off from work, which meant she would not be able to accompany me to Gibraltar to go sailing, or on the drive back to England. In for a penny, in for a pound. I made up my mind, for the same reasons, to tell her a little white lie and say that I was going back to Northern Ireland the day after she was to leave Ibiza in a week's time. I promised myself that it would be the last lie, however well intentioned, that I would ever tell Sands, but that did not make me feel any more comfortable about it. I would have more time to think about it later, but also decided while sitting on that boulder to ask Sands to marry me as soon as I arrived back in London. If she refused my proposal I would try to break off the relationship. It was not fair to either of us to carry on as we had been for the last eighteen months.

If it is wondered why I find it necessary to talk so publicly of so private a matter, it is not easy. I do so because it became something that the Swedish Prosecutor made a great deal of in an attempt to prove his case against me, and consequently it needs explaining. My motives have also been misrepresented in at least one national newspaper.

By half past three Christopher had still not turned up to take me to the airport. He is notoriously unpunctual and unreliable and this was typical of him. Feeling angry and frustrated, I could see poor Sands waiting alone at a strange airport and having no idea of how to find me. Jamille's old Renault 4 was outside the villa, its reliability too was very much in doubt, but in desperation I decided to chance using it. I need not have worried for when I rattled and jolted into the airport car-park there was the Jeep. Chris and Jamille had decided to go straight there to collect Sands. I mentally apologised for my unbrotherly thoughts as I found them waiting in the Arrivals Hall. They laughed when I told them how I had been cursing all the way from San Juan, not knowing if the wretched Renault was going to give up the ghost at any moment.

Sands arrived looking wonderfully attractive, and finding myself overjoyed to see her I felt even more ashamed of my deception. She is a large-boned, tall girl with shoulder-length blond hair and beautiful blue eyes. Her ready smile, quick wit and loving nature endears her to all who meet her. On more than one occasion I have quietly watched her talking amongst friends, without her realising it, as she threw her head back in laughter or leant forward to gently touch someone's arm to emphasize a point, and felt how lovely a person she was and how lucky I was to have her. In the ensuing months Sands was to stick by me through thick and thin, when no one would have criticised her for turning her back on me and walking away.

We left the airport and made our way through the afternoon traffic to Ibiza City where, after a quick drink at the Montesol to help Sands recover from her journey, I hired another car, this time from a small agency where Chris had a friend who gave me a good discount. Then, in a three car convoy, we set off for Santa Gertrudis, a small village ten minutes drive from the Capital, where Chris rented a second house.

One might question why my brother kept two houses. The point was used by the Swedes to support their description of Christopher's supposed freewheeling expensive life style, financed through the sale of drugs. In fact there was a perfectly reasonable explanation for him to have rented both.

He had taken out a year's contract on the one in Santa Gertrudis in July 1986, paying the year's rent in advance. It was in a convenient location for him being both close to the marina where he moored *True Love*, and to Chantal's house so that he could see as much of his son as possible. By Ibizan standards this villa was modern and fairly sizeable, but it was charmless, and lacking in all character. It was in a poor position and could boast neither a garden nor a swimming pool. However, it had the benefit of mains electricity and water (including hot water) and being right next to a main road there was no tortuous camino to conquer before arriving at the front door. Another drawback was its bad design, for instance the only entrance was via the kitchen. Apparently its only redeeming feature was that it had a washing machine, a luxury in Christopher's circle of friends.

In November the house above San Juan became vacant, and since he had had his eye on it for several years, Chris immediately rented it before anyone else could beat him to it. He then tried unsuccessfully to persuade the Santa Gertrudis landlord to release him from the remainder of that contract, but he would have none of it. Therefore, it was not that he maintained two houses by choice, but rather that he had no other option except to present the first landlord with nine months' free rent, something that he was quite naturally loath to do. The situation had its benefits, I was told, because it meant that Chris could bath in the house, which had a plentiful supply of water, use it as a store house for equipment from his boat, and allow visiting friends to stay there, as I was about to do. He also intended to sublet the place to tourists that summer. In any case the rents on both were reasonably low.

When we arrived at the villa in Santa Gertrudis I saw for the first time, parked outside, the green Jaguar XJ6 that was to be my Nemesis.

The following week passed all too quickly and we kept ourselves very much to ourselves, content in each other's company. That is not to say that we did not see Christopher and others from time to time, but we did not go out of our way to socialize. Our daily routine remained fairly constant. We would normally have breakfast at the Montesol, before exploring parts of the island. It was still too cold to swim but we went for frequent strolls along nearly deserted beaches. In the evenings we would find a restaurant and while away the time with friendly small talk.

If our routine was constant, to us at least, it was not in any way boring. We were enjoying the relaxed holiday atmosphere, and the opportunity of being together for a whole week, the longest period we had managed since the previous August. Apart from Chris and Jamille, when I took Sands up to the mountain villa to see the view, stopping off en-route in the village for coffee at Fernanditois Café, a local watering hole, the only people we visited were Chantal and her boyfriend, Jim White. They lived at the end of a slightly less difficult camino in a tasteful and comfortably converted farmhouse, typical of most of the homes in the inner areas.

Chantal was a lovely person, tall and slim, in her mid thirties with long brown hair. I did not know her that well but she always showed genuine pleasure at seeing me, and we got on famously together. As my sister-in-law and the mother of my only nephew, I was extremely fond of her. She was a perfect mother, loving, caring and gentle, but at the same time firm and encouraging to Tarik. She was Swiss and spoke English with a soft French accent that I found attactive.

Chantal had settled with Jim, a well-built, jolly Canadian in his early forties. He obviously loved her and had become a warm, affectionate 'step-father' to Tarik. Tarik, in turn, was a happy, confident little chap, obviously very content with his lot and unaffected by the fact that he came from a broken home. In any case, he saw his father whenever he wished, often choosing for himself which parent he wanted to be with at any particular time. He attended the local English school, and had many friends his own age in the area.

Two events took place during the week Sands was on Ibiza that at the time seemed unimportant and innocent enough but were to acquire real significance as events turned out.

The first was on the Wednesday morning, the day after Sands arrived. Chris appeared alone shortly before ten a.m. I heard the crunch of wheels outside on the drive. There was an Alsatian belonging to the landlord that went beserk whenever anyone approached, giving us plenty of warning. I went out to meet him.

'I've just come to collect the Jaguar,' he told me, 'it's time I took it for a run. I'll leave the jeep here for a few hours.'

There was something wrong, I could tell. My brother looked deeply worried, even scared. He would not look me in the eye and seemed flustered and hesitant.

'What's the matter Chris? Something is wrong, isn't it? Can I help?'

'No, no. Nothing. It's nothing. I must be going!' I reached out and caught him by the arm.

'Come on Chris! We're brothers. I can tell that there is something worrying you. Let me help.'

He looked at me, as if inwardly fighting to come to a decision. 'Honestly, it's nothing really. I've got to go to meet someone and I think there may be trouble.'

'Well if that's the case, why go? It's a free world.'

'No, I have to!' The words rushed out. 'And if I don't leave now I'm going to be late.'

'Right. I'm coming with you. No arguments. Let me just tell Sands, she's in the bath. How long will we be away?'

'About an hour,' was the reply. He looked relieved. I told Sandra what was happening and that I would not be away long.

It turned out that the meeting was due to take place in Santa Eulalia, a popular seaside tourist resort about fifteen minutes' drive northwards. At this time of year, however, it would be fairly quiet.

'Who are we going to see?' I asked.

'Do you remember meeting someone called Duke during your last visit?'

'No I don't think so,' I replied, trying to recall.

'He invited us both over to his catamaran for a drink one afternoon, when *True Love* was moored nearby. He had a little fair-haired boy called Alvi, a year or so older than Tarik.'

'Ah yes, the Irishman, but why are you expecting trouble from him? He seemed harmless enough.'

'Well he isn't,' was the only response. It was clear that whilst he was pleased to have me along, Chris did not want to elaborate further on the nature of the forthcoming confrontation. I decided not to push him.

Santa Eulalia has all the trappings necessary to satisfy the undemanding tourist and is consequently an uninspiring mess although it is still just possible to disentangle enough of its original features to see that it must once have been agreeable enough. We parked just off the main square and Christopher led the way to a café on its north side. Sitting at a table on the pavement outside it was a dark-haired woman of about thirty-five, with an angular face and wearing sunglasses. I can remember nothing else about her except that she seemed vaguely familiar and was holding a small child, or was it a small dog, in her lap. I am almost one hundred per cent certain that she was Duke's wife, a Dane called Gitta or something similar. She appeared to recognize me and I in turn realised why she looked familiar. She had been on Duke's yacht when we had gone to it for a drink on my last visit.

The three of us sat and chatted for a few minutes, ordering

coffee and beer from the waiter. Gradually in dribs and drabs more people came and joined the party, in rather typical Ibizan style, until we numbered about six. All the newcomers were men, in their thirties, but as yet there was no sign of this Duke character. The common language was Spanish, of which I was the only one with a total lack of knowledge. In consequence I found myself, not unwillingly, demoted to observer status. In any event, I was finding whenever I moved into these circles that I was only tolerated because I was Christopher's brother, and no one seemed overly keen to talk to me.

There still being no sign of Duke, or trouble of any sort, I slipped away to a nearby kiosk to find a newspaper. Armed with a copy of the previous day's *Daily Telegraph* I rejoined the table and contented myself by reading and taking frequent sips of my ice-cold beer.

Duke arrived with another man a few minutes later. They pulled up chairs and sat either side of Chris, who appeared nervous but otherwise outwardly composed. The atmosphere became frosty, losing its previous joviality, but the conversation, now a mixture of English, Spanish and a smattering of French, remained general and even casual.

Duke seemed surprised to see me but said hello and even asked how Army life was treating me. I replied in equally monosyllabic terms. He was small, about five foot seven, slim and wiry, in his late thirties or early forties. His hair was blond to gingerish, and on this occasion he was clean-shaven, although I remembered a beard from our previous meeting. When he spoke his accent was soft Irish, probably originating from the Republic. He and Christopher were soon holding an animated conversation in hushed tones, with Duke doing most of the talking, sometimes emphasizing a point with a threatening finger. Eventually the two of them got up and went into the café together, re-emerging after a few minutes. Whatever the topic of conversation, some understanding must have been reached because they now stopped their whisperings and joined in the general hubbub. A few minutes later I suggested to Chris that it might be time to go. I was a little concerned for Sands, who must have been starting to wonder at our continued absence. As we stood up to take our leave,

Duke rose with Chris and turning to face him gave a final:

'Don't forget what I've said, will you!' It was delivered with a poker face and not a little menace. Chris just nodded, tight lipped.

We had agreed to give an American who lived in San Juan a lift, but he lingered at the table saying his goodbyes, so Chris and I walked back to the Jaguar alone. He was still troubled by something, looking haunted and apprehensive. As we sat in the car waiting, I pondered over what I had seen. Although the meeting had indeed been frosty, and the little Irishman nastily unfriendly, there had been no indication of any of the physical trouble that Chris had been expecting – perhaps my presence had prevented that.

'Chris, what on earth was that all about? The atmosphere back there was electric to say the least. What are you so worried about, and what did this Duke person want? You obviously aren't on friendly terms. If he's being a nuisance and threatening you, why not go to the Police?'

'Look, drop it will you, it's nothing. Just a stupid argument over money. Now please don't ask any more questions.' And, raising his voice, 'Learn to mind your own damn business, can't you!'

I stared at him in astonishment. I had only been trying to help. Wasn't that why I had come along in the first place? Before I could protest, however, the American opened a back door and climbed in. We returned to Santa Gertrudis, where Chris exchanged cars, and together with his friend drove off to San Juan.

The second event in question occurred on the Friday morning at the villa in Santa Gertrudis. Again, on hearing the dog barking and the sound of an approaching car, I went out to investigate. This time it was not Christopher's Jeep but the white Volvo I had seen at the petrol station a few days before. The same couple were inside it. The man jumped out, and I walked over to the driver's door to greet him. He was about my height, six foot, and older, about fortyish at a guess. He had tight, curly, short black hair, and a sallow complexion with a prominent forehead. Not an unhandsome face. He was dressed in casual clothes. The woman, as at the petrol station, remained in the car and ignored me. As we shook hands he held onto mine longer than I thought necessary, something that I always find slightly embarrassing.

'Hello, I'm Lokesh. You must be Chris's brother, Simon.'

'Yes I am. How do you do? I'm afraid he's not here, but can I offer you a drink?'

'No thanks, we just dropped in on the off chance of catching him. How are you enjoying your holiday?'

'Fine thanks, but the weather could be better.' There had been a light rain shower that morning, and I was falling into the old British habit of 'when confronted by a stranger, talk about the weather'. 'Are you sure I can't tempt you with a beer or a glass of wine?'

'No. Must be going. Can you tell Chris that I called?' And with that he was in the car and away before I had time to say anything else.

The entire visit cannot have lasted more than a minute or two. Sands had come out to stand beside me at one point but there had not been an opportunity to introduce her and she had wandered off. I could now hear her in the kitchen, pottering, and I went in to her.

'Who was that?' she asked.

'A Swedish friend of Christopher's and I think his wife. I asked them in for a drink but they seemed in rather a hurry.'

'He didn't sound Swedish to me, rather more like Scottish.'

'No', I replied, 'I'm sure Chris said he was Swedish; we bumped into him at a petrol station the day before you arrived. His name's Lokesh: that doesn't sound very Scottish to me.'

I rarely get the chance to see Tarik, and being my only nephew I dote on him. Consequently Sands and I visited Chantal's house a couple of times during the week, and on the Saturday we took the little fellow out for the day, to allow me to spoil him. We arranged to hand him back at a barbeque that we were all going to that evening.

It was to be a barbeque and fireworks display to celebrate some kind of local fete given by a Spanish couple, I believe of South American descent. They were friends of both Chantal's and Christopher's and had invited Sands and me when they had heard we were on the Island. It turned out to be a fairly boisterous party: whilst the children enjoyed the fireworks, the adults enjoyed the wine, but I found it next to impossible to communicate with any of the other guests, and after attempting to break the ice with several cold shoulders I took myself off to a quiet corner to fall asleep.

Before I did so Chris took me aside and told me that he had telephoned Gibraltar to check on *True Love*, only to find that she was still not ready. Sadly there was no hope of going sailing now. He added that I might as well leave for England whenever I liked, even taking Sandra with me. I reminded him that she had to be back at work the following Wednesday and, therefore, did not have the time necessary to accompany me on the drive. I asked him not to mention it to her and we agreed to finalise plans later.

Sands had been having more success with the locals than I, at one point being surrounded by Latin admirers, but she too finally tired and woke me up to suggest we call it a night. I said goodbye to Chantal as we left. It was to be the last time I ever saw her.

Whenever I have been sailing in the past, the enjoyment has invariably been sullied by the nightmare of having to enter an unknown, or for that matter a well known, harbour at night. With this in mind I had brought with me a military night sight, known as a pocket scope, from Northern Ireland. It effectively gives its user total night vision, albeit in only one eye and with limited range, and would be, I had thought, a tremendous sailing aid. However, I had hidden it on the boat, rather than carry it about and risk losing it when we had decided to come to Ibiza. Before I could drive home I was now going to have to return to Gibraltar to retrieve it.

Sands left on the following Tuesday morning. I was sorry to see her go and very nearly decided to fly back to London with her. If it had not been for the damn night sight, I probably would have. Ten days later I was to wish more than anything in the world that I had. When she passed into the departure lounge I hurried out to the car and drove to a beach near the end of the airport runway to see her plane take off. I watched as it roared overhead and continued staring at it until it became a distant speck on the horizon. Then, feeling rather lonely, I made my way to the Montesol for a consoling drink and afterwards drove up to San Juan to find Chris.

The conversation that took place when I arrived at the

mountain villa changed the entire course of my life.

After asking me if Sands had got away safely, Chris told me that there had been a change of plan. He had found a buyer for his Jaguar and there was now no need for me to drive it back to England. This came as quite a surpise but I really had no strong feelings about it one way or the other. True, I had been looking forward to the journey home and had intended to stop off in the Alps, en route, for a couple of days skiing, but it would now be only too easy to fly to Gibraltar, collect the things I had left on the boat, and then go directly back to London. There might even be time to revert to my original plan of buying a car in Germany. The £7,000 was still burning a hole in my pocket.

Then Chris added . . . 'Si, would you do me a real favour? This buyer is an Englishman living in Sweden of all places. He has offered a fantastically good price, much more than I could hope to get in England, and I badly need the cash.' I could sense what was coming next. 'Would you drive the car up there for me? I would do it myself but I should stay here to sort out *True Love* and get her ready for the chartering season. I'll lose clients if I don't and I can't afford that risk.'

'Sweden,' I exclaimed, 'but that's miles away. I've got to be back at work in a couple of weeks and I still have to go to Gibraltar. I've missed the only flight today, so I can't even set off for there until tomorrow.'

'It's not actually that much further than driving direct to London,' Chris persisted. 'I will pay all the expenses and you could fly home from Stockholm. You would be back in plenty of time. Please Si, you would be doing me a great favour. I know it's asking a lot but you were taking it back to England in any case, and this won't take much longer.' He looked desperate.

'Well look. I'll go and buy a map and have a think about it. I'll let you know later.'

'Righty-ho. I'll be here all day. I would be very grateful if you could, Si. Let's have dinner somewhere this evening and we can talk about it some more.' I drove slowly into Ibiza City. Sweden! Christ that was right up in the north of Europe, in fact, you could not go any further north. However, Sweden was one of the few European countries I had not visited, so I thought it might be quite fun to have a look at the place. If I arrived there in good time I could even go skiing. There had to be plenty of snow that far north. I also felt that I owed Chris this favour – after all he had lent me his villa for a week, and I knew he was short of money. If the Jaguar was sold that would be a great help to him. I would buy a map and then make a final decision. I managed to find one in a small bookshop and took it to the Montesol to study it whilst I had some lunch.

In fact the distance was not that much further than the drive to London via the Swiss Alps. The journey would be an easy one, on good roads, much of them motorway, and should not take me longer than two days, three at the most, barring any mishaps. And I was quite used to driving on the Continent. If I could fly to Gibraltar tomorrow, be back on Thursday and leave on Friday morning's ferry for the mainland, I could be in Sweden on Sunday afternoon. Plenty of time, therefore, to deliver the Jaguar to this Englishman and get at least a week's skiing in before having to catch a London flight on Tuesday the 17th. I had to be back at work on the 18th at the latest.

By now I was quite excited at the prospect. I had heard a lot about Sweden. Hadn't everyone? The land of freedom, democracy, human rights, pretty girls and liberalism. Wasn't it the 'world's Moral Superpower?' A week's skiing up there would be just the ticket. I finished my lunch, had an extra beer to celebrate, paid the bill and set off back to San Juan, feeling that 'all was well with the world'.

Christopher was obviously pleased with my decision and showed his gratitude by taking me out to dinner that night. He did add, though, that he did not think I could leave until the weekend because he wanted to ensure that I was properly insured to drive the Jaguar and he expected that to take a few days. He explained that he had been having some problems with his insurance company and had yet to receive his policy, although he had paid a premium of over £800. There were also final arrangements to be made with the purchaser.

I caught the next morning's eight o'clock flight to Malaga (via Madrid), eventually arriving in Gibraltar in mid-afternoon, after a hot and stuffy bus journey from the airport. The weather on the Rock was beautiful, much warmer than it had been on Ibiza. Since there was now no hurry to rush back, I stayed on there for two days, sunning myself on *True Love*'s deck and generally being lazy. It was not until Saturday morning that I eventually set off back to Ibiza – not, as I had originally intended, by air from Malaga but at the wheel of an old Mercedes saloon that Chris kept in Gibraltar to use when the yacht was there. He had asked me to bring it back to Ibiza for him, so that it could be used to carry new equipment for the boat back to Gibraltar. That way, he had explained, he would avoid having two cars stuck there when he sailed back to Ibiza. I had readily agreed to this additional 'favour' because by the time I had taken a bus to Malaga, and a plane via Madrid to Ibiza, the two journeys would be about the same timewise. I also preferred driving to sitting around for interminable hours at airports, waiting for connecting flights. As it was I missed the ferry to Ibiza and so had to leave the car in Valencia and fly the last leg of the journey.

So it was late Saturday evening before I again found myself back on Ibiza. I hired a car at the airport and drove straight to the villa above San Juan. Chris had some friends around for dinner, but when I arrived they were on the point of leaving. I flopped down in front of the fire and listened to the noises of slamming car doors, revving engines and shouted goodbyes. With the sound of cars diminishing into the night, Chris and Jamille came back inside.

'I'm sorry, I hope I didn't break up the party. Your friends never seem too pleased to see me.'

'No it's okay, they were leaving anyway, but I'm surprised to see you back so early. Where's the Mercedes?'

I explained about missing the ferry and told him that his car was now parked at Valencia airport. He didn't seem to mind.

'Anyway, Chris, I want to be off tomorrow morning and if I had come across by ferry tonight I would have missed the one in the morning.'

'I'm afraid you are going to miss it anyway,' he said softly, and went on to explain that he had not heard from his insurance company, nor had he been able to finalize the sale details. He was expecting to do both on Monday.

This was typical of Christopher: I should have expected it. A schedule to him was only something to be broken: he had no sense of urgency and was more than prepared to take events

as they came. Punctuality was not a word in his vocabulary.
Rather irritated I exclaimed:

'I had been hoping to have some time to go skiing in
Sweden, Chris. At this rate I'm not even going to have time to
get there!'

'You will still go?'

'Yes, I said I would, and I will, although if I had known it
was going to take this long to begin with I would probably have
refused. As it is I seem to have wasted most of my leave. I
suppose it would be too optimistic to hope for Monday's, so
let's go firm on Tuesday morning's ferry. Okay?'

At first he tried to argue the point, trying to persuade me to
leave on Wednesday's boat, explaining that he and Jamille
were going to accompany me as far as France in the Jeep so
that he could buy the spares that were needed for it, and he had
one or two things to do himself before he could leave. Besides,
by Wednesday he was sure to have a firm answer on the
insurance. However, I was having none of it, saying that if I
didn't take Tuesday's ferry I wasn't going at all and he finally
agreed, adding that he did have a few details we could discuss
now.

Apparently I was to deliver the Jaguar to Lokesh. 'The man
you met at Santa Gertrudis,' Chris explained, 'he lives in a
town south of Stockholm called Linköping, but his house is
damn difficult to find so I've arranged for you to meet him at
the local railway station. That should be easy enough to find,
but he hasn't phoned with the timings yet, that's the problem.'

I wondered if I was ever going to get them. I also forget now,
whether he said if Lokesh was actually buying the car himself
or merely handling its sale. Perhaps the point was never made
clear, but in any case Chris told me not to worry about the
detail of the sale, I just had to deliver the car and someone who
knew the local system would handle everything else.

We pored over the map and decided on my best route north,
and I was shown Linköping's exact location. I also suggested
that we drive via Andorra, because it was a duty-free haven
and almost en route. I thought I might be able to buy some
cheap skis there; perhaps Chris would also be able to find his
Jeep spares in the place.

'By the way, did you come via Santa Gertrudis tonight?'

Chris asked, and when I told him that I hadn't, 'then you won't have seen my message. The house was burgled whilst you were away, but as far as I can tell nothing has been stolen. Your bag was ruffled through, but even your camera and torch were not taken. I had also brought an expensive torch for the sailing trip. Strange isn't it? Perhaps they were just after cash, that seems to be the norm with house break-ins on the island.'

He then went on to ask me if I would sleep down there that night because the house could not be locked until a carpenter could come to fix the broken doors. He said that he had moved the Jaguar away from the house to be on the safe side. It was now parked in San Juan. However, since I had wanted to drive it, albeit without proper insurance, to get the feel of it before my long journey, he agreed to return it the next morning. It was getting late and I was tired after my travels that day, so I took my leave and made my way to Santa Gertrudis and bed.

I awoke late the next morning and wandered dozily out into the sunshine. Both kitchen and annex doors had been jemmied open, bits of doorpost littered the floor. I checked my kit, the only things missing were a shirt and a pair of jeans. Cheap at the price, but odd that the thieves had not taken anything more valuable. I wondered if Chris had inadvertently mentioned to anyone the cash I had been carrying around for the last three weeks. If so they might have thought I would leave it behind during my trip to Gibraltar and taken the opportunity to try and steal it.

There was no food in the house, so I walked into the village for a breakfast of coffee and warm bread. I must have been away for about an hour, for when I returned the Jaguar was once again parked outside the villa. There was a note on the kitchen table with its keys.

'I couldn't wait. Drive carefully. NB The insurance. See you later, Chris.' I was in no hurry to do anything. I cleaned up the house in preparation for my departure, and then had a long soak in the bath. At about four o'clock I decided to take the 'Green Machine' for a spin around the island, really only out of boredom and to check to see if it had any problems. It seemed to work perfectly and I did the grand tour before ending up in Ibiza City shortly after six. The Jaguar was an unusual car for Ibiza and it attracted more than a few stares from the local people.

I parked opposite the sea front, and ambled along through the marinas, looking at the myriad of yachts of all shapes, sizes and design. It was a peaceful evening with a light breeze, the sun shining, halyards tapping anxiously against masts. The sound of water lapping against innumerable hulls, the creaks and groans that are always heard around boats. The smell of salt on the air. I made my way slowly along, pausing every now and again to admire one of the finer yachts.

Eventually I found myself opposite the Casino, which faces one of the marina gates. The bar was open so I ventured in for a drink, wasting an hour or so by downing the odd gin or two. I was becoming increasingly angry and bored by this unnecessary delay. Here I was kicking my heels in this wretched place when I should have been en route to Sweden. In fact according to my original plan I would just be arriving. I ought to have taken this morning's ferry and damned the consequence. Looking back, apart from the week with Sands, I had wasted my entire leave. I should never have even contemplated this 'sailing' holiday. Why hadn't I taken Sands off somewhere special for a month? What a wasted opportunity! I was more angry with myself than anyone else.

I vented some of my frustration by walking briskly into town, muttering to myself as I went along, my subconscious guiding me unwittingly to the Montesol. I woke up from my reverie as I stopped outside, wondering for a second where I was.

I took a table inside and ordered another couple of gins. I realized that I was getting mildly drunk, but 'so what!' I thought. 'There's nothing better to do.' I found the Montesol depressing now that Sands had gone. We had spent too many happy, laughing hours there. Now it was cold in comparison and the waiters ruder than ever.

I decided to try another bar almost opposite and made my way rather unsteadily towards it. Choosing a table in a corner, I ordered a whisky and sat down to read a trashy book I had picked up at Santa Gertrudis; something about hidden Nazi gold. I can only have been there for a few minutes when three men came bustling in, chattering noisily in Spanish and occupying the table adjacent to mine.

'Aren't you Chris's brother? The soldier?' A voice broke in on my concentration. I glanced up. One of the three had spoken and was now looking at me expectantly. It had been an English voice – a London accent.

'Yes I am. How did you know?'

'Oh I've seen you about with him. Like to join us for a drink?' and before I could answer, with a nod at one another they got up and came over to sit at my table. We swapped introductions. The chap who had spoken called himself Brian. He was indeed a Londoner, but now resided on the island, making a living doing odd jobs. 'This and that,' he explained. Of his two friends, one was Spanish, I think called José, who hardly said a word during the next couple of hours. The second could have been any nationality, speaking English with a sort of trans-Atlantic drawl. I forget his name, let's call him Dennis. All three were in their late twenties and not dissimilar in appearance. José was typically swarthy, with a couple of days growth on his chin, longish black hair and a gold pendant around his neck. Brian and Dennis were fair skinned, but with deep tans and mousey coloured hair.

For two hours they plied me with drink, and if I had been pleasantly well oiled before, by the time they finished with me I was outrageously paralytic. Consequently I can remember very little of the evening's entertainment. The conversation was general. They asked me about life in the Army, I asked them about life on Ibiza. We talked about sailing, about the only topic we had in common. At one point, growing tired of their company, I made excuses and tried to escape, but they would have none of it. They asked me where I was going and instead of saying home to bed, I stupidly replied 'to another bar'. They came with me. Outside in the street we stopped for a breath of fresh air and Brian prodded a little tin and offered me what I initially thought was a cigarette. It took me a couple of moments to realise that it was a joint. I slurred at him that not only did I not want it but if he and his pals were going to smoke marijuana they could do it by themselves and f--- off! They looked at me as if I was mad, but the last thing I wanted was to be arrested for smoking pot. Rather ironic as events turned out.

In the second bar the heavy drinking continued until

eventually at what must have been shortly after eleven Brian suggested we go to a discotheque. I saw my chance and this time was successful in getting rid of them, but . . . was legless.

I cannot remember when it was that I was last in such a state. I oscillated my way back to the main square and lurched into the Montesol, even ordering a final whisky though I could not bring myself to touch it. I was quite incapable of walking as far as the Jaguar, let alone of driving it home, so I took a taxi back to Santa Gertrudis. Once there I collapsed into bed.

I did not wake up until past one o'clock the next afternoon and to have described myself as crapulent would have been an understatement. My hangover was extraordinary. There must have been at least a dozen little men inside my head working on the backs of my eyes with pneumatic drills. To stand was a nightmare in itself. I made the age-old promise.

'I'll never touch another drop, as long as I live. So help me God!' Chris and Jamille turned up later in the afternoon for a bath and found me nursing my hangover on a chair in the sunshine. They laughed when I told them where the Jaguar was and why I had been unable to drive it home the previous night, and suggested that we go into town later on for a meal and to collect it once we had eaten.

We had dinner at the Casino Restaurant. It was a jolly evening despite the remnants of my hangover, and I already found myself breaking the 'promise'. The more I saw of Chris, the more I realised how much I liked him. He had a genuine heart of gold, and a generous, gentle nature. He never ceased to surprise me, displaying what a year ago I would have described as uncharacteristically moderate views. He was obviously enjoying life, who could argue with the path he had chosen?

During dinner Chris told me that he had bought the tickets for the morrow's ferry and that it left at midday. He had also finalized details with Lokesh. I was to meet him in Sweden at ten o'clock on the next Friday evening. I asked for his telephone number in case we missed each other for any reason, but Chris explained that he was not on the telephone, hence the choice of the railway station for the rendezvous. If he gave me directions to Lokesh's house and I got lost, there would be no way for me to contact him. Better to choose a local landmark and wait to be collected.

Under the circumstances that seemed reasonable but I insisted that Chris ring Echo – an office answering service that many people in the San Juan area use because few have telephones of their own and there is no door-to-door postal service – every day until the weekend so I could at least leave a message there for him in case something should go wrong. It may seem strange that a time late in the evening was chosen for the meeting, but I had been expecting that. Up at San Juan on the Saturday night when I arrived back from Gibraltar Chris and I had made a rough approximation of the most likely time I could arrive in Linköping, and we had agreed that it was unlikely to be before Friday afternoon. I presumed that ten p.m. was, therefore, chosen to give me some additional leeway.

We said our goodnights outside the restaurant. Needing the walk to the Jaguar to clear my still throbbing head, I arranged that they would meet me in the morning at Santa Gertrudis in plenty of time to take my hire car back to the airport, before catching the ferry.

I made my way slowly to the car park, enjoying my final walk along the seafront and the evening's breeze. The Jaguar was not there. The car park was an empty plot of land, presumably where another block of flats would one day be built. There were numerous cars standing on it, but not the Jaguar. Puzzled I made another thorough check, but still no Jaguar. My initial thought was that there must be two parking areas exactly the same, and I had come to the wrong one. It also crossed my mind that in the previous evening's drunkenness I might well have forgotten where exactly I had left the car. I searched unsuccessfully for the next thirty minutes, my anxiety mounting as time went by. Finally it dawned on me, there could be no other explanation. Someone had stolen the damn thing! I found a cab, telling its driver to step on it and take me to the nearest police station. 'Pronto!' It turned out to be in a disused hospital, three minutes away on the outskirts of the city just off the main road leading to the airport. I paid off the driver and went inside.

In the reception area sat three rather sleepy policemen. The immediate problem was one of language, making me wish that

Chris had stayed with me. I speak not a word of Spanish and the bobbies on duty that night, no English. We communicated with hand signals and sound effects.

'My car' I said holding an imaginary steering wheel between my hands and going 'broom, broom', 'Has gone, stolen, finito!' I then shrugged my shoulders, opened my arms out wide and looked about feigning puzzlement.

They too looked puzzled, except genuinely so, glancing at one another as if to say 'Holy Mother, we've got a right one here!'

After many more expansive gestures, vroom vrooms, and pretending to make off with one of their hats, they finally seemed to understand, with beaming smiles and many Ahh's all round. I was told to follow one of them down a side corridor, which made me wonder if they had indeed understood or if I was being led away to cool my heels in a cell for the night.

I was taken to an office which was obviously used to take down public complaints. There was no one inside it. I was asked to wait. The room had a drinks bar type counter stretching across it about six foot in front of the door, presumably to keep people like me at bay. On my side there was a bench to sit on, nothing else. On the official side there was the expected clutter of metal filing cabinets, desks, telephones, typewriters and swivel chairs. It looked like organised chaos. I sat on the bench and waited.

A couple of minutes later I heard muttering voices and footsteps approaching along the corridor. The door swung open and two policemen entered. One passed through a flip-top segment of the counter, closing it behind him before settling himself behind a desk. He took out paper forms and carbon paper and, after sorting them into a bundle, rolled them into an antiquated typewriter with a flourish. He looked up expectantly.

His colleague stood beside me at the counter and started to ask questions. He spoke one or two words of English but otherwise we were back to the hand signals. Each time he acquired an answer that satisfied him he would translate it for the typist, who would then fill out another caption on his form. I handed over my passport which saved a lot of time and effort. The questioning, translating and typing were eventually done and the triplicated form brought over for me to sign. The questions on it turned out to be written in both Spanish and English, so why hadn't they just given it to me to fill out? But who was I to argue? All the form stated were my personal particulars and that I had reported a vehicle stolen, as well as listing all items that I could remember had been inside it, which included the car's documents and a radiocassette player. Nothing should have been simpler but it had taken the best part of forty-five minutes to complete. I signed all three copies with not a great deal of interest because I realised that Chris would have to come down to sort things out in the morning. The typist took the signed documents into a side room where there must have been someone sleeping, for I heard him being shaken awake, followed by a loud yawn and a gabbling of fuzzy Spanish. Eventually the man returned with my signatures countersigned. I was given one copy and asked to telephone for news the next day. A taxi was called and I was on my way back to Santa Gertrudis a few minutes later.

I was in bed and asleep before midnight. I awoke the next morning wondering what to do, as well as being concerned for my brother's car. The trip to Sweden was now an obvious non-starter. Even if the Jaguar was recovered within the next couple of days, I was sure the police investigation into its theft would take a long time. In any case, unless I succeeded in departing Ibiza that morning, I was never going to be able to make the journey, leaving enough spare time for mishaps, to ensure a timely arrival back in London in exactly a week's time. I might as well fly home as soon as possible.

Chris and Jamille put in an early appearance at nine o'clock. I rather apprehensively explained what had happened, after all if I had not left the Jaguar downtown none of this would have happened. I would have forgiven Chris if he had been more than a little angry with me. However, he took it rather philosophically:

'Shit! An effing wonderful time for this to happen.' Then, after a short pause: 'Not to worry, it's a small island and that car sticks out like a sore thumb. I'm sure the police will find it soon enough, unless that is, the thieves managed to get it off the island before you reported it stolen last night. Lucky it's insured. Look, I've arranged to see my bank manager and Jamille needs to do some shopping. Why don't you go to the Police Station to see if there is any news? We will join you there as soon as possible.'

'Yes okay,' it was the very least I could do, 'but I want to return my hire car first. Unless I get it back by ten I will have to pay another day's full charge and it has already cost me a fortune. I'll take a taxi to the Police from there, but do be quick, it's damn difficult not being able to speak Spanish.' I added that I would be catching the next plane to London now that the drive to Sweden would have to be called off. He looked a touch crestfallen but he must have realised that he had to face facts. We made a contingency plan of meeting at the ferry terminal at midday, if we missed each other beforehand. Looking back I think Chris may have been intending to check all vehicles boarding the ferry to ensure his was not among them, being spirited away, but he did not actually say as much.

I returned the hire car with seconds to spare, thus avoiding an extra day's charge, and then taxied to the Guardia Civil Station, but not before checking the departure times for flights to England.

As I entered the by now familiar reception area, a rotund officer came jollying towards me, his face a huge smile.

'Ah, Ah, yer car, eet ees . . . .umm, er . . .,' his English failed him. He turned about, went to a desk and fished out a paper form. He thrust it towards me, on it among other things was printed: LOST/RECOVERED. He pointed gleefully to 'RECOVERED', puffing out his chest as if to say, 'Aren't we the Ibizan Police terribly, terribly efficient.'

I had to admit, it had been quick work. I could not help wondering what state the car was in though. My jolly friend led me importantly back to the previous night's office. Once again triplicate sheets of paper were rolled into ancient typewriters. Once again a report was maddeningly slowly tapped out. I tried to explain that the owner was on his way down to complete any formalities, but that produced nothing by way of response. In turn they explained to me, using the same old hand signals, that I must now go to the Guardia Municipal, they were the Guardia Civil and made it clear that they did not like dealing in such lowly matters. There I would be given back the car.

'What today?' I asked.

'Yes, immediately.'

It was a quarter past eleven. I might just make the ferry if I hurried. 'Me take boat (finger tips touching together in front of me forming the bows of an imaginary ship) with Jaguar, to Valencia today. Please (hands clasped as if in prayer). Quick, quick. No Guardia Municipal. You!' (pointing).

They looked at one another, shrugged their shoulders and sighed at the ceiling. They caught my sense of urgency. A telephone call was made, presumably to their poorer cousins. I was shown a map, and a grotty finger nail pointed to a spot where again presumably the Jaguar was to be found. A taxi was called, the driver given instructions, there was much excited shouting and waving of arms. I was literally manhandled into the back seat, the door slammed. We roared away. I sat back – the driver seemed to know the way. He took me to an apartment building in the northern outskirts of Ibiza City, a few blocks away from the Casino and the marinas.

When we arrived, there was the Jaguar, apparently undamaged, with a Police tow truck parked alongside. I told the two policemen leaning against it that I had come for the car, showing them the ignition keys. They looked at me blankly. I gave them this morning's form, typed out at Police HQ. This they understood. They radioed base to check and after receiving what must have been the correct reply, removed a huge padlock and chain that had been looped through the steering wheel and around the brake pedal. Meanwhile I inspected the car. The only apparent damage was a broken rear quarter-light on the driver's side. Shattered pieces of crystallised glass littered the back seat. On the inside the car had been stripped of all moveable objects: gone were cassette tapes, loose change, all documents and every other piece of the clutter that seems to accumulate in any car. The thieves had made an attempt at removing the radio, but had only succeeded in buckling its facade before giving up. The ignition switch and steering lock had not been interfered with; normally they have to be broken off before a stolen vehicle can be hot wired, but I remembered that Chris had kept a spare set of keys in a pocket in the driver's door, along with the car papers. The bad guys had been given an easy time of it.

The police were totally uninterested in any kind of investigation, not even taking fingerprints. It was obviously enough that the car had been recovered. They drove off towards the city centre and I put my foot down back to Santa Gertrudis, where I had left my luggage. With luck I would just have sufficient time to collect it and make it to the ferry terminal on time.

Chris and Jamille were waiting, taking a cup of coffee in the terminal café. They seemed astonished at seeing me appear in the Jaguar, and after a hurried explanation we raced onto the ferry, fortunately it had been delayed and we were the last to board. Chris thrust a newspaper into my hand once we had climbed to the passenger decks. Its headlines were full of the capsizing of a Townsend Thoresen cross-Channel ferry, the *Herald of Free Enterprise*. There was a large picture of the stricken vessel lying on its side. The death toll was expected to be high, rescue teams were still searching. A tragedy. We looked at each other; not good news especially when we were now about to spend five hours on a similar ship ourselves.

The ship berthed in Valencia that evening and we drove in convoy to Barcelona, where Chris led the way to a small hotel he knew in the Port District, called the Monte Carlo.

I was up early the next morning but it was not until shortly before eleven that we found ourselves back on the road. Travelling with Christopher was proving to be at the same lethargic pace that typified his habitual lifestyle. En route to Andorra we stopped for a late lunch while a roadside workshop welded the Jaguar's exhaust pipe that had started to blow, and I took advantage of an industrial vacuum cleaner to hoover up the broken window glass.

There was not even a hint of snow in the Principality's capital when we arrived late in the afternoon, too late as it turned out to make any real effort at buying a pair of skis. I did try in a couple of shops but the only ones available were of the wrong sort and far too expensive, even at duty-free prices. I have skis at home and I did not want to waste money buying a second set for just a week's skiing, unless they were really cheap. I could always hire some at the resort. We did manage to find a new spare tyre for the Jaguar, the old one being totally worn out and, therefore, useless. I was not going to drive 2,500 kilometres across the Continent without one, and Chris in any case wanted the car to be in as good a condition as possible for its new owner – hence his insistence that we stop to weld the exhaust earlier. We did try looking for a Jaguar agent to buy a new quarter-light but without success. It was the same story with spares for the jeep.

After stocking up with duty free, we headed for the French border, at last encountering snow at the very top of the pass, but the slopes appeared deserted and there was no sign of any après-ski. Perhaps it was too late in the evening. Once in France we made for Narbonne, eventually stopping for the night at a motel in its outskirts.

I left Chris and Jamille at eight o'clock the next morning and my onward journey proceeded without any major problems. It was easy driving, purely a question of sitting on one motorway after another for the entire length of Europe. The route I had chosen taking me past Lyon, Dijon and Nancy; crossing into Germany at Saarbrücken, then northwards again to Cologne, through the Ruhr Valley to Dortmund, then Hannover, east of Hamburg and finally to Travemunde, from where I intended to catch a ferry to Trelleborg in Sweden.

At one point when venturing into Lyon to find a bank and buy some French money, I had to brake hard, not realising that the lights had changed, and I noticed that my driver's seat shifted on its foundations. It did not worry me to begin with, but once you realise that a fault exists you begin to notice it more and more. I began to feel the seat rock whenever I accelerated, slowed down, turned a corner, or adjusted my position, and it seemed to be growing worse. I became concerned that I might at any moment be pitched into the back seat without warning – not to be recommended while travelling along at over 100 miles per hour. I felt down with my left hand and found that the screws attaching the seat to the floor were loose. In fact, at least one appeared almost out of its socket.

The next time I stopped for petrol I asked the attendant if I could borrow a screwdriver, but all I received in return was a gruff 'non', and a typical Gallic shrug of the shoulders. I tried again in Germany and this time succeeded in borrowing one, but not of the right size. The attendant tried to help and together we discovered that the screws had star-shaped heads, like a Phillips head but with six points. The attendant told me that I would need 'ein spezial . . . ' referring to the screwdriver. I was in a hurry and did not labour the point. Later on Friday morning, having run out of Deutschmarks, I left the motorway and drove into a village called Bad Nenndorf to find a bank. Having changed my money I took the opportunity to try and buy a suitable screwdriver, but although I tried in two shops, neither could help me. I tried again in Denmark with no joy, and because I was determined not to be beaten I had one last go on arrival in Sweden.

I slept in the car on Thursday night, just outside Cologne, where I had become hopelessly lost because I had run out of Marks and the only motel I found wouldn't take my credit cards. On arrival in Travemunde on Friday morning I found that I had missed that morning's ferry and would have to wait all day for the next one, not due to sail until eleven that night. At least that is what I was initially told but a kindly girl selling the tickets told me of another ferry terminal at Puttgarden that had sailings to Denmark every hour or so. 'Why not drive up through Denmark to Sweden?' she asked me, 'you will save many hours that way.' That is how I was able to try again for the screwdriver in Denmark, and why I entered Sweden via Helsingborg and not Trelleborg.

Having passed through customs at Helsingborg, I again had to stop for petrol. I had another 350 kilometres to go and since it was past six thought it best to top up straight away in case everything closed. The first petrol station I came across had a large display of tools on sale so I had a look for the elusive screwdriver. Again no luck, but the cashier told me that there was another garage just three miles up the road that would certainly have what I wanted. I did not realise at the time that the Swedish mile is ten kilometres long, so after approximately three British miles I turned off the main road into a village called Åstorp where I found a garage.

When I entered its kiosk I immediately realised that I had been wasting my time, but I asked anyway. The lady cashier could speak no English but she pointed to a man standing behind me. I explained what I was looking for and he told me

rather hesitantly to . . . 'come, come,' and led me outside. At
first I thought he was taking me to the garage workshop but
instead he jumped into an old Volvo waving at me to follow
on behind. Time was running short, it was close to six thirty
and I had to meet Lokesh at ten, but I felt I could not just
ignore this man who was obviously trying to be helpful.
Another five minutes would not hurt, so I climbed into the
Jaguar and did as I was bid. The Volvo sped around a couple
of corners, eventually stopping outside a hardware shop. It
looked closed.

My new friend got out of his car and approached the shop
door, taking a bunch of keys from his pocket. I realised that
he must be the shopkeeper and was about to open up his
premises just for me. 'Very kind chap,' I thought. We went
inside the dark and quiet shop. A light was switched on and
at the same time an older man emerged from a door behind
the counter. The two men, who looked as though they could
have been father and son, spoke to each other briefly in
Swedish, then I was asked over to a large display of
screwdrivers and told to take my pick. After searching through
several rows I found one that looked as though it would do the
trick. I asked if I might borrow it, but the younger man looked
pained that I didn't want to buy anything after he had taken
so much trouble to give me what I wanted. I suppose he had
a valid point so I amended my request to simply see if it fitted
the seat screws, assuring him that if it did I would indeed buy
his screwdriver. I went out to the Jaguar and leaning through
the passenger door tested to see if the tool fitted one of the
loose screws on the driver's seat. It did, so I returned to the
shop and made the purchase.

I was pleased to have won my battle with the troublesome
seat, and expressed my pleasure by saying:

'Thank you very, very much. You have been extremely
kind. You have saved my life.' I don't know how much he
understood, but my obvious exaggeration appeared to please
him, and he beamed at me as we said our goodbyes.

Once back in the car I quickly tightened every loose screw
I could find on the seat. It was dark by this stage and I had to
work by touch, but I cured the problem in about thirty
seconds. Throwing the screwdriver into the glove box, I

retraced my steps to the main road and headed as quickly as I could northwards on the final leg of my journey to Linköping.

If I have dwelt on the issue of this screwdriver, it is because it became a lynchpin of the prosecution case against me.

I must have broken all the speed limits in my drive to Linköping, although at the time I did not realise it. I knew I was driving fast but was travelling with the flow of traffic and most of the vehicles I passed were heavily laden lorries. There was a good deal of snow about; it was piled up on either side of the road, but the surface was dry enough. I did not want to risk missing Lokesh, otherwise I could give up all hope of going skiing.

Shortly before nine-thirty I left the motorway and followed the signs for Linköping town centre. I could not have known that I had barely an hour's freedom remaining. I stopped by a pretty blonde girl:

'Excuse me, can you tell me the way to the railway station, please?'

Four

'Drugs.'

Before I could ask for more detail the fat sergeant turned on his heels and left me. The cell door clanged shut with a rattle of keys.

My initial reaction was one of relief, almost amusement. So it had all been a ghastly mistake, there was no cause for concern. My earlier confusion gave way to a sudden feeling of confidence, I was positive I would be set free as soon as this mix-up was sorted out, probably in the morning. After all I knew that I had no connection with drugs of any sort – I certainly had no drugs on me, I had never even experimented with illicit drugs of any sort. The whole idea was too ludicrous for words.

I sat on the cell bunk, wrapped in the thin blanket, my back against the wall and my knees drawn up to my chin. I was too keyed up to sleep and as the hours passed worries and uncertainties began to creep into my consciousness. My arrest had been no chance affair. It had been conducted effectively, with purpose, and in a fairly professional manner. Those policemen had known exactly who they were after and they must have known why. That must mean they had good grounds for believing that a crime was being committed. Since I knew that I had done nothing untoward I came to the not unnatural conclusion that they must have been after Lokesh or his friend, and I had been arrested purely on the grounds that I had been seen with them. But why? Was Lokesh involved with drugs? Was the driver of the Saab? The answer was that I did not know. I suppose anything was possible, but all I did know was that it did not concern me.

All these thoughts and more went drifting through my mind.

If Lokesh was a drug smuggler, did that mean Christopher was? Surely not, and even if he was he would never have involved me. Never! I felt certain that whatever the case he was not a party to it. The more sinister possibilities were unthinkable. I realised that there was little point in further speculation – the situation would be clarified soon enough.

I tried to rest but sleep came only in fits and starts; it had been a pretty frightening night and I was finding it impossible to relax. Concern for one's future is a powerful stimulant. Even to be suspected of a drugs crime was bad enough, indeed a stigma that might prove difficult to live down. I was going to have some explaining to do.

I knew that it is normal practice for a suspect to be interviewed as soon after his arrest as possible, whilst the shock of capture is still strong. The truth has a habit of tumbling out of a confused mind, and I was therefore expecting to be called for questioning at any moment, but morning came and still no one disturbed my nervous slumbers. I could hear nothing outside my cell, the silence was eerie. It added to the sense of unreality that had long ago gripped me.

In mid-morning a policeman brought me a roll and a plastic cup of lukewarm coffee. He said nothing except to ask me if I wanted to go to the lavatory. I went, not through any bursting need but merely to relieve the boredom. I padded after the man in my stockinged feet, trying to question him on what was going on but he would have none of it, returning me immediately to my cell after I had finished. Once there I ate my 'breakfast' with a hunger but not a great deal of relish.

It was not until early in the afternoon that my cell door opened again to reveal a tall man in civilian clothes. He introduced himself as Kriminalinspectör Jan Bihlar from the Uppsala Drugs Squad. His smile was friendly and he shook my hand in an almost warm greeting.

'What in God's name is going on?' I demanded.

'Come. We will discuss matters.'

He took me to a small, bland interview room of the type that anyone who has seen a thriller on television would recognize, where we sat facing each other across a wooden table.

The man who confronted me was in his mid forties, with a

muscular build. He looked fit and I would guess that in his younger days he might have been quite an athlete. He was good-looking, his face suntanned with a strong jaw, large nose, and prominent forehead exaggerated by a receding hairline. His hair was brown and brushed back. He completed the image with a droopy moustache. He was dressed in the type of casual clothes that I was more used to seeing on teenagers – a fake Lacoste sports shirt, baggy grey trousers and white sneakers. He spoke passable but far from fluent English, with a 'Hurdy Gurdy' accent, and frequently referred to a dictionary in this and subsequent interviews.

Bihlar started the interview by asking me if I was prepared to admit my guilt.

'What guilt? What crime? No one has even told me why I have been arrested, except for some mumbled mention of drugs. I will certainly not admit to any guilt because I have committed no crime. I have done nothing wrong,' I cried. I was trying to remain calm, but I was becoming angry and I suppose it showed in the tone of my voice. 'I have nothing to admit to.'

Bihlar looked at me, then reaching into his briefcase he took out a pad of lined paper and a ballpoint pen, and without a word started to write something down. There was a pause whilst he did so. When he looked up again I asked him what he had written.

'I have written that you deny the accusations.'

'What accusations?' I snarled.

He stared me straight in the eye, and after a theatrical lull sighed with feigned resignation.

'We know that you and your friends are drug smugglers, and we believe that you have smuggled a large consignment of hashish into Sweden. You are accused of a serious drugs crime, and serious smuggling of goods.'

'But that is ridiculous, I have done nothing of the sort.'

'We shall see,' he said.

'Yes we shall. Have you searched my luggage, my car? If so you will find that there are no drugs anywhere. This is stupid.'

'Maybe, maybe not. But now I want you to tell me exactly why you have come to Sweden, and why you met up with those two men at Linköping station.'

My mind was racing; the situation was getting serious, but

I was fortified by the fact that I had nothing to hide and therefore nothing to fear. Although this man seemed so sure of himself, I was confident that once the police had conducted a thorough search they would let me go. There was, however, one nagging doubt at the back of my mind, and that was Christopher. Whatever was going on I was as convinced as I could be that he had no part in it, but I also realised that because he was a friend of this Lokesh, because he had asked me to drive to Sweden, and due to the very lifestyle he chose to follow, a shadow of suspicion would almost certainly fall his way. I therefore, on the spur of the moment and without time for additional thought, made a snap decision to leave his name out of the issue. In other words not to mention that he had asked me to deliver his Jaguar to Lokesh.

It was an incredibly stupid thing to do and one that I was later to bitterly regret, but I have to admit that faced with a similar situation again I would probably make the same decision. I will not try to justify myself except perhaps to say that it was an instinctive act made under great pressure, at a time when my mind was far from clear, to protect a member of my family who I thought would otherwise come under needless suspicion.

For the next two hours I told the inspector who I was and gave him an outline of all that had taken place in the preceding 24 days. He made notes in Swedish throughout. Everything I said was the exact truth except in one vital area. I needed a reason for my meeting with Lokesh. I stated that I had come to Sweden to go skiing. That was true. I stated that I had been invited to stay the night at Lokesh's house. That was true. But it was still not an explanation as to how these arrangements had been made. There was no alternative but to make something up. I therefore said that after seeing Lokesh at the petrol station on Ibiza we had bumped into each other a couple of days later outside the Montesol. Over a drink he had asked how I was enjoying my holiday on the island.

'It's been great fun, but it's almost over now. I'm leaving next week to drive back to England. I'm taking Chris's Jaguar back to London to sell it for him. However I am planning on stopping en route to go skiing in the Alps.'

'Oh you ought to go skiing in Sweden, it's fantastic up there this time of year. I'm flying up there myself next week, if you want I could always give you a bed for the night on your way to the slopes.'

I told Bihlar that this conversation had planted the idea of visiting Sweden in my mind and that days later when Lokesh had dropped by at the villa in Santa Gertrudis, I had told him that I had decided to drive up there. We had then arranged the meeting at Linköping railway station.

Pretty thin? Yes, but short of telling Bihlar that Christopher had asked me to deliver the Jaguar, it was the best I could do. I was not telling the whole truth but not so much through mendacity as through omission. I did not feel at all pleased with myself, but I was comforted by the belief that in the long run it would make little difference. They were going to have to let me go in the very near future. I would have to live with my conscience.

Inspector Bihlar brought his interrogation to an end by asking me if I had used both the Jaguar's petrol tanks on my drive through the Continent. I replied that I had. He asked me if I had made any telephone calls during the journey. I replied that I had tried to leave a message for Christopher with Echo at one point when a warning light had started to flash, but I had been unable to get through. In any case the problem with the light must have been a short circuit, because it had had no effect on the running of the car. Finally he asked me if I wanted a lawyer, and also if I wanted to notify the British Embassy in Stockholm of my arrest. I pondered these questions for a few seconds. I considered that I had no need of a lawyer and being more than a little embarrassed at my arrest, and convinced that I would soon be released, I decided that it would be better to keep as low a profile as possible. I refused both offers.

As he escorted me back to my cell, there was obviously to be no release that weekend, Bihlar asked me in a conversational tone what my job in Northern Ireland had entailed.

'I was a staff officer working in the Army Headquarters, but really I do not see what it has to do with your investigation.'

'No I am just interested, but I think you are in the British SAS.'

At the time I passed this remark off as a joke and thought

nothing more of it, but as events were to turn out this subject was to become an absolute fixation with Inspector Bihlar. Quite why I shall never know.

On the following Monday the police transferred me to a remand centre in Västerås, a town about 120 kms north west of Stockholm. I was driven there in a Prison Service Volvo estate car with blacked out windows, and apart from the driver, an elderly man with a large beer gut, my only guard was a woman in her late thirties. I was not even handcuffed. On arrival in Västerås the driver lost his way and at one point left the car to ask directions in a shop. It would have been a cinch to escape, but the thought never crossed my mind. Perhaps if I had known what was in store for me at the hands of this supposedly enlightened country I might have reacted differently.

The reception awaiting me at the remand centre was similar to the one I had received at Motala, except in this case it was handled by prison guards, not the police. Again there was a stripsearch, my belt and shoes returned to me hours earlier were once more removed, but this time I was allowed to keep my watch. I was placed in an identical cell to the one I had left in Motala: the same double-glazed window with drawn blinds; the same bunkbed fastened to the wall; the same table, fastened to the wall. The same bench to sit on, fastened to the wall. An internal air-vent hissed noisily at me from the ceiling but it was not enough to keep the air fresh or cool. There was however one improvement; this cell had a wash basin with a tap I could actually control myself. The quality of life was improving.

This was the third day that I had been totally isolated from the outside world. I had not been allowed to make any telephone calls, not even to my family to report what had happened and to say I was safe and well; nor was I allowed to see a newspaper or listen to the radio. My guards would not talk to me. I could not have felt more alone.

In fact, as I was to learn as the months rolled by, this was normal procedure for all suspects held in custody. The concept of bail is unknown in Sweden, due to the mistaken notion that it favours the rich. Anyone arrested is placed under the direct control of a public prosecutor, who has the power to detain him without charge for an indeterminate period whilst he conducts his enquiries and decides whether there is sufficient evidence to make a formal charge. Furthermore everyone, regardless of the type of crime, is placed in solitary confinement to avoid collusion with others arrested or those still being sought. To this end there are remand centres, known as Häktets (pronounced 'Hektet') attached to every large police station, but usually run by the prison service. I was to get to know the system well.

Inspector Bihlar came to see me for the second time at 1300 hours on Tuesday, the day after my transfer to Västerås. He appeared well pleased with himself and informed me immediately we were alone together in an interview room that a large quantity of cannabis had been found hidden in the Jaguar. He again asked if I was prepared to admit my guilt.

I was stunned; the feeling of shock was numbing. I just stared at the man in astonishment. The enormity of my position flooded over me. It could not be true, it just couldn't be true. Surely there had been some mistake? Everything seemed so totally unreal, a nightmare from which I would suddenly wake up.

'I have no idea how those drugs came to be in the car. I have no idea what is going on,' I said quietly, and then with my voice rising. 'You have got to believe me! What possible motive have I to smuggle drugs? Why should I risk my career, my well-being, everything, to smuggle drugs? I am not short of money, I have a well-paid job. I would never do anything so irresponsible. For God's sake man, do I look like a drug smuggler?'

He agreed that I was certainly an unusual drug smuggler, and then asked: 'If you are telling me the truth, then who could have done so ghastly a thing to you in luring you to Sweden under such circumstances?'

'I don't know, I just don't know.' I should have told Bihlar the complete truth then and there, but I held back. I was still totally convinced, more so now than ever, that Christopher would never have used me in this fashion. If I had been tricked then so had he, and I could not bring myself to point the finger of suspicion at him. I felt certain in any case that as soon as he learnt of my arrest he would find out what had gone on, and then come forward to clear the matter up. It would not help the situation if he was to be immediately arrested as well. It also crossed my mind that the police could be trying to deceive me into believing that drugs had been discovered in the car in order to gauge my reaction to the news, to establish whether I was involved in whatever the others had been arrested for.

If there was cannabis in the Jaguar, I had no idea how it had got there, nor who could have hidden it there. However, it would not have been that difficult for anyone to have done so, after all the car had been sitting unattended outside the villa in Santa Gertrudis for months. I pointed this out to Bihlar, adding that it might be no coincidence that the villa had been broken into during my return visit to Gibraltar, and that the car itself had been stolen just days before I left for Sweden.

We spent the next hour going over parts of my previous statement but the inspector was obviously not that interested into delving into much more detail at this stage.

I told Bihlar that I now needed a lawyer, and that I wanted to telephone the British Embassy, my Commanding Officer in England, and my family. This last request was refused but when he grew tired of questioning me we went to an office to make the other calls. He did the dialling and sat facing me listening in on an extension whilst I spoke to a member of the Embassy staff who promised that someone would come to see me at the first opportunity. I then rang my Commanding Officer, telling him what had happened and that I hoped to be back at work by the end of the week. This comment brought a caustic smile to Bihlar's lips, he also winked at me knowingly once I had put the receiver down, and tapping the side of his nose with his forefinger he accused me of being an army spy. Again I laughed this off as some kind of silly joke.

It was an extremely worried man that was returned to his cell at 1430 hours.

The next morning I was informed that a lawyer was waiting to see me, and I was escorted to the by now familiar interview room. As I entered a portly man in a dark suit rose from a chair to greet me. He introduced himself as Tom Placht, an advokat from Uppsala. We shook hands, it was good to see a friendly face wearing what looked like a genuinely sympathetic expression.

Tom Placht is in his forties, about 5ft. 9ins. tall, and will I hope not mind if I describe him as slightly rotund. He has deep set eyes, short dark hair, and a Scandinavian style beard and moustache groomed to hug the contours of his round face.

I was to find out later that he had been specifically approached by the District Court of Uppsala to represent me in view of the fact that his knowledge of English was considerably more sophisticated than that of most of his colleagues; his academic record was impressive and he had for some years taught at the Faculty of Law at the University of Uppsala (the main University town in Sweden). Furthermore, and this may be more relevant, he was not considered to be a 'crony' of the prosecutor in charge of my case.

I will not let this opportunity pass without praising the dedication that Placht was to show in representing me. Also the courage and considerable sacrifice made by him on my behalf throughout. He was to prove fearless in defence of my interests and on numerous occasions was to express embarrassment as a Swede for the attitudes and actions of some of his fellow countrymen. He has become a firm friend and ally.

On that first morning he sat me down and explained the severity of the situation in which I found myself.

'I understand you are denying the charges, Captain Hayward, but let me tell you that you are in a very unenviable position. It is going to be difficult to prove your innocence, very difficult.'

'But surely,' I interrupted, 'it is up to them to prove my guilt, and they will not be able to because I have done nothing wrong.'

Placht held up his hand to stop me. 'When you have been arrested at the wheel of a car full of cannabis, the boot may be on the other foot, I think that may be the correct English expression. But we shall see. Before we go through your story, let me explain my position to you. I will represent you to the best of my ability regardless of how you plead, but what I will not do is defend you as an innocent man if you tell me that you are in fact guilty. Is that understood?'

'Perfectly, but you need have no fears, because I am pleading not guilty, because that is exactly what I am. Not guilty.'

'Good,' he said.

'There is one more thing I should tell you. There is no such thing as a deal with the police in Sweden. No such thing as plea-bargaining. So that is not an available possibility for you.'

'Again I understand that, thank you, but since I have nothing to bargain with the thought had not crossed my mind.'

We then went through my statement, just in outline to give Placht a background picture. I wanted to tell him the complete truth, I very nearly did, but after what he had just told me I held back, and repeated the exact same story to him as I had previously related to Bihlar. He made notes throughout.

When I finished he took a blank piece of paper and on it drew a chart. He swivelled it around to face me. The chart was a long line marked off into segments. He used his pen as a pointer. He explained that one extreme was innocence and freedom, the other guilt and prison. The half way mark between the two was the point of indecision, in other words doubt, and this point at least had to be reached. Because I had been arrested in a car loaded with cannabis my own position on the chart, at that precise moment in time, was a great deal closer to the guilt extreme than the innocent. It was his job now, if we were to win, to bring it back the other way, but it was going to be an uphill struggle all the way. My own analogy was that it was rather like starting a football match six goals down.

The doldrums struck in a major way once Placht had left me. He had painted a very black picture indeed and I could not have felt more dejected. How could I have possibly found myself in this position? Another fundamental concern was what my Regiment would make of all this once the news broke. It was clear now that I was in an extremely serious predicament. I asked for pen and paper, and sat down to compose one of the most difficult letters I have ever felt it my duty to write. It was to Colonel James Emson, the Regimental Lieutenant Colonel Commanding The Household Cavalry, and its purpose was to explain the situation and to resign my commission.

There now followed a period of waiting. They continued to keep me totally isolated. Apart from an hour's 'exercise' each morning, and when I went for a shower or to relieve myself,

I was left alone in my cell. I was given books to help pass the time, nothing else. The exercise was not really exercise at all: I was taken by lift to a small walled cage on the roof of the building. It was about five feet wide by ten long, and open to the elements. All I could see was the sky through the roof bars, and the guard watching me through the gated entrance. I could hear other prisoners, presumably in similar boxes, but I could not see them. In fact I never saw another inmate: even the corridors were empty whenever I was permitted to venture into them. My 'cage' supplied me with some much-needed fresh air, a change of scenery (although scenery is hardly the word to use), but little else. There was scarcely room to move, let alone exercise, especially since snow had been brushed into a frozen bank at one end. However I found the cold air exhilarating after the stuffiness of my cell.

The days went by and I slowly became used to the routine. Breakfast, a sandwich and coffee, at 0700 hours. Lunch, actually not too bad, at 1100 hours. Dinner, or rather high tea and again not bad with a varied menu, at 1600 hours. Exercise and ablutions in the mornings.

Placht came to see me twice more. We went through my statement in exact detail, more so than I had yet been asked to give the police. He told me that 50.5 kilos of cannabis had been found hidden in the bodywork of the Jaguar, and to find it the police had had to strip the car down completely. There had been pictures of it in the papers and on the television. He could not say anything else about the case, nor what was happening in the outside world. It was clear that he was very concerned not to breach the prosecutor's restrictions.

On the second occasion he informed me that I was to be brought before a Court in Uppsala on the following Tuesday 24 March. He explained that this was normal procedure – an arrested suspect had to be brought before a judge within nine working days. It would not be a trial, purely a hearing to ascertain whether I should continue to be held in custody. My hopes rose only to be immediately dashed.

'The prosecutor is going to request that you be detained for a month to allow him to complete his enquiries,' Placht said almost casually.

'A month! But that's impossible. I can't stay here for another

month. I'm already late for my new job in London as it is. Can
we fight this, Tom? Can I have bail?'

'I can ask that the prosecutor be only granted two weeks, but
I do not honestly think that it will do the slightest good. And
Simon,' he looked me straight in the eye and paused, 'there is
no bail system in Sweden. You must understand that they will
keep you in custody until they decide to charge you or not. I
should also warn you that solitary confinement will be used as
a weapon to break you in order to obtain a confession. They
will not admit this, of course, but it is what always happens.'

For the second time in a week I found myself too shocked
to speak. How could this be true? Wasn't Sweden known as the
world's moral superpower, the great bastion of human rights?
Was it not supposed to have a liberal and open society? And
here I was being kept without charge, in solitary confinement,
and now being told that the authorities could keep me for at
least another month, and that they would use passive coercion
as a weapon to break me. In other words to force a confession
from an innocent man at any cost. It was unbelievable. The
sense of unreality gripped me anew.

'Tom, this cannot be happening! This is 1987, we are in
Western Europe. Surely I must be charged within a few days
or released? Surely they cannot continue to keep me in solitary
confinement indefinitely?'

His only answer was . . . 'It is the Swedish way.'

The police did not come to question me again before the
court appearance, my only other visitor was a Vice Consul
from the Embasssy called Jenny Cummings. A woman of
about my own age, tall, thin and with shoulder-length dark
hair. She was sympathetic to my position but unable to do
much to help. She explained that there were numerous British
citizens either in prison or awaiting trial in the country.

All the Embassy was able to do was ensure that they received
the same treatment as indigenous Swedes. That was no help
at all. I asked whether, since there was no bail system in
Sweden, the Embassy would be prepared to request to have me
released into its custody. Miss Cummings appeared rather
taken aback by this suggestion and her reply was a very definite
no. There was no contingency available for such a move, and
in any case the Swedes would almost certainly refuse to

contemplate it. She promised to get a message through to my family to say I was okay, and left me feeling very alone and helpless indeed.

Tuesday morning found me in a somewhat apprehensive mood due to the forthcoming court hearing. However, I also felt a keen sense of anticipation because I was going to be able to put my case before an impartial judge. Despite being told to expect a further month's detention, I could not help but feel a ray of hope that the court might side with me and order my immediate release.

I was driven to Uppsala by minibus, this time handcuffed to a guard, arriving shortly before midday. I remember little of the journey, which took a few minutes over an hour. Whilst I enjoyed my first view of normal people for eleven days, I was too preoccupied with my immediate future to take much notice of the passing scenery.

The Press were awaiting my arrival. There was a crowd of TV cameras and reporters standing sentinel at the entrance to the police station underground car-park, and I presume another at the main station entrance. I found it disconcerting in the extreme that so much interest was being shown in me. The minibus had the customary blacked out windows so I must have been invisible, but nevertheless there was a flurry of activity and much taking of photographs as we swept down the entrance ramp and through a set of automatic doors that closed behind us.

We halted in the relative tranquility of the basement car-park, and I was marched a few feet to an awaiting lift that whisked me up four floors to another Häktet. My guards were in a state of excitement at this obviously unaccustomed media attention and chattered away like children amongst themselves. I found the very thought that I was the cause of it all highly embarrassing.

They put me in an empty cell: this time I was allowed to keep my shoes but not my belt. I had no idea what was going on nor why I had been brought to a remand centre rather than a court building. I had still not grown accustomed to not being my own master and to being treated like a farm animal which needs no explanation as to what is happening to it.

I sat alone and miserable, the future looked bleak: it was

incredible to think that life had sunk to this level in less than two weeks.

The door opened and Placht came bustling in, a bright smile on his face. He was trying to cheer me up.

'Well you have certainly attracted a good deal of attention. There are so many reporters at the courthouse that the judge has decided to hold his hearing here in the police station. It is better this way, you will not be seen by any of them.'

He handed me a tie I had previously asked to borrow from him. I felt and looked scruffy, totally inadequately dressed, in my old sailing clothes, to face a judge in front of whom I was going to have to plead for my freedom, not to mention my future. The tie made a big improvement, at least psychologically. Placht advised me to speak out confidently for myself when the time came, and to emphasise the lack of motive to change my entire lifestyle to suddenly stoop to the level of a drugs courier. I had already mentally prepared a short address. As for himself, he was going to demand my immediate release, but he could not have looked less optimistic.

The time came and we were escorted to the temporary court, which was to be held in a conference room. As I entered several people were already seated around one end of a long table. The man I took to be the judge was at the head. My first impression was that he appeared to be rather young for the role, reminding me more of a doctor than a judge. He was a clean cut man in, I would guess, his early forties but looking rather younger, with fair hair going bald, a weak chin and thin face. He wore a dark blue suit and gave off a quiet, almost nervous aura. Beside him, but set slightly off to one side, sat a young female clerk, who took notes throughout the following proceedings.

My guards detached themselves from me and sat along the wall near to the door. Placht and I sat on one side of the table to the judge's right, beside an elderly woman who whispered to me that she was my interpreter. Facing us were two men I had not seen before. The judge introduced them as Prosecutor Ulf Forsberg and Kriminalinspectör Jan-Erik Nilsson, and himself as Ulf Hellbacher.

So there we sat, Tom Placht, the interpreter and I, facing the prosecution along opposite sides of a table, with the judge and his clerk at the head of it. It hardly looked or felt like a Court of Law.

Forsberg was a small man, sported a walrus-style moustache and his mousy-coloured hair was cut so that it just covered the tops of his ears. He was always to look unkempt whenever I saw him, even when wearing a suit, always leaving his collar unbuttoned and his tie loose as if he was unused to wearing one. He was in his mid-forties and spoke with a grating nasal accent.

Inspector Nilsson was about the same age as Forsberg but tall and well built. He too had a moustache, on a strong long face with sad eyes. Of the three men who were to feature predominantly in my prosecution, the other two being Forsberg and Bihlar, this man was to be the most sympathetic, and at times even treated me with a modicum of kindness and understanding.

The hearing did not last long – at the most half an hour. Forsberg outlined the case – there had been several arrests, a large quantity of cannabis recovered, investigations were proceeding. He required a month to complete his enquiries and requested that I be kept in custody during that period. It was then my turn, I gave a brief account of myself emphasizing that I was innocent of all the accusations made by the prosecutor. I knew nothing about the drugs, indeed I had no motive whatsoever to turn my hand to drug smuggling. After every few words I had to pause to allow the interpreter to translate.

The judge turned to my lawyer. 'Advocate Placht, have you anything to add at this stage?'

'Yes your Honour, although my client has been arrested at the wheel of a car in which 50.5 kilos of cannabis have been discovered, the Prosecutor has no proof whatsoever that Captain Hayward knew of their existence. As he has explained there is no motive for him to commit such a crime. He has given a full and credible account of his actions and how he came to be in this predicament. He holds a responsible position in society, and can be believed. I demand that this Court release him immediately.'

Under the circumstances it was all he could do. Inspector

Nilsson asked that he be allowed to put some questions to me. Permission was readily given.

'Simon Hayward, you say you have met Forbes Cay-Mitchell's girlfriend. What is her name?' The interpreter repeated the question in English.

'I do not know who Forbes Cay-Mitchell is let alone his girlfriend.'

'Forbes Cay-Mitchell is the man you call Lokesh.'

'Well I did not know that, I have only ever known him as Lokesh. As I have explained to Inspector Bihlar, I did see a woman who I believe may be his wife or girlfriend but I have never spoken to her, nor do I know her name.'

'Does the name Prita mean anything to you?'

'No, it does not.'

'If these drugs were planted in your car, as you claim, who could have done such a thing to you?'

'I'm afraid I have no idea, none at all. I only wish that I did.'

He had no further questions. We all looked expectantly at Judge Hellbacher. I uttered a silent prayer, crossed my fingers and held my breath. After a pause when the judge appeared to be considering all that he had heard, he said.

'There is a case to answer. Simon Hayward is to be kept in custody for one month from today.' He set the next hearing for Friday 24 April.

I knew what he had said before the interpreter could relate the 'sentence' to me in English. I could tell from the satisfied expressions on the faces of the two men sitting opposite me. I turned to Placht.

'I thought we were going to ask that the prosecutor be granted only two weeks?'

'Simon, there is no point, believe me.'

I could not have felt more dejected. My shoulders slumped and I looked down at my hands, tightly clasped together in my lap. However, there was no point in whingeing – that would achieve nothing. Better to accept my fate, put on a brave face, and get on with it. I took a deep breath, stood up and thanked the judge.

Placht said that he would visit me in the next few days. I was led away.

The difference between being merely an arrested suspect and

being an arrested suspect who had been up before a judge became apparent as soon as I arrived back at Västerås. To begin with the guard who took my shoes and belt tried to put me into prison uniform. I refused. It was bad enough being treated like a criminal but I was not going to be made to look like one. After some energetic discussion the guard relented, he was a young man in his early twenties and did not put up much of a fight. There were also to be some minor improvements. Instead of paper sheets for my bunk I was now given proper linen ones, and best of all a radio to listen to. The guard having failed to persuade me to wear his uniform was not going to let me have the final word, however. Before locking my cell door he smiled at me, but there was no warmth in his eyes. He slowly looked about the cell and then purposely back at me.

'Get used to all of this,' he said with a sweep of his arms, 'you are going to be here a long time.'

Alone once more I sat down and surveyed my surroundings. The bleak little cell with its off-white graffiti-covered walls, its clinical furniture, the ugly strip-light in the ceiling over which I had no control, the wash-basin and the blinded window, which for all the light it let in might having just as well not have been there. The thought of having to spend a full month in this box was demoralizing in the extreme. It was not so much the loneliness that got to me – not in the beginning at any rate – but the silence. On a normal day, apart from the guards when they came to bring me food, or to take me to wash or to exercise, I never saw, spoke to or heard anyone. The exception was Saturday nights when the police must have rounded up the local drunks and put them in cells on the floor below me. Their screams and shouts, and hammerings on the walls could be heard for hours. It made a welcome change. The radio was also very welcome, but it was a cheap model, which although I tried tuning it for hours refused to pick up any English-language channel. Its tinny music however was a godsend.

The police were obviously in no hurry to question me further – the softening up process must have started. When Bihlar did appear again on Thursday 26th, it was not to interview me but instead . . .

'You have visitors. Your mother and girlfriend are here.' My

heart leapt. 'But,' he continued, 'you are not to discuss the
case. If you do I will terminate the visit immediately. Do you
understand?' I said that I did. 'Good, you have half an hour.'

They were waiting for me in an interview room and stood
up smiling as I entered, but I could see as I embraced each in
turn that both 'girls' appeared tired and drawn. Both had red-
rimmed eyes and tears were very obviously not far from the
surface. We sat down around the table, I beside Sandra, Bihlar
making up the foursome next to my mother. She spoke first.

'Darling what is going on? We have been so worried.'

'I cannot tell you I'm afraid; if I mention the case Mr Bihlar
will throw you out.'

'Yes we know, we have been briefed,' Sands interjected with
a withering smile at the policeman.

'All I can say is that drugs are involved,' I looked at Bihlar
to see if I was breaking the rules but he seemed relatively
content, although watchful, 'but let me assure you that I am
innocent, they have not even charged me yet.'

'We know, we have never doubted that for a second.'

We talked on for half an hour, each trying to reassure and
comfort the others, holding hands and occasionally swapping
squeezes of encouragement. Apparently my mother had been
having trouble with the press, but she was not allowed to say
exactly what. She was able to tell me that the story had broken
and had made the headlines in a major way. It was the first
piece of news I had had for almost two weeks, but it was the
very last thing I wanted to hear. As a family we have always
guarded our privacy jealously and now it seemed that
everyone in Britain was reading about us. The one bonus was
that luckily no one had latched onto Sandra yet.

Our time together felt as though it was over almost before
it had begun but Sands managed to charm Bihlar into granting
us more time. In relenting he said we could have half an hour
more, but only after lunch because he had things to do.

The three of them returned two hours later, this time armed
with a thermos flask, coffee, tea, sugar and dried milk. Boiling
water being readily available, these purchases would make my
existence a great deal more comfortable. My mother also
brought a suitcase of extra clothes and, to help pass the time,
another full of books.

This period too went all too quickly. My mother told me she had spoken to the Army (quite who she meant by 'Army' I was not sure and she was not allowed to say) and that everyone was being supportive. She was also going to instruct the best lawyers she could find.

It was a straining time for all of us but we managed a few laughs, mainly at the expense of my prison issue plastic sandals (the only part of the uniform I had to use) which we all agreed I would not bother to bring home with me.

I hugged tightly two of the people I love most in the world as the time came for goodbyes. We felt confident that I would be home soon but that did not make our farewells any easier. Sandra came with me as far as my cell door, it was only some fifteen feet down the corridor from the interview room. When she saw inside the tears she had been holding back all day burst forth and she clung to me until the final second. When that metal door closed on me the weight of despair was crushing and the sense of loneliness almost overpowering.

Bihlar returned some minutes later.

'I will be back in a few days. We are going to have a long talk.'

I do not know if this revelation was made to scare me or not, but my only emotion was anger that he was not going to question me at the earliest opportunity and eager anticipation for the forthcoming interview. After all, the sooner the police had all the facts, the sooner they would become assured of my innocence, and the sooner I would be released. Before leaving me Bihlar added:

'Your mamma and Sandra were very upset and crying as they left.' He stared at me straight in the eyes. I did not give him the satisfaction of a reaction to this obviously nasty little quip.

The waiting continued, time pased very slowly. The hours crawled by, making each day unbearably long. Reading became my only pastime.

April 1 came. I could not help reminiscing over another April Fool's Day twelve years before when a fresh faced young Second Lieutenant had reported to his Regiment in West Germany for the first time. So much water had flowed under the bridge since then, but no one in their wildest dreams could possibly have guessed that this would be the eventual outcome.

The door opened, Bihlar again. 'You have another visitor.'
'Who is it?' I asked.

'A Colonel from your army.'

I thought at first that it must be the Embassy Military Attaché, they are usually colonels or lieutenant colonels, but it turned out to be Colonel James Emson. I was quite surprised but very pleased to see him.

'Good Lord, hello Colonel.' We shook hands. He was a tall, wiry man just turning fifty and about to be promoted to brigadier. He had commanded The Life Guards in the early 1980s and we knew each other well.

With Bihlar present he now proceeded to give me the third degree. We were allowed to go into rough detail about the events that had put me behind bars. He asked me a list of pertinent questions and interrogated me in an extremely professional and thorough manner. I was quite shocked and taken aback, but there was 'method in his madness'. He was to tell my lawyers a few days later in London that he had travelled to Sweden with an open mind, unsure of my innocence and quite prepared to believe that I had been tempted into drug smuggling. Anything was theoretically possible. However having questioned me in depth and in an intentionally harsh manner he had come away convinced that I was indeed innocent. He related that I had not flinched under his barrage and replied to everything unhesitatingly and with conviction.

His probing examination of me and the drug question over, he finally changed the subject. He opened a file that had lain in front of him on the table throughout the interview, holding it in such a manner that I could not see its contents.

'As you may know Simon, your arrest has attracted a great deal of publicity and more than a healthy amount of interest in you personally. I have here one quite worrying article from the *Daily Express* because it claims to quote you. Mr Bihlar will not let me read it out to you in full but, and I quote, "Life Guards officer . . . claimed to police he is a British spy." "My life would be worthless if the IRA ever got hold of me." ". . . recruited for 'special ops' in Northern Ireland." Have you ever said any of these things?'

It seemed a stupid joke. 'No Colonel, I most certainly have

not. Of course I haven't, why should I?' And, turning to Bihlar: 'Ask Inspector Bihlar, he has been the only person to question me. Have I ever mentioned such things Mr Bihlar?'

Bihlar was looking extremely sheepish and blushed with obvious embarrassment.

'Well?' the colonel enquired, looking at him.

'No, Simon has never said these things,' he muttered slowly, almost unwillingly.

'There is one last thing Simon,' Colonel James turned his attention back to me, 'I have received your letter. Thank you for it but I am taking no action on it.'

He stood up to leave, smiling confidently at me.

'Don't worry boy, we'll sort this matter out and have you home in no time. Keep your spirits up, and don't let them get you down. Continue to behave as you have been doing: I will support you in any way I can.'

I thanked him. We shook hands again. Seconds later he was gone. He was to prove as good as his word and became one of my staunchest supporters.

As Bihlar took me back to my cell, I stopped and turned to face him in the corridor:

'That was you wasn't it? You gave that story to the newspapers. All that nonsense about spies and the IRA. I told you the other day when you mentioned it, for God knows what reason, that because a soldier serves in Northern Ireland it does not make him a spy or a member of the SAS. You obviously have a very vivid imagination.'

He looked flustered and secretive. 'No, no, it was not me. I have said nothing to the press. It came from your Ministry of Defence in London. Yes, that's right, they did it.'

'Ha! That is rubbish, why should they? No you did it! Well let me tell you Bihlar, it is bad enough being here accused of a crime I know, and I think you know, I have not committed, but I will not have you lying and spreading rumours about me to the media.' I was wagging my finger at him, my voice as cold as I could make it. He stared at me for a few seconds clearly at a loss what to do. Eventually . . .

'It was not me. Come, you must go back to your cell.'

The next day Bihlar came back to Västerås to interview me, but before he did so he kindly allowed me another visit. This time it was Sandra accompanied by a very close mutual friend of ours called Simon Falkner, also an officer in The Life Guards. We were allowed almost an hour together, with the same rules on not talking about the case in force as before. Simon is a handsome man of just under six feet, with a thick-set build and piercing blue eyes. He combines a strong character with an equally robust and dry sense of humour. A popular professional soldier who had served in the Guards Independent Parachute Company before its disbandment in 1974, I had known him since my first days in the Army and although four years my senior, we are firm friends. He had made the visit to Sweden that Thursday 2 April not only to lend moral support to Sands and me, but also in a semi-official capacity, because he had information that he and senior Household Cavalry officers believed would have a bearing on my continued incarceration.

In 1984 I had, quite by chance, discovered the identity of a London drugs dealer. The man, called Brian Walsh, was plying his filthy trade from a flat on the Fulham road, dealing in heroin and cocaine. He was an addict himself, but much worse than that he had a sixteen-year-old son whom he had personally turned into a heroin addict at the age of twelve. Any father who could do that to his own son deserved no quarter. My initial gut reaction had been to pay the low-life a visit, with a few select friends, to give him an offer he could not refuse. However, on calmer consideration I had realised what an incredibly stupid thing to do that would have been.

Instead I had consulted Simon Falkner who I knew was friendly with the police officer in charge of the Notting Hill Gate area of London, later to be the Head of Scotland Yard's Serious Crime Squad, Chief Superintendent Basil Haddrell. The two of us had gone to see him one Sunday morning at his home and I had told him all I could, but in fact it was all old news. The police had already known all I could tell them and a lot more, even down to the fact that Walsh kept a converted deodorant aerosol in his bathroom which could be twisted open to conceal money or drugs.

As far as I know no action was ever taken by the police on the information I supplied. Walsh was eventually arrested, but only after his son had gone to the authorities in desperation, informing on his father in a determined effort to win a chance to rid himself of his addiction.

By the time I saw Simon and Sandra that day, Simon had already related this story to Bihlar to demonstrate to him my attitude to drugs in general and in particular to those who deal in them. It was an attempt to persuade the Swedish police that I could not possibly have become knowingly involved in drug dealing. Indeed, my past record clearly proved my aversion to drugs and those involved with them.

Simon now told me what he had done and we both instinctively looked at Bihlar to see what kind of reaction he was registering. Not a lot, was the answer, he just shrugged his shoulders. It looked as though he was not about to let anything influence his investigation or his opinion of me.

Bihlar had a habit of trying to ingratiate himself with all newcomers, and he did not draw the line at my visitors. For our part we, at least subconsciously, realised that he was the man who held my immediate future in his hands, and we were therefore not prepared to make an enemy by alienating him. Consequently, this visit went in a good humoured way, and we included the Inspector in our forced merriment. Sands even went as far as a little good natured teasing.

'Come on Mr Bihlar, you know Simon is innocent, why not let us take him out for lunch. We will bring him back, I promise.'

'Aha, I cannot. You have the British SAS waiting outside to rescue him.' Came the reply with a waved finger.

Again this was an indication of the fixation that Bihlar was to hold throughout his investigation. On this occasion I decided to ignore him.

On a more serious note, Sands asked: 'When can he come home?'

'As soon as we are sure he is not involved in this crime then Simon will be released immediately. But until then he must remain here.'

Immediately my friends had said their goodbyes and departed, Bihlar began his third interview with me. It followed the same pattern as before, with the policeman taking notes in Swedish throughout. I should explain the nature of police interviews in Sweden as I experienced them, because Bihlar's method was to become a bone of contention when the prosecutor eventually presented his case against me. The procedure was that no contemporaneous notes were taken, either handwritten or tape-recorded. Instead a general record was made in the form of a precis, and all notes were in the words of the police officer conducting the interview, not mine. Seldom therefore was a complete and thereby accurate record of the proceedings made, and certainly never a record of every word spoken. Clearly such a system is wide open to abuse as what appears on record is entirely at the whim of the officer.

This session was a reiteration of our first but in much greater detail. Again I repeated all that had happened since the day I left London for Gibraltar, this time adding the background of my meeting with Christopher in London in September and his open invitation to me to go sailing with him.

I talked for over two hours with Bihlar asking the occasional question. When I had finished, for the first time he tried to put the pressure on.

'Simon, it is strange what you say, because other people I have spoken with disagree with much of your statement, especially over these meetings you claim to have had with Lokesh.'

This did shake me, although I had been expecting it of course. Lokesh or Mitchell, or whatever his name was, would know nothing about these imaginary meetings when questioned, nor I presume of my intention to go skiing in Sweden. I have never been closer at that point to telling Bihlar the whole truth, although at later dates I came as close, but again I held back. Telling a deliberate lie was not easy: it went against everything I had ever been taught, but my reluctance to incriminate Christopher and, I have to admit, a certain amount of fear, prevented me from telling the total truth.

Not only did I not want to implicate my brother in this mess, but in addition I now felt 'stuck with' my story, even trapped by it. I realised that to change it at this stage would severely damage my credibility, and being certain that the truth behind those drugs found in the Jaguar would out, and that I would in consequence be released, I knew that I needed all the credibility I could muster.

I remembered a lesson taught me at Sandhurst: once you

have made a decision, stick to it. To be indecisive creates uncertainty and confusion.

'What I have told you is the truth, word for word. I don't know who could have told you otherwise.'

'Lokesh denies holding these meetings with you, and Sandra's story appears to match his statements.'

'That cannot be, I have told you the truth. I have nothing further to add.'

These comments drew the interview to a close, but as he was packing up his notes another thought must have struck Bihlar. He paused and looking at me said: 'I do not believe you, and I will tell you why. In all your statements you have mentioned very few names, whereas Sandra has talked of several. She has been more open than you, and that is a sign of the truth. And what she says differs from what you are saying.'

'That cannot be possible, what I have told you is the truth and I do not believe you when you say our statements differ. And the only reason I haven't mentioned names is that you haven't asked me for any.'

I then reeled off all the names I could remember having heard whilst on Ibiza. They varied from the Café owner in San Juan to Chantal and the list must have been about a dozen strong.

Christopher	Ingrid
Chantal	Mario
Jim	Jamille
Fernandito	Brian
Lokesh	David
Duke	

Bihlar wrote them on a separate sheet of paper from his main notes: a factor that was to become highly important during my trial, because he was to deny ever having received the list in the first place.

Having just told me that he did not believe a word I said, Bihlar left me saying: 'Simon, either you are telling me the truth or you are a very good actor. Which is it?'

I laughed. I have never been able to act, nor could I then – not even to save my own life.

The police chose not to question me again during my time at Västerås, and on 8 April transferred me to Uppsala. There was no warning or explanation of what was happening, I was just told to collect what few belongings I was allowed in my cell and driven off in a car. My initial reaction was one of cautious optimism, and with hindsight not a little naivety, in that I believed I was about to be released, especially since the escort guard did not handcuff me. However, this hope was soon dashed because once in Uppsala, a town about 75 kms north of Stockholm, I was taken to another Häktet.

After the usual reception they placed me in an identical cell to my previous two – this one however, had a very real bonus, the venetian blind in between the window panes being partially open. This meant I was able to look out on some semblance of normality, to watch normal people walk by. It was a constant reminder that there was life on the outside, and consequently my horizons felt slightly improved.

Indeed there were to be several improvements to the quality of life in the Uppsala remand centre. The conditions in which I was held were by English standards even good. The prosecutor must have taken this opportunity to relax some of the more Draconian restrictions he had placed on me. I was now allowed a short-wave radio, which Jenny Cummings kindly bought for me, enabling me to listen to the BBC World Service; my new home was also equipped with a black-and-white television set, which made the long evenings bearable. In addition I was permitted as many books as I wanted and English newspapers sent out by my mother, though only once they had been censored and any mention of me removed. There was no limit to the number of letters I could write or receive. My cell, although small, was spotless and hygienic, and the food was under the circumstances very good. A 'Tuck Shop' trolley would be brought around twice a week to sell cigarettes, sweets, coffee, biscuits and other 'goodies'. One could take a shower every day. Therefore the physical conditions under which I was kept were clearly more comfortable than if I had been remanded in custody in a British prison.

I came to know some of the guards at Uppsala well. The vast majority of them were highly sympathetic to the needs and feelings of their inmates; some even expressed extreme embarrassment at the way they were forced to handle them. Prisoners with no restrictions applied on them by a prosecutor were allowed out of their cells for short periods to talk and drink coffee together in a recreation room, or to take exercise in a small gymnasium. However, those like myself with severe restrictions and not allowed to see, let alone speak to, another inmate, would sometimes be invited to do the same with a guard, and let me assure you that after weeks of isolation any human company became a blessing.

This was how I came to meet Inger Jonsson, whose role was more that of a social worker than warder. Because it must have been very time-consuming to take the high-category restriction prisoners out from their cells, due to the fact that only one could come out at a time, many of the guards did not bother. Inger did. And she did so not so much out of a sense of duty but out of real human compassion. To me she became one shining light in the gloom that otherwise surrounded me.

Inger was a jolly, gregarious woman in her late thirties, and I am very pleased to be able to call her my friend. At my lowest moments, and I was to have many of them, she would come into my cell to comfort me, often insisting, even when I felt too lethargic to do so, that I came out to talk and drink coffee with her. She also encouraged some of the other warders to do the same. Occasionally I would find myself surrounded by the girls who worked in the Häktet, all of whom were seeming to take a personal interest in my welfare. They certainly made my existence much more bearable and I will always be grateful to them. Simple manual work, such as sorting and counting postcards for a local manufacturer, was available to keep prisoners occupied in their cells and to supply them with some cash to enable them to make purchases from the trolley shop. Inger, realising how important it was for me to get out of my cell as frequently as possible, would as often as she could take me into the Häktet workshop to do this work with her there. When no one else was interested she did her best to keep me occupied.

There can be no doubt that the physical conditions of my remand in Uppsala were comfortable, especially when they are compared to those that exist in Great Britain. However, all the good aspects were more than negated by the fact that I was held in solitary confinement.

If you want a taste of what it is like to sit in solitary confinement, try locking yourself in your bathroom, stay there for a month and let the only contact you have with the outside world be with your worst enemy who comes with food three times a day. That is how a Swedish journalist, Claes Britton, who as a student worked as a part-time guard at the Kronoberg Remand Centre in Stockholm, described it. I can find no better analogy.

I found solitary confinement to be an increasingly disorientating experience, as well as a mentally debilitating and exhausting one. It is a recognized form of psychological torture, a technique that slowly brainwashes its victims. I knew this, and realising what might start to happen to me I initially set myself a strict routine. I worked to a programme each day, forcing myself out of bed in the mornings; regardless of the weather I would always take the hour's exercise on the roof, and I would reserve a period at the same time each day for letter-writing, for reading, for exercise, for washing myself and for cleaning my cell. Knowing the importance of remaining active both physically as well as mentally, I would exercise as much as I could, but for all the press-ups, sit-ups, and running on the spot that I did I found it impossible to keep fit, and I therefore started to lose condition, and with it my energy, my appetite, and consequently over a stone in weight. And, persevere as I might, as the weeks passed by I began to find my programme next to impossible to adhere to.

My great pastime became reading: I read book after book after book. Those on travel I found most enjoyable but I read anything I could lay my hands on. For example, I lost myself in Wilfred Thesiger's autobiography, *The Life of My Choice;* Lawrence's *Seven Pillars of Wisdom;* Bernard Levin's *To The End of The Rhine,* and *Hannibal's Footsteps;* Quentin Crewe's *Touch the Happy Isles,* and *In Search of The Sahara.* And so the list goes on, varied and endless. These men with their talent took me beyond the surrounding grey walls, far away into different worlds, and whilst I was reading the worries and agitations would be forgotten. But eventually I would always return from these mental travels, and always the walls would once again close in on me with their terrible pressing silence.

There is a limit to how much reading one can do, so when it became too much I would fall back on my own imagination. I would lie on my bunk and enter a world of my own this time, attempting to re-live past experiences. I would run through an old holiday step by step, and thus return to Africa or Greece; the Middle East, the Far East or America. I would play a mental exercise by choosing any month of a particular year and try and work out precisely what I had been doing at the time. It all helped the hours to pass.

I would also go forward in time and plan future ideas and holidays in precise detail, promising myself that I would actually carry them out as soon as I regained my freedom.

Gradually time lost all value in the cell's loneliness. The hours, days, and weeks – eventually even the months – became a meaningless blur. I became increasingly lethargic, reacting to the isolation by becoming apathetic. I would lie on my bunk for hours without thinking a single thought.

The effects of prolonged solitary confinement are difficult to explain. One feels trapped, smothered, enclosed. The walls close in. The air feels heavy, the atmosphere suffocating. You long to be able to run clear, gulp down great lungfulls of fresh air, to feel the wind, the sun, the rain, grass beneath your feet, to hear wind in the trees; to stroll down a street, to enter a shop. You start to realise just how much in life we all take for granted. You look at that terrible door with longing, willing it to open, for some kind, warmhearted, fatherly figure to beckon to you, to take you by the hand and lead you to freedom. To give you a final gentle push that propels you through the final gate. Such is the stuff that dreams are made of.

By itself I could put up with the isolation, but it was the isolation combined with outside concerns that made the situation close to intolerable. I could not help but worry about my immediate future, about my family and the nightmare it was being forced to live through, about Sandra and her family, about my career, about what the Army would be making of all of this, about what I was missing as life passed me by, and so the list went on. The strongest emotion I felt was one of extreme embarrassment, even shame.

As hard as I tried to remain active strange things started to happen to me. I would wake up from a daydream crouched in a corner of my cell hugging my knees, and rocking back and forth, or hidden under the desk, without the faintest idea of how I came to be there or what I was doing. Increasingly large blank spots would appear in my memory, and I began experiencing fierce headaches during which my eyes would refuse to focus.

I found that sleep became a major safety valve because whilst I was asleep time passed quickly and my worries receded. I would often sleep for anything up to sixteen hours a day with little difficulty.

I am not an emotional person, and I pride myself as being as resilient as the next man, but in this harsh environment I began to find that if anyone, especially visitors who I realized were genuinely sympathetic, showed me the slightest kindness, even as much as a kind word, my emotions would run high and tears would well up in my eyes – a reaction that became next to impossible to control and consequently rather embarrassing.

This regression occurred more rapidly than I realised at the time. I was visited in early May, only some seven weeks after my arrest, by John Gorst, the Member of Parliament for Hendon North and a friend since 1983 when he had helped me in the planning stages of a Regimental Trans African Expedition. He came to Uppsala in his official capacity as an MP and we were able to spend about half an hour together in the presence of the police. For some reason known only to themselves the Uppsala authorities decided to take umbrage at this visit, but that is another story and one that at the time I knew nothing about.

Gorst became very concerned for my well-being and horrified at the circumstances under which I was being held. He was also to become an outspoken critic of the Swedish judicial system and one of my greatest allies. On his return to England, after seeing me, he decided to make a speech about me during the May Parliamentary Adjournment Debate in which, amongst other issues, he described my state of mind and the possible effects of solitary confinement:

Captain Hayward is a healthy, resilient, 31-year-old man. There is no doubt about his healthy physical condition. However, the same cannot be said of his psychological state.

When I saw him nine days ago in the presence of the police and of the British Consul, he had red rings around his eyes, his manner was subdued and apologetic, his speech was hesitant and faltering, and at times he gave way silently to totally untypical emotion.

The day I left him he wrote me a letter which the authorities allowed to get through to me. In it he said:

'May I apologise for being so wet and for letting my emotions show but as you will realise I am not in the best frame of mind at present. One day I must sit down with you and analyse the effects of all of this, but perhaps now is not appropriate. I am afraid though, that the pressures of my situation have slowly built up on me. It is not so much being in solitary confinement but all the other factors accumulating with isolation that seem to make one feel so miserable. I don't wish to be seen to be stooping to self pity but I hope this explains my behaviour during our discussions.

'This whole affair is so unreal – I still can't believe it is happening ... Above all I have a feeling of intense embarrassment ... I also hope that my answers to your questions were satisfactory – my mind is not very clear at the moment and I am having difficulty in concentrating, so please forgive me if I was less than verbose.'

Contradictorily, he ended his letter by saying:

'Despite appearances I am fine.'

The letter deeply disturbed me after my observations of Captain Hayward. It is absolutely clear – I have consulted many people who know him intimately – that he is significantly disorientated. I have now pursued a number of other inquiries to establish what may be happening to him.

I described to Dr Paul Bowden of the Maudsley Hospital – he also works for the Home Office entirely in connection with prisoners – what I had observed of Captain Hayward. I also read him the entire contents of the letter I have just referred to.

Dr Bowden's comments were as follows. He said 'His response to the conditions of this detention reflect that he has been improperly detained. I don't know the details of the conditions of this detention. All I know is that, however he is being detained, it is having an adverse effect on his mental health.'

I asked, 'What do you mean by improperly?' He replied, 'To an extent that he is becoming mentally disordered as a result of the conditions of his detention, his detention is not conducive to good mental health.'

I asked, 'Might his treatment prejudice him at his trial?' He said, 'Even if he is innocent, he might come to believe he is in some way guilty and, in that frame of mind, he would be unable to effectively defend himself against the charges.' I asked, 'What is your opinion of Captain Hayward's present condition judged from my description of his state when I saw him on 5 May' – after he had been in detention for 54 days – 'and from the evidence of his letter to me written on that day?' Dr Bowden replied, 'He is undergoing severe emotional reaction. His mental state is precarious. Unless the situation is altered, he will get a good deal worse. This view, incidentally, is irrespective of whether he is innocent or guilty.'

I asked, 'How might his condition deteriorate from now onwards?' He replied, 'He would start losing his sense of identity. He would begin to create around him an artificial world. At the extreme he would go mad in trying to make his own illusory world.'

With hindsight, I can now see that the descriptions given by Dr Bowden and the other psychiatrists Gorst consulted were accurate indications of what was happening to me, and the other unfortunates held in the cells around me. Not infrequently I would hear someone go berserk. Without warning the person would start to scream and shout, and beat against the walls with his, or her, fists. Occasionally these tantrums would go on for hours, but all would invariably end in muted sobs, and I could imagine the prisoner reduced to crying like a baby and fighting for his, or her, sanity.

There seemed to be no fixed official reaction to an inmate behaving in such a manner. It would very much depend upon which warders were on duty at the time, and how busy they were. Sometimes the individual would be taken out from his cell and counselled; on other occasions he would simply be left to get over the problem by himself. Not surprisingly the suicide attempt rate in Swedish remand centres is high.

Months later, after my trial, I was asked by a reporter if I would ever 'crack'. I replied that I did not understand the question. I did not. What would have been the point in breaking down? What would have been the point in crying and shouting, in screaming out and beating against the walls? It would not have resulted in my early release, but only in the loss of my last vestiges of human dignity and self esteem. The only way to get out of solitary confinement quicker would have been to confess to a crime I had not committed, which of course is what the police wanted, and was something I was not about to do, although I must admit that in my lowest moments it was something that I momentarily contemplated, if not seriously. The very thought would always surprise me, and it was one that I would immediately put out of my mind.

In fact the worse they treated me, the stronger my resolve became. If it was to be a battle of wills, I was not about to be beaten. Certainly life got bad, but never that bad.

Sadly the authorities took my quiet resolve as quiet acceptance of their treatment, and therefore as an indication of my guilt. They were obviously more used to prisoners breaking down than showing signs of silent determination. Indeed Bihlar was to say at a later stage that one of the reasons he became convinced of my guilt was just because I did not scream out my indignation at every possible opportunity.

In Uppsala every possible psychological tactic was brought to bear to reinforce my isolation. The warders were instructed to disturb me as seldom as possible and not to remove me from my cell unless absolutely necessary. Consequently for several weeks after my arrival I was not taken out to the recreation room; I was not permitted to use the gymnasium (indeed I did not even know of its existence), and I was not supplied with work – and, this work was important because when mentally exhausted it kept you physically occupied. The fact that these illegal additional restrictions were ever lifted was only due to several of the warders deciding on their own initiative to ignore them.

Any visits that I was allowed were at the whim of the police or of the prosecutor and the length of them similarly depended upon their goodwill. The only private visitor I was permitted was my mother, but she too, unknown to either of us, was used as a means of applying more pressure. On paper it may appear that the authorities were even generous with the number of visits they allowed – my mother flew over seven times before my trial – but that would be a false picture. The longest we were ever allowed together was an hour, but usually the visit would only last minutes. On one occasion, when my mother had travelled the 1,200 miles to see me, Bihlar told us we could have an hour together but after only ten minutes he then looked at his watch and suddenly announced that he was too busy to let the visit go on any longer, and called a halt. The resulting effect on my morale, and that of my mother, was easy to appreciate. On this occasion Inspector Nilsson took pity and gave us half an hour together later in the afternoon.

Another favourite trick was to tell me that a visit had been arranged for a certain date, usually about a week in advance. Not unnaturally I would then greatly look forward to it – it was something to work to and my morale would take a leap – only to be told at literally the last minute that it had been cancelled. Or worse still I would not be told of the cancellation at all, so when the time arrived and no one came to collect me, and no one could give me an explanation as to why they had not, I would start to worry that something terrible had occurred. I would imagine the worst and fret for hours. Consequently my morale would plunge.

Yet another ploy would be to allow us a short time together on one day, and tell us that on the next no time was available, everyone was too busy, but that if my mother waited until the day after that we could spend a full hour together. The knowledge that my mother was in town, so close but not allowed to see me, was miserable for both of us.

On another occasion Bihlar went to great lengths to explain to my mother where the window of my cell was, so that after the visit she would be able to stand outside and we would be able to wave to each other. To want to do so may sound fairly pathetic, but when you consider that I was alone all day every day, to be able to look out of my window at all was a pleasure, and to see someone I cared for through it, a real bonus and a comfort. The experience however was to be short lived. No sooner had my mother arrived at the position indicated than a guard, one of the bullying kind, burst into my cell, ushered me outside, and locked the window blind tight shut. This deprived me of all natural light and my only contact, albeit a rather artificial one, with the outside world. In fact I could still just see my mother, through a tiny chink in the blind, defiantly waving at my window.

Bihlar's malice had yet to reach its limits. During the same visit, which took place at the end of June, he volunteered to collect my mother from her hotel for another session with me early on the second morning of her stay in Sweden, on his way in to work. It appeared to be a kind gesture, especially since the weather was foul, and one that was gratefully accepted. However I should have realized that he had an ulterior motive, for no sooner was my mother in his car than he turned on her, verbally abusing her, shouting at her that her son was guilty, that there was positive proof of his guilt, and that it was her duty as a mother to persuade him to plead guilty.

When I saw my mother that morning I was shocked by her appearance, she was shaking like a leaf, as white as a sheet, and, it was clear that she had been crying and was in great distress. Whilst I recognize that it is a policeman's duty to investigate an alleged crime to the best of his ability, I can find no reason for Bihlar to treat my mother in such a fashion. His argument was with me – if he had wanted to give me a rough time, that I could have understood, but he had no right whatsoever to try and get at me by attacking someone I loved. As it was my mother is made of stern stuff: as upset as she was she thought only of me, and when we embraced she said to me, with a defiant look at Bihlar:

'Be strong darling, be strong. We will prove your innocence and get you out of here.'

The way my mail was handled was another deliberate attempt to further weaken my morale. When one is away from home, especially in my circumstances, mail takes on enormous importance. My family and friends, and a great many people who had simply read about me, began to write so regularly that letters would arrive by the handful every day. This annoyed Bihlar, and he made no secret of the fact, because he wanted to censor everything, and consequently he must have found himself fairly busy. However he discovered that it supplied him with another lever to use against me. He would inform me that mail had arrived, frequently coming up to my cell to see me for no other reason other than to tell me, always taking special care to say if one was from Sandra or my mother, then adding that he was too busy to check them and that he would not give them to me until the next week. Not infrequently he would also hold letters back on the pretext that they had some relevance to the case. Some of these would eventually get through, but days or even weeks late. Others were retained for months, and when they were finally given to me in the following November not one proved to have any relevance to the case in even the most oblique sense. For instance one was from James Emson, and the only reason I can think for it to have been withheld was that in it he stated that my brother officers were behind me, and cast doubts about my chances of receiving a fair trial.

Outgoing mail came up against similar obstructions. I was not allowed to write to my younger brother David simply because Christopher's second name was David, and regardless of anything I might have written. In other letters whole paragraphs were censored, and on other occasions no letters posted on a particular date would arrive. Bihlar would also become extremely irate if I tried to write too many, making it impossible to reply to everyone who was kind enough to write, although officially there were no limitations.

All in all the official attitude seemed to be: 'This man is not confessing, make life as difficult for him as possible until he does!'

There is little doubt that the prosecution began to play a game with me. Despite four court appearances, at month-long intervals, where each time Judge Hellbacher granted extensions to my detention on the given excuse that more time was needed to complete the investigation, the police were obviously in no hurry to question me. Indeed they rarely did so. During the nineteen weeks leading up to my trial only nine interviews took place, most lasting barely half an hour, some as little as five minutes, and at least one on my own bidding.

If the investigation was slow, it also appeared to me at the time to be inadequate and fragmentary. In all fairness I should emphasize that I made these observations whilst in isolation, gleaning my conclusions from the type of questions put to me during interviews, and from what little Tom Placht was allowed to tell me. Events were to prove me correct.

The most glaring flaw seemed to be in the refusal on the part of the prosecution to conduct inquiries on Ibiza. Since it was there that the drugs had originated, and it was from there that the drugs ring must have operated, it was surely obvious to even the most dim-witted individual that if the truth was ever to be properly established, the means of doing so were only to be found on Ibiza itself. However, the police made no effort to visit the island before my trial and as it turned out, according to the Ibizan police, no request was made for even the most rudimentary inquiries to be carried out on the island until June, and then only to establish if Christopher was still living there.

Tom Placht was enraged at the superficiality of the investigation. In April he urged Forsberg, with my blessing, to broaden the scope of his investigation to include Ibiza. When no result was forthcoming he decided to make an official request on paper. Therefore on 4 May he wrote to the prosecutor demanding that inquiries be conducted on Ibiza, that Mitchell's common-law wife be questioned, and that I be given English translations of all my statements. Placht explained his interest in Prita to me by saying that since she had lived closely with Mitchell she might be able to throw some light on the affair, and that it was vital that she be questioned before the two of them were given the chance to confer. In actual fact, and this Placht could not tell me at the time, Mitchell had implicated Prita in his operations, and therefore it was imperative that she be questioned because she obviously knew exactly what had gone on. This letter, like the previous verbal requests, was ignored.

An hour after my arrival in Uppsala, on Wednesday 8 April, I was taken downstairs to the police station to be questioned by Inspector Jan-Erik Nilsson, whom I had last seen in court. It was a short interview lasting no more than fifteen minutes, and Nilsson did not even bother making an official record of what we discussed. I believe he was just taking the opportunity to have a look at me, and to turn the screws a little tighter.

The thing that struck me immediately on entering Nilsson's office was a large poster of me stuck on the wall. It was of the kind that newsagents use to advertise the daily headlines, and the caption below the photograph read 'British Spy Officer in Häktet'. What I should have realised, but didn't, was that the Uppsala Drug Squad officers were extremely pleased with themselves. They were proud to have arrested a British Army officer, especially one belonging to what they perceived as an upper-crust elite regiment. Hence the poster on the office wall, but more importantly – and again I failed to realise this at the time – it was an indication that once they had their teeth in me they were going to be very loathe to let me go. Especially after publicising their 'achievement' so widely.

Nilsson started the interview in the by now familiar way: 'Why don't you admit the crime, we know you did it.'

'No, you don't know anything of the sort, because you can't. I had nothing to do with those drugs.'

'We have sophisticated methods on Ibiza which prove you are guilty. We know when and how the car was loaded, and exactly when you left to come to Sweden.'

'Well if you know all that, you will also know I had no part in it. So why not release me?'

'Yes we know,' he spoke ponderously, his English not as good as Bihlar's. 'We know you are guilty. We have sophisticated methods.'

I made no reply. There seemed little point in doing so. Instead I just looked at him blankly. He grew tired, obviously coming to the conclusion that he was not going to get a confession that day, and gave up.

'You have my bags here, I would like to check my property,' I said. I had asked Bihlar at Västerås if he would account for my possessions but he had told me that there was no reason why he should. I had been surprised at this apparent lack of proper accounting procedure, especially since I had been carrying a large sum of money at the time of my arrest, and now that I had the opportunity I was eager to ensure nothing had gone astray. Bihlar had already told me that the police who carried out the arrest had handed in £6,700 with the rest of my luggage. Since there had been £6,800 of the original £7,000 remaining, one hundred pounds had mysteriously 'disappeared' but there had seemed no point in making a 'song and dance' about this. I had more important problems to worry about.

Nilsson agreed and took me along the corridor to another office. It had Bihlar's name on the door. I was to get to know it well. My suitcase was lying in one corner, and other assorted bits and pieces were on an adjacent bookshelf. The suitcase had quite clearly been thoroughly searched, its contents thrown back in a crumpled bundle. I emptied it out onto the floor and carefully re-packed it. Checking as best I could that everything was still present. Some of the contents of the Jaguar had found their way into it, perhaps during the initial search. Some assorted tins of oil and spray-paint from the boot, and the screwdriver I had bought in Åstorp. These I put in a separate grip and I told Nilsson, who asked what I was doing, that I did not want them mixed up with my clothes. I also found the note Christopher had left me, saying that the villa in Santa Gertrudis had been broken into. Stupidly, as it was to turn out, I left it where it was and did not draw Nilsson's attention to it. At a later stage when I was accused of making the villa break-in up I was to ask the police to look for this note, but by then it had mysteriously disappeared. There was a copy of the 'Spy poster' on the wall in this office as well. Bihlar interviewed me for the first time in Uppsala on Monday 13 April. It was a short session lasting only twenty minutes.

'Will you now admit your crime?' he began.

I was by now becoming very bored with this question. 'No I will not, and what is more I have nothing further to add to my last statement. The truth is the truth.'

He gave me his usual penetrating stare: 'Did you have any tools with you in the Jaguar?' He pronounced it 'toys' which initially confused me.

'That's rather an odd question. Why on earth should I want any toys with me?'

He appeared to get rather angry at what he must have taken to be flippancy on my part.

'To get at the drugs!' he retorted.

This was really confusing, I could not help laughing. 'I think you are using the wrong word Mr Bihlar, I don't understand what you're trying to get at.'

'You know. TOYS! Hammers, screwdrivers, things like that.'

'Oh, I'm sorry, you mean tools.' Now even he laughed. 'Yes as far as I know, I had just one. A screwdriver that I bought outside Helsingborg, in a place called Åstorp if I remember correctly.'

I then went on to explain what had happened with the Jaguar seat.

'How many screws did you tighten?' he asked.

'About two or three I think. I'm not exactly sure now.'

'What did you do with the screwdriver when you had finished with it?'

'Let me see,' I pondered the question, 'I either put it in the car glovebox, or on the passenger seat. I can't remember which – I was in rather a hurry.'

He then changed the subject by asking me how I had intended selling the Jaguar in England. Again it seemed an odd question, I replied that I would have advertised it in a London newspaper. This appeared to satisfy him.

'Tell me about the money you had on you. It was a very large sum to be carrying around. We think it was part payment for the drug run. What is your excuse this time?'

'I don't need an excuse Mr Bihlar. It is really very simple, I withdrew it from my bank in London before leaving for Gibraltar. As I have already explained to you, it was my original intention to fly to Germany, after the sailing holiday, to buy a car. The money was for that.'

'Why did you take it in cash? Surely that was rather dangerous? What would you have done if you had lost it, or if someone had stolen it? Why did you not buy traveller's cheques? That would have been wiser.'

'Yes it would have been, but sadly I did not have time to organize any. My bank always takes a day to issue them and I had been unable to order them in advance. With everything else I had to do on my one day in London I just did not have the time. I had no choice but to take it in cash. As to losing it, or having it stolen, I kept it on me at all times. The only way someone would have been able to steal it would have been over my dead body.'

'I do not believe you, Simon. What were all these other things you had to do in London?'

'Before you go on any holiday there are always a million things to organize. I had to buy sailing waterproofs. I had to do a job for the Army. I had to go to my bank. I took my mother out for lunch – it was the first time I had seen her for weeks. I had to buy an air ticket. And all sorts of other odds and sods.'

'No Simon, this money was part-payment for the drugs run. It proves your guilt, so why don't you confess.'

'It proves nothing of the sort. I am telling the truth. In any case there is an easy answer to this problem. Why don't we telephone my bank manager right this minute and ask him if I withdrew that money in London? If he confirms what I say then you will know I am not lying, and we will be able to put this matter to rest.'

He refused to carry out this suggestion.

My spirits rose as the date for my second court appearance drew near. Surely the authorities would have to release me? As far as I was aware the police had not been able to produce a scrap of further evidence against me. I was sure that by itself the cannabis found in the car was not proof of any guilt. How could it be? After all, I had not known of its existence. However Placht once more warned me to expect another month's detention. I found this news upsetting in the extreme, not only because the prosecution had been unable to establish any corroboration of their case against me, but also because it appeared that they had made little effort to do so. The past month had been difficult – I make no bones about it – and I did not even want to think about having to spend another in solitary confinement.

This time the hearing took place in the Uppsala District Court House, and although it was held *in camera*, I had to brave the press who crowded about in the corridor outside the doors to the courtroom. I felt more comfortable this time wearing a suit, but none the less it was incredibly embarrassing to emerge from the lift, handcuffed to a guard, to face a barrage of clicking cameras and shouted questions. Placht had predicted that this would happen and had advised me that I could go in under a blanket. I did not want to. If I had to appear in court, I was going in with my head held high, not skulking about under a blanket like a common criminal with something to hide. I faced the ordeal looking straight ahead and ignoring all questions.

The hearing was short. Forsberg stated that Mitchell had named Christopher as the 'Mr Big' behind the drugs ring, and that I too was involved. I could not believe my ears. He added that he expected Christopher to be apprehended within the next few days. He asked that I be detained for a further month to allow time for the investigation to be brought to a conclusion. Placht pointed out that in the past month the police had been unable to prove anything against me. It did not the slightest bit of good. The judge granted Forsberg his wish.

That was it. Back to the cells for another month.

I was left to soak. The next interview did not take place until Wednesday 13 May, two weeks after the last court appearance and a full month since the previous session. On this occasion both Bihlar and Nilsson questioned me, and the interview was distinguishable by the fact that it was the only time either of them ever tried to get rough with me. As per usual I sat in front of Bihlar's desk, he placed himself opposite me, with Nilsson standing at his shoulder and occasionally pacing about.

Anyone who has ever watched a detective thriller on the television will know roughly what it is like to be interrogated by the police. With or without the amateur dramatics it can be a highly intimidating experience. Because it goes without saying that they disbelieve everything that is said because they try to blow even the smallest of details out of all proportion and because they leap at every opportunity to catch you out, it all becomes rather daunting. Automatically you start to try and justify everything you utter, and for no reason you start to feel a little guilty.

This interview started quietly enough but soon both policemen were shouting and firing questions at me in rapid succession. To begin with Bihlar ordered me to explain again why I had bought the screwdriver. I did as I was bid, describing how the seat had loosened, how I had attempted unsuccessfully to borrow, or buy, a screwdriver to fit its screws on my drive up through the Continent, and how I had eventually bought one in Åstorp soon after six on the evening of Friday 13 March. The police had a receipt from when I had bought petrol in Helsingborg, and it confirmed my stated timings.

When I finished they smiled at one another, and then the rough stuff started. It was obvious that they thought they had at last caught me out and that I could now be browbeaten into making a confession.

'How many screws did you tighten?'

'Two or three.'

'Last time you said only two!' Fist banging on the table.

'Last time I said two or three!'

'Were they at the front or the back of the seat?'

'I think . . . '

'How loose were they? . . . Did you have to move the seat to get at them? . . . What else did you use the screwdriver for? . . . Who else used it? Did you touch the passenger seat? . . . Come on admit it, you used this screwdriver to open the drugs compartment!'

The questions came at me without pause, leaving me little or no time to answer. Frequently I would start a reply but then another question would be barked at me before I could finish. Finally I gave up trying and just sat back and looked at then as they rabbited on. Eventually they fell silent. They thought they had me, it was written all over their faces. Smug, self-congratulatory expressions.

'I tightened up two or three screws, they were very loose. I can't remember offhand if they were at the front or the rear of the seat, I believe at least one was at the front. I did not touch the passenger seat. I used the screwdriver for nothing else, nor did anyone else because I was alone. I know nothing about any drugs or where they were hidden.' I spoke as calmly as I could.

Bihlar now spoke, also calmly.

'You should know that the front seats had to be removed before we could remove the cannabis from the car. What do you have to say about that?'

'I have nothing to say about that.'

Nilsson then took his turn. 'We have found traces of green paint on the screwdriver. We have also established that it would have been impossible for you to have scratched them onto it by merely tightening the seat screws. There is no paint on those screws, nor in the vicinity of them. We believe them to come from the drug compartment, and the screwdriver has been sent to the laboratory to confirm this.'

Bihlar interrupted, raising his voice again.

'Come on Simon admit it! These paint scratches prove your guilt. You did not buy this screwdriver in Sweden, you brought it up with you all the way from Ibiza. It is not even new. The paint came from the drug compartment when you loaded the car. ADMIT IT!'

Before I had a chance to refute this latest ridiculous accusation Nilsson joined in the affray.

'We have bought an exact replica of your screwdriver, and have scratched paint from the Jaguar onto it,' he said, producing the tool for me to see the traces of green paint. 'Not only could you not have put this paint onto the screwdriver if, as you claim, you only used it on the seat screws, but nor could you have done so by mistake. I had to really scratch hard against the car's bodywork to mark this copy. Therefore you can only have done it by levering open the drug compartment hatch.' He made levering motions with his hands. 'Now come on let's stop fooling around. ADMIT YOUR GUILT. THERE IS NO OTHER EXPLANATION!'

I stared at them both in mild astonishment and because I knew I was on firm ground, with a certain amount of amusement.

'What you are saying is nonsense and totally illogical. All you have to do is question the shopkeeper in Astorp and you will find that I am telling the truth. I did not bring this screwdriver up with me from Ibiza but as I have tried to explain to you, I bought it in Sweden.'

'We do not believe you,' Bihlar replied, 'but if you did buy it in Åstorp you must have stopped on your way to Linköping to check on the drugs.' He sounded menacing.

'How else could the paint have been scratched onto the screwdriver?' Nilsson added.

'Now that really is stupid. You know from the petrol receipt that I was in Helsingborg at six p.m. How long does it normally take to drive from there to Linköping?'

'About five hours.'

'Well, since you also know that I arrived in Linköping at half past nine. How on earth would it have been possible for me to have stopped en route, removed the front seats, checked on the drugs, and still managed to reach Linköping in only three hours? That does not make any sense. Does it?'

The two policemen could see that their argument was not quite watertight. They had not done their homework properly. Far from forcing a confession out of me, they were making themselves look vaguely ridiculous. Their earlier exuberant confidence was now replaced by subdued glares.

'If what you are saying is true,' Nilsson growled, 'how can you explain the paint traces?'

'I cannot explain them. Nor do I have to. Perhaps they were already on the screwdriver when I bought it and therefore the paint won't match the car's, or they were put there by the police. Either deliberately or to give you the benefit of the doubt, perhaps when the Jaguar was being searched. In any case it matters not. All you have to do is interview that shopkeeper to clear the question up.'

I was taken back to my cell.

A few days later Bihlar came to collect me and told me, as he led me to the lift, that there was going to be a film show. He took me down to the basement carpark where the Jaguar was being stored. 'The film show' turned out to be the filming of a video of me demonstrating to the police how I had tightened the seat screws. As well as Bihlar, Tom Placht was present, making verbal notes throughout into a pocket recorder, Nilsson, Forsberg and several others.

'We want you to show us exactly what you did with the screwdriver,' Bihlar demanded, 'You will be videoed as you do so.'

'I can't show you exactly for the simple reason that I can't remember exactly where the screws are. Please do not forget that I tightened them over two months ago, in the dark, and when I was in a tearing hurry. The whole process took only a few seconds to boot. It is not the sort of thing that sticks in your mind, especially when you attach no importance to it at the time.'

'Just show us.'

I did my best, but I do not suppose it looked very convincing. I sat in the drivers seat and felt down with my hands. The screw by my left leg, the one I had originally fiddled with when I had first noticed the seat was loose in France, was easy to find. Its opposite number to the right was covered by the seat cushion, which looked as though it would have to be removed before you could get at the screw. Therefore it was obviously not one of the ones I had tightened in Åstorp. I climbed out of the car and leaning in through the door slid the seat forward to reveal the two rear screw positions. One, on this occasion, was missing altogether and the other was hanging loose. I seemed to remember there had previously been two of them. I stood up and looked inquisitively at Nilsson and Bihlar.

'You do not seem very sure of yourself,' Bihlar said.

I made no reply. For the next half an hour or so the two policemen fiddled with the seat and its screws, occasionally barking a question at me. Two things became apparent. The first was that I was not totally sure of the positioning of the screws. But there again, and as I tried to explain to my audience, I would certainly have known the exact locations if I had helped to load the cannabis into the car on Ibiza. The same would also be true if I had just been shown where the drugs compartment was located and told to buy the screwdriver to remove the front seats.

Secondly, the seat rocked in precisely the way I had claimed it would, once at least two of the screws were loosened. Indeed Bihlar and Nilsson were videoed as they agreed that they could feel a 'rocking motion'.

Again Bihlar did his best to catch me out. I mean no criticism of him in stating this, it was after all his job to establish the truth. He asked me to explain once more how I had borrowed a screwdriver in Germany only to find that it would not fit. Once I had finished doing so, his eyes gleamed and with an exclamation of triumph he said:

'Right Simon, now I am going to prove that you are lying, because I am going to demonstrate that any screwdriver will fit these screws.' Whereupon he produced a medium-sized screwdriver from his pocket and thrust it under my nose. The camera zoomed in to catch the moment when the great detective at last revealed the dastardly Guards Officer in all his devilry to be a liar and a crook.

'Is this the type of screwdriver you borrowed?' It was a

normal flat ended screwdriver of the type that everyone has used at one time or another. I replied that it looked similar.

'Then watch carefully.' The note of triumph in his voice could not be mistaken, and must have been more than apparent to all the men standing around us, as Bihlar leant down to attempt to unscrew one of the seat screws. It would not fit! He tried again, but with the same result. It was now my turn to be triumphant.

'You see Mr Bihlar,' I said quietly, 'just as I told you, and exactly what happened to me in Germany.'

He looked livid, and blushed to the roots of his hair. I'm sure with embarrassment as well as anger. Without a word he turned on his heel and stalked off, to return a few minutes later with a handful of different sized screwdrivers. He tried them in succession and eventually found one that turned the screw. He looked up.

'There, you see, it fits. You must have been lying.'

I felt as though I was replying to an indignant child. I smiled at him.

'Of course it fits Mr Bihlar. If you find one of the correct size, of course it will fit. None the less, the one I borrowed in Germany must have been of the incorrect size because, just like the first one you tried, it did not fit.'

Bihlar's little demonstration, far from proving me to be a liar, strengthened my case because it clearly showed that I had been telling the truth. And even more importantly it proved that the posidrive screwdriver I had bought in Åstorp was not required to remove the seat screws, as long as a flat ended screwdriver of the correct size was available. Since the drug smugglers would certainly have realised this, it raised the question why, if I had been involved in the operation, I had been ignorant of this fact and had gone to all the trouble of finding exactly the right tool when it had not been needed in the first place. The one plausible answer, which the police obviously did not want to consider, was that not knowing of the drug's presence, I had innocently discovered the driver's seat to be loose and after a quick examination had come to the mistaken conclusion that a specialized implement was required to rectify the problem. As any layman would have.

Placht then drove another nail into the coffin lid of this

particular police argument. He asked how long it had taken to remove all the car fittings necessary to gain access to the drug compartment, after Bihlar had shown us exactly where the cannabis had been hidden.

'About an hour,' was the reply.

'So are you trying to tell me,' Placht continued, 'that although Simon made the drive from Helsingborg to Linköping in record time, that you really want us to believe that he also stopped beside the road, spent an hour removing bits and pieces of the car's interior, for which incidentally he did not have any tools, to check that the drugs were still okay, which was an unnecessary task, in so doing scratched those paint traces onto the screwdriver, then spent another hour replacing everything, and still managed to arrive in Linköping only three hours after leaving Helsingborg. That is plainly ridiculous.'

Forsberg and his police officers looked extremely glum.

On Wednesday 20 May Nilsson came up to speak to me in my cell. On this occasion he wanted to know if I recognised any of a list of names. There were about half a dozen of them. I remember thinking it strange that they all appeared to start with 'M'. Macunda, Mary, and Meru are the ones that have stuck in my mind, probably because they were to be mentioned again at later dates. At the time they meant nothing to me.

On Monday 25 May Bihlar interviewed me for the sixth time. It was another short session, lasting only half an hour.

He did not mention the screwdriver except to say, with an accusatory smile, that he had not been able to locate the shop I 'claimed' to have bought it from. Instead he asked me to run through exactly what Mitchell and I had said to each other during the meeting at Linköping railway station. It took me only a few minutes to do as I was bid.

'Did Mitchell mention a garage to you?'

'No he did not, only a house.'

'He never told you to drive straight into the garage when you arrived at the house in Motala?'

'No, as I have just told you, he never mentioned a garage at all.'

'Did he mention the Jaguar's broken window to you?'

'No, it was dark, I doubt whether he even noticed it.'

'Are you sure, Simon? Mitchell's statement does not agree with yours.'

'I am absolutely positive.'

And that was that. Bihlar concluded by telling me that I would be going back to court for the third time on the following Wednesday, adding that they were going to ask for yet another month. This was not good news, and it was delivered in a very unsympathetic fashion.

As each month drew slowly to its close my spirits would rise accordingly. I saw the final days of each as the last I would have to spend in solitary. Consequently each time I was told that another month was going to be requested my morale would nose dive. The very thought of what lay ahead would make me feel almost suicidal, and I had to concentrate hard to force myself to take a grip on reality and to continue the fight.

I wonder if Bihlar was aware of the effect of his casually stated and almost nonchalant comment, informing me that I would have to spend another thirty miserable days alone in a stuffy little box! I rather think that he was more than aware.

So on Wednesday 27 May I once again found myself up in front of Judge Hellbacher. The fact that this day was the anniversary of my father's death fifteen years earlier did not bode well for me. As on the previous occasions Forsberg demanded that I be detained for another month. It was of course what I had been expecting, but that did little to soften the sting. The excuse on this occasion was the screwdriver. He explained to the judge that it could only be used on the seat screws, that much the defendant admitted, and that both front seats had to be removed before access could be gained to the drugs compartment. He explained that some highly incriminating traces of green paint had been found on the screwdriver, that laboratory tests proved came from the Jaguar's bodywork. He added that these traces could not have been scratched onto the screwdriver if I had only used it to tighten the seat screws. He said that the police had been unable to find the shop from which I claimed to have bought the screwdriver, and that it was almost a certainty that I had in fact brought it with me from Ibiza, where it must have been used to load the cannabis.

He went on to say that the police officers who had been
involved in my arrest and in the subsequent search of the
Jaguar all denied having seen the screwdriver, let alone having
used it, and therefore could not have been responsible for the
paint traces. Indeed the tool had been found in my suitcase,
not in the car where I had claimed to have left it. He concluded
by saying that there was no other explanation for the paint
traces except that they proved I was lying and that the
screwdriver was a vital implement for the unloading of the
drugs, which is why the defendant had it in his possession.

I sat and listened to the interpreter as this mish-mash of
unverifiable nonsense unravelled before me. All the police had
to do was find the shop in Åstorp to disprove this theory. I felt
angry and helpless.

When it was my turn to speak I pointed this fact out to the
judge, adding that if this screwdriver was so terribly
incriminating, why was it that I had brought the authorities'
attention to it in the first place. It would have been quite easy
for me to have denied ever having seen the damn thing before.
After all there are usually tools to be found in a car. I also
pointed out that although the police refused to believe that I
had tried to buy the screwdriver before my arrival in Sweden,
all they had to do to establish that I was telling the truth was
go to the shop in Helsinger and ask a few questions. Why had
this not been done?

Placht emphasised that no real attempt had been made to
verify my story, that the screwdriver was not essential to the
removal of the drugs from the car, and that there had to be a
logical explanation for the paint traces. He also pointed out
that in the demonstration carried out with the prosecution,
both Bihlar and Nilsson had verified that the seat rocked in the
way I had indicated. He again demanded my immediate
release, reminding the judge that nothing further had been
found against me since the day of my arrest, and despite
intensive interrogation I had stuck religiously to my original
statement. He finished by telling the court that no proper
investigation was being conducted since no attempt had been
made to hold inquiries on Ibiza.

It was all to no avail. It appeared that little reason had to be
given for Hellbacher to remand me in custody. However, on

this occasion he granted Forsberg only three weeks, adding that it would also be the final time he would remand me, and that the prosecution should get a move on. Although the hearing was held *in camera*, the judge allowed the press in to listen as this 'sentence' was passed.

Once again I found myself being taken back, in handcuffs, to the Häktet.

A few days later at Tom Placht's insistence the police made a proper effort to locate the Åstorp shop, and of course succeeded in doing so. They never actually went to see the shopkeeper in person, but merely relied on a telephone call. The question therefore remained as to how there came to be traces of green paint on the screwdriver. Since laboratory tests had proved that they originated from the Jaguar, and since it had been established that neither I nor the police officers who arrested me or searched the car could have been responsible for their presence, I believe that they became something of an embarrassment to Bihlar and Nilsson.

Although the subject of the paint traces was never raised again, the prosecution continued to insist that the screwdriver was a vital implement for the unloading of the cannabis, and that I had bought it on my arrival in Sweden once I had passed through the final customs post, to minimise the risk of the drugs compartment being discovered. This theory was weak, not only because it had been demonstrated that the screwdriver was not required to remove the seat screws, but also because it could have been easily disproved by visiting the shops in Helsinger and Bad Nenndorf where I had tried to buy the screwdriver en route to Sweden. The police never bothered.

Perhaps the most important point, that the prosecution refused to consider, was that it was only by a stroke of luck that I managed to buy the screwdriver after closing hours. If it had been so vital to the unloading of the drugs, such an important purchase would hardly have been left to chance.

In early June Bihlar asked me to provide him with a list of every car I had ever owned. There were about a dozen or so, dating back to 1973. A couple of days later on the 4th he brought me to his office for another interview. Again on this occasion Nilsson was present.

I was asked whether I was sure the list was complete. I told them I was certain it was. Nilsson, standing as usual at Bihlar's shoulder, was holding what turned out to be a statement, the contents of which he was obviously taking great pains not to let me see.

'I have here a statement,' he began, 'it is from a man who has spoken to the Thames Valley Police in England. We have been supplied with this copy on the condition you are not allowed to read it, however . . . '

He then went on to read me parts of it. It was from a man who claimed to have met me in 1978, and who had been employed by me repairing and servicing my cars for several years since then. This man was apparently claiming that I had been running a racket since the 1970s smuggling drugs into the United Kingdom in used cars. He said that I had paid him to convert several cars for this purpose, one of them being a Sunbeam Rapier, from which he had removed the overdrive unit from the gearbox in order to lighten it. This he stated was to make the car appear to weigh the usual amount when loaded with cannabis.

Nilsson finished his rendition by telling me that this informant was prepared to give evidence against me, 'any time, any place,' as long as his expenses were met and that I was not informed of his address.

I sat and listened with incredulity. I guessed immediately who this individual was (I will call him 'Ronnie Butcher'), and he was lying through his teeth. The only item of truth in the entire statement, at least in that part that had been read out to me, was that he had serviced my car during the time I had been based at Windsor in the late seventies. I had never even owned a Sunbeam Rapier. 'I know exactly who made that statement. It will be signed by a man called Ronnie Butcher. Correct?'

Both policemen looked crestfallen. They were obviously embarrassed that I had identified their informant correctly.

'I cannot tell you,' was all Nilsson replied.

I explained how I knew it was Butcher, and told them everything I could about the man, including the reason I believed had led him to make this false statement. In 1978 I had owned an old Fiat 124 which needed attention before it would pass its MOT test. To this end I had taken it to a garage in Windsor only to find that it was too busy to carry out the necessary repairs immediately. Instead the receptionist had recommended me to another customer who happened to be standing beside me at the counter. This man was Ronnie Butcher.

At the time, as it turned out, he was a self employed mechanic, working from a domestic garage beneath his council flat in Windsor. However he told me that he was planning to move to an old barn on the outskirts of the town, where he was hoping to expand his business. He repaired my car well and at reasonable cost, and it passed its MOT. In the months that followed, until the Regiment was posted to Germany, I used his services as a mechanic frequently, as did several other Life Guards.

On one occasion when collecting my car from him, Butcher had asked me if I was interested in buying a small sailing dinghy, which I saw was parked on a trailor alongside his barn. If I did not want to, he had continued, had I any friends who might? I refused but to cut a long story short, some friends of mine did eventually buy the thing.

However, and again to cut a long story short, it turned out to be stolen, and rather smarter than I had surmised. Not surprisingly the people who bought it, when collared by the police in 1981, mentioned my name. In turn, when interviewed, I reported that the boat had originally come from Butcher. I had no idea if he had stolen it, but he had certainly sold it.

I was asked by the police to be a prosecution witness at Butcher's trial and I naturally enough agreed to this request.

At his trial I gave the only evidence that I could. That the boat had been purchased from Butcher, but that I had no idea how he had come by it, nor if he had stolen it. He denied the charge, attempting to make out that I must have stolen the dinghy and once caught had tried to pass the blame onto a man with a known criminal record, who could therefore not defend himself. That was nonsense, but eventually Butcher was found not guilty. Despite this, he vowed to get even with me.

When I finished this account, it was once again clear from the faces of the two policemen that evidence they had thought would make their case against me was, like everything else they had so far found, proving to be of a highly dubious nature.

Bihlar then went on to question me on the details of how the meeting at Linköping had been arranged. He asked me if any other time but ten o'clock had been agreed upon. I told him that ten had always been the only time discussed. He seemed to be convinced that there had been alternative timings, and that Christopher had arranged them. I replied:

'Mr Bihlar, I organized my holiday; Christopher had nothing to do with it.'

'If that is so, why did your brother telephone Mitchell here in Sweden, to inquire about the possibilities of leaving the Jaguar at Stockholm Airport and if it would be safe there?'

'I have never heard anything about such a call, my brother certainly did not mention it [which was the truth]. Why should he have done, I was going to drive the car back to England?' [Which was not the truth].

'This call was made from Ibiza on Monday 9 March, the day before you left for Sweden.'

'Well I did not make it, and I had never heard about it before you mentioned it in court the other day.'

'Mitchell says he received this telephone call on the 9th, and had replied via Echo saying that he would bring the meeting with you at the station forward to an earlier time.'

'I know nothing about this Mr Bihlar, and I doubt whether it is true because not only were the timings not brought forward but as it was Mitchell was late for the meeting at ten.'

Bihlar then continued to question me on unimportant issues relating to the journey from Ibiza to Narbonne. For instance he asked me why I had paid for the spare tyre we had bought in Andorra. I told him I had done so, because Chris had been short of money and I had had the right amount of pesetas left. I did not understand the relevance of these questions and I said as much, but Bihlar just shrugged his shoulders in response.

'Did you not find it strange that Mitchell did not leave you a telephone number in case of emergencies. There was one where he lived?'

'He never offered me one, and I forgot to ask for one,' was all I could think of by way of reply.

'If the meeting with Mitchell was not that important, why was it that you drove from early morning to late at night for two days to get to Linköping at the agreed time?'

'I drove that quickly because I wanted as much time to go skiing as possible. The longer I took over the journey, the less time I was going to have on the slopes. Mitchell lived on the way and it was convenient to stay the night at his house. That is why I met him.'

Bihlar brought the interview to an end by asking me to list every military course I had ever been on:

1974 – Recruit training. Guards Depot. Followed by the RCB.
1975 – SMC 7, Royal Military Academy, Sandhurst.
1975 – Young Officers Specialist to Arm Course. Royal Armoured Corps Centre, Bovingdon.
1976 – Long Equitation Course, Melton Mowbray.
1978 – PQS 1, Lieutenant to Captain Promotion Test.
       – Returning Officers Course, RMAS. RCC 17.
1979 – Regimental Gunnery Officers Course.
1987 – PQS 2, Captain to Major Promotion Exam.

'Did you not attend any courses before being posted to Northern Ireland?'

So that is what he had been fishing for. 'Anything to do with Northern Ireland is classified. I would have to get permission before talking about it, but of course all soldiers going to Ulster receive additional training.'

On 11 and 12 June I was interviewed by two officers from Scotland Yard. This visit was to cause more concern and trouble than could possibly have been foreseen at the time. Of all the interrogations I was to undergo it is ironic that these ones, at the hands of British detectives, turned out to be the most alarming and intimidating.

Tom Placht warned me on the morning of the 11th that the visit was going to take place, and advised me that when it did he ought to be present. Advice that I readily accepted.

Bihlar came for me late that afternoon.

'There are two of your friends to see you,' he said with a sarcastic smile.

This caught me off balance. 'Who?' I asked.

The fixed smile remained on his face, the man was enjoying himself. 'Two English policemen. They want to talk with you.'

'Is my lawyer here?' The reply was negative. 'Then I refuse to see them.'

The smile dropped from his features, he went puce with anger and slammed the cell door in my face. A guard told me later that she had never seen Bihlar so furious, he had almost knocked her off her feet in the corridor outside my cell, as he stalked off to telephone Placht. He returned to me a few minutes later.

'Your advokat is on the telephone,' he barked.

Placht told me that he could not come over right away but that he had arranged for a meeting to take place the following morning. However, he added that Bihlar was keen for me to see the detectives that afternoon and he thought that there was no harm in me doing so, as long as there was no discussion about the case. He had made this stipulation to Bihlar. On this basis I agreed to see the two men straight away. It was to be a mistake.

They were waiting for me downstairs in an office close to Bihlar's, who once he had shown me in left the three of us alone together. They were smartly dressed in collar and tie, and dark suits, which made a stark contrast to the casual get-up I had grown accustomed to seeing the Swedish police wear.

We introduced ourselves, although of course they already knew who I was. They were Detective Inspector Dave Morgan and Detective Sergeant Brian Moore. Morgan was short, dark haired and in his late thirties or early forties. Moore was tall, thin, red haired and in his late twenties. For some reason something made me suspicious of them, so I asked to see their warrant cards. They were who they claimed to be.

I sat beside Morgan and opposite Moore. They were as professional as Bihlar was clumsy, and I must admit quite frightening with it. Morgan explained that although they were in Sweden officially, they were out of the jurisdiction and were therefore seeing me as private citizens. They had no control over me. He added that they were not going to discuss details of the case, that could wait until the next day.

'We realize that you are in a difficult position, Captain

Hayward,' Morgan began. 'What with all these senior Army Officers and Members of Parliament trying to help you, when really the three of us in this room know that you're guilty. You are going to look pretty bad when the truth comes out.'

I said nothing.

'We know you're guilty Simon. Don't mind if I call you Simon, do you?' The younger man asked. 'We know, for instance, that your brother Christopher is a professional drugs smuggler. Not big time, you understand, but the odd 200 kilos here and there. He brings them in from Morocco on his boat. We know that you willingly and knowingly worked for him as a courier.'

'You cannot, because I did not,' I interrupted. He held up his hand to stop me.

'Don't talk, just listen. We've done quite a lot of checking on your family. Your younger brother Justin's company for instance. What's its name?'

'I don't know.'

'Gold-Tip, it's called Gold-Tip,' volunteered Morgan.

I just looked at Moore in amazement. This was extremely frightening. These men seemed so sure of themselves, so confident, but I knew that what they were saying was absolute nonsense. But nonetheless these detectives sounded so convincing that they even had me wondering.

'Look, we are not interested in the little people,' Morgan continued, 'we just want the chiefs, the international crime syndicate. Fifty kilos, even two hundred kilos is very small time to us. It might be enormous to the Swedes, but hardly worth bothering about to us. Help us and we will help you.'

'We are going to get these people,' Moore took over again, 'with or without your assistance. If you cooperate with us we can bypass your family. If you don't we will have to go through them to get at the big timers. It's like going along one side of a triangle, straight to the main goal, or along two sides arresting minor criminals like your family on the way. It is up to you.'

I was finding this impossible to take in. It was so unreal. I sat gawping at Moore.

'If you confess and tell us all you know, especially about the big smugglers you met in Spain, we might be able to make a deal with the Swedes. As I say, fifty kilos to them is heavy, but to us it's peanuts. We will be able to get the charges dropped or at least reduced. Come on Simon, what do you say?'

'I cannot help you. I have nothing to say, except that everything you have stated is rubbish. Total rubbish. You could not be more wrong, sergeant.'

Morgan spoke for the first time in a while. 'Well, we will know soon enough. A man answering your brother's description, and sailing a catamaran, has been arrested in the West Indies.' He stared at me straight in the eyes when he said this. If he had been hoping for a reaction he did not get one. 'Right, that will do for this evening. We said we would not talk about the case.' Which of course was all we had been discussing from the moment I had entered the office. He rose to his feet, nodding at Moore.

'Now hang on a minute,' I said, 'you are not going to make all these accusations and then just walk away. I want to help you in any way possible, but the fact is I do not know anything about the drugs world, nor anybody involved in it. Let's talk about this some more. I want to clear this matter up. I want to convince you.'

'No, that will do. You sleep on it tonight. We will see you again in the morning. In any case we may not be needing your help, we're off to visit your mate Mitchell now. He will cooperate.'

They became very pally, insisting on escorting me back to my cell, remarking that it looked just like a Section House room, where young unmarried policemen apparently live. They laughed and joked before leaving me.

I asked the guards if I could telephone my lawyer, and seeing the state I was in, they kindly allowed me to. Tom Placht must have detected the panic in my voice and came straight over.

I related to him all that had taken place. He too was astonished, not only at the methods Morgan and Moore had adopted, but also at the content of my discussion with them. In the next hour he did his best to calm me down and reassure me.

'Simon,' he said finally, putting his hand on my arm, 'do not worry too much. Now we know their tactics. They were just trying to scare you. Let us wait and see what happens tomorrow before deciding what to do about it.'

The morning's session was more formal, and was held in

Nilsson's office. Besides myself and Placht, Bihlar, Nilsson, Morgan, Moore and Forsberg were present; and an eighth man who was introduced as Inspector Gunnar Larsen, a Norwegian Police liaison officer, attached to the Norwegian Embassy in London. He was a small, dark, wiry man in his late forties. The interview was chaired by Morgan who sat with Moore behind a desk. The rest of us sat down facing them. The office was rather cramped.

Morgan started by questioning me on the statements I had given to date, not in great detail but specifically on my reasons for coming to Sweden. He ended by saying:

'Well, from what you have just told me and from studying the details of the case, I think you are lying. Your story is weak, very weak, and what is more it doesn't hold water. It's not up to me, but I don't think you stand a chance.' He had written out two lists, alongside each other. One with the details of my statements, the other with Mitchell's. 'Mitchell is pleading guilty, so he will be believed, and besides which his story is more credible.'

'We saw him last night,' Moore spoke for the first time, 'and he has confirmed all the information we hold. So it does not really matter what you say now.' Both men stared at me.

'I have told you the truth. I am not going to allow you to force me into confessing to something I have not done.'

Morgan then dropped his bombshell. 'I have given a statement to the Swedish police, listing the information we have on you, Simon.' He also called me by my Christian name now – all pretence at formality had ceased. 'I, and Sergeant Moore, have signed it. And, if we are asked to, we will come to Sweden to testify against you.' Moore added threateningly. 'You are going to prison for a long time Simon.'

As I sat in that office, listening to these two detectives, the true enormity of my situation flooded over me. It was not until that moment that I had ever considered the possibility of being sent to prison, now it seemed more like a certainty than a probability. I suddenly felt deeply depressed and more than a little concerned for my immediate future. Which is probably exactly how the police had wanted me to feel, and the result they had wished to achieve.

'Inspector Bihlar,' Morgan asked, 'Did you find any

fingerprints on the cannabis. They were vacuum-packed weren't they?'

'Yes they were, and we did find some prints, but not Simon's.'

'Have you tried the new laser technique?' he was talking to Bihlar but watching me intently, 'that will show up much more. Even prints that have been wiped off will become clear.'

It was as though he was expecting me to say: 'You won't find mine, I was wearing gloves.'

'No we have not,' Bihlar answered, 'but we will now.' It sounded as though they had been rehearsing their lines.

Finally as the meeting broke up and everyone was rising to their feet, Morgan turned to Moore, and said in a stage whisper that was obviously intended for my ears: 'Get on to our man in the West Indies immediately, Brian, and see if that bloke they've caught is Christopher Hayward.'

Placht came back to my cell with me. 'Don't worry about that,' he squeezed my arm, obviously pleased with how the morning's events had turned out. I wish I could have shared his optimism. 'They were fishing, and all that rubbish about laser fingerprinting, and their man in the West Indies. It's a joke.'

I was to see Morgan once more. Bihlar brought him up to my cell that evening, just after I had had my dinner. He sat on my bunk, Bihlar gave him a cup of coffee and left us alone together.

'You know where I've been this afternoon?' and, when I didn't answer, 'I've been to Mitchell's trial.' He had a kind of sick smile on his face. 'He pleaded guilty, told the Court the whole story. He says that Christopher was his boss, and you agreed to act as the courier for the thrills. He was very convincing. They believed him.'

I wasn't in the mood for this. I just looked at the man, expressionless.

'I really hope you get away with this Simon,' he continued. 'In England you probably would, but not here in Sweden. I think you will get between five and six years. As far as I'm concerned, cannabis smuggling isn't such a bad crime these days. In fact I think they ought to legalize it, that would make my job a lot simpler. Leave me more time to have a go at the hard drug smugglers – they're the true criminals. Mitchell agrees, he even said as much this afternoon.'

'I have not done anything wrong to "get away" with,' I snapped at him, 'and I don't agree with you on the cannabis issue, and I don't give a damn what Mitchell said this afternoon.'

'It's incredible,' he said, changing the subject, 'my visit to Sweden was supposed to be confidential but it's already in the newspapers. Even in the *Daily Telegraph*. How do you suppose that happened?'

'Well don't look at me. I don't exactly have easy access to the outside world from this cell. However it does not surprise me, apparently Forsberg and his men have leaked everything possible about this case to the press. Not that I'm allowed to read any of it. They cannot keep anything secret, and what they don't know, I'm told they make up.'

'Yes,' he replied, 'I rather agree, it could only have come from them. What strange behaviour.'

We sat looking at each other in silence for a few seconds.

'Look, I realise you can't tell me now, not with your innocent plea, but after your trial, and hopefully over a pint in a London Pub, you might feel like telling me what really went on. If they convict you, which is more likely, I will come and see you in prison.'

'I won't be able to tell you anything, for the simple reason I do not know anything. You will be wasting your time.' I stood up to rinse my coffee cup out in the handbasin. I turned to face him. 'I don't want to talk to you any more. Please leave!'

Once he had gone, I sat and gazed at the wall opposite me. I must have been in a state of semi-shock for the next few hours passed by without notice. My mind was reeling from the events of the last two days. Until that very morning I had been convinced that I would eventually be released without charge, and now it seemed that not only was there a better than good chance that I would be put on trial, but that the popular consensus of opinion was that I would also be convicted and sent to prison for a very long time. A daunting and terrifying prospect.

The truth could be my only defence: there was no other way

for me to beat these allegations, especially since with all this false evidence starting to emerge, the picture was starting to look extremely bleak. There was only one irrefutable fact in the whole affair, and that was that fifty kilos of cannabis had been found in the Jaguar. That alone could not constitute proof of my guilt. Although they had suspected their presence, it had taken the police three days to locate those drugs, which on their own admission had been professionally hidden. Therefore, anyone who had simply driven the car, could easily have done so without definite knowledge of their existence. However the fact that they had been found in the car certainly did not make my case any stronger and had the effect of placing more onus on the defence to prove my innocence.

I realised that was going to be a very difficult task, indeed almost impossible, unless it could be established who had secreted the drug consignment in the Jaguar, and at their present rate there was not much likelihood of the police doing that. Having tricked me into taking their risks for them, it was obviously too much to hope for that the true culprits would come forward to help me, now that I had been arrested.

Christopher was an obvious key to the mystery, and I had been hoping that he would come forward to explain what had taken place on Ibiza, but instead he had disappeared, not even sending a statement to divulge his knowledge, if any, of the affair. I could not understand what had got into him. By running away he was making himself look guilty. Perhaps he was involved? However, even if he was in some way responsible, surely his guilt was not indicative of my guilt.

However, with Mitchell apparently claiming that he worked for Christopher, and that I had known exactly what I had been doing, together with this so-called evidence from Scotland Yard, the strength of my position had deteriorated. In fact it had nose-dived. The case against me was starting to look strong, and that scared me. Indeed, the authorities appeared to be giving no consideration to the difficulties that an unwitting courier would have in proving his innocence.

If I was going to stand trial, I had to go to court on the basis of the truth, the whole truth, and nothing but the truth: otherwise I might just as well plead guilty to a crime I had not committed. I now bitterly regretted my decision not to tell the complete truth from the very beginning. It had been the worst possible thing I could have done. The desire to protect Christopher had been strong; to be totally honest with myself it was still strong, but if he had committed a crime he did not deserve my protection, and if he had not committed a crime he did not need it. I was being a fool only to myself by remaining silent.

If the realisation had finally dawned on me that it was time to make a clean breast of things, it also did not escape my notice that to do so was to risk damaging what little credibility I may have had left. Indeed a month earlier when I had very nearly told Placht everything, he had, before I could do so, explained to me that the one strength of the defence case, and the fact that was causing most concern to the prosecutor, was that after so long I was still sticking religiously to my original statement.

I found myself therefore in something of a dilemma. Whereas I felt that the best hope of salvation lay in telling the complete truth, this feeling was also tempered by a fear of the consequences of changing my story at this late stage.

I spent a nervous weekend pacing my cell and the exercise pens, but in reality my mind was already made up. The next time Tom Placht came to see me I was going to tell all. Forsberg of course would probably leap at the opportunity in an attempt to discredit me completely, but that was a risk I was going to have to take.

At least, I reassured myself, he would not be able to accuse me of changing my account of events to make it coincide with the statements of others. I had no idea what anyone else, not even Mitchell, was saying, except in the barest of detail. Solitary confinement had seen to that.

Placht was unable to visit me again until Tuesday 16 June. We sat together in my cell. I looked at him, he could not have known what was coming. Taking a deep breath, I began.

'Tom, I have something to tell you. Something that I've been wanting to tell you for some time.'

He looked nervous himself now, almost as though he had been expecting this conversation for weeks but was not sure what sort of confession I was about to make.

'Stop Simon, before you say anything, remember our first conversation together. Whatever you are about to tell me I will have to pass on to the prosecutor.'

'I realise that, and I want you to do so.' I took another deep breath, that damnable uncontrollable emotion was starting to raise its ugly head again. I could feel tears beginning to well in my eyes. 'Tom, although the vast majority of what I have told you has been the truth, I'm afraid to say that it has not been the whole truth.'

He stopped me again. 'I think it would be better if we went to an interview room so that I can make proper notes.'

There were rooms attached to the Häktet, almost opposite my cell, for just this purpose. We went to one of them. I started for the third time.

'There is actually not much more to tell. My main reason for coming to Sweden, Tom, was not to go skiing but to deliver the Jaguar to Mitchell for my brother. I was not going to sell it in London for him, although initially he had asked me to do so. However a few days after that request he told me that a buyer had been found in Sweden and asked me if I would drive it up here instead. It is really as simple as that, I was going to go skiing as well, I was going to spend the night at Mitchell's, but instead of taking the car back to England, I was going to travel on to the ski resorts by train, or possibly by hire car, and then fly back home. All the arrangements for the meeting with Mitchell at Linköping were made by Chris, I never spoke to Mitchell about them. In fact the only time I spoke to Mitchell at all on Ibiza was when he visited Santa Gertrudis, and that was about little more than the weather. We never met outside the Montesol. I made that up.'

Placht was watching me carefully whilst these words spilt from me. When I finished there was a long-drawn out pause.

'You bloody fool, Simon! You stupid bloody fool. If you had said this right from the beginning, you would now be free!'

He could not have better described how I felt. He told me to run through the whole story again, whilst he made notes. I also explained my reasons for not telling the truth from day one, and my decision for doing so now. I felt much better once everything was out in the open.

'Right, I will see Forsberg tomorrow, and presumably Bihlar

will question you sometime soon after that. It fits Simon, it fits. I just wish you had had the sense to tell me earlier.'

'I almost did, on several occasions. It has not been easy for me to tell deliberate lies Tom, but you remember telling me that the one strength of my position was the fact that I had kept to my original statement, despite everything. I do not mean to pass the buck at all Tom, but it became a very difficult decision to make. I feel much better now, however.'

'Yes, I understand that. When you were telling me the story, you looked as though a great weight was being lifted from your shoulders. But I must ask you. Are you sure this is all you want to say? Is this the complete truth?'

'Yes Tom, that is everything. You now know the whole story.'

'Do you promise me? Even if I were to ask you the same question in ten years' time, would the answer be the same?'

'I promise.'

The expected interview with Bihlar took place the following morning at 11.20, with Tom Placht sitting in to ensure fair play, and to lend me some moral support. On this occasion we insisted that Bihlar tape the proceedings, so that there could be no controversy at a later stage. With hindsight I now wish that I had insisted that all my statements had been taped, it would have avoided a great many problems during my trial.

To start with the session was an exact repetition of my conversation with Placht the previous evening. Bihlar took his customary notes despite the recording, and did not say a word until I had finished. He then asked me the obvious question.

'Why did you not tell me this before?'

I told him of my belief that Christopher was innocent, and of my initial wish to protect him. He then continued to question me for some fifteen minutes on different aspects of my complete statement, most of it was old ground and he already knew the answers, but he was clearly trying to catch me out. One question, however was on a totally new tack.

'We have a receipt showing you bought 31 litres of petrol in Helsingborg. Why did you buy it in Sweden and not in Denmark?'

'I don't know, It was not through any definite choice, I just stopped to fill up at the first petrol station I came across.'

'Why only 31 litres?'

'Again, I'm not sure. I suppose that was all I needed.'

At first this line of questioning puzzled me but soon it became clear what he was getting at. He was attempting to prove that I had deliberately arrived on Swedish soil with one of the two Jaguar petrol tanks empty, so that the car would appear to weigh the correct amount, even with the 50 kilos of cannabis, if the customs became suspicious.

I could only laugh at this. 'Mr Bihlar, this is so ridiculous. I am sure that if the customs became suspicious enough of a car to want to weigh it, that they would have the sense to check how much petrol was in its tanks before doing so.'

He did not seem very pleased with my logic, and just glowered at me. Sometimes I could only doubt the man's perspicacity.

'Look, Mr Bihlar. I had no idea that anything was hidden in that car!'

'We know that you knew that drugs were in the car!'

'You cannot know that I knew, because I didn't know!' I began to hope that he wouldn't pursue this line of argument or we would be in danger of becoming bogged down in strings of 'I know's' and 'you know's,' and 'we knew that you knew's'. Luckily he decided to draw the interview to a close.

'Has the lawyer got anything to say?'

'Not for now.'

The petrol station question was never mentioned again. I cannot think why it was ever brought up in the first place, especially since petrol is considerably cheaper in Sweden than Denmark, which would have been an obvious reason for me to have waited until my arrival in Helsingborg before buying fuel.

On 18 June I returned to the Uppsala District Court for the fourth time. Not surprisingly, but just as upsettingly, Forsberg requested that I be bound over for yet another month. He gave two excuses on this occasion. Firstly he told the judge of Morgan and Moore's visit, and presented the statement they had submitted. It was the first time that Placht and I had physically seen it, and Tom asked for, and was given a copy. It was short, highly damaging, and to the point.

12 June 1987

Report of Brian Moore, Detective Sergeant and
David Morgan, Detective Inspector, of the
National Drugs Intelligence Unit,
New Scotland Yard,
Broadway,
London SW1.

We have information in relation to the seizure of 50.5
kilos of cannabis resin made in Linköping, Sweden, on
13 March 1987, when Simon HAYWARD was arrested.

1. Christopher HAYWARD is a professional cannabis
    trafficker.
2. Christopher HAYWARD acquired the Jaguar motor
    car index number MHM 795X in the United
    Kingdom, in which his brother Simon HAYWARD
    was arrested and in which the drugs were concealed.
3. Simon HAYWARD had full knowledge that the
    drugs were concealed in the vehicle.
4. Simon HAYWARD was to be paid £20,000 for
    providing this courier service for his brother
    Christopher HAYWARD, by Christopher.
5. Simon HAYWARD also became involved in this
    offence because of the 'excitement' that it would
    provide.

On Thursday 11 June 1987 we spoke to Forbes Cay
MITCHELL, also arrested for this offence. Without being
prompted in any way he FULLY corroborated the above
information that we had previously acquired, before our
visit to Sweden.

DAVID MORGAN   BRIAN MOORE

Secondly Forsberg reported my change of statement which,
he said, now required further investigation. Once again I was
asked to give an account of myself and my reasons for not
telling the complete truth right from the beginning. In so
doing I made an impassioned plea to Judge Hellbacher to

understand my shock and confusion at being arrested, and my natural wish to protect a member of my family. If he felt any sympathy for my situation, he did not show it.

In summing up his request Forsberg stated that more time was needed to complete his investigation, and that he expected more information to emanate from Scotland Yard, where enquiries were also progressing. There seemed little point in either Placht or me saying much. The judge, as on all previous occasions, granted Forsberg his wish. This time giving him a full month and thereby ignoring his warning that the last remand was going to be the final one.

When I returned to my cell I could not have felt more crushed and demoralised. I lay back on my bunk, unable to think, to take in what was happening to me. I felt numb and although it might sound pathetic all I wanted to do was curl up and go to sleep, and stay asleep until this nightmare came to an end. Tears rolled down my cheeks, my breath came in short, sharp, heaving gasps. It was as though the past fourteen weeks had suddenly become too much to handle.

I felt someone sit on the bed beside me. I opened my eyes, it was Inger. I had not heard her come in. She obviously knew what had happened. All I could mutter to her was:

'Another month, oh my God, another month.'

She sat me up, and put her arms around me. I was touched by her generosity of spirit, she was a kind and gentle person, who really felt for her prisoners and understood what they were going through. I put my head on her shoulder, and found myself crying like a baby.

Bihlar was to interview me formally twice more before my trial. On Tuesday 23 June he questioned me for two and a half hours, making me run through my entire statement again, from start to finish.

'If what you are saying is true Simon, your brother is a real bastard. What type of man would do such a thing to his own brother?'

'What I am saying is the truth, but don't jump to conclusions Bihlar. Neither of us knows for certain if Christopher set me up, you are only assuming that he did. Perhaps he was tricked as well? I do not believe that he would have done this to me, and ask yourself this question. Who in their right mind would smuggle drugs in their own car, registered to them? That would be just asking for trouble, not to mention taking totally unnecessary risks. He might just as well have driven the car himself.'

He ignored this, and just said: 'We shall see, we shall see.' Then:

'What arrangements were made for the registration and sale of the Jaguar in Sweden?'

'I have no idea. Chris told me not to worry about that, it was going to be handled entirely by Lokesh. I was asked to deliver the car, nothing more. In any case I presume nothing could have been done until duplicate papers could be arranged. Don't forget the original ones were stolen from the car.'

The last session took place on Friday 26th and lasted only five minutes.

'You should know that I have spoken to Mitchell about your new statement. He says you are lying, and that he was not going to buy the Jaguar. His very words were: "I am a hash dealer, not a car dealer".'

'I have never said that he was definitely going to buy the car, all I know is that he was going to take delivery of it. All I was told, as you know, was that it was going to be bought by an Englishman living in Sweden. That may or may not have been Mitchell, I don't know for certain but I assume that it was him.'

'So you stick to your statement?'

'I most certainly do.'

In the last week of June the prosecutor and police announced that they were all going on leave, indeed Bihlar who it should not be forgotten was personally in charge of my investigation would be away until Monday 27 July. I found it amazing, in view of the fact that I was being kept in solitary confinement with the leave of the Courts, ostensibly so that evidence could be gathered and the matter brought to trial as quickly as possible, that Forsberg and his men should immediately go off on holiday. Surely if it had been necessary for him to obtain a further period of remand, at the very least one would expect him to do all he could to have his case ready by the next hearing date.

I found it even more difficult to sit in my little box knowing that the police were doing nothing to further their enquiries. As time passed it would obviously become increasingly difficult to establish the truth, but the Swedish authorities appeared not to care.

However if my case officers being away on holiday was frustrating in the extreme, it also carried with it a bonus. Suddenly previous visiting restrictions were greatly relaxed. This meant that for the first time since April Sandra was allowed to come to see me. She travelled to Sweden with her mother and the three of us were given time together on three consecutive days, the final period even lasting for two and a half hours – far longer than any previous visit.

Whilst it was wonderful to see Sands again, even in the company of a police officer, she was the bringer of bad tidings. On our third morning, she quietly told me that Chantal had been found dead in her bed ten days before. She was not certain, but a drugs overdose was suspected. She added that Tarik was now with my mother in London. It was indeed bad news. Whereas I had not known Chantal well, I had been fond of her and I was greatly saddened by her death. I was also more than a little shocked that drugs had been the cause, for as far as I knew she never touched them. Even more I felt for young Tarik, who it would seem had now lost both his parents. He was only seven, the same age as my brother David had been when our father had died. I remembered only too well a little boy's pain and tears on that occasion, and I knew that Tarik would be going through the same hell, and confusion, now. We adults never properly appreciate just how much young children actually understand. I felt terrible not being able to go to him.

I could not have known at the time, but as events were to turn out it became a very strong probability that poor Chantal's death was not an accident.

During the afternoon of Thursday 16 July Placht came to the Häktet, accompanied by a young woman in her early twenties, whome he introduced as Hanna Pontein, to inform me that Forsberg had charged me on the previous day, and had served on the defence the statements and exhibits on which the charge was based. We had been expecting this but I was more than surprised that there had been no formal charging

procedure, as there would have been in England. It seemed
odd that it had occurred without my presence, or knowledge,
and that it had been left up to my lawyer to tell me. None the
less, the following charges had been laid against me:

1. GROSS SMUGGLING.
That Hayward wilfully imported 50.5 kilos of cannabis
into Sweden via Helsingborg without notifying the
relevant authority.
   The offence is to be considered gross, since it concerned
goods of significant quantity and value.

Section of Act.
Section 3 of Penal Act on Smuggling. (1960:418)

2. GROSS DRUG OFFENCE.
That Hayward, during the period 10-13 March 1987
transported the 50.5 kilos from Ibiza, Spain, to Vastra
Ryd in Motala municipality, in a Jaguar, registration
number MHM 795X. On 13 March 1987, in Sweden, he
was illegally in possession of the 50.5 kilos, and illegally
transported them from Helsingborg to Vastra Ryd.
   The offence, which was wilfully committed, is to be
regarded as gross, since it concerned a particularly large
quantity of drugs.

Section of Act.
Section 3 of the Penal Act on Narcotic Drugs. (1968:64)

Special Claims.
1.   That 50.5 kg cannabis, a Jaguar registration number
MHM 795X and a screwdriver of BACHO 8930 TX 30
type, be forfeited. (Confiscated item nos. 0303-178-87,
0303-249-87, 0303-256-87 p 1)

2.   That Hayward be deported from the country.

The trial had been fixed to commence on Thursday 23 July,
only one week away. This left the defence with an enormous
problem, because he had not known what the exact charge
would be, or what evidence the prosecution would present,
Placht had been quite unable to properly prepare himself.

Forsberg, on the other hand, had had 125 days in which to prepare his case, and although Placht had on 4 May requested that the evidence be translated into English, the entire prosecution bundle was in Swedish, a language of course that I did not speak nor understand. To make matters worse the documentation ran to 186 pages. We had now barely a week to prepare my defence.

To this end Placht told me that he was flying that day to London to consult with Kingsley Napley, the solicitors my mother had instructed, and he had taken on Hanna Pontein to help work through the evidence. Time, he explained, was against us.

Hanna was a short, square featured girl, with a bubbly character and a delicious giggle never far from the surface. I took to her immediately. She was a law graduate and, due to the fact that she had spent many of her formative years in America, spoke perfect English. She was also, as I discovered later, one of Sweden's leading horsewomen.

We spent the next four days together poring over the prosecutor's documents, she translating everything possible in the time available. There was too much to do the job comprehensibly. It was mainly comprised of written statements from me and numerous other witnesses, including Mitchell, other members of his gang, and several police officers. There was also an accumulation of other papers involving the screwdriver, how the drugs were found, and how Forsberg had built his case against me. I had been through some of my own statements, when Placht had been handed them the week before, with an interpreter and as Hanna and I now finished the job, we made a list of the mistakes and misunderstandings we found within them. A copy of this list was later presented to the prosecutor, and was also used to some effect at my trial. It would have saved a great deal of time and trouble on all sides if Bihlar's method of statement-taking had been a lot more accurate and a lot less amateurish.

The level of improbity that the prosecution was prepared to stoop to became more than apparent two days before my trial was due to begin. Placht requested that the defence be allowed to view the video made of the Jaguar being searched, and the one of me explaining how I had used the screwdriver, since both of them were mentioned in the documented evidence we had been supplied with.

Seeing the cannabis being discovered was interesting enough, but totally irrelevant as far as evidence was concerned, for no one was disputing the fact that drugs had been stashed in the car. The copy of the second video was. however extremely alarming. It was clear that it had been carefully edited. The part showing Bihlar exclaiming that he could prove I was a liar and trying to use the normal screwdriver on the seat screws had been partially cut. Gone was the sequence showing the screwdriver not to fit, instead, all that could be seen was Bihlar standing up and turning to me saying:

'There you see it fits. You must be lying,' and my reply. 'Of course it fits, Mr Bihlar, if you find one of the correct size . . .'

To anyone watching the film for the first time, like the judge at my forthcoming trial, it would appear as though the demonstration had been successful in its aim to prove I had been making things up.

I was appalled and angrily remonstrated with Nilsson, who was conducting the showing. After some argument the very red faced inspector grudgingly admitted that the demonstration had actually taken place in the way I have described earlier in this chapter. He refused however, to admit that the video had been deliberately edited. What the film did still show was Bihlar and Nilsson agreeing that the seat rocked. That at least was something. We had obviously made a major mistake in not demanding a copy of the video on the day that it was made.

Wednesday 22 July was an eventful day, and one that was to instil more hope in me than I had felt in almost twenty weeks. Placht telephoned me in the afternoon.

'Simon, I cannot tell you what is going on, but there will be no trial tomorrow. It has been postponed for at least one day. And Simon, I don't want to give you too much hope either but . . .', and he paused '. . . there may be no trial at all.'

I thought I must have misheard him. My hopes soared.

'You mean, they're going to let me go free?'

'I can't tell you more yet, all I can say is there now may not be a trial. You must be patient.'

That night I prayed like I have never prayed before. I wrote in my diary. 'Tom doing good work.'

The following day I was finally allowed to meet Christopher Murray. He and James Emson, now promoted to Brigadier, had flown out to Sweden the evening before. They came to see me with Tom Placht. Murray was a tall, well-built man in his early forties, with brown hair and a full beard. He and Brigadier Emson did most of the talking, with Placht adding the occasional word.

It appeared that at this late stage the authorities had suddenly hinted that they might be prepared to release me on some form of bail, into the custody of the Army. Quite why this compromise was now being offered, no one seemed to know, or, were not allowed to tell me. The general feeling was that the Swedes did not have a strong enough case against me and, having backed themselves into a corner with their continuous press releases declaring that there was definite proof of my guilt, were now trying to find a face-saving formula to release me.

'I hope that what is about to happen,' said Brigadier Emson, 'is you will be released into military custody, and be allowed to fly to England. Then in a couple of months the charges against you will be quietly dropped. Of course, you would have to give a personal undertaking, guaranteed by the Army, to return if required.'

'That is really your only chance Simon,' Murray added, 'Statistics show that little more than two per cent of defendants are acquitted at trial. This way you will have to remain in some form of military custody, probably at Windsor, but you should be free in a few weeks.'

'The figures that you are quoting are true,' Placht, who had been listening quietly, interrupted, 'but that is because most defendants plead guilty in Sweden. It is unusual for them to go to court pleading otherwise.'

We chatted on for some time, going over details of the case, but I could see that my visitors were hopeful that a trial would not take place. As they left Brigadier Emson turned to me:

'Keep your chin up boy. Let's not be too optimistic, too early, but there is hope.'

My mother was due to visit me the next morning at nine o'clock, but still by half past no one had come to collect me. As always I began to imagine that some terrible accident had happened, but I need not have worried, and on this occasion the police were not playing their little games with me.

Eventually, almost two hours late, we were allowed to see each other for some thirty minutes. The reason for her tardiness was that the police had been interviewing her since early morning. She was not permitted to tell me why, but everything about her oozed new confidence and hope. A marked difference from her last visit.

Nilsson interviewed me later that afternoon in Tom Placht's presence. Apparently my mother had informed the police that Christopher Hayward had telephoned her at the beginning of the month, he had refused to reveal from where, to say that the man behind the entire business was an Irishman by the name of Dook.

'Have you ever heard of, or met this man? His name is Dook, spelt D-O-O-K.'

'You know damn well that I have. I have already told you that I met him on Ibiza with my brother.' I went on to describe, yet again, the meeting at Santa Eulalia.

'Yes, you have told us about that meeting, but you have never mentioned a man by the name of Dook before.'

'Yes I have, both when I described the meeting soon after my arrest in March, and his name was one of the ones on the list I gave Mr Bihlar in April. However I spelt it D-U-K-E, but I presume we are talking about the same man.'

'Well I have never heard it before today,' he persisted.

Nilsson went on to explain that my mother believed Chantal's death was not an accident, and that she herself had been threatened outside her London house recently. This was very worrying news, but there was nothing I could do about it.

'Now you must tell the truth Simon. You must confess to protect your mother from this man Dook, and you must tell me all you know about him.'

'Look Mr Nilsson, I have told you the bloody truth. For God's sake man, do you think I would tell lies and put my family at risk in the process? I have already told you all I can about this fellow Dook, but I should point out to you that I have no personal idea if he is responsible for those drugs or not. However, if my brother says that he is, that is good enough for me.'

'Well since we know nothing about him, there is little we can do. We do not even know his real name.'

'Yes and that might not have been the case if you had done as Mr Placht and I requested months ago, and carried out some enquiries on Ibiza! I snapped at him. He looked sick. 'The only other thing I know about him is that he keeps his yacht, a catamaran, at a marina in Ibiza City. You might be able to discover his true identity from there.'

I went on to explain in detail and with a sketch map, where the marina was situated and gave the best description of Dook as I could remember. In his forties, about 5ft. 8in., tall, thin muscular build, fair hair, soft Irish accent. It was not much to go on. The reason I knew of his yacht was that Christopher had pointed it out to Sands and me during a walk one afternoon as being similar to his own. I also remembered it from my visit to the island in 1984..

Nilsson had been conducting this interview because Bihlar was still supposed to be away on leave until the following Monday. However just as he was drawing the session to a close the office door opened to reveal a tanned and healthy looking Bihlar. I was surprised to see him, it was most unusual for him to return early from a holiday, his third since I had been in custody. He smiled at me as he entered, it was more of a sneer.

'There is going to be a trial,' he said. 'It's going to start on Tuesday.'

Five

What Forbes Cay Mitchell and his cronies failed to realise was that the Swedish police had been on their trail for two years. When Mitchell arrived in Sweden, on 7 March, the police were preparing to move in for the kill. He was expected and from the moment he touched foot on Swedish soil a surveillance team followed every move he made.

Consequently, when the operation culminated on that icy road just outside Motala on Friday the 13th the police had a comprehensive picture of who was involved in the ring. Over the ensuing weekend a total of twelve arrests were made. The police had also been expecting a shipment of cannabis, their only surprise – on their own admission – was my presence.

In fact they were sufficiently surprised that after the initial searches of the Jaguar revealed nothing I was very nearly released. To his credit it was Bihlar who insisted that I be retained, and when the cannabis was eventually found his stand was vindicated.

To begin with the Swedes kept my arrest secret, but as soon as the British authorities were notified, Colonel James Emson telephoned my mother with the news, although initial reports were confused and stated that I had been stopped at Arlanda with a suitcase full of drugs. The story broke days later with a television announcement on 22 March.

The following days became especially difficult for my family, with reporters laying siege to my mother's London house. No holds were barred in an attempt to get a story. Journalists camped on the doorstep, knocking on the front door at all times of the day and night, hounding anyone who came and went, asking for interviews. Microphones were stuck through the letter box to eavesdrop on any conversation taking

157

place inside the house, and all the neighbours were questioned. The most persistent went as far as to climb in through a basement window in an effort to achieve their aims others remained satisfied with banging on the windows and continually calling to those inside. When no interviews were forthcoming, 'phantom' quotes started to appear in many of the tabloids.

It is not difficult to imagine how my mother felt, already confused and greatly upset at the news of my arrest, to find herself besieged in her own home, with hordes of strange people attempting to break in, hammering on the doors and windows, calling out her name persistently at all hours; and then, having made little or no comment, to find herself widely quoted in the national newspapers.

I, meanwhile, was able to glean the most general and patchiest idea of events as they unfurled in the nineteen weeks leading up to my trial, because of the nature of my remand I had no way of knowing exactly what was going on around me. Nor the extent to which Tom Placht in Sweden and others in England were endeavouring to help me. Indeed by the first day of my trial I knew but a fraction of what had actually taken place.

What follows in this chapter is a chronological list of the more important events which occurred either without my knowledge, or at best without my detailed knowledge.

The week after my arrest Christopher telephoned home to ask my mother what was going on. When she told him, his spontaneous reaction was to blurt out:

'Oh no, the set-up was meant for me and I have passed it on to Simon!'

According to Inspector Bihlar, Christopher also telephoned him during the same week. For some reason known only to himself he did not bother to keep a record of the conversation that took place, the only official contact ever to be made with my brother, so we have only Bihlar's memory to go on as to the accuracy of its content.

Apparently Christopher asked if Lokesh had been arrested, and although he refused to answer this question Bihlar asserted that it must have become obvious during the call that Mitchell was indeed in custody. Christopher refused to say where he was, except that it was somewhere in France, and when he was asked to come forward Bihlar claimed that his reply was:

'I am too busy at the moment.'

It became clear that Forbes Mitchell, a Scot with four minor previous convictions, had run a very successful cannabis distribution network and importation business from Ibiza to Sweden for some years. He had attracted the attention of the Swedish police and I had unwittingly stumbled into this. It also became evident that all members of the ring were members of the Rajneesh Cult, and they all used Bhagwan names. Mitchell's was Lokesh.

During my trial Mitchell was to claim, presumably for the benefit of the many press and radio reporters present, that he had remained silent for months after his arrest; and when he did eventually make a statement he only ever confirmed what he found the police already to know. In fact a study of the case records reveals that this is actually far from the truth. He started to talk, 'sing like a canary' is how one official was to describe it later, almost from the first moment.

It would appear that Mitchell kept silent for the first couple of days, probably to give him time to catch his breath, try to establish what the police knew, and to enable him to concoct a plausible story.

In any event by 19 March he was 'spilling the beans' in a major way, telling everything he knew about his Swedish colleagues, including Prem Lennart Viryo, the driver of the Saab; Åsa Hoffman, Viryo's girlfriend; another woman called Nasim Tervaniemi; and Joachim Anderson, who would appear to have had his own ring but who bought cannabis from Mitchell. All of these people were eventually to give evidence at my trial.

By the end of March Mitchell had revealed the entire machinations of his organisation, from the Ibiza connection to Sweden. However he was claiming to be a small fish in a large pond, denying that he ran the show in Sweden, and stating that he worked for a 'Boss' on Ibiza, who he would only name as Mr X.

His statements reveal that Mitchell talked extensively about a man named Macunda, stating that he was his partner, that they had always shared the profits of their 'dealing' with each other on a fifty-fifty basis, and that Macunda always acted as the ring's courier. Nilsson at one time asked me if I recognised any of a list of names, therefore it was presumably Mitchell who had given them to him, especially since one them had been Macunda.

He had also implicated his girlfriend, Prita, both as a material witness, and as an active participant in the ring. Among other roles, he stated that she would take messages and run errands.

When I appeared before Judge Hellbacher for the first time on 24 March I gave no thought to Mitchell or anyone else in his ring, indeed at that time I had no idea who else existed. In fact five of the twelve people arrested, including myself, appeared before Hellbacher on the same day, one immediately after the other. All were remanded, and since I was the last of the five it was very much a foregone conclusion that I too would be remanded in custody.

On that same day Forsberg gave a press conference to explain about the arrests. He refused to name me, describing me as a Guards captain, and stated that I was denying any involvement, but added: 'It would be easier if I had his confession, but I do not need it.'

In other words, he was declaring his belief in my guilt. In a newspaper report, printed again on the same day, the prosecution declared that I was some kind of 'undercover military specialist', that Mitchell and I knew each other well, and that there were several other facts, which could not for the moment be mentioned, pointing to my definite guilt. I had, it was declared, given a statement but they did not believe it.

Outside the police station after my hearing Tom Placht did his best to even the scores, stating in the strongest possible terms:

'The Captain is innocent!'

On Friday 3 April my mother engaged the services of Kingsley Napley, a well known and highly reputable firm of London solicitors. She visited the firm's offices to speak to Sir David Napley, the senior partner, and one of his colleagues Christopher Murray, who was to handle the case. They in turn immediately telephoned Tom Placht to discuss the matter with him, but because the case was under investigation, and due to the general fear of collusion, Placht was forbidden from informing Kingsley Napley of what was going on, even of the exact detail of the content of the court hearing. All Murray was able to do was ask for arrangements to be made for him to be allowed to visit me in the Häktet.

On this same day Mitchell gave a statement in which he spoke at length about Nasim Tervaniemi, naming her as the mastermind and principal of the drugs ring in Sweden. According to him she was responsible for the distribution of the cannabis once he had safely organised its delivery to the country, for collecting the money resulting from the sales, and for handing the residue to him, which he would then, after taking his cut, deliver to the Mr X on Ibiza. Mitchell's testimony against this wretched woman could not have been more damning.

On Monday 6 April Sandra and her father Rodney Agar, a retired Royal Navy Commander who left the Navy to take up a successful business career, visited Kingsley Napley to enable Sandra to give a full statement to Murray about her time on Ibiza with me. This at least was to provide him with a starting point. As it turned out, and contrary to what Bihlar had told me, Sandra's statement was almost identical to my own.

Since my own father was dead, Rodney Agar was to assume the role of paterfamilias and became a staunch ally to both me and my mother. His support was both generous and enduring. He co-ordinated the actions taken in England by the various factions involved in trying to help me and worked tirelessly in an attempt to win my earliest possible release. I owe a great deal to him.

On 7 April Tom Placht telephoned Christopher Murray to inform him that Forsberg had refused Kingsley Napley access not only to their client but also to any information held by the police in relation to him and upon which the prosecution had relied at the first court hearing to justify my remand. Kingsley Napley were therefore forbidden from seeing me and from knowing on what grounds I was being held in custody. On the following day Murray tried to speak to Forsberg direct, only to find that he was 'unavailable'. He left a message with an assistant asking Forsberg to return his call, but was told that this would probably not be possible on the rather weak excuse that international telephone calls were not allowed due to economic restraints. Murray therefore made four further attempts that day but still no reply was forthcoming. I was being refused the legal aid of my choice. Consequently Sir David Napley wrote to Sir Geoffrey Howe, the Foreign Secretary, explaining what was happening and asking for assistance.

On 13 April Bihlar refused my mother access to me: it was to be the first of many such blocking attempts. Happily, on this occasion, Kingsley Napley were able to resolve the problem, with the help of the British Embassy, and she was allowed to visit me in Uppsala on the 14th and 15th, but only for a few minutes each day. It was obvious that Bihlar was extremely put out by having to permit the visit. He was equally obviously not used to prisoners having support.

On Thursday 16 April Mitchell named my brother Christopher as the Mr X. As events were to turn out, the fact that he chose this particular date to do so was to assume great significance.

It was not until Wednesday 22 April that Murray was eventually able to speak to Forsberg in person. In a somewhat blunt conversation Forsberg confirmed the information that he had given to Tom Placht, and again refused Kingsley Napley access to their client. As far as he was concerned I had a perfectly good Swedish lawyer and he could see no reason why he should allow me to see an English one as well; albeit that Kingsley Napley were acting for me and that there were numerous enquiries to be made on my behalf in England. I suspect Forsberg found the concept of defence lawyers collecting evidence somewhat odd, and it became clear that he was most put out at the fact that enquiries could be made over which he had no control.

On this same day Kingsley Napley received a letter from Mr Tim Eggar, the Parliamentary Under-Secretary of State for Foreign and Commonwealth Affairs, on behalf of the Foreign Secretary, regretting that he was unable to assist. It was not Government policy to interfere in the internal affairs of another state.

On Thurday 23 April, Ulf Forsberg, on the strength of

Mitchell's testimony, applied successfully to the Courts for Christopher Hayward to be 'arrested in his absence'. An international arrest warrant was issued via Interpol a few days later.

The following day Murray again managed to speak to Forsberg and again renewed his request to be allowed to see me. Whilst Forsberg was quick to deny any suggestion that he distrusted Sir David or Christopher Murray, he stated that he was still not prepared to allow a visit, adding that had they been Swedish lawyers the answer would have been the same. During the course of this conversation he indicated that there was no doubt in his mind that he believed me to be guilty.

One aspect of Forsberg's behaviour caused both Tom Placht and Kingsley Napley considerable concern, and indeed I found it, as already mentioned, extremely frustrating. Despite the fact that the drugs had obviously originated from Ibiza, no attempt was made by the prosecutor to make enquiries on the island, either by sending one of his police officers, as would have been the case in England, or by asking through Interpol for enquiries to be made by the local police.

On Wednesday 29 April John Gorst came into the picture for the first time. He had read of my arrest and had written to me as a friend in March. He now telephoned Kingsley Napley to offer all the help that he felt he could. He and Murray had a long discussion, as a result of which the following day he spoke to the Prime Minister and to Merlyn Rees, who was showing support. Big guns were being brought to bear. After various other discussions with Kingsley Napley it was decided that it might help were he to visit me in his official capacity as a Member of Parliament. He therefore made the necessary arrangements, via the Swedish Embassy in London and the Foreign and Commonwealth Office, for such a visit to take place. It became clear at a later stage that this visit both greatly annoyed and embarrassed the Swedish authorities – in particular the police.

It is the duty of a Swedish prosecutor to investigate all evidence, both on behalf of the prosecution and the defence. This fundamental principle of objectivity is imposed in a chapter laid down in the Swedish Code of Judicial Procedure, which clearly states that not only circumstances which appear to be against a suspect but also those in his favour are to be investigated and taken into account.

In accordance with this duty, and because he had been ignoring verbal requests, Placht wrote to Forsberg formally on 4 May demanding that he make enquiries of various witnesses on Ibiza, with a view to those enquiries assisting the defence and establishing his client's innocence. As with the verbal requests, Fosberg ignored this letter.

John Gorst travelled to Sweden on Tuesday 5 May, and was able to see me, accompanied by a British Consul called John White, in the presence of Bihlar and Nilsson. For the first time I was permitted to discuss the case with someone other than the police or my Swedish lawyer. Gorst was also allowed to tape record the entire conversation. We went through the whole ghastly mess in general outline, with Gorst asking me one or two questions on the more important points. During the discussion he told me that he had spoken briefly to the Prime Minister and that if possible he would do so again now that he had seen me. He also added that he would do all within his power to help me and that in his opinion, although anything of course was possible, he considered it improbable that I would have been so stupid as to start smuggling drugs, and that he believed me to be innocent.

After the interview was over, and once I had been taken back to my cell, Bihlar obviously had second thoughts about the recording, and asked for the tape to be handed over, which Gorst refused to do. He agreed, however, to give a somewhat unnecessary undertaking that it would not be played to anyone who was likely to be involved in drug trafficking.

. Gorst also asked Bihlar if an investigation was going to be conducted on Ibiza. To his astonishment the Inspector replied that he was too scared to go to the island to make enquiries, because if he did he would be murdered.

For some reason the Uppsala authorities belatedly decided to take exception to this visit and to blow the incident out of all proportion. I believe what really upset them was that I had been told by a British Member of Parliament that I had support in high places, and this did not comply with their policy of trying to break down my defences in a bid to force a confession from me. This contention is strengthened when one remembers that any letter from any kind of even vaguely official source that even hinted at support was withheld. For example, one from Brigadier James Emson, and even a copy of *Hansard* which recorded a speech made by Gorst about my detention.

For whatever reasons, the incident appears to have soured relations, and undoubtedly resulted in Forsberg and the police accusing Gorst through the Swedish media of having lied to them and having posed as visiting me in an official capacity on behalf of the Prime Minister.

Press reports were subsequently carried in the British press, and in particular the *Daily Telegraph* which printed the headline:

'MP lied to Swedish Police for interview with Guards Officer.'

The article quoted Nilsson as saying:

'We were given the distinct impression by Mr Gorst and the British Consul that the visit was on the personal orders of the British Prime Minister . . . We trusted the word of a British MP and of the British Consul that this was an official visit we could not refuse.'

And Forsberg as saying:

'He (Gorst) knew the conditions of the meeting and seems simply to have lied to us to gain access to a prisoner our courts have accepted should be confined . . . We expect a serious diplomatic complaint to be made to the British Embassy and Foreign Office.'

This feature prompted defamation proceedings by Gorst against the *Telegraph* which were settled in his favour out of court.

This affair is a perfect example of how incredibly short-sighted Forsberg and his officers could be. Their spontaneous and usually thoughtless reactions to events occasionally bordered on the inept. Press statements were often made that, had they paused to think or investigate, they would have quickly realised could never be substantiated. In this instance they publicly accused a British Member of Parliament of deception, and the British Embassy of being a party to that deception, without bothering to check their facts. Had they done so they would have found that the visit had been arranged officially via the Swedish Embassy in London, the British Foreign and Commonwealth Office, the Swedish Ministry for Foreign Affairs, and the British Embassy in Stockholm. Gorst's reasons for requesting the visit were on record, had been accepted by all of these institutions, and were clearly only in the capacity of an MP. Indeed he could not have 'lied' or been involved in 'deception' because he had had no contact whatsoever in the fixing of any of the appointments made on his behalf. The Vice Consul of the British Embassy, who made the final arrangements for his meeting with Bihlar and the subsequent one with me, had read a letter from Mr Landelius, the First Secretary of the Swedish Embassy, to Gorst and was under no misapprehension that he had not established his bona fides through the proper channels. Nor did the visit have anything to do with Mrs Thatcher and Gorst never claimed that it did, the Consul's recollection of events was in exact accord with his own, and the tape recording Bihlar permitted Gorst to make during the interview with me confirms it. He only stated that he had mentioned my case to the Prime Minister and a senior member of the Opposition before his departure for Sweden, and said to me that he intended to do so again on his return. He never claimed, nor would it ever be likely, that he was acting as an emissary for Mrs Thatcher.

On 12 May Gorst wrote a very polite letter to the Swedish Ambassador to London, Mr Leafland, asking for the misunderstanding to be properly resolved. He would have been within his rights to have demanded a public apology from Forsberg but refrained from doing so. He received an acknowledgement stating that the matter had been passed on to the Ministry for Foreign Affairs, but never heard anything further. Needless to say, Forsberg never succeeded in having a 'serious diplomatic complaint' made against either the British Embassy or the Foreign and Commonwealth Office. I suspect the Swedes were only too happy to allow the matter to quietly drop.

On Thursday 7 May, and no doubt as a direct result of the Gorst visit, attempts were made to transfer me from Uppsala to a remand centre some 100 kms north. There is also no doubt that the reason for this was to make it far more difficult for me to see my lawyer or to be visited by my family. This threatened move was in fact cancelled but only after a great deal of fuss had been made by Tom Placht, Kingsley Napley and John Gorst himself.

The next day, and again as a result of the Gorst visit, Dihlar informed my mother that there could be no future visits from either family or friends. He told her:

'Under no circumstances can you see your son, it's your own fault!'

Forsberg was eventually to lift this needless restriction, but not before three weeks, and only after concerted intervention from Kingsley Napley and the British Embassy.

If Mohammed cannot go to the mountain, let the mountain come to Mohammed. On Wednesday 13 May Tom Placht flew to London, with the Court's permission, to consult with Kingsley Napley. During meetings over the following two days he briefed Christopher Murray on all aspects of the case that he was able, and together they tried to formulate the best policy for my defence. They agreed that it was going to be a difficult case to win unless concrete evidence could be produced supporting my innocence. On Friday the 15th they attended the House of Commons where John Gorst addressed the House on my behalf.

In his speech Gorst outlined the details of my arrest, and the conditions under which I was being held. He criticised the Swedish pre-trial procedure and attacked the country's human rights record in this field, accusing the Swedish Government of being in violation of the Convention on Human Rights and quoting examples of cases it had lost before the Court on Human Rights. He urged the British Government to suspend its extradition treaty with Sweden until this record was improved.

I suspect that many of those present inwardly agreed with everything Gorst was saying but due to diplomatic and political constraints were prevented from publicly siding with him. In any event the official response, given by Mr Eggar, was sympathetic but not very helpful. It was not Government policy to interfere in the internal affairs of another sovereign state. In concluding, Mr Eggar said:

'While I can understand my honourable Friend's concern,

I am afraid that the Swedish legal process must take its course. Her Majesty's Government has no standing to intervene in that process, although, through our consular officials we shall continue to monitor the case closely and to offer all the assistance to Captain Hayward that we properly can.'

Throughout the pre-trial period, and I should add that it did not stop after my trial, Forsberg and his officers made almost continual press statements, not only about how their investigation was progressing, but also leaving no doubt as to the fact that they were convinced of my guilt and that they had the evidence to prove it. For example, in the Swedish newspaper *Expressen* on 28 April, Forsberg stated:

'Both oral and technical evidence have shown that he smuggled the drugs knowingly.'

Again in the *Expressen* on 30 May, Forsberg is quoted as saying:

'I believe him to be guilty and I will prove that at the trial.'

In the *Daily Telegraph* on 8 May the Uppsala Drug Squad claimed to have firm evidence that I was a courier in a cannabis syndicate with an Ibizan connection run by several Britons – something they never had.

Tom Placht wrote to Forsberg in May complaining precisely of this behaviour, it was not to have the slightest effect. Indeed there can be no doubt that the manner in which the issue was reported in the Swedish press was to highlight what has been described by one Swedish correspondent to Kingsley Napley as, 'coverage by the socialist leaning journalists in the mass media in terms of a class struggle in such a way as to tend to incite public wrath against the "upper class" fellow who could afford extra legal counsel and mobilise friends in high places in England.' There is no doubt that 'class' was very much a live issue amongst the Swedish media. My lawyers were amazed on occasions to read the articles that were published describing my 'position' in society, bearing as they did no relation to the true situation. I was described throughout as a super-rich aristocrat, part of the Queen's bodyguard, and a man who had guarded the Prime Minister. The struggle became one of this image of me versus the 'people's police'; the Guards Captain vs poor old Inspector Bihlar, who became something of a celebrity.

Additionally, the question of the British Army's involvement in Northern Ireland has caused considerable ill feeling in Sweden; and our presence there is portrayed almost daily in the Swedish press as an example of 'British imperialism'. Once again the prosecution exploited these feelings. The fact that I had just completed a two-year posting to Northern Ireland was widely publicised. Stories began to appear, which have subsequently been traced directly to the offices of the Uppsala Drug Squad, claiming I was some kind of 'Army Spy' an undercover agent, a member of the Special Air Service Regiment. All of which, again, was total anathema to the Swedes, especially when the British press jumped on the bandwagon with articles claiming that I had been responsible for the deaths of several terrorists, copies of which received headline treatment in Sweden.

Against this background there can be no doubt that when the trial commenced there was considerable antipathy towards me and what, in the eyes of the Swedish media, I stood for.

In early June the situation started to get nasty, as so often happens in criminal cases involving drugs. At nine-thirty on the evening of the 6th my mother was threatened by a man as she returned home. She was approaching her front door when he suddenly appeared from beside a car parked outside the house. He calmly asked her if she was Mrs Hayward, and having confirmed that she was, snarled at her:

'Tell Chris if he even thinks he knows anything and talks, we'll kill his boy.'

He then quickly moved away. My mother was horrified and not unnaturally extremely frightened. She rushed into the house and after composing herself steeled herself to take a peek outside again, but there was no sign of either the man or the car. This was to be the first of several such threats.

The next week Morgan and Moore paid their visit to Sweden. As it turned out, and I fail to see why they chose not to tell me, especially since it was published in the newspapers during their visit and it would have meant nothing to me in any case, these police officers came from the National Drugs Intelligence Unit; a body set up in response to the increased sophistication in drugs trafficking, manned by officers from various police forces around Britain, and officers from HM

Customs and Excise.

Where British nationals are arrested abroad for drug trafficking offences, officers from the NDIU will visit these Britons in custody in an attempt, if possible, to obtain drugs intelligence from them. Similarly there are occasions when NDIU officers have received information regarding those in custody abroad that they wish to check with the individuals concerned. This would appear to have been the case with me.

For reasons which perhaps will never be fully known Morgan and Moore filed the one-page report that Forsberg was to rely on so heavily. However, with the benefit of hindsight I am now of the firm belief that they gave it to the Swedes purely as a lever to be used against me, never dreaming that it would actually be presented as evidence before a court of law.

Having arrived in Sweden on an intelligence mission, I believe they agreed unofficially to help the Uppsala Drug Squad in trying to persuade me to confess, and the statement they subsequently made out was merely intended as a way of frightening me into making that confession.

What Morgan and Moore had obviously not fully appreciated was the mentality of the Swedish police, and the readiness of the Swedish courts to accept hearsay as evidence. They knew that hearsay was acceptable because they told me as much, but to give them the benefit of the doubt, a courtesy they never extended to me, they may not have known the extent of that acceptability.

To Forsberg the statement must have been a godsend, a dream come true and a golden opportunity not to be missed. He immediately pounced on it and lost no time in presenting it to the Court, where of course it was all too readily accepted.

This horrified Kingsley Napley, not only because of its totally prejudicial effect, but also because it was hearsay upon hearsay, and they knew only too well that it would be impossible to challenge because police officers refuse to identify their informants. The fact that the information appeared to have come from New Scotland Yard, with its international reputation, magnified its prejudicial effect. Consequently Sir David Napley arranged to see Assistant Commissioner Hewett, who before his retirement in 1988 was unarguably one of the most experienced officers in the country and perhaps unrivalled in his experience of criminal intelligence. He undertook to look into the matter and eventually wrote the following letter to Sir David:

C V Hewett, OBE, QPM, Assistant Commissioner
NEW SCOTLAND YARD
BROADWAY, LONDON SW1H 0BG

                                        15 July 1987

Dear Sir David,

Thank you for your letter of 14 July.

Firstly, I can confirm that the wording of your note of the information supplied by the two officers of the National Drugs Intelligence Unit when they were in Sweden, is essentially the same as the report which they provided.

I understand that this report was made available to the Court and is being retained. I have written to Mr FORSBERG, the District Public Prosecutor dealing with the Simon Hayward case, regretting that I was unable to accede to his request for the attendance of the two officers at the hearing. The reasons I gave were that the officers are unable to vouch for the truth and accuracy of any of the information in the paragraphs numbered 1-5 in the report, and that all the information within their knowledge would amount to hearsay evidence and this would be inadmissible in similar proceedings in an English criminal court.

I am unable to comment on your understanding that the Swedish authorities intend to rely on the report of the two officers even in their absence, except to say that I have received no information on this particular point from the Swedish authorities or anyone else. If any notification has indeed been given to this effect I would appreciate knowledge of it.

I see no point in your interviewing the two officers. They are strictly forbidden to reveal the source of their information because this was an intelligence source which has to be protected.

                    Yours sincerely,
                    COLIN HEWETT

Despite the final paragraph Sir David and Christopher Murray were in fact allowed to interview Morgan and Moore the next day. However the ensuing discussions were clearly a stonewalling exercise on their part and consequently of little value. Understandably, and as expected, they refused to identify the source of their information, but for no apparent reason they also refused to state the purpose of making the statement in the first place. Whenever questions became embarrassing they would attempt to hide behind a cloud of confusion, invariably falling back on the old maxim, 'I cannot answer that question for security reasons.'

At one juncture, in an attempt to make the officers at the very least explain their motives and justify their actions, Sir David commented:

'To the outside observer such as myself, it's quite an amazing document for a senior police officer to have given in a country where it can be used as evidence. If it is ever, as doubtless it will be, made public it will fill people with horror. You can appreciate that? People will be horrified that a senior police officer has made statements of this sort which he is not prepared to explain, which are going to be used with the strong possibility that some, possibly innocent, person is going to get up to ten years in a Swedish prison.'

The only thing that Morgan was to admit to during the interview was that the information appearing in the statement came not from one source, but several. He refused to name any of them. However it is not hard to deduce that one of them must have been Butcher, after all, I had seen his statement, and at a later stage a 'concerned individual' (and now it is my turn not to reveal my source) told my lawyers that if they wanted to know the origins of at least some of the information they should look to 'Simon's cars'. Another was certainly Mitchell.

The final paragraph of the NDIU statement should not be forgotten:

'On Thursday 11 June 1987 we spoke to Forbes Cay Mitchell, also arrested for this offence. Without being prompted in any way he fully corroborated the above information that we had previously acquired, before our visit to Sweden.'

In fact this was denied by Mitchell when he eventually gave testimony at my trial. Under cross-examination he stated that he had said nothing spontaneously but that Morgan and Moore had asked him leading questions, had asked him to make a professional guess at the amount a courier transporting fifty kilos of cannabis could earn, and finally had asked him to speculate on my alleged role.

To emphasize the weakness of this statement it emerged that no information had been forthcoming from any source until my case had received wide publicity in the British newspapers. It cannot be discounted that this was the source of the informants' information. The possibility should also not be ignored that whoever was behind the drugs ring had a prime interest in trying to shut any inquiry down at the earliest possible juncture. In other words, whoever put the cannabis in the Jaguar would be more than happy if the police investigation did not go beyond the people already arrested and charged. It would therefore not be surprising to find these people trying to feed through false information to make it appear that the real ringleaders had been caught, or to identify as a ringleader someone totally unconnected, who of course, having no knowledge of the affair, would have little chance of repudiating the information.

It is also not beyond the bounds of possibility that a terrorist organisation could have manufactured the information which eventually reached the NDIU. As already mentioned there was wide publicity in both the Swedish and British press, whether true or false matters not, to the effect that I had, prior to my arrest, spent two years 'under cover' in Northern Ireland on active service, with specific coverage of an incident in Strabane, which infuriated the IRA, where three terrorists were shot dead by the security forces. My arrest could well have been seen as an ideal opportunity to take a swing at an army officer who had supposedly been 'killing our boys'. The planting of such disinformation is well within the capabilities of the IRA.

Two other factors disturb me about the NDIU report, and must have a bearing on its validity. Source reports of any value will always contain details: places, dates, times, and personalities. The Morgan and Moore statement contained nothing but generalisations, and information that was available to anyone who read a newspaper and with a basic knowledge of how the illicit drug trade works. If the data held within it had been genuine and worthy of note, and any experienced handler will know that informants are notoriously unreliable at the best of times and are to be treated with extreme caution, it would have included such detail as: when and where the cannabis was loaded into the Jaguar, who was present at the time, who carried out the actual packing, where meetings to organise the run took place and who was present at them, the identities of the principals involved, where the cannabis originated from, and so the list goes on. The second factor is that the NDIU intelligence originated in the United Kingdom whereas the crime was of course perpetrated on Ibiza.

The very fact that Assistant Commissioner Hewett was prepared to write his letter to Sir David Napley, and another very similar one to Forsberg, speaks for itself. Hewett's letter leaves no doubt that the information contained in their report was not only unreliable but was merely a piece of criminal intelligence passed from one police force to another, and was never intended to be, and should never have been, used as evidence in court.

On Thursday 11 June my mother received another telephone call from Christopher. The conversation she held with him was to put her in something of a dilemma. Christopher told her that he had read about the statement I had given to the Swedish police in March, and from that moment he had known that I was lying to protect him.

'Mummy, I may have been involved with some things in the past, but I am not involved with this business. You have to believe me.'

'I want to believe you . . . '

'Simon has been lying to protect me. He did not go to Sweden because Lokesh invited him, he went because I asked him to deliver the Jaguar to Lokesh. I told him it was going to be sold in Sweden, and at the time I thought it was.'

'My God Chris, this makes all the difference. Why have you not said this before?'

'I couldn't, I just couldn't. In any case I thought Simon would have been released immediately. He is innocent after all. If I had suddenly come up with a different statement it would have made him look guilty. However, since they have had him for three months, I presume it must be looking bad for him?'

'It is, darling, it is. You must come forward now and give this evidence. Where are you?'

'I can't tell you, and I can't come forward. Go to Simon's lawyers and tell them this. He will be alright, he knows nothing.'

My brother refused to say where he was, and refused to go into any greater detail. Apparently he sounded frightened and at times during the conversation was reduced to tears.

The next morning my mother went to Kingsley Napley to tell Murray of the telephone call. It put everyone into a dilemma, and caused not a little embarrassment. Murray had no access to me and therefore could not tell me to change my statement, in any case that would have smacked of collusion, the very reason why Forsberg would not let anyone near me. He did not want to put Placht into an embarrassing and difficult position by giving him information that he might have to pass on to the prosecution, and which might weaken his client's position. Placht would have to tell Forsberg where the information had come from, and he in turn would almost certainly have immediately accused my mother of collusion with Kingsley Napley and, or, my brother, to put words in my mouth in an attempt to add credence to my story. Placht too would not have been immune from such accusations. It must have been a delicate situation for everyone, and they decided to sit back and do nothing for the time being.

On this same day Mitchell appeared in court in Uppsala, I of course was being interviewed by Morgan and Moore. He pleaded guilty to all charges. His lawyer described the relationship he had with his client as an extraordinary one, stating that his part in acting for Mitchell was really that of a by-stander. Everything appeared to have been pre-arranged and he was there merely to do as he was told. Mitchell knew exactly what he was doing, saying that he would admit his guilt on this, that and the other aspect; he would talk freely about this part of the proceedings but would say nothing about that part. The lawyer said almost nothing throughout the entire trial, which lasted but one afternoon.

It would also appear that Mitchell put on something of an act for the benefit of the court. Bursting into tears at one point he deplored the 'grief and trouble' he had caused Sweden and his family, and later made an impassioned statement regarding the use of cannabis, which he condoned and admitted using personally.

He also admitted during the trial to making six drug shipments to Sweden between September 1984 and the summer of 1986. The Jaguar run was to have been the seventh. He claimed that Nasim Tervaniemi, who he said had been smuggling drugs into Sweden prior to his involvement with her, always took receipt of the consignments in Sweden for onward sale. Afterwards she would render payment to Mitchell. He claimed that for each run his fellow Scot, Makunda, acted as the courier; Christopher Hayward was the principal of the operation and had been from the second shipment onwards.

As to my involvement, Mitchell stated that Christopher had told him that I had agreed to act as the courier on the final run, Makunda being unavailable, for the money, the excitement and because I could easily get out of trouble if caught. He added, that since he had only been expecting 25 kilos at the most, I must have been planning to sell the other 25 elsewhere.

On 15 June John Gorst received an anonymous letter:

Dear Mr Gorst,

In today's *Daily Telegraph* you were quoted as saying you believed Captain Simon Hayward to be innocent of the charges of drug smuggling. This may well be so.

The man arrested with Captain Hayward, Cay Forbes Mitchell and also Christopher Hayward, Captain Hayward's brother, are both members of the Bhagwan Shree Rajneesh cult, so too is Macunda, spelt wrongly in the *Telegraph* as Macumba.

I first met these three men in Poona, India, in 1977, even then they were making a living from smuggling drugs to Europe, or rather getting others to do it for them.

I know several people who were told by Christopher Hayward and Macunda that the drugs they were carrying was cannabis, when in fact it was heroin, and some were caught and imprisoned.

Christopher Hayward, his Rajneesh name is Lokesh, is the organising force behind the smuggling. He has disappeared from his home in Ibiza several weeks ago, and his mother Mrs Hazel Hayward is terribly worried and believes he may have been murdered by his contacts in the drugs world.

Also involved with the men arrested in Sweden is Michael Scott who was arrested at Dover early in May of his year when returning from Amsterdam with £5,000 worth of drugs.

Scott is also a Rajneesh follower, his name is Meru and is a long time friend and fellow drug dealer with the three men mentioned above. Scott is on bail awaiting trial.

I could give you names of other Rajneesh followers who are also drug smuggling, but so far there is no evidence against them.

As my MP perhaps you could do something to bring this into the open. The Rajneesh organisation is deeply involved in drug smuggling, here in England, in Europe and also in India.

I was a Rajneesh follower for eight years, and saw what was going on.

Please excuse me if I don't give my name, the risks involved are quite real.

Yours sincerely, etc.

Gorst passed this letter on to Scotland Yard. It is interesting despite its obvious inaccuracies. Lokesh is Mitchell's Rajneesh name and it was later established that Christopher had never been to Poona. Meru however, was one of the names that Nilsson had asked me if I recognised in May, supplied to him by Mitchell.

On 16 June Åsa Hoffman was tried and also pleaded guilty. She was later sentenced to five years' imprisonment. Both Viryo and Anderson received identical sentences when they were eventually put on trial.

On the same day, of course, I admitted to Placht the true reason for my visit to Sweden. This relieved Kingsley Napley of the problem of how best to use the information given to them by my mother. However, due to the highly suspicious nature of the Uppsala authorities, and because to an outside observer it might have appeared as if some form of collusion had taken place, it was decided not to draw needless attention to Christopher's telephone call. Looking back I find this decision a pity, because there could not possibly have been any deception. The last visit my mother paid me prior to my statement change was on 10 June. Christopher telephoned London on the 11th, Kingsley Napley were informed on the 12th. Nothing further was said about it; Tom Placht was not even informed, and I changed my statement on the 16th. Since I had had no communication with anyone 'in the know' I could not possibly have been prompted. It may seem a convenient coincidence that Christopher's call and my change of story occurred within a week of each other, but that is all it could have been – a coincidence.

On Thursday 18 June Mitchell was sentenced to seven years' imprisonment. From the trial judgement document, which Kingsley Napley had translated, it would appear that the Court believed every word he told it, including the remarkable claim that he had only made £16,000 from smuggling a total of 112 kilos of cannabis worth £350,000, over a four-year period. These figures do not include the final fifty kilos.

Forbes Mitchell must have been well satisfied with this sentence because he chose not to appeal against it. One could easily spend hours speculating on the reasons for this, but what became apparent at a later stage was that only a portion of his smuggling activities had come to light at the time of his trial, so it is not difficult to assume that he did not appeal because he wanted the full picture to remain hidden. Perhaps under the circumstances he got off lightly. It also became abundantly clear that he was protecting somebody, and he must therefore have hoped that by not appealing there was a good chance that the investigation into his organisation would be closed.

On Monday 22 June Kingsley Napley were again in touch with the British Embassy to ask the Consul to renew Murray's request to see me. The Consul agreed to do this through the Ministry of Foreign Affairs.

On 23 and 24 June my mother was allowed to visit me, and

it was during this visit that Bihlar sprung his 'ambush' and verbally attacked her in an attempt to pressurize her, in view of my change of story, into thinking that it was now her duty as my mother to persuade me into pleading guilty.

On Wednesday 24 June Rodney Agar also travelled out in a bid to see me, but despite waiting in Uppsala for two days the police refused to allow him to visit me. To be fair they had warned him that this might be the case prior to his departure from England, but he came regardless because he wanted to confer with Tom Placht. It is ironical that the given excuse for the police refusal to allow his visit, was because they were too busy, but in the event they wasted more time in their determination to prevent the visit, than if they had permitted us ten minutes together in the first place.

On Monday 29 June John Gorst tabled an Early Day Motion before the House of Commons. It was eventually signed by seventy-seven other Members of Parliament, from all political parties. It read as follows:

That this House notes that on 30 June Captain Hayward of The Life Guards will have been detained by the Swedish authorities, in solitary confinement, and without any charges, for 109 days; that, despite deliberate disorientation through isolation, he has consistently denied all knowledge of the drugs found in the car he was driving but did not own; that, except for consular visits and irregular ones by his mother who is prohibited from discussing his case or offering reassurances, he is now denied all visits, including that of a British lawyer; that this ban was introduced on the pretext that a visit by a British honourable Member, arranged through both British and Swedish embassies, was controversial; that he is forbidden to receive the Hansard Official Report of his case (15 May); that he is expected to be held indefinitely until he confesses; that he is meanwhile serving a penal sentence of solitary confinement in breach of all the basic principles enshrined in the European Convention on Human Rights; that this penal servitude is imposed before charges, without trial and in the absence of a conviction; and calls upon Her Majesty's Government, in taking appropriate steps to insist upon Sweden observing its obligations under the Convention, to emphasise that the Convention is based upon the premise that individuals have a right to humane treatment and justice, and further deplores the hypocrisy of the Swedish Government, which parades itself as a champion of human rights and is always the first to meddle in the affairs of other countries whose human rights records it criticises.

On 30 June there was another dramatic development. Once again Christopher telephoned my mother.

'How is Simon?'

'You can imagine how he is. He has been in solitary confinement for 110 days, he is appalling. Can't you help him?'

'Mummy, do you remember what I said to you on the first time I spoke on the telephone, "The set up was for me"? This man asked me to do something for him and I wouldn't do it, and Simon is suffering because I wouldn't do that. By the way, what's happened to Lokesh?'

'He has been tried and sentenced to seven years, and he has implicated both you and Simon.'

'Yes, and everybody believes him because you are all stupid. Lokesh is protecting someone who he is much more frightened of than he would be of anyone else.'

'I can understand that because I have had threats against Tarik.'

'Oh God! Where is Tarik.'

'He is in Ibiza but I think he is going to Canada with his mother next week. You have got to help Simon, you must say what you know.'

'I don't know anything but I suspect very strongly an Irishman who has about six passports and who travels under lots of different names, but on Ibiza is known as Dook.'

'Dook?'

'Yes, D-O-O-K, but Mummy he is ruthless and Lokesh will be terrified for his girlfriend and her child.'

'I have to tell someone about this.'

'Not until Tarik goes to Canada, Mummy. I am not coming forward. Simon will be alright as he doesn't know anything about it and he is innocent.'

'I have told Kingsley Napley about you asking him to

deliver the car to Sweden to sell.'

'I understand, but it makes me look guilty and I am not.'

'An MP called John Gorst, who has been helping Simon, has received an anonymous letter relating to this business. I want to ask you some questions arising from it.'

'Go ahead.'

'Were you in Poona in 1977?'

'No, I have never been there in my life.'

'Are you sure, it's very important?'

'In 1977 I was in Switzerland and Ibiza, and I didn't go anywhere else.'

'When did you become a Sannyassan?'

'I can't remember but not until the 1980s, and I am not one now.'

'Are you on your boat in the West Indies? Because that is what all the press are saying.'

'No, I'm not even on my boat, nor am I in the West Indies.'

'You put me in a very difficult position.'

'Well I won't ring you any more.'

My mother was terrified at what Christopher had told her, adding weight as it did to the threats she had already received. She became extremely concerned for Chantal and Tarik's safety. This concern was greatly heightened when Chantal failed to reply to any of the telephone messages my mother left for her. Her immediate reaction was to fly to Ibiza but Kingsley Napley advised against this on the grounds of safety. Instead she decided to send a friend who had volunteered to help. The problem was that she had no idea exactly where Chantal lived, except that it was in the Santa Gertrudis area, and had no idea how to contact her, except via Echo.

With a certain amount of ingenuity however, the friend managed to locate Chantal. He found it next to impossible to get directions from anyone, because the very close community had become used to protecting one another from the bands of reporters, many of whom had been claiming to be close friends of the Hayward family, who had been roaming the island since my arrest. Eventually he managed to find the remote farmhouse where she lived, and spoke to Chantal.

He explained the situation to her, and my mother's grave concern. In reply she told him that she was aware of the danger but could not leave Ibiza for another week, after which she, Tarik and Jim would be flying to Canada. She was sure they would be safe until then. He begged her to leave with him immediately, but she refused. There was nothing more to be done; my mother's friend returned to England alone.

A couple of days later Chantal telephoned my mother to say that she knew who was behind the drugs run to Sweden.

'It had nothing to do with Simon, and neither was Chris directly involved. I am flying to London en route for Canada next week, and I will tell you everything then. I will speak to Simon's lawyers if you wish, and I am also prepared to testify in his defence, on Chris's behalf, in court.'

She added that everyone on Ibiza was terrified of saying anything or of becoming involved, and she asked my mother to keep her call a secret until her arrival in London. Again my mother begged her to leave Ibiza immediately, but again she refused.

On Wednesday 1 July Forsberg informed Tom Placht that Scotland Yard had refused permission for the NDIU officers to return to Sweden to give verbal evidence. Apparently Forsberg was incensed at this news, being convinced that it was a British conspiracy to pervert the course of justice. What is perhaps more interesting is that he never mentioned to Placht the letter he received a few days later from Mr Hewett explaining the reasons why Morgan and Moore were not being allowed to give evidence.

C V HEWETT, OBE, QPM, Assistant Commissioner
NEW SCOTLAND YARD
BROADWAY, LONDON SW1H 0BG

6 July 1987

Dear Mr Forsberg,

Simon Francis Hayward, detained in Sweden
for Drug Trafficking

I have today received via Interpol telex your letter requesting the attendance of Detective Inspector MORGAN and Detective Sergeant MOORE to give evidence in the proceedings against Simon Francis Hayward.

On 12 June, in Sweden, these police officers had supplied a report which each signed, and I have subsequently reviewed the content. The officers are unable to vouch for the truth and accuracy of any of the information in the paragraphs marked 1–5 in the report. All the information within their knowledge would amount to hearsay evidence and this would be inadmissable in similar proceedings in an English criminal court.

I regret, therefore, that I am unable to accede to your request and the two police officers will not be permitted to give this evidence.

A separate request has now been received through Interpol channels for enquiries to be made in the United Kingdom in relation to this case. Every effort is being made to complete these latter enquiries expeditiously. I hope that the results will assist your investigation, and that where relevant and supportable evidence is obtained the police officers will be able to attend the proceedings to present it.

Yours sincerely,
Colin Hewett.

On 26 June I had finally been allowed to receive a copy of the Hansard report on John Gorst's speech. On 1 July Gorst tabled the following Early Day Motion:

That this House notes that on the 105th day of his solitary confinement without charges, the Swedish authorities have finally, after 42 days, permitted Captain Hayward to receive a copy of the Hansard Official Report of the debate of his case on 15 May; and congratulates Her Majesty's Government for the persistence with which they have argued for this to be allowed.

Also on 1 July my mother was told by the Swedish police that they would be on holiday, as would the prosecutor, until 27 July, which in any case was untrue, and that therefore no visits could take place during this period. This prompted John Gorst to table his third Early Day Motion a week later:

That this House notes that on 9 July Captain Simon

Hayward will have been held by the Swedish authorities for 118 days in solitary confinement and without charges; that on 18 June the authorities were granted permission to retain Captain Hayward for an extended period of solitary confinement; that since that date the two senior police officers as well as the prosecutor in charge of the case have all gone on their annual holidays; and urges the Swedish Embassy in London to explain and justify to the British public how these pre-trial procedures are not only in accordance with natural justice and the principles that vindicate the European Convention on Human Rights, but also how they further any investigations that may be deemed necessary.

On Friday 3 July, eleven days after his initial request, Christopher Murray was told by the British Embassy that Forsberg was still reluctant to agree to allow him to visit me. Also to their total astonishment Forsberg had expressed surprise that neither Placht nor I had requested an end to my solitary confinement. The Embassy Staff and Kingsley Napley were dumbfounded at this comment in view of the fact that it was an open secret that everyone was extremely concerned at the treatment I was receiving at Forsberg's hands. Accordingly Murray immediately telexed the following message to him requesting permission for a visit to see me, and also an end to solitary confinement:

Dear Sir,

As you know, we act on behalf of Captain Simon Hayward and have recently renewed our request to visit our client. This request was made through our Stockholm Embassy to the Swedish Ministry of Foreign Affairs. We have today been informed by the Embassy that they have been notified of your extreme reluctance to agree to such a request and you would not allow a meeting if our client's case was to be discussed.

Additionally, in the week commencing 5 July you do not have available an officer with sufficient command of the English language to attend such a meeting. Our client's mother has been granted permission to visit her son on Monday 6 July, an English speaking officer seems to be available for her but not for us. We can only assume therefore that there has been some misunderstanding and await confirmation that a visit will be possible in the week commencing 5 July.

You have apparently expressed surprise to the Foreign Ministry that neither Advokat Tom Placht nor Captain Hayward has requested Captain Hayward's removal from solitary confinement. It is difficult to imagine how you could be under any illusions that Captain Hayward's continued detention in solitary confinement was one to which he consented. We have only this week been informed that at long last a copy of Mr Gorst MP's speech in the House of Commons has been passed to Captain Hayward. That speech concentrated solely upon what is generally considered in this country to be the inhumane treatment of a prisoner awaiting trial.

For the avoidance of doubt therefore and in Mr Placht's absence we formally request that Captain Hayward be released from solitary confinement forthwith.

We await your confirmation and immediate reply.

Yours faithfully,

Kingsley Napley never in fact received a written reply to this telex save through the columns of the press a few days later. On 8 July Forsberg informed Tom Placht that under no circumstances would he permit Murray to visit me, even in the presence of a police officer.

Wednesday 8 July was a sad day. Jim White telephoned London to say that Chantal had been found dead on the morning of the previous day. My mother, accompanied by my brother Justin, flew straight to Ibiza to collect Tarik. In fact they were to stay on the island for three days to attend Chantal's funeral.

There is very little doubt in my mind that Chantal was murdered. The circumstances of her death have never been satisfactorily explained. Spanish postmortem examinations have always been at best abysmal, and at worst non-existent.

There is even some confusion as to whether she was ever the subject of a postmortem at all, indeed the Ibizan authorities released the body for burial within two days. The initial cause of death was given as pulmonary oedema, or fluid on the lungs, but it was later revealed that she died from a massive drugs overdose and inhalation of her own vomit.

Even more sinister, the undertaker pointed out to my mother the existence of a needle mark on Chantal's left forearm, just beneath the elbow. The Guardia Civil, investigating her death, had dismissed this as an insect bite, but the undertaker assured my mother that it was a needle puncture wound. There was only one.

There is no evidence to support the suggestion, made by Mitchell amongst others, that Chantal ever used hard drugs. Certainly when I saw her on Ibiza she had been her normal healthy self. I am sure I would have noticed puncture wounds in her arms, or if she had been 'unwell' in any way. I had neither seen, nor heard mention of, any drug taking. This was borne out by the doctor who gave regular check-ups to both Chantal and Tarik, when on being questioned she stated that Chantal was definitely not on hard drugs and never injected herself with anything. Indeed she described her as an athletic, fit mother with an obsession for her own health and for that of her son.

So the question remains, 'How did Chantal die?'

The British Consul on Ibiza described the circumstances of her death as suspicious; the police on the other hand, after a superficial investigation, closed the case.

Apparently there had been a party of sorts at Chantal's house on the evening before her death, at which a good deal of drinking had taken place. Jim White explained that he had suddenly felt unaccustomedly tired and had collapsed into bed. The last time he had seen Chantal alive had been just prior to this, then she had looked fine, happily talking with a group of friends. In the morning he found her dead in bed in a pool of vomit.

The crucial factor is that the needle mark was found on Chantal's left arm, and she was left-handed. To state that the drug overdose was self administered pre-supposes that a woman who had never taken hard drugs in her life, suddenly decided to experiment, for the first time, in the middle of a party, with a syringe containing a lethal cocktail. And, in so doing, injected herself using her completely unfamiliar right hand. That is beyond plausibility.

It can also be no coincidence that this highly suspicious death occurred just days, even hours, before she was due to fly to London to give evidence that might have cleared my name and presumably would have indicted the true culprit.

I believe Chantal was murdered to keep her quiet, and her death would have had the additional bonus of scaring any other would-be witnesses into silence. However, one way or the other, it was at least mysterious enough to merit proper investigation.

Whilst on Ibiza my mother and Justin attempted to do some detective work of their own, and made as many enquiries as they could under the circumstances. However they found that no one was willing to divulge anything, although they were both convinced that some of the people they spoke to knew more than they were saying. Fear is a great deterrent. They were eventually warned that it was very dangerous to poke around too much, and that it would be better if they left the island. They heeded this advice and immediately after the funeral returned to London with Tarik. Chantal's grief-stricken parents also arrived from Switzerland to attend the funeral. It was obviously an extremely harrowing time for them – my mother did all she could to comfort them.

There was to be one last sinister postscript to this unhappy affair, which adds weight to my belief. My mother returned to Ibiza with a private detective in early September. Following this a very distraught friend of Chantal's told her that the grave had been disturbed. There has never been an investigation into what exactly happened, but it would be interesting to see if evidence of a murder has been removed?

On 10 July John Gorst obtained information that the Swedish equivalent of a 'D Notice' had been issued on the Swedish press, preventing them from commenting upon a discussion of civil rights issues arising from my detention. He tabled another Early Day Motion to this effect:

That this House notes that unconfirmed reports emanating from Stockholm indicate that a Swedish equivalent of a D Notice has been issued for guidance to the country's newspaper editors; that this guidance has been given by Mr Bo Heineback who is both head of the Press Department in the Ministry of Foreign Affairs and Chairman of its Psychological Warfare Contingency Committee; that the guidance advises newspapers not to discuss the civil rights issues arising from the detention of Captain Simon Hayward, who will have been held in solitary confinement without charges for 120 days on 11 July; questions whether a fair trial can ever take place in a country whose legal system permits the prosecutor to hold a suspect in indefinite isolation while he and his police colleagues issue damaging and inaccurate briefings, both on and off the record, to members of the domestic and foreign press, and while free comment on the issues that are raised is inhibited by edicts from other official quarters; and in drawing attention to these matters, invites the Swedish Embassy in London to deny them or, in confirming their accuracy, to justify them in terms that will be comprehensible to the British public.

On Wednesday 15 July, Tom Placht received a telephone call from a man who identified himself as a Mr Ter Brake, a lawyer acting for Dook, asking to be put in touch with Mitchell's lawyers. The very existence of the mysterious Dook, in connection with this affair, had been kept a closely guarded secret. It was also puzzling that he was now indirectly asking to be put into contact with Mitchell who by this time was in prison, with none of the restrictions still in force against me, and able to talk to anyone he pleased. The tone of his conversation with Ter Brake left Placht in no doubt that he was receiving a thinly veiled threat, which he took seriously enough to contact the police immediately the call was over. They in turn took it seriously enough to advise him to move his family out of their home to stay with relations, and for himself to be put up in hotel accommodation at public expense. The existence of this man Ter Brake, his relationship with Dook, their connection with Mitchell, and the attitude of the Swedish police to them, was to become significantly more relevant as time wore on.

It was on 17 July that Forsberg decided finally to charge me. This news prompted John Gorst to lay down the following two

Early Day Motions in the House of Commons:

That this House notes that the Swedish prosecutor in the
case of Captain Hayward has laid charges against him on the
125th day of his solitary confinement; that he will face trial
seven days later; that there will be no jury at his trial, that
he remains in solitary confinement and unable to discuss his
case with any British person; that there is no sub judice rule
in Sweden and that the authorities continue to feed the
media with comment and information relating to his case;
that the prosecution has lodged with the court hearsay
evidence from British sources so that it cannot be
withdrawn even though the information would be
inadmissible in an English criminal court and that it cannot
be challenged by cross-examination in a Swedish court; that
the truth and accuracy of this information, although
incriminating if it were true, is such that those who supplied
it cannot and will not vouch for it; that even if this
information is not referred to in open court it has already
been made available to the presiding judge who must by
now be influenced by it; that any guilty verdict, in the light
of the foregoing and preceded by procedures in which the
defendant has been isolated and disorientated, cannot be
regarded as a fair one; and that any guilty verdict arrived at
in the absence of searching cross-examination and based on
anything less than grounds that are beyond reasonable doubt
would be a travesty of justice . . .

That this House notes that all evidence served upon
Captain Hayward prior to the start of his trial in Sweden on 23
July is in Swedish despite the request of his Swedish defence
lawyer that it be in English; that the Swedish prosecutor has
had 125 days in which to prepare his case; that statements
taken from Captain Hayward as well as from one of the
prime prosecution witnesses against him were in English but
have only been made available in Swedish; that the volume
of documentation served upon Captain Hayward runs to
about 200 pages; that Article 6 (3a) of the European
Convention on Human Rights states that everyone charged
with a criminal offence has the right to be informed

promptly in a language he understands and in detail of the nature and cause of the accusation against him'; that Article 6 (3b) states that he has a right to have adequate time and facilities for the preparation of his defence'; that Swedish law requires the trial to take place within seven days of charges being preferred; and that the treatment of Captain Hayward is in direct, specific and flagrant breach of the provisions of the European Convention.

Tom Placht himself rushed to England with a spare set of papers to serve on Kingsley Napley. Christopher Murray spent the whole of the following weekend with his Swedish mother-in-law, who translated the most important statements while he took longhand notes.

Kingsley Napley also received help in this translation from a most unexpected source. On the day Placht arrived from Sweden they were approached by a man called Jens Nilsson, no relation to Jan-Erik Nilsson, with the news that on 8 June he had been handed all the statements, taken from me by the Swedish police to date, by the translation agency of a Fleet Street newspaper for translation. In view of the fact that at that stage no evidence had been served on the defence and Kingsley Napley were still trying unsuccessfully to gain access to their client, and to any information relating to his case, it is somewhat ironic that Fleet Street should have obtained copies of this evidence.

It was only due to the integrity of Jens Nilsson that the matter was ever brought to the attention of Kingsley Napley. He had heard Sir David in an interview on Monday 13 July on Radio 4 in which he complained of the lack of access to his client and to the evidence, if any, against his client. Nilsson thought it improper that others should have access to my statements and my lawyers should not. He therefore telephoned Kingsley Napley.

In July *Private Eye* published an article on the 'Hayward' case in which they mentioned this episode. This is an extract from that article:

Simon Hayward has been held in solitary confinement for more than 100 days and has been denied the opportunity of

seeing his solicitor, Sir David Napley – allegedly because
they (the Swedish authorities) feared possible collusion to
obstruct the course of justice. The Foreign Office has made
various overtures to the Swedes and it was only last
Thursday that the Swedish authorities claimed that access
was not granted because a proper request had not been
made – a demonstrable lie.

More interestingly, though, is the trial by public
interview. It seems that *habeas corpus* does not exist in
Sweden, nor does the obligation to provide the accused's
lawyers with the evidence against him. Hayward's solicitors
Kingsley Napley have not even been able to get a copy of
their client's statement to the Swedish police. They might,
however, if they were prepared to go into an auction with
Fleet Street. Last week the statement was on offer to hacks
for a price – leaked from the Swedish prosecutor's office.

Better still, perhaps, would be a toll call to Sweden where
the prosecutor will talk to anyone in the greatest confidence
about matters that he has denied to Simon Hayward and his
lawyer and family.

On Saturday 18 July, *The Times* published an article written
by John Gorst which could not have better summarised the
entire situation. It was entitled 'SWEDEN'S DARK AGE
JUSTICE'.

After being held in solitary confinement for 126 days,
Captain Simon Hayward of The Life Guards was charged
yesterday with smuggling 110 lb of cannabis into Sweden.

From the moment of his arrest he has protested his
innocence – the car in which the drug was found belonged
to his brother, who immediately disappeared. His was the
only completely unknown face among the dozen or so men
and women detained after the find, all of whom had
apparently been under Swedish police surveillance for some
time. Yet until recently he had been denied the most
elementary comforts; he had even been denied consultation
with Sir David Napley, the family's solicitor.

Since I visited him 11 weeks ago the only people allowed to see
him have been consular officials and his mother, who was

told she must not discuss any aspect of the case with him, apart from one visit from his girlfriend. To incarcerate a man, particularly one of Captain Hayward's standing, for so long in conditions of such severity would, to most people in this country, perhaps presume a guilt that has still to be tested in a court of law. And there, indeed, is the nub of the matter.

In Britain, a prisoner is considered innocent until proven guilty. In Sweden, there is a presumption of guilt from the moment of arrest. Here the law, administered by a completely independent judiciary, provides a shield for the individual against any misuse of power by the state. In Sweden the judiciary is conceived as a servant of the state, and the law is regarded as an instrument for its protection.

In British trials, in open court before judge and jury, the truth is arrived at in the process of searching examination and cross-examination. In Sweden the meaningful examination takes place in the pre-trial process, when, as in Captain Hayward's case, the suspect can be held if necessary in total isolation. This stage is confined exclusively to the public prosecutor and the police, with the suspect merely represented by a court appointed defence lawyer. During this process the State virtually decides whether he is guilty; if he protests his innocence, the figures clearly show what little chance he has of being released after being put on trial.

A survey of the results of nearly 100,000 trials in Sweden reveals that in only one or two cases in every 100 does the defendant secure release. Essentially, the function of a Swedish court is not to decide whether a suspect is innocent or guilty, but to make a record of the evidence, and then to decide what penalty is appropriate once the defence and prosecution have had their say.

The treatment of evidence in this country and in Sweden is so different that it would be more appropriate to describe what they call evidence as testimony, much of which would be inadmissible in a British court, and even more, would collapse under cross-examination.

The Swedish public are well prepared in this particular case. For four months, both prosecutor and police have conducted a sustained campaign to denigrate Captain

Hayward through the columns of a docile press and over radio and television. Overt and covert briefings have disparaged anyone who has spoken well of him. Some at least of their 'disinformation' has been both defamatory and untrue. In addition, it has been 'suggested' to the media that they should not raise the issue of his civil rights.

Captain Hayward's defence lawyer, Tom Placht, normally reserved and taciturn, has expressed concern about the handling of this case. Last week he told an *Expressen* reporter, 'I have never experienced a case which is so surrounded by question marks that will not be investigated.'

'What mystifies me is how an otherwise enlightened people, with so much of its culture respected and admired by the rest of the world, can accept a system of "justice" that harks back to the Dark Ages. For arbitrariness and denial of human rights it is exceeded in modern times only by totalitarian states. In fairness to the Swedish people, however, I must add that a growing body of opinion is deeply critical of the law and its administration.

'Captain Hayward's guilt or innocence is not for me to determine, although I confess that were his guilt to be established "beyond reasonable doubt" I personally, together with those who have served with him, and are familiar with his detestation of drugs, would be as surprised as they would be shocked.'

What action should the Government take? Opinion is stirring across the entire political spectrum. About 80 MPs have signed a motion calling for pressure to be exerted on Sweden to observe the Spirit of the European Convention on Human Rights, of which it is a co-signatory. Some MPs intend to raise the matter at the next Council of Europe meeting in the autumn.

Whatever the verdict in the Hayward case, the Swedish Government's daily violation of human rights will not simply disappear. More voices will be raised in protest. More questions will be asked. Public concern everywhere will continue until Sweden joins the rest of the civilized world in its respects for the rights of man.

Sir David Napley held a press conference on Tuesday 21

July which was also addressed by John Gorst. Sir David in talking about the many 'disturbing aspects' of the case against me said that he feared I would not receive a fair hearing in Sweden where the police were 'paramount' and the courts really only an 'arm of the executive'; where it was regarded as a rebuff if the police failed to produce enough evidence to obtain a conviction. Indeed, a fair trial could not but be in doubt due to the level of publicity surrounding the case.

Sir David went on to express concern at my physical and mental condition, saying that I was bearing up but that I had lost over a stone in weight, suffered from severe headaches and dizziness and had difficulty in concentrating. He was also highly critical of the involvement of the National Drugs Intelligence Unit, whose officers had attempted to 'exhort' me into admitting guilt.

Gorst added that he had been told in a written Parliamentary Reply that Mr Hurd, the Home Secretary, had asked the Chief Inspector of Constabulary to look at the exchange of criminal intelligence between the United Kingdom and other countries in the light of the Hayward case.

The flurry of activity that took place on 22 July was much more involved than I could possibly have known. At the time I was told but a fraction of what was actually taking place, and the defence came within an ace of gaining my release. Discussions went on all that day between Tom Placht and the prosecution with a view to me being released on some form of bail, into the custody of the Army. On the following day Brigadier James Emson and Christopher Murray, together with Placht, continued the battle by carrying out long and involved negotiations with the senior prosecutor for the area, Alf Juhlin, his deputy and Forsberg throughout the morning in an endeavour to explain what powers the Army would have were I to be released into its custody.

These negotiations continued the next day at the Ministry for Foreign Affairs in Stockholm with a view to their interceding. When this meeting broke up it looked very much as though I was about to be released and returned to England. Indeed, a month later when John White, who had been present at this meeting, visited me he told me that he had been 99% certain that I was to be released and was shocked at the news that a trial date had been set. However it was stressed at the time that the final decision rested only with Forsberg. On this occasion Forsberg was put firmly on the spot by his superior, and apparently it became obvious that he was under great strain.

It is still not clear exactly what went on during this period, nor the motives for this sudden indecision as to whether to press ahead with my trial. However, what is clear is that Placht decided at the last moment that he should inform the prosecutor of the existence of Dook, and what was known by the defence about him, which led to my mother being questioned by the police on the 24th. It would also appear that the authorities suddenly became extremely worried as to the security of the trial proceedings because of the possibility, in their eyes, of IRA reprisals. This was a home-grown, probably fictitious problem of their own making since it was a direct result of the rumours spread by Forsberg and Bihlar. Dook being an Irishman only compounded the problem.

It is another strong possibility that Forsberg had justifiable doubts as to whether he had enough evidence against me to secure a conviction. He had backed himself into a corner with his many public statements of my guilt, and now that he was shortly going to have to put his money where his mouth was he may have been getting cold feet. He must have considered that a conviction was expected of him for the same reasons. If there was doubt in his mind, he probably considered it preferable to release me on bail into military custody 'on humanitarian grounds whilst more evidence was being collected', and then to quietly drop the charges, when all the hue and cry had died down, a couple of months later, than to go to court and lose.

In any event it was not to be. Late in the afternoon of 24 July Christopher Murray received a telephone call from Inspector Nilsson to inform him that the prosecutor had decided (I am sure with not a little coercion from the case officers), to proceed against me, but that for security reasons the trial location was to be moved to the Appellant Court building in Stockholm. A press release was put out explaining, to justify this decision, that there was a 'double threat' to my life, not only from international drug dealers believed to be behind threats to members of the Hayward family, but because the danger of an 'IRA attack' was regarded as a real possibility.

In the meantime Kingsley Napley had sent Richard New, a retired Customs and Excise investigator, now a private detective, to Ibiza to see what, if anything, he could find out in general about the Mitchell drug ring, and in particular about Dook. In other words we were having to employ investigators to do what the Uppsala Drug Squad, on their own admission, were 'too afraid' to do. As it turned out the police may also have had ulterior motives in not wanting to conduct their own enquiries on Ibiza; in case the results proved to be in my favour.

My trial started on Tuesday 28 July 1987.

Readers of this book brought up under the British legal system, or one originating from it, will already have realized that the legal system I encountered in Sweden differed in significant respects. Before going on to discuss my trial, it is perhaps worth looking at some of the differences, since they were so influential on the outcome of my case.

Sweden is a signatory of the Eurpoean Convention on Human Rights, and as such it theoretically at least takes the view, in common with Britain and other democracies, that prisoners should be held innocent until proven guilty. In practice, however, it's not that simple – as I was to discover to my cost.

In the first place, the independencc of the judiciary, so prized as a part of the British system, does not exist in Sweden, where the judiciary is openly regarded as the instrument of the state (or), as government officials would say, 'the people'). Swedish judges are in effect civil servants, employees of the state and although they have degrees in law they are not drawn from the legal profession, but instead trained for the sole purpose of working as judges. Naturally, their first loyalty is to their employers, not to any idealistic notions of the rights of the individual.

In addition, there are no juries in Sweden. Instead, the judge is helped to his verdict by a team of 'lay assessors'. Far from being the randomly-picked teams familiar elsewhere, these assessors are, like the judges they serve, political appointments. Each of Sweden's political parties gets to nominate a certain number of assessors, in proportion to the percentage of the national vote it receives at election. Like British juries, the Swedish assessors tend to have no legal training. Unlike them, however, they have a strong political interest in backing their government's 'line'.

The absence in Sweden of laws governing the reporting of cases, like Britain's 'sub judice', or 'Contempt of Court' rules, means that policemen and prosecutors are free to say what they like to the press, and judges and assessors are free to read their comments. In a case like mine, then, where the trial comes at the end of months of extravagent claims from police and prosecutor, and sensational speculation by the journalists themselves, dominating the newspapers day after day, it's difficult to see how they can approach the hearing with an open mind.

It's not just the press who are allowed to speculate however. Sweden's attitude to evidence admissable in court seems astonishingly slack to the foreign observer, hearsay is readily accepted, as are the suspicions and 'educated guesses' of prosecutors and police. In any case, thanks to the notorious 'Sanalika Skal' clause, to achieve a conviction the prosecution are required only to prove that the defendant *could* have committed the crime of which he is accused. As long as they can produce a plausible story, then, the prosecution need not worry about proving that their charges are actually true. So much for 'innocent until proven guilty'!

In fact, it is assumed that most people who end up before the judges are indeed guilty. The police and prosecutors, it is thought, would certainly have released anyone of whose guilt there could be the slightest doubt, long before he came to trial. To be fair, the authorities do sometimes quietly drop charges against people, and let them go, when their guilt begins to look doubtful. Most prisoners, however, end up admitting their guilt, if only, as some Swedish critics of the system point out, because they're kept in solitary confinement until they do.

A system weighted so heavily in favour of the prosecution does place an enormous burden of integrity upon them – a burden which, given their status as political appointees, Swedish officials cannot really be expected to bear. Even the well-meaning official will find it difficult to embarrass the state by admitting error, especially in a well-publicized case where the prisoner's guilt has been triumphantly proclaimed to the press for weeks on end. Similarly, where such a loathsome crime as drug-smuggling is involved, it may seem more important to 'make an example' of someone for the good of Sweden than to bother too much about the rights of the accused.

My prosecutor, Mr Forsberg, could not under any circumstances be described as a well-meaning official. He very quickly made it clear that he was entirely without scruple. Not content with exploiting the advantages the system gave him, he denied me the rights that Swedish law – in theory, at least – gave me. His constant obstructing of my lawyers in their attempts to build a case for the defence, and his total failure to investigate the truth of my case, either in Sweden or in Ibiza, were both in flagrant breach of his duty. The defendant in Sweden, however, has no recourse against the injustices of such officials.

Six

'Let the jury consider their verdict,' the King said, for about the twentieth time that day.

'No, no!' said the Oueen. 'Sentence first — verdict afterwards.'

'Stuff and nonsense!' said Alice loudly.

Lewis Carroll

DAY ONE — *Tuesday, 28 July 1987.*

Our footsteps echoed noisily in the concrete emptiness of the tunnel. Pipes, lining the ceiling, stretched away into the distance. Every fifty yards, or so, the impersonal eye of a video camera monitored our progress.

I had been brought up from Uppsala early in the morning, handcuffed and guarded by three warders. The Prison Service Volvo was escorted by a police car, its blue lights flashing, which had pushed its way through the rush hour traffic as we entered Stockholm, clearing a path for us.

The tunnel was over one kilometre long. It led from the Kronoberg Police Station underground carpark, into which we had sped unchecked, to the Svea Appellant Court building, a gaunt pile on Scheelegatan. It enabled prisoners to be taken to their trials without seeing the light of day, and avoided distasteful overexposure to the public.

I took a deep breath, involuntarily releasing it in a long sigh. The guard beside me sniggered.

'They all do that.'

'Who all do what?' I asked.

'Prisoners,' came the reply, 'they always sigh like that in here. That's why we call it the "Tunnel of Sighs". You know, like the bridge in Venice.'

I made no comment. 'They always sigh more deeply on the way back,' he added, looking at me knowingly.

Armed police were everywhere, in blue jump-suits and heavy bullet-proof flack-jackets. Two of them led the way along the tunnel, their radios chattering exuberantly. Another showed us into what must have been the oldest and slowest lift in Sweden. We had to stand tightly pressed, shoulder to shoulder, as it moaned and groaned, and creaked its exhausted way up to the fifth floor. Yet more officers, some with sub-machine guns, were standing guard in the hall into which we finally emerged. It had a high vaulted ceiling with great stone pillars and a rather grand staircase, up which I was unceremoniously ushered into a not so grand holding cell.

The cuffs were removed. I sat alone. 'I should be nervous,' I thought to myself. I was not. I didn't feel even slightly apprehensive. This was just another stage in my seemingly unending nightmare. It was all too unreal: was it really happening to me? If anything I felt oddly cheerful. Cheerful at the prospect of being amongst people again for the first time in 138 days. Cheerful, because I thought I could see a light at the end of the tunnel. Cheerful, because I could not fathom how Forsberg could think he had a case against me, now that he was going to have to present it to a court of law.

The door opened. Tom Placht came bustling in, with a bright step and a reassuring smile, offering me his hand.

'Morning Simon. How are you feeling?'

'I'm fine Tom, just fine. When do we start?' We shook. 'Very soon now, the court is filling up. Feeling nervous?'

'No, not really. I just want to get it over with, and then get out of here.'

'Good, I am pleased you are confident. Christopher Murray is downstairs talking to journalists, and you will see your aunt and John Gorst in the courtroom. Your mother and James Emson will not be permitted to sit in until after they have given evidence.'

'Okay, are there many reporters here?'

'Yes, I would guess at around fifty.'

I laughed. 'Well Tom, there is nothing like being famous, even if for all the wrong reasons.'

We talked for a few minutes about minutiae, Placht briefing me on what to expect and on how he expected the first day of the trial to proceed.

'When is Forbes Mitchell going to testify?' I enquired.

'Oh, not until the end of the week.' With that he left me to my thoughts.

A loudspeaker, high in one corner of the cell, made a ping-ponging noise, like one hears in airport terminals. A woman's voice came on. A stream of Swedish followed. I heard my own name being mentioned. The broadcast came to an end with a final *piinngg*.

A few seconds later my guards came for me.

There was a hush as I entered the courtroom through a side door. All eyes were on me. It was a large, rectangular, oak-panelled room with tall windows running down the left hand wall. At one end, to my right, was the Judge's Bench, raised on a dais. Placed centrally behind it a heavy door led to his chambers. At the other, the main entrance beckoned. The public gallery, like rows of pews in a church, filled half the room. Directly in front of it, in the centre of the floor facing the Bench, stood the empty witness box. Immediately on my right, the defence stand and opposite it, across an open expanse of blue carpet, that belonging to the prosecution.

The public gallery looked full to capacity, and judging by appearances, mostly with reporters. My aunt and John Gorst were seated in the front row. I smiled and nodded to them. There was no prisoner's dock; I hesitated, not sure where to go. Placht stood up from the defence stand and pointed me towards an empty chair beside him. To my left was the court interpreter, a man called Martin Naylor, actually an Englishman whom I had met on previous court appearances. Beyond him sat Christopher Murray. On Placht's right was Hanna Pontein, surrounded by bulging law books. I winked a hello to her. Forsberg sat devoid of all expression opposite, beside him Bihlar, who smiled at me in recognition. I did not return it. Judge Hellbacher, flanked on both sides by five middle-aged assessors and a young woman clerk, looked down at me from his bench. My guards detached themselves to sit along the wall beside the public gallery, close enough to grab me if I was to make a sudden break for freedom.

I took my place, knowing that I was the focus of scrutiny; knowing that Forsberg was about to do his damnedest to denounce me before all who were prepared to listen; knowing that the most ordinary privileges of a decent life – common trust, personal respect, the right to freedom – had been taken from me, like a coat that one checks in at a theatre door. I wondered whether I would ever be able to retrieve them?

The court looked informal to the point of matter-of-factness. There were no gowns or wigs, no affectations of office. When speaking no one was to stand up, little obvious respect was paid to the Judge. A buzz of whispered conversation resumed, someone laughed. People were eating sweets, crackling the papers, others drank cans of coke. Guards, looking bored, sprawled in their seats. The Judge and male assessors wore suits, as did Forsberg – but with a thin grey leather tie in its customary position two inches below his unbuttoned collar. Bihlar was wearing a short-sleeved pale green shirt, a tie but no jacket. The impression given was of a people's court with a distinct lack of discipline. I hoped its sense of justice was on a higher plane.

Forsberg commenced the proceedings by reading out the charges against me. It was shortly before 10 am.

'Simon Hayward is charged with Gross Smuggling in that he ... Also with a Gross Drug Offence in that he ... The prosecution calls for a long sentence to be handed down.'

This was the first time I had ever heard the charges put to me officially, and even at this stage I was not to be allowed to make a formal reply. Instead Placht answered for me.

'Simon Hayward categorically denies all charges, and pleads NOT GUILTY.' The judge scribbled with his pen.

Forsberg began by putting the case for the prosecution. He spoke for an hour and twenty minutes. His grating, nasal delivery becoming increasingly monotonous as the time ticked by. I noticed a growing amount of inattention amongst the press, marked by yawns and muted whispers; and this was only the very start of the first day; I wondered what it would be like on the final day. At least they could get up and walk out. The prosecutor was reciting from a script as if reading a litany, slowly and uttered phrase by phrase, so that it could be more easily translated.

What he had to say was very much as expected, with no great surprises. He explained the background to the case – the police had become aware of the existence of a well organised drugs ring. Cannabis arriving regularly from Spain in specially fitted vehicles. Telephone conversations were intercepted, people followed. Gradually a picture had been built up. The operation had culminated in the arrest of Hayward, Mitchell and several others in March of 1987. 50.5 kilos of cannabis had been recovered. Mitchell had been tried, found guilty and sentenced to seven years' imprisonment. He had fully admitted his crime and had been of great assistance in helping the police with their enquiries. His account differed totally from Hayward's.

Not unexpectedly, he made much of my change of statement. Not describing it, as indeed was the case, as one lie to protect a brother, but instead blowing it out of all proportion, driving each and every possible point home with a vengeance. Referring to me in a rather patronising manner as 'Simon', as though detailing the misdemeanours of a naughty little boy, he spelt out how I had invented the meeting with Mitchell outside the Montesol, the discussions about Sweden, Mitchell's suggestion that I go skiing there, and the invitation to stay the night at his house in Linkoping. He punctuated each point with 'This was a lie.'

'This was another lie; and yet another lie.' He made it sound as though I had not told the truth in any part of any of my statements to the police, and at the same time it became blatantly clear that he was attempting to build Mitchell up to be an honest and totally reliable witness, in direct contrast to myself.

'On 17th June Simon changed his statement on important points, making it tie in better with Mitchell's story, obviously hoping it would become more credible.'

This was a shocking claim, it was the only thing I had not expected him to try on. How could he assert that I had altered my account to make it coincide with Mitchell's when he had kept me in solitary confinement precisely in order to prevent such a possibility from taking place? I had no idea what Mitchell had been saying in detail, and the police had been very careful not to tell me.

I found myself staring at Forsberg with a burning sense of anger and frustration. He continued by ridiculing my plans to go skiing, saying that he could not ask the court to believe that anyone would travel the length of Europe to ski for just one or two days, for that is all the time I could have had, he stated, by the time I had reached the slopes, not forgetting I had to be back in London by the 18th. At the same time he denounced my belief, as he saw it, that Mitchell was a Swede. 'The man speaks with an unmistakable Scottish accent.'

The Screwdriver received a more than prodigious amount of attention. He pointed out that I had bought it only after arriving in Sweden, when my journey was almost at an end, and having passed through the final customs post, despite having had every opportunity of doing so beforehand. He refused to believe that the driver's seat had become loose and instead told the court that it was his conviction I had made the purchase solely to unload the drug consignment, reminding us that the car seats had to be removed before access could be gained to the secret compartments, and that this special screwdriver only fitted the seat screws.

Every now and again he would pause to take a mouthful of water. He had a peculiar way of speaking, as though chewing each word, the corners of his mouth making exaggerated movements. Throughout Bihlar sat motionless beside him, also looking bored. His eyes roaming from one person to another, sometimes stopping at me whereupon he would again smile faintly, either in recognition or vindictiveness; it was almost as if he was saying – 'I've got you now, just you wait and see.' I noticed he had a mannerism: one finger poised across his lips as if calling for silence. The Judge sat impassively, only stirring to make the odd note.

Most criminals need a motive for their crimes, mine it was stated was a yearning for excitement and a desire for money. The defence had put forward the car theft on Ibiza as a theory for how the drugs came to be hidden in the Jaguar; this Forsberg said was nothing more than a smoke screen, it had been staged to help the courier if caught. Since Simon's arrest his brother had disappeared.

He continued by angrily demanding, no doubt for the sake of the press, that Scotland Yard allow Morgan and Moore to attend the trial, calling the refusal to permit them to testify 'a travesty of justice'. He submitted their report as evidence and told the court that Inspector Larsen would give testimony in their place. The clear implication was that the British establishment was protecting one of its own, but he made no mention of Assistant Commissioner Hewett's letter explaining his decision not to allow his officers to attend.

There was a pause to allow Forsberg to present some written evidence, the document detailing the examination of the Jaguar and some photographs of the work in progress. Court exhibits B and E.

The monologue started once more as he described the technical examination of the car, explaining exactly where and how the drugs had been found. As he did so the Judge and assessors studied the photographs, passing them, one to another.

It became clear from this opening address that the prosecution case rested on:

1. My arrest at the wheel of the Jaguar.

2. My brother's disappearance.

3. The presence of the screwdriver.

4. My change of statement.

5. The Morgan and Moore Report, supported by Larsen.

6. Mitchell's evidence. (Whatever that was going to be.)

Placht now opened the case for the defence. 'The mere fact that there were drugs in the car does not mean Simon Hayward is guilty. Under Swedish law the prosecution must prove that he knew they were there. As far as I am aware no such proof exists. The prosecution case is based on the fact that Hayward gave two versions of his story, but he provided incorrect information regarding only a couple of details that are quite marginal to the case, for a reason that is understandable. Much rests on Mitchell's information, but as far as I know he has yet to implicate my client directly.'

He told the court of Christopher's telephone call to my mother – '. . . the set up was meant for me, and I passed it on to Simon . . .', and continued by providing information about Mitchell that Forsberg had omitted. Police evidence stated that since 1984 Mitchell had transported only 112 kilos of cannabis from Spain to Sweden, and yet there was further evidence to suggest the quantities were much larger. This last consignment of 50 kilos was unusual, with a new courier, carried out in a hurry, the consignment itself larger than normal.

The prosecutor was setting much store by the purchase of the special screwdriver by Hayward, yet the plausible reasons my client has given for buying it cannot be refuted. The driver's seat does rock in the way he describes, and as the court will soon be able to see for itself, any screwdriver could have been used to remove the seats. There were tools in the house in Zinkgruvan, where the car was due to be unloaded. Why had the police not made a proper inventory of these tools? There is a photograph that shows one screwdriver remarkably like the one Hayward bought. 'So he did not need to buy one to be able to get at the drugs. A fact he would have known had he been a member of this drugs ring.'

He criticised the police handling of the case. Why had no enquiries been carried out on Ibiza? Even Scotland Yard agreed to co-operate with such investigations, he said, producing a letter to prove it. And yet none were carried out, despite defence requests that they be conducted. Mitchell's common law wife, Prita, should have been interviewed. Why was she not?

At this juncture Forsberg interrupted to say that contact had in fact been made with Prita, and he mumbled something about a telephone call between her and Bihlar. Placht looked visibly taken aback. 'Why was I not told? Why was I not invited to be present during this call?' He did not receive a satisfactory explanation. Forsberg just turned puce with embarrassment. We did not realise it at the time, but this was to prove a highly significant revelation.

The eyes of the suntanned Inspector Bihlar were suddenly more alert, his attention focused intently on Placht. He swayed ever so slightly in his seat, obviously very annoyed.

'The entire investigation has been conducted in such a way as to be extremely prejudicial to my client.'

As a finale, Placht produced Hewett's letter written to Sir David Napley, and read it out to the court. '. . . unable to vouch for the truth nor accuracy . . .' Forsberg's face dropped in surprise. He clearly could have had no prior warning that the defence had seen this letter, and had quite obviously decided not to tender his own copy as evidence. Placht now called upon him to place it before the court.

I find it inconceivable that a British prosecutor, or for that matter any other Swedish prosecutor, would have acted in such an underhand and deceitful fashion. Forsberg's bias, not to mention dishonesty, was compounded when one recalls that the evidence in question was hearsay upon hearsay originating from an unnamed, unproduced informant. Any pretence of impartiality on his part had by this stage completely disappeared. I looked up at the Judge to see what action he would take. The answer amazingly was none. He remained sitting in his characteristically impassive pose; it was as though he had not understood what had taken place. I began to have my first doubts about the fairness of the trial I was receiving.

Placht drove the point home by reminding Forsberg that in June the defence had asked for charges to be made against me within two weeks. He had disagreed because Larsen was not going to be able to produce a memorandum on 'my guilt' for another three weeks, the result being that I had been held for another month. This memo had still not been produced, nor had a similar one from Scotland Yard. 'Could the prosecutor do so now?' Needless to say, he could not.

Placht ended his opening address with Forsberg looking extremely glum and embarrassed. Round One to the defence?

Throughout the trial the Judge was to call the occasional break to give everyone a chance to stretch their legs, as well as recessing the court for lunch each day for an hour, or so, at around noon. Every evening proceedings would draw to a close between five and six pm. During the daytime adjournments I would be led back to the holding cells, or to the Kronoberg Häktet for lunch. At the end of each day I would return to Uppsala. As soon as Placht finished his address Hellbacher announced an interlude for lunch.

Members of the 'Home Team' had been playing cat and mouse with the press ever since arriving in the country. Now, as my aunt and John Gorst left the courthouse, shepherded by Hanna Pontein to where my mother and Brigadier James Emson were hiding, a bevy of cameramen followed them, hoping no doubt for photographs of everyone together. First, the vultures completely missed my mother sitting right outside in a parked car which my aunt and Gorst purposely ignored. Then, in their clamour they failed to notice the brigadier who stood on a street corner hidden beneath a giant umbrella, hissing at Gorst to move away when he approached him.

'Pssst, John it's me, James. Don't come this way! Go away. GO AWAY!'

Reporters soon established that they would have more luck with members of the prosecution, and even the Judge; all of whom would grant off-the-cuff interviews at the drop of a hat during these intervals.

After lunch it was my turn to give evidence. I spoke for over two hours, going into as much detail as possible, running through everything that had happened to me, in relation to this affair, since meeting Christopher in London in September 1986 to the moment of my arrest in Sweden. I mentioned nothing new, my testimony was an exact replica of all that I had told the police in the various statements I had given them.

By the time I finished it was half past four, and the Judge decided that my cross-examination could take place the next day. This day's proceedings would be concluded with a showing of the two video tapes submitted by the prosecution. To this end three television sets had been positioned in the centre of the floor, facing in different directions so that all spectators would have at least a partial view.

The first film was the one showing the Jaguar being searched – men hacking and scraping away at its interior. All the seats had been removed; packets of the consignment, wrapped in transparent plastic eventually being discovered and removed with difficulty from the door sills. A square of metal appeared to have been cut out of the inside of each of them, and then glued back into position once the drugs had been hidden. They could now clearly be seen being prised open with a chisel.

I still could not understand why this film was being shown; neither side was disputing the fact that the drugs had been found in the car, making it totally irrelevant. This graphic demonstration can only have been designed to play on the emotions of the assessors. The showing dragged on; I had seen it all before; my mind began to wander. I glanced across at my aunt, Myrtle Matthews, sitting no more than ten feet away, but it might just as well have been ten miles – I could almost feel the invisible wall that stood between us. She was my mother's identical twin, younger by ten minutes, and had decided to attend the trial to lend moral support. Her presence had apparently caused a certain amount of consternation among the court ushers and guards because they had mistaken her for my mother, who as a witness was not allowed to sit in court until after she had testified. This new twist had only added to the confusion of an already complex affair that the locals were finding something of a handful. I smiled at the thought of the dignity of all those heavily armed and self important guards being thrown by such a 'worrying matter'.

I was brought back to reality with a jolt as the court clerk changed tapes in the video machine with a loud snap. The second film was my demonstration of how the seat had become loose. The police editing had not been corrected, needless to say, but Placht could put that right later. At least this showing was relevant, albeit somewhat inconclusive.

Shortly before six the Judge brought the proceedings to a close, announcing that the trial would reconvene temporarily in Uppsala in the morning with an examination of the Jaguar, before resuming once more in Stockholm.

I was allowed to say a quick hello to Myrtle and John Gorst before being taken back to my cell in Uppsala. I did not know what to think of my chances after this first day, indeed I did not want to think about them.

DAY TWO – *Wednesday, 29 July 1987.*

The Jaguar stood gleaming under the strip lights, someone must have given it a polish for the occasion. As on the previous day I was the last to join the 'court', now occupying a workshop in the basement carpark of the Uppsala Police Station.

If the situation had not been so serious I could not have helped finding the scene that confronted me rather comical. A cluster of journalists was being kept at bay by a strip of white tape; they looked all set to pounce,with their notepads and pencils held expectantly. Forsberg stood to one side flanked by his minders, Bihlar and Nilsson. They were holding a whispered conference. Judge Hellbacher was touring around the car as though he had never seen a Jaguar before, followed in single file by his five assessors. They reminded me of frantic, panic-stricken ducklings following their mother on the first excursion to a pond, wings flapping excitedly, bottoms waddling madly. The court clerk completed the batty scene. She had her arms full with a huge pile of ring files, the top one open, ready for note-taking. At the same time she was struggling with a somewhat overlarge tape-recorder and like an eager correspondent out on her first big scoop, she would poke the microphone under the nose of anyone talking, desperately transferring it from one face to another, in the meantime getting the trailing wires into a frightful tangle. The set-up did not look like any court I had ever seen before, and I suspect most people present felt likewise.

The prosecution obviously intended making as much as possible out of the screwdriver, the car seats and the seat screws.This demonstration was to be an attempt on Forsberg's part to disprove my stated reasons for having the screwdriver in my possession.

My arrival was the cue for everyone to gather around into a confused mass by the open driver's door of the car, while the judge kicked off the morning's play by swearing in the first and only witness, Inspector Bertil Olsson, who had been responsible for searching the car and discovering the cannabis. I found myself standing next to Christopher Murray who had been watching everything with a look of incredulity on his face.

Olsson was a tall, somewhat podgy, round-featured individual in his mid- to late-forties, with black hair, and a beard exaggerating his puffy cheeks. He was dressed in a well-laundered boilersuit, complete with police badges, and was clearly highly nervous. During his cross-examination he blushed continuously, often pausing to wipe perspiration from his brow. He reminded me of one of the old school of loyal but dim-witted lance corporals, given his rank, not on merit, but out of courtesy to his age and long service. However, like many such men he was apparently clever with his hands and had done a thorough job in stripping the Jaguar, but, as we were to establish, not such a thorough one in putting it back together again.

Admitting that it had taken him three days to search the car, he described how he had eventually found the cannabis, pointing out the location of the secret compartments and proudly displaying one of the metal cutouts that had sealed the openings. All this was of course just as irrelevant and boring as the video had been the previous afternoon. He demonstrated how the bottom cushion of the driver's seat could be removed, explaining that it had to be lifted before access to all four seat screws could be attained. He loosened each screw in turn, using a normal screwdriver, until the seat frame could be rocked on its foundations. With much open discussion, every possible combination was tried, first one, then two, three and all four screws were loosened and tightened by a varying number of turns. It was a rather one-sided demonstration, with the Judge and assessors refusing to sit in the car to establish for themselves if the seat rocked despite Placht's remonstrations for them to do so, and it was also clear that Olsson had been well briefed, even primed, on how to answer Forsberg's questions. However it was equally clear, however hard the police tried to conceal the fact, that the seat did indeed move as I had described, once the screws were loose.

Asked if anything else of interest had been discovered in the car, Olsson produced one of those magnetic key boxes, designed to be clipped to the underside of a vehicle to avoid people locking themselves out, and stated that he had found it hidden on the inside of the back bumper. In the box were the spare keys that had disappeared during the theft on Ibiza. Why should the robbers have wanted to secrete a spare set of keys on the car? Was it because they planned to re-steal it at a later date? Was this evidence of a back-up plan, in case I had missed the rendezvous with Mitchell at the station? The possibilities were endless; but this did show that the theft had not been a chance affair, unrelated to the drugs.

Now it was Placht's turn to cross-examine. 'Inspector Olsson, did you attach any relevance to the front seats before you discovered the cannabis?'

'No, I just removed them along with all the other inside fitments.'

'As the work progressed you must have had dozens of loose screws, nuts and bolts. What did you do with them all?'

'Yes, there were a great many, I put them all in a box for safe keeping.'

'We can all see that the car has been put back together again now. Did you have any odds and ends left over, once the job was complete?'

Olsson smiled sheepishly. 'Yes, there were a few. Some would have been too difficult to replace and I had forgotten where others went. Please don't forget, it was an enormous job.'

'Oh, don't worry, I do not mean to be critical. We have all taken things to pieces only to find parts left over once we have put them back together again. However, you signed a statement to the effect that you returned the car to the condition in which you found it, once the search was complete.' He produced a copy of this statement, dated 20 March 1987, which formed part of the prosecution's documented case against me.

'Yes I did,' said the unsuspecting Olsson.

'Well, when I inspected the car in May I noticed and drew your attention to the fact that there were only three screws holding the driver's seat to the car floor. In other words one was missing. I see now that there are four. Can you explain that?'

'Yes, I could only find three, so I must have lost one of them. Therefore I had to buy a replacement. That was not easy because the retaining nut, which had also disappeared, is a very unusual one.'

'Ah,' said Placht with a note of triumph creeping into his voice, 'how can you be so sure that there were four screws in the first place, and not just three?'

'Because I can distinctly remember finding four.'

'That's very interesting. Do you honestly expect the court to believe that despite the fact you removed so many screws you could not remember where to put them all back; despite attaching no relevance to the seats; and despite the fact that you very carefully kept all loose articles in a special box, that you can still manage to distinctly remember one set of screws above all the others. And not only that, but you also lost one of them and its retaining nut. I would suggest to you that there were only ever three screws and that you have produced the fourth purely to make the seat appear firmer on its foundations, because of course with one missing, and it would have to have been the one hidden by the seat cushion, there is an even better possibility that the seat rocked in precisely the way my client has described.'

Olsson looked even more nervous now, but he stuck to his story. 'N-N-NO,' he stammered, 'I-I can p-positively remember that there were four.'

Placht changed tactics. 'What tests did you carry out on the Jaguar?' at the same time taking avoiding action from the microphone that was stuck into his face.

'I don't understand. What do you mean?'

'Well, Captain Hayward has stated that the seat rocked when he was driving at speed, and when he had to brake suddenly. Did you conduct any tests to establish for yourself if that can happen? Have you test driven the car at speed, and with the seat loose?'

'No, I have only driven it here in the garage; at about 5 kph.'

'So in effect you can have no real idea if the seat rocks or not!?' Placht drove the point home. Olsson looked aghast, glancing at Forsberg for help, but the prosecutor was suddenly extremely interested in his shoelaces.

Since the defence had now proved that this entire demonstration was a sham, based as it was on biased speculation not on proper tests of any sort, I expected the Judge to order correct tests to be carried out forthwith. However, he did not bat an eyelid.

'One more question,' Placht continued. Olsson looked relieved that his ordeal was nearly over. 'How many tools, and of what kind did you need to remove the cannabis from the car?'

'Let me see now,' the inspector assumed a pensive look, 'a

small Phillips for the seat cushion retaining screw; a flat-ended
screwdriver for the actual seat screws; an assortment for the
side fitments that needed to be lifted before the carpet could
be removed; a chisel to open the drug compartments, and
some steel wire which I bent into hooks in order to pull out
the drug bags.'

'Did you find any of these other tools in the car?'

'No I did not.'

'So,' said Placht, turning to the Judge, 'the only tool my
client had on him was one that was not required to unload the
cannabis. If he had known about the drugs and had needed to
purchase equipment to remove them from the Jaguar, would
he not have bought all these others that Olsson has mentioned?
Ones that were actually needed to complete the job.'

The Judge shrugged, obviously not willing to commit
himself. Instead he called a halt to the session, ordering the
court to reassemble in Stockholm at 10.30 hours. Round Two
to the defence?

My cross-examination started immediately the court
reconvened in Stockholm. Forsberg began by asking me a few
questions on what I took to be undisputed minutiae.

'When did you decide to go sailing?'

'When did you decide to travel to Gibraltar?'

'Why did you have so much money on you and where had
it come from?'

'Why did you have a sophisticated nightsight and powerful
torch in your possession?'

'Why did you not go sailing and travel to Ibiza instead?'

And so the list went on. Of course the court already knew
the answers because of the detailed statement I had given the
previous day, but I answered everything as I was bid, making
a point of being as polite as possible, calling the odious
creature 'Sir', something he must have been totally unused to;
but still, there has to be a first time for everything in anyone's
life.

This cross-examination was not as I expected. There was no
rush of questions, fired in ever-increasing numbers and
volume, designed to catch me out and produce a 'dramatic
courtroom confession'. Instead Forsberg's manner was quietly
subdued, even pedantic. Having to leave long pauses to allow

the interpreter to do his bit did not help the flow of his delivery either. All in all, Perry Mason would have been appalled.

Eventually the more important issues were broached, or at least the ones Forsberg must have considered more important.

'Why did you not tell Sandra that you were intending to drive to Sweden?'

This question annoyed me because the subject had been thoroughly covered during the pre-trial investigation, and I had thought the police satisfied with my motives for not telling Sandra of my plans to drive back to London. Indeed Forsberg had even hinted to Placht that the subject was closed. The very last thing I wanted to do was to start delving into so delicate and personal a matter in public, beneath the gaze of so many hungry reporters.

'I could not have told her, even if I had wanted to, sir,' I spoke slowly and deliberately, letting my anger show, 'because, as you well know, my brother did not ask me to drive to Sweden until after she had left Ibiza.'

'Then why did you not tell her you were driving back to London?'

So I had to explain all about our relationship, how I had wanted some time alone to think matters through, and to unwind from Northern Ireland. How Sandra had only had one week off from her work and could not have accompanied me, and that I had tried to avoid upsetting her. It was clear from his expression that the prosecutor did not believe me, or at least did not want to believe me, but he let the matter drop. In any case he had made his point.

Having set the scene he then launched his major offensive. 'Soon after your arrest Simon, you made a statement saying that you had come to Sweden to go skiing and that you had arranged with Mitchell to stay at his house in Linköping on your way to the slopes. In June you changed your story, saying instead that your brother Christopher had asked you to deliver the Jaguar to Mitchell for sale. In other words, you lied; you lied about meeting Mitchell on Ibiza; you lied about discussing skiing with him; you lied about . . .'

Realizing that my credibility was at stake, I could not afford to let Forsberg get away with making a great issue out of this. Placht did not look as though he was about to make an objection, so I took it upon myself to interrupt. If the Swedish system was more like an open debate than a trial, then I was not about to let the prosecutor bend the issue against me.

'Excuse me sir. Hang on a minute please!' I had won the floor, which was a first step at any rate. 'I have already told you why I did not tell the complete truth from the very start, but you are attempting to make it sound as though I have not told the truth in any part of my statements, which, as I think you are more than aware, is far from correct. Yes, you may be right in saying I lied, but for what I considered was a good reason at the time, and concerning only one very small portion of a statement that took me over two hours to read out to the court yesterday. And for what it is worth I am not very proud of myself for behaving in such a manner, but . . .'

I expected him to re-interrupt me in order to regain the initiative, but to my surprise he let me continue, so I described how I had felt on the night of my arrest, and what had been going through my mind.

'. . . put yourself in my position. I had just arrived in Sweden after a long drive, I was tired, hungry and looking forward to a good night's sleep followed by a few days' skiing. Instead I found myself being arrested in a very aggressive manner. I was driving along when suddenly my car was forced off the road and boxed in by others that did not look like police cars. I was dragged from my driver's seat by men who did not look or identify themselves as police officers . . . I was handcuffed and taken to a police station, stripped, searched and put in a cell. No explanation was given. I found myself in a state of shock, I had no idea what was going on. I was confused and rather frightened. It was only after two or three hours that someone came and told me that I had been arrested on drugs charges . . . I knew that I had absolutely nothing to do with drugs of any sort . . . I came to the natural conclusion that a dreadful mistake had been made, and as soon as the authorities realized this I would be released . . . I had become mixed up in something outside of my control . . . as I sat in my cell I realized, I assumed, the only reason I was arrested was because of the people I had been with – a feeling reinforced by the fact that the arrest appeared well planned.'

I continued by describing my reaction to being told that

cannabis had been discovered hidden in the Jaguar:

'. . . this only served to increase my state of shock and confusion . . .'

And my total conviction that Christopher was not involved in drug smuggling, despite the circumstances, and my consequent decision not to mention that he had asked me to deliver his car to Sweden,

'. . . with hindsight, I realize it was an incredibly stupid thing to do, but I can only explain it as an instinctive act to protect a member of my family, and I could not help myself . . .'

How, as time had passed, I had become stuck with my story, and . . .

'. . . eventually I did realize that I would be going on trial and that it was at least a possibility that I could be convicted for a crime I had not committed. I was told repeatedly by the police that I would be going to prison for at least seven or eight years. It also became a stronger possibility that my brother was in some way involved – after all he had not come forward – and if he was, he did not deserve my protection and if he was not, he did not need it. I therefore decided that my only real chance of beating these allegations was on the grounds of the complete truth and not just part of it.'

I concluded by telling the court that the final factor had been my visit from Morgan and Moore, and their attempts at blackmailing me into confessing:

'. . . I knew what they were saying was absolute nonsense, but they made their accusations with such authority and conviction that the situation became very frightening. I thought that if people like police officers were saying these things about me then my only chance of clearing myself would be on the basis of the complete and utter truth. That is why I changed my statement.'

Whatever views Forsberg held of this plea in mitigation he chose to keep them to himself. When I finished speaking he contented himself with a long stare in my direction – the courtroom fell silent. I presume this intentionally dramatic pause was his way of conveying to the bench that he did not believe a word I had said.

'You have described the theft of the Jaguar on Ibiza. Don't you think the way in which it was stolen and recovered so quickly was rather strange?' he asked, with a rustle of his notes that broke the silence.

'No, I don't think so. It depends I suppose on whether you consider it had anything to do with the smuggling operation. I have only put that suggestion forward as a possibility, I have no idea what actually happened. Cars do get stolen, of course. The fact that the spare keys have been found hidden on the car is also of interest, don't you think?'

Ignoring my question he continued. 'Can you tell us again briefly what happened at the police station when you reported the car missing, and later when you were told it had been recovered?' I did as I was bid.

Forsberg now produced the forms that the Ibizan Police had given me.

'Do you make a habit of reading a document before signing it?' he asked me.

'Under normal circumstances, certainly. I would always read it first.'

'Did you read these police forms before signing them?'

'Probably, I can't remember off hand; but don't forget there was a language problem and also I attached no significance to them at the time. The car was not mine, I was merely reporting it stolen and I assumed that my brother would eventually be handling the situation.'

'The first form is in English and Spanish, and it establishes you as the owner of the car, which was, I believe, the whole point of the exercise – to supply you with documents making it look as though you owned the car. How can you explain that?' he was looking pleased with himself.

'I cannot, and I was not aware that it did.' I was puzzled by this new twist, however Placht came wading in to the rescue. Addressing the court he said:

'This document establishes nothing of the sort. Opposite the caption – OWNER – it states simply "el mismo", not my client's name,' and turning to me, 'Captain Hayward, do you know what el mismo means because I don't.'

I didn't have a clue. 'I don't I'm afraid. I did not then, although I didn't notice it at the time, and I do not now.'

'But you read the form before signing it,' insisted Forsberg, 'and el mismo means "the same", in other words it is referring

Life Guards tank and crew on exercise on the West German plain in 1980

A Chieftain engine chan

Forbes Mitchell's villa In San Miguel

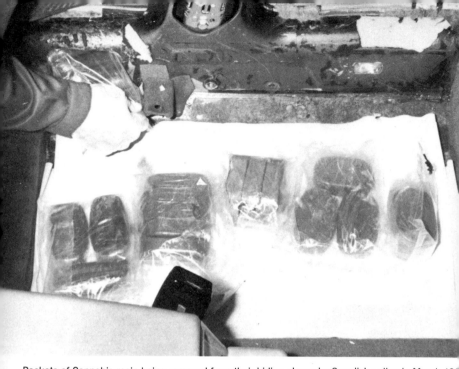

Packets of Cannabis resin being removed from their hiding places by Swedish police in March 198

The court's inspection of the

Malmo Prison

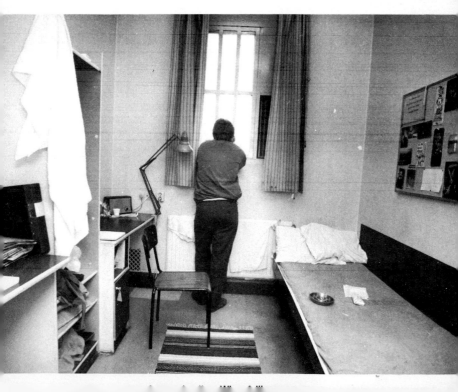

back to your name which is on the top of the paper.'

'I suppose I might have read it, I'm not sure, but at no stage did anybody ask me if I was the owner, if they had done so I would have told them that my brother was. It must have been their assumption that I was the owner.'

'Did the police officer who took down your particulars speak English?' asked Forsberg.

'No, as I have already explained, no one spoke English, barring one or two words, no more than that. Look sir, you are obviously trying to prove that I tried to establish myself as the Jaguar's owner with this line of questioning. Well, we have a saying in England – "The proof of the pudding is in the eating". If I had gone through this elaborate charade to make it appear as though I owned the car, why is it that I have never actually claimed to be the owner? From the very first time I was questioned by Inspector Bihlar I have always said it belonged to my brother. Your questions do not make any sense!'

'What was Christopher's reaction when you told him the car had been stolen? Was he concerned?'

'Yes, of course he was concerned. His initial reaction was one of anger, and I think he said "Oh shit!" [there was some levity in the court over the translation of "shit"] but because the island is so small and the car sticks out like a sore thumb, I don't think he took it as a major disaster.'

'Why didn't he go with you to the police station in the morning? Since it was his car it is rather strange that he left that to you.'

'Again I do not think so. I was only going to report back because the police had asked me to. It never crossed my mind that the car would have already been recovered. In any case Chris said he would meet me at the station; and when, and if, it was eventually recovered I presumed that he would have to reclaim it as the owner. As we know now, that proved not to be the case, but on that morning Chris said something about an appointment with his bank manager, and with the benefit of hindsight, I believe he may also have wanted to check the ferry to ensure that whoever had stolen the Jaguar did not immediately take it off the island. That is only speculation on my part, I hasten to emphasize, but it would explain why he arranged to meet me at the ferry terminal as a back-up plan in the event of us missing each other at the police station.'

'If you had cancelled your plans to leave that morning, why did you bother to return your hire car?'

'Simply because I had decided to fly home on the first available plane, and I therefore had to return the car before 10 am or incur another day's charges.'

To this very day I cannot understand the logic of Forsberg's next question. 'Why did you leave your luggage at the villa in Santa Gertrudis? Why didn't you give it to your brother to take to the ferry terminal? I find this very strange.'

I was beginning to wonder if there was anything Forsberg did not find 'strange'.

'Since the car had been stolen, surely it must be obvious to you now, as it was to me then, that I was not about to be going anywhere immediately. I would have thought it much more suspicious if I had taken my bags with me, under those circumstances; that is if you are trying to make out I staged the theft and therefore by implication, would already have known that the car had been recovered. I am afraid I fail to understand your logic.'

Forsberg was proving to be nothing if not pertinacious. He made one final effort to prove that I had staged the theft.

'Why is it that the police were able to find the Jaguar so quickly?'

'I have no idea. Indeed Christopher was quite surprised at this piece of uncharacteristic efficiency on the part of the Ibizan police. To get the correct answer to that question you had better ask them.'

At this juncture Forsberg changed the subject matter of his questioning. 'Why did you choose to drive via Andorra? It was a long way off your route to France.'

'Well in actual fact it was not that much out of our way. I had never been there before so I thought it would be fun to see what it was like en route, and at the same time to take advantage of its tax-free status to buy some cheap skis to use in Sweden.'

'Was it your brother's idea to go there?'

'No, it was mine, but he also thought it was a good idea because he wanted to buy a spare tyre, and perhaps a replacement for the broken quarter-light.' I went on to explain for a second time why I had not managed to buy skis. Then ... 'I would like to point out, sir, that if there had been anything sinister about my decision to drive via Andorra I would hardly have told the police about it in the first place. They would never have been any the wiser.'

'He ignored this', I thought, valid comment. 'Do you really expect us to believe that you would drive the length of Europe to go skiing in this country for just two days? No one would do that.'

In answer to this I explained how my departure from Ibiza had been delayed by the insurance problem. 'If I had left on the date I had originally planned on, I would have had four or five days' skiing.'

'If you were really visiting Sweden to go skiing, as you claim, why didn't you have any skis with you in the car?'

'Because I left England to go on a sailing holiday, not a skiing holiday. And as I have tried to explain, I did not manage to buy any skis in Andorra, therefore I had decided to hire some in Sweden.'

He continued to ask me questions on varying subjects, all of which I had covered in my opening statement to the court, and in even greater detail during the police interviews. Finally he gave up and handed the cross-examination over to Placht.

'Can you describe your relationship with Christopher?'

'Relationship would be the wrong word. We really did not know each other that well ... '

'What type of lifestyle did he lead on Ibiza? Was it an extravagant one?'

'No it was certainly not extravagant, in fact he had very little money.'

'How did he earn his living?'

'Chartering his yacht mostly.' I went on to explain in detail the way Chris lived.

'Did you at any stage, during your time on the island, see any indication of, or suspect that any criminal activity was taking place?'

'No, none whatsoever.'

'Did you see any sign of drugs or Christopher taking drugs?'

'No I did not. I realize that my brother has been described

as a hippy, and that people naturally associate hippies with drugs, but I never saw any. Indeed I would not describe him as such, nor the way he lived as a hippy lifestyle. Simple, maybe non-conformist, but not hippy.'

'The prosecution has made much of your military training, saying that it would have helped you in acting as a courier. Can you comment on this?'

'Well, I don't mean to be flippant but the British Army does not train its officers to smuggle drugs. My regiment is equipped with armoured cars, I fail to see any connection.'

'How would you describe your financial position?'

'I think the best way to do so, would be sound. I have not got much money, but enough.' At this point Placht produced a letter from my bank manager which described my account as typical of an army officer's.

'When you passed through Andorra what customs checks were there?'

'We were stopped going in, both Christopher and I, and our passports were checked. On leaving, the French customs stopped us again and made a quick search of the cars. Because Andorra is tax free, I presume they check people more thoroughly when they leave to ensure they haven't exceeded their allowances. It would be logical for the checks coming out to be more strenuous than those going in.'

Placht's questions continued along this theme, clearing up any misconceptions that may have arisen. He finished by asking me about an Englishman I had spoken to briefly at a barbeque during my first visit to Ibiza in 1984. It was a good example of how many people reacted to my presence.

'How did your brother's friends take to you? Were they friendly?'

'Most of them were totally indifferent. Indeed I got the impression that they tolerated me simply because I was Christopher's brother. I suppose it boiled down to the fact we had nothing in common.'

'Didn't you play a little trick on one man you met?' he asked me with a smile.

'Yes, it was at a barbeque at some woman's house, and because nobody was interested in me I was standing to one side in the garden enjoying a quiet drink, when an Englishman walked up to me and started to chat. He was a bit of a spiv in his late thirties, and dripping in gold pendants and bracelets. He knew I was Christopher's brother but not my profession, so as a means of breaking the ice he asked me. For a laugh, and because he looked rather a dubious character, I told him that I was a policeman. On hearing this, his face dropped a mile, and without another word he turned on his heel and walked away.'

There was a titter of amusement from the public gallery as I recounted this tale, but it grew into raucous laughter when the interpreter, who had been doing an outstanding job to date, quite obviously got stuck on the translation of 'spiv'. He turned to me in confusion, his expression matched only by the puzzled faces on the Bench.

'There isn't a word for spiv in Swedish.'

'Well, try "wide-boy".' I volunteered, trying not to join in the infectious laughter.

This suggestion only made matters worse. 'No can do!' he whispered, looking desperate.

We got there in the end with – 'Haj' – Swedish for shark.

Before testifying the Judge had asked if I had any objection to the press using tape recorders. On advice from my lawyers I replied that I would prefer if they did not. The reason was quite simple, and at the time seemed a logical one. I did not want extracts broadcast out of context. With the benefit of hindsight however this decision was a mistake. Public opinion holds some sway over Swedish court verdicts, and because the prosecution case was weak, first impressions, especially those given by me, were of the utmost importance. Nobody, least of all the defence counsel, could have anticipated what a convincing witness I would make, how well I would be able to stand up to cross-examination, and what an excellent overall impression I was to give. I put this performance down, not to any natural ability to speak in public on my part, but to the anger that had been gradually building up inside me since the date of my arrest. Anger at the way the police had conducted their investigation; anger at the weak character and improbity of the prosecutor; anger at the way in which I had been held; but perhaps most of all a deep sense of anger and bitterness towards the criminals who had put me in this position in the first place. Now for the first time I was being given the opportunity to explain myself, not only before a court, which I had no reason to believe would be anything but strictly impartial and just, but also before a mass of journalists who I hoped would report the situation effectively, and thereby help to have an innocent man released. I gave vent to all my pent up anxieties.

John Gorst described my testimony thus: 'Simon's evidence took two hours and 17 minutes. He was dignified, clear and unruffled, and went into plenty of detail. He was fluent and made an excellent impression. Comments from journalists afterwards showed that they too thought he made a most unlikely drug peddlar.'

Christopher Murray had this to say: 'As a lawyer who has practiced for nearly twenty years in criminal courts, I have never before seen or heard such a remarkably impressive performance, particularly when one bears in mind that until the moment he walked into the full glare of the trial court and was expected within a couple of hours to commence a long address, he had been in solitary confinement for a period in excess of four months.'

Forsberg must have thought so too, for when Placht had finished his cross-examination I glanced across at him to find him once again looking extremely forlorn. Round Three to the defence?

The Judge made one of his infrequent announcements – 'The Scotland Yard officers will not be attending.' I must admit to a feeling of relief when I heard him say this. Although I had known that they would not be coming, I would not have been that surprised if they had suddenly walked through the door. Despite being so totally false, their report was so damning and delivered with such authority and confidence that it scared me. In their place Inspector Gunnar Larsen was called to the witness stand. Hellbacher swore him in.

Larsen was in his mid-forties, of medium height and slight build. He had a dark complexion, black hair thinning to a bald patch on the top of his head. Deep set eyes in an aquiline face. As he gave his testimony he appeared nervous to the point of embarrassment, and I got the clear impression that he was present very much against his will and better judgement.

Although his evidence was deeply damaging I could not help feeling sorry for him.

Under cross-examination by Forsberg he told the court that for the past two years he had been stationed in London as the Drugs Liaison Officer between the Nordic countries and Great Britain. When the Hayward case had received attention in the British mass media a flood of information had started to come into Scotland Yard; both from persons who refused to reveal their identities and from those who were known to the police but who wished to remain anonymous, due to the fear of reprisals. He had met one particular informant belonging to this latter group, initially with Morgan and Moore but again at a later date on his own, who had supplied the information detailed in the report submitted to the court. When information of this kind is given, the informant's credibility and motives for supplying it are always thoroughly investigated. The man in question was a person who had himself been a criminal, and who had often informed to the British police on other cases, particularly involving drug crimes. His information had always been 100% correct. His motives for supplying information was that he was totally opposed to drug trafficking, but had no objection whatsoever to other crimes. His information in this case had been corroborated by more that had been received, and furthermore, when Mitchell had been questioned he had spontaneously given a statement that supported the informant's.

'Why have Inspector Morgan and Detective Sergeant Moore not come to this court to testify in person?' Placht asked.

'They wanted to, but their superior officer, Assistant-Commissioner Hewett, refused to grant them permission.'

'Would you say that Mr Hewett is an experienced police officer?'

'Yes, most certainly. He has a background in Special Branch and would not hold the position he does without being highly experienced.'

'Doesn't it surprise you therefore that he has refused to allow his police officers to come to Sweden to testify, because in his opinion ... ' and now Placht recited from Hewett's letter, ' "the two officers are unable to vouch for the truth and accuracy of any of the information in paragraphs 1–5 of their report." And may I remind you, this refers to the same information as you have testified to here today.'

Larsen was looking even more embarrassed than ever by this stage. 'I am not going to sit here and criticize Mr Hewett,' he hedged and wriggled, 'all I can say is that he is basing his opinion on the British system.'

'But surely,' Placht jumped in, 'under any system, if the accuracy of a piece of information cannot be vouched for it makes it highly unreliable.'

'I will not comment on that, except to repeat that Morgan and Moore wanted to give evidence before this court.'

'Why should they want to do so, if they are unable to vouch for the reliability of their information?'

'Those are Mr Hewett's words, not Morgan and Moore's.'

'So what you are saying is that they disagree with their commander?'

'I will not comment on that either, but as the officer in charge Mr Hewett may not have been as in touch with everyday matters as his men, and may therefore have held different opinions.' His clear implication was that Hewett had made a mistake, was not as competent as his subordinates, and ought to have allowed them to testify.

Placht had removed his spectacles and was pensively chewing on one of the arms while fixing Larsen with a bland stare, his pale blue eyes remained expressionless.

'Who is the informant, Inspector?'

'I cannot say.'

'Does he come from Ibiza?'

'No, he does not.'

'Is he British?'

'Yes, and he is resident somewhere in Britain.'

'Was this person told by my client himself that he was being paid to transport drugs into Sweden in the Jaguar, owned by his brother Christopher?'

'No, he was not.'

'That means that your informant was receiving and passing on second hand information. Indeed it might have been third or fourth hand, perhaps even older still. Is that not so?'

'Yes, that is correct.'

I could not believe that this nonsense was being accepted as evidence. A prosecution witness was supplying information from a man he would not name, whose address he would not give, whose whereabouts he did not know, and whose statement had been effectively disowned by the organisation which had originally received it. I had to pinch myself to believe I was in a court of law in a civilized country.

'The problem,' Placht continued 'is that we are in a Swedish court, and it is naturally interested in this informer. It is apparent, from what you have just said, that his information is second or third hand and is therefore very hard to evaluate, especially since it comes from an individual with a criminal record. We should like you to tell us who your source is!'

'But I cannot do that,' insisted Larsen, 'for two reasons. Firstly for his own security, and secondly for the safety of myself and my family. I will not serve up my head on a platter by publicly naming a member of a British criminal organisation.' An incredible statement for a police officer to make; it was clearly an excuse.

Placht leapt at this admission. 'So this informant is still a member of a criminal organisation; is he?' No comment from Larsen.

Placht now called upon the court to order Larsen to reveal the identity of the informant, stating that only his doing so could permit the so-called evidence to be properly evaluated. If he still refused, he asked for the policeman to be fined or arrested, until he changed his mind.

'I demand a decision on this immediately.'

Looking somewhat perplexed, the Judge and his assessors retired to consider this request. It would be a nice touch, I thought, if Larsen was to end up in the cell next to mine in the Häktet. Indeed, he was looking rather perplexed himself.

In the ensuing recess Placht told John Gorst that if Judge Hellbacher consented to his demand it would be the first time an Interpol Officer would have been ordered to reveal his source by a Swedish Court. However it was not to be. The Bench returned twenty minutes later to state: 'The court finds that Inspector Larsen has justifiable professional reasons for not revealing the name of his source, and therefore will not order him, either on payment of a fine, or a remand in custody to do so.'

'I passed a note to Placht telling him to ask Larsen whether Ronnie Butcher was his informant. He refused, saying that at this stage there would be no point in doing so. He did, however, make one final effort, by asking that the 'evidence' be rejected under the terms of The European Court of Human Rights. Since it was not open to cross-examination, the evidence was not compatible with Article Six, he claimed. This threw Hellbacher, who replied that he would give an answer the following day, once he had had time to consider the point.

I could not help feeling deeply worried by this testimony, the court had seemed far too eager to accept it, but Placht smiled confidently at me when I expressed these fears to him. 'Do not worry. It has no value. It means nothing.' I was not so sure. Against the run of the evidence, Round Four had gone to the prosecution, and Forsberg and Bihlar were looking extremely pleased with themselves.

Next came the cross-examination of four Swedes who, despite being total strangers to me (I did not know any of them from a cake of soap), were described as my 'co-defendants'.

Åsa Hoffman and Prem Lennart Viryo had lived together for many years. It was at their house that drug shipments were unloaded, and to which Mitchell had been leading me on the night of our arrests. It was also apparent that, on each delivery, they would receive a few kilos of cannabis to sell for themselves. They had already been tried and sentenced to five years' imprisonment apiece. Joackim Anderson ran a separate network, distributing drugs supplied by Mitchell, as well as by other dealers. He had been sentenced to six years.

These three witnesses had been called by the prosecution and gave very similar evidence to each other, but with important contradictions as far as the defence were concerned, specifically in relation to the number of runs Mitchell had organized. Each agreed they had never met nor seen me before that day, and could only repeat what Mitchell had told them about me. It became evident that he must have gone out of his way to tell these people that the consignment was being delivered by a serviceman who would be acting as courier for the first time, agreeing to undertake the task not only for money and excitement, but also because he wanted to help his brother. None of them would look me in the eye as they testified and all fidgeted nervously.

Åsa Hoffman was the first to take the stand. She was a beefy girl in her early thirties, dressed for the occasion, somewhat ironically, in virgin white; with long hanging gold earrings. She was not unattractive, had a smiling complexion, and wore her brown hair in a bun. Her eyes seemed glassy, as if she had been crying.

'I want to point out,' she volunteered almost immediately, 'that everything I am saying is total hearsay. It all comes from Mitchell (she called him Lokesh). I know nothing about this man,' throwing a surreptitious glance in my direction, 'and I have never seen him before.'

She expressed surprise that Mitchell had said so much needlessly about the organization of this final run, describing his actions as both unusual and out of character. Apparently he had done so to reassure her, but she had still found it puzzling and unnecessary, especially since he had also told her that she was not to meet the courier under any circumstances. She admitted there had been something strange this time, not only because of the quantity of drugs involved much larger than was normally the case – but because it had been organized in such a hurry, with a new courier that nobody was going to be allowed to meet. When asked, she stated that Mitchell had told her the courier would unpack the drugs from the car. She said there had been six previous consignments, and that on one occasion in 1986 Mitchell had visited her and Viryo in Sweden, accompanied by Prita and her son. She refused to say whether drugs had been discussed during the stay.

Bihlar was looking pleased with events, an almost gloating expression on his face as Placht put his questions.

Viryo was a tall, slightly greying man in his mid-forties, wearing a blue sweater and pale trousers. Deep sunken eyes, behind thick glasses, were the most prominent feature in a long face. He was obviously very nervous, making exaggerated gestures, and looked as though he would have preferred to have been anywhere but sitting before this court giving evidence. He looked a weak character, and there was little doubt in my mind who was the dominant partner in his relationship with Hoffman. He had been the man who had met

Mitchell in Linköping, but I would not have recognized him. He was able to add little to the court's knowledge, corroborating much of Hoffman's testimony, but he did say that he had found Mitchell to be unusually nervous at the railway station, and that he had told him that they would probably have to give the driver of the Jaguar a bed for the night (which of course contradicted what he had told Hoffman about not meeting the courier under any circumstances). He too expressed surprise that Mitchell had found it necessary to talk so much about this new courier. He said there had been seven previous runs.

Bihlar fingered his lips, beaming protectively at his witness.

Anderson was a tall, fat man dressed in a blue denim shirt and jeans. He wore metal, rimless glasses and his brown hair long onto the shoulders. He had a moustache and was in his early thirties. Once again Bihlar was beaming with satisfied expectancy as this man took the stand. His evidence was much the same, the only new item he was able to add was that there had been a total of nine consignments organised by Mitchell since 1985.

These statements can have been of little value to the prosecution, and I took it as an indication of the 'strength' of their case against me that they had to rely on such weak, almost irrelevant hearsay evidence. All it proved was that Mitchell had taken the highly unusual step of telling his contacts too much about his 'new courier'; and that there was a good deal of confusion as to the exact number of drug runs, which if anything helped the defence case by casting doubt on the accuracy of Mitchell's evidence.

Nasim Tervaniemi made an altogether different impression to her three compatriots. She was vivacious where they had been lifeless. She was convincing and clear where they had been fumbling and nervous. She also differed in that she had been called by the defence.

She was an attractive, self-possessed woman of below average height, with long brown hair drawn up into a ponytail. Her eyes were piercingly bright and her prominent teeth flashed when she smiled. She had long manicured fingernails and must have been in her early thirties.

Although pleading guilty to involvement in the ring she was

denying the extent of the accusations made against her. She had yet to go on trial and was, like me, still being held in solitary confinement. She appeared to be bearing up to her ordeal remarkably well. Mitchell was claiming that she was ' . . . in charge of the Sweden end' and that she always took the lion's share of each delivery for herself. In denying these charges she stated that she only worked for Mitchell and normally only handled money, not the actual sale of narcotics. She was ultimately to be sentenced to six and a half years' imprisonment, a conviction based almost entirely on Mitchell's testimony.

She spoke in a clear, strong voice and was not afraid, when referring to me, to look me straight in the eyes, even bidding me a 'hello' when she too explained that she had never clapped eyes on me before. Her evidence was detailed and interesting, supplying a hitherto unseen look into Mitchell's activities.

The two had met each other at an Ashram in India in the late seventies where Mitchell had apparently led a 'flashy existence', living in a large house with a pool, having bags of money, and owning a discotheque. He had been involved with drugs, openly boasting that he was 'heavily into LSD' and mixing with that ilk. She could not say if he had dealt in them, but she suspected as much.

Mitchell had moved to Ibiza in 1984 where, before his arrest in Sweden, he had continued the high life, renting a distinctively large and expensive villa outside San Miguel. Of greater significance, he and Prita had been caught carrying cannabis on a train in West Germany, just prior to taking up residence on the island. For some reason only Prita had been arrested, but she had managed to escape.

'Succeeded in escaping from the German police?' queried Placht, 'that was well done.'

'Yes, I think so too, especially since Prita had lost her passport.'

'What nationality is she?'

'German, but of Polish origin I think.'

As far as Nasim was aware, Mitchell ran the ring in an uneven partnership with Makunda. The cannabis was always collected from Morocco by someone working for Mitchell, who owned a boat. She knew this man was called Poonananda but had heard during the pre-trial investigation of someone else called Chris, but she did not know if they were the same person. Mitchell would pay this boat owner to sail to Morocco to buy the cannabis and deliver it back to Ibiza.

'It was cheaper that way,' Nasim explained, 'the price in Morocco is about half that on Ibiza.'

'What is the price?' asked Placht.

'I do not know for certain but I would guess at between 5,000 and 7,000 Krona a kilo in Morocco, and between 12,000 and 15,000 Krona on Ibiza; but it would depend on the quality.'

'Mitchell claims he paid 27,500 Krona a kilo to Christopher Hayward on Ibiza.'

'Take everything he says with a pinch of salt. I once bought a kilo from Mitchell on Ibiza for 18,000, and he would have made a healthy profit on that.'

Nasim continued by explaining that the drug consignments were packed into cars on Ibiza by a mechanic, and then women would be paid to courier them to Sweden. Makunda and Mitchell would travel up independently, the former rendezvous-ing with the courier on the 'Swedish side' before delivering the car himself to Mitchell. The women would be paid off immediately and normally return to Ibiza by train. This was Mitchell's way of protecting the security of the distributors in Sweden.

'That is why I find it incredible that Simon was being taken all the way to the end of the line,' she stated.

'Did you ever meet any of the couriers?'

'I drove back to Ibiza with a courier once, a German girl.'

She obviously knew more than she was prepared to reveal, refusing to go into greater detail, even to name the people Mitchell mixed with on Ibiza.

When Mitchell arrived in Sweden in March 1987, she had been struck immediately by his nervousness and strange behaviour.

'He was very unlike his normal self. Totally different from my previous meetings with him. He would often telephone Prita who had remained on Ibiza, presumably to check on the run.'

She had been greatly concerned by the state he was in and said that she had therefore decided to opt out of any further involvement with the ring, something she had been thinking about anyway because she had recently opened a small boutique with a friend, and would soon be going to drama school. When she had told Mitchell that she 'wanted out', he had turned on her and threatened:

'I can tell this guy to kill anybody at any time.' And refused to release her.

'This guy,' she said meant Makunda, whom she described as being totally under Mitchell's influence, and although she liked him as a person, she considered him to be very dangerous. She added that her story could be confirmed because she had telephoned Hoffman to discuss the problem, and the police would have a tape of the call since the telephone had been tapped.

Placht ended his cross-examination by asking if there was anything else she would like to add. 'Anything you can think of that I should have asked you about?'

She paused for a few seconds – 'Well Makunda was due in Sweden again at the end of April, so I had been told this run would only involve a small amount of cannabis.' She had therefore been surprised when she was told fifty kilos had been found in the car. She concluded by giving perhaps her most significant piece of information.

She claimed that the police had asked her leading questions during their investigation, even going to the extreme of supplying her with information before interrogating her on a specific issue. 'My case officer, Jan-Erik Nilsson would come up to my cell in the Häktet, sit on my bed and tell me everything Mitchell had been saying, even showing me copies of statements. He would then question me, asking detailed questions which of course he now knew I had answers to.'

Placht bristled on hearing this news. 'Can you be more specific. What exactly did the police tell you?'

'Everything, sometimes in great detail. For example, something about one of the Jaguar's windows and its insurance. I realised then that Mitchell had been talking a lot and making up stories. At first Åsa would admit to nothing and then suddenly she started repeating the same stories as Mitchell.'

'So, what you are saying is that Åsa and Viryo are making

statements to match Mitchell's, having first been given the necessary information by the police, and that these statements are incorrect. How can you be so sure about this?'

'Because I have been shown their reports, and like Mitchell they are trying to reduce their own responsibility, by passing culpability on to me.'

'Could Mitchell and Makunda have hidden hash in a car and tricked someone into driving it to Sweden for them?'

'They are capable of anything, including violence.'

'Have you actually heard of this type of thing taking place?'

'No, not that I know of anyway, but they would be capable of doing such a thing.'

The day came to an end with Forsberg looking worried and Bihlar looking furious.

DAY THREE – *Thursday, 30 July 1987.*

The morning was to be taken up with witnesses called by the defence; the entire afternoon with the cross-examination of Forbes Cay Mitchell.

Chief-Superintendent Basil Haddrell came first. He related to the court the details of the Brian Walsh affair, speaking in a firm, rather clipped voice, full of self assurance. Every inch the experienced professional police officer who had spent a lifetime giving evidence to the courts, he was smartly dressed in a dark suit, collar and tie. His testimony was of great importance, not only because it gave a totally independent and impartial verification of my attitude to drugs and those who dealt in them, but also because he had been granted permission to attend the proceedings by Scotland Yard and my lawyers felt that this permission would certainly have been withheld if there had been any firm indication of my guilt. As such his presence went a long way in offsetting the Morgan and Moore Report.

Major Simon Falkner took the stand to demonstrate how it was perfectly in character for me to travel long distances on impulse, and indeed he felt that there was nothing unusual in, and he had not been the slightest bit suprised to hear of, my journey to Sweden. He gave examples of how, when based in West Germany, soldiers often drive hundreds of miles to go skiing in the Alps for a weekend; and how on one occasion he and I with two other friends, feeling bored one Saturday morning, had suddenly decided to drive to London for dinner. We had set off immediately in the fastest car available, having telephoned our respective girlfriends to say we were on the way, arriving in London late that evening. We had made it back to Germany, tired but exhilarated, in time for first parade at 0800 hrs on the Monday morning. He mentioned another instance in which I had flown out to Greece, when he had been spending seven months sailing around the Mediterranean, on the off chance of finding him to cadge a week's sailing.

It was clear that Forsberg was finding all of this quite incredible, and from the look on his face I was not at all sure whether he believed what he was hearing. He was the sort of mousy little man who did nothing on impulse and who probably planned his holidays months, if not years, in advance. He had no questions for Falkner who finished by saying that he knew me to be ' . . . revolted by drugs.'

Brigadier James Emson gave me a character reference that could only be described as a 'rave' notice. To hear myself being described in such glowing terms was rather embarrassing, and I found myself staring fixedly at my hands clasped firmly together on the desk in front of me.

' . . . Simon Hayward is a first-class soldier and citizen, a man of great integrity and of the highest personal standards, . . . he is robust and brave, . . . it is guaranteed that he will reach the rank of Lieutenant-Colonel . . . '

At this point Tom Placht whispered in my ear, 'Lieutenant-Colonel, Simon? That's not very high?' I explained to him that it was too early to say whether any officer of my rank would progress any further.

' . . . all in all,' the Brigadier continued, 'he has demonstrated unequivocally the sterling qualities necessary for a first-class offer in a cracking Regiment. However, if he has one flaw it is that on occasion he can display signs of otherwise uncharacteristic naivety and gullibility; in other words he can be too trusting.'

He went on by giving a very brief run-down of the duties

of The Household Cavalry and of my own military history. He also supported Falkner's testimony:

' ...it would not be abnormal for a young officer like Hayward to drive a Jaguar at breakneck speed across Europe.' Recalling his own earlier career he said: 'We would frequently drive all night Friday from northern Germany to Switzerland to ski, be on the slopes on Saturday morning, drive back on Sunday to work and feel all the better for it... I've known young officers to club together, drive to London for dinner and drive back to Germany. It may seem a little crazy, but young people with a lot of spirit do these things.'

As to buying cars on the Continent? All soldiers did this, many while based in Britain, because of the savings available. In fact he had bought his own mother a car in this fashion, saving her several hundreds of pounds.

Seeing my mother in court giving evidence was a somewhat harrowing and moving experience for me. To anyone not knowing her she looked small and vulnerable, especially at the times when she gave way to quiet emotion, but this appearance only hid her strong and generous character. It must have been an utterly distressing occasion for her and she handled it with great composure. Someone was later to remark that she had reminded everyone of a tigress fighting for her offspring. That was no exaggeration, and as well as being moved I felt very proud.

The Judge informed her once she had taken her seat that as the defendant's mother she was not under any obligation to be a witness, nor was it necessary for her to take an oath.

'Thank you, I understand that but I am here because I have information that I believe is both of relevance and importance to this issue. I would also like to take an oath.' On receiving no reply from Hellbacher she added, 'In any event I will testify as if I am under oath.'

Looking pale but unruffled she related in a low voice the contents of Christopher's telephone calls to her; of his spontaneous reaction on being told of my arrest – 'Oh my God, the set-up was meant for me and I have passed it on to Simon'; of his eventual admission that he had sent me to Sweden to deliver the car for sale; and finally of his belief that the mysterious Irishman 'Dook' was the mastermind behind the affair and that Mitchell was lying to protect him.

For the first time that week the courtroom was totally silent, with no quiet whispers, no rustle of papers, no noisy movements, not even a stifled cough to break the electric atmosphere as my mother's faint but dignified voice kept everyone spellbound with an account of how she had been threatened – 'Tell Chris that if he even thinks he knows anything and talks, we will kill his boy'; of her efforts to persuade Chantal to leave Ibiza, and of her strong conviction that her daughter-in-law had been murdered to keep her quiet, and perhaps 'pour encourager les autres'; and of her efforts, while on the island, to attend Chantal's funeral, to make enquiries about Dook and the true background into her son's drive to Sweden – endeavours thwarted by everyone's reluctance to say anything beyond warning her to take great care and to mind her own business.

When she described the circumstances of Chantal's death she was unable to hold back the tears. They flowed freely down her cheeks and with her voice cracking under the strain she was forced to pause frequently to dab at her face with a tissue. It was a tremendously courageous performance, and I am not ashamed to admit that my own eyes were not exactly dry at the sight.

My mother made no mention of Chantal's planned visit to London. It would be easy to say that this was a mistake using the benefit of hindsight, but at the time she quite rightly decided that Tarik's safety was paramount and that it would therefore have constituted an unnecessary risk. One death in the family was enough.

Forsberg asked but one question. Had my mother met Mitchell during a visit to Ibiza? The answer was no.

Before Mitchell was brought in after lunch to testify, the Judge re-affirmed his decision to allow Larsen's evidence to stand, and announced that he found the Morgan and Moore Report to be admissible under Swedish Law, quoting Rule of Procedure 35 para 14. This piece of bad news came as no surprise to me, although I looked upon it as a grave injustice, especially so since my lawyers were in little doubt that it constituted a breach of the European Convention.

It soon became apparent that Mitchell, dressed for the

occasion in a loose black jacket and white trousers, considered himself to be something of a card. He delivered his word perfect testimony, initially reading from a prepared text, with an unconcealed air of boredom, slouched deep into his chair, often needling the defence and enlightening the court in a patronizing tone about the mechanics of wholesale hashish dealing.

This was the first real opportunity I had had of studying the fellow at close quarters for any length of time – on all previous occasions our meetings had been too fleeting and I had taken little interest in him. Indeed my first impression was that I must have forgotten what he looked like because I would not have recognized the man sitting before me from Adam. Listening to him now, I found him to be a self-possessed, rather arrogant smart-alec of international proportions, and I was left in no doubt that he was cleverly attempting to reduce his own culpability by passing as much blame as possible onto others, specifically my brother on Ibiza and Nasim Tervaniemi in Sweden. However, to give him his due, he handled himself with a good deal of skill and only those who had thoroughly studied the facts of the case would have realized that his evidence was, at least in part, confused and contradictory. In fact to the uninitiated he would have sounded plausible and convincing.

It was Placht's job now to highlight these flaws to the court. If I was to have any chance of acquittal he had to discredit this witness.

'Simon Hayward,' Mitchell said under cross-examination by Forsberg, 'was the perfect courier. No one would believe this guy was a hash smuggler.' He claimed that Christopher had told him that his brother was in it for the adventure, 'and perhaps there was something about money too, but I was not particularly interested.'

'When did you move to Ibiza?' asked Forsberg.

'I think that it was in August 1983.'

'How many shipments of cannabis did you organize from Ibiza to Sweden?'

'Six,' Mitchell replied.

'Was Christopher Hayward involved in any of these shipments?'

'Yes, in five of them.'

'When did you first meet Christopher Hayward?'

'In 1984.'

He gave a laconic description of his life on Ibiza, how he had met Christopher and how this particular run had been set up. In contrast to earlier statements to the police he now took pains to emphasize that he kept his 'business' activities totally separate from his social life, telling the court that Christopher had wanted to bring me to his house to be briefed but that he had refused to allow this to prevent the possibility of Prita becoming embroiled in the affair. He concluded by recalling that during the drive from Linköping he had become nervous about some cars that appeared to be tailing him:

'To my relief they began to overtake, but unfortunately they turned out to be the police and I was seized and taken into custody.' He recounted this in such a resigned, matter of fact voice that it drew laughter from the public gallery. In retrospect, he added philosophically, it was clear that the authorities had been onto him from the start.

To the suggestion that it was inconceivable a man like Captain Hayward would risk everything he stood for, not to mention severe punishment by smuggling drugs, he reminded the court wearily of the criminal's golden rule:

'If you can't do the time, don't do the crime.' More laughter.

'Have you any comments,' asked the prosecutor, 'about one of the Jaguar windows being broken?'

'I could make a hypothetical statement about it, but it would not be based on fact. However if you would like to hear my hypothesis then I can tell you about it.'

'Yes, I would like that,' replied Forsberg.

Since the witness was clearly being asked to speculate, Placht whispered to me that this would not be allowed by the Judge. However Hellbacher made no move to intervene.

'I have heard,' continued Mitchell, 'that in cases where there is special concern for the courier's safety something is concocted to make it look as if the car he is going to drive has been broken into. Then if he is stopped at a border crossing by customs and the consignment is discovered, he can always claim that the car had been stolen and that someone else must have hidden the hash inside it. This is only speculation, I must add, and I am not actually aware of this practice being tried out. It is therefore, broadly speaking, tittle-tattle.'

'Normally who was responsible for placing the drugs in the car, and who was responsible for their removal?'

'There is no normal method, and I have never been involved in that aspect of the operation. On this occasion, however, I know the courier was going to unpack the consignment.'

I stared with mounting anger and frustration as this wretched fabulist subtly drove yet another nail into my coffin.

'Do you know anyone by the name of Dook?' asked Forsberg.

'I do not know him, I am only acquainted with him.'

'Is it correct that Nasim was one of your receivers in Sweden?'

'She was the principal receiver in Sweden.'

'Have you been good friends with her in recent years?'

'Yes, to the extent that anyone can be good friends with Nasim, then I was a good friend of hers. I had a certain disadvantage, and that was that I am a man. She generally does not get on well with men.'

'Have you ever met Mrs Hayward?'

'Yes, she once came to my home on Ibiza with Chris for a few minutes.'

Forty minutes after Mitchell had entered the courtroom the cross-examination was handed over to Tom Placht.

'How many times have you met Simon Hayward?' was his first question.

'I have actually met him twice; I was physically close to him on a third occasion, at the time I talked to his brother at a petrol station, but then I was unaware who he was.'

'So you have actually spoken to him twice; is it correct that in these conversations there was no discussion whatsoever of any drugs business?'

I held my breath. This was the 64,000-Dollar question. If Mitchell chose to lie now he could sink me. For some reason, that was later speculated upon by the Bench in justification of their decision to convict me, he chose not to.

'I have never discussed drugs with Simon Hayward,' he replied.

'So it is correct then that the information which you received about my client's involvement in this affair, and which you have related to this court, derives from some other person, and is therefore hearsay? '

'Yes, I obtained it from his brother, Chris.'

'Therefore you have no first hand knowledge of any crime committed by Simon Hayward?'

'That is correct,' replied Mitchell.

'Did his brother at any time say that Simon Hayward was aware that there were drugs in the car?'

'I think so, in that Chris said that he was doing it for the sake of adventure, which would imply that he knew.'

'Chris told you that?' queried Placht.

'Yes, he did.'

'But in an interview with the police conducted during the pretrial investigation you said, and I quote from your statement: "Mitchell said to Chris that he was surprised that his brother was willing to drive the car, and Mitchell ASSUMED that he was doing it for money and excitement." Which would mean that Chris never mentioned money or excitement.'

'No,' Mitchell insisted, 'Chris actually told me that, and from it I assumed that Simon knew what he was doing.'

'So you want to alter your earlier statement?' No comment from Mitchell.

I felt enormous relief flood over me. Surely, now that Mitchell had admitted that he had no first hand knowledge of any involvement on my part, and could only repeat hearsay, this would greatly weaken his evidence. I was also fairly sure he was lying about my brother, a fact highlighted by his mix-up and uncertainty over what Christopher had or had not told him, but that was a problem that could be sorted out later. However, even if Christopher had told him I was driving the car to Sweden for the adventure, it did not necessarily mean the adventure of smuggling drugs, he could have meant the adventure, the fun, of the drive itself.

The prosecution case was starting to look decidedly thin, and judging from Forberg's gloomy expression the same thought must have occurred to him.

'You seem to have taken very few precautions with this new courier. I would myself – purely from a logical point of view, if I had been in your situation – have been extremely interested in him; to find out who he was exactly, and to ensure he was properly briefed. But you did nothing! For all you knew he could have been a policeman.'

'I knew he was Chris's brother and that he was a soldier.'

'In that case, why did you not invite Simon to your villa to discuss the run and any security problems?'

'As I have already said, I originally agreed with Chris that Simon should come to my house, but then I thought the matter over and felt that it would be better if he did not do so.'

'Yes, you said that you were not keen on discussing drugs business within your home and in front of your girlfriend.'

'That is correct,' said Mitchell.

'But that did not stop you from discussing this particular shipment with Christopher in your home. Did it?'

'Yes, I know, but Chris was not a stranger!'

'I do not understand. Simon was Christopher's brother, and if you were trusting him with a car full of your cannabis, surely you could trust him enough to bring to your home?'

'At the beginning of this entire business, I did not want Simon to know anything about me. I only wanted to introduce myself to him so that he would be able to recognize my face again, that is why I visited the villa at Santa Gertrudis.'

'Well Mr Mitchell, I can tell you that I, and I am certain this court, find your behaviour extremely illogical. It seems to me that you were taking an enormous and unnecessary risk using a totally unbriefed courier who you must have realized had never done this sort of thing before. And if you did not want him at your house, why did you not take him elsewhere to be properly briefed?'

Mitchell had a sardonic answer to almost every question put to him. It appeared to be his way of avoiding difficulties.

'On previous runs, who were the girls you and Makunda used as couriers?'

'I never employed any girl as a courier,' Mitchell replied.

'Boys then,' asked Placht.

'What do you mean by 'boys'?'

'The opposite to girls?'

'Yes, but "boys" for me means ten year olds.'

'Okay, let me be more exact . . . male persons.'

'No, my only courier was Makunda.'

'Why should Nasim Tervaniemi say differently? She even claims to have driven back to Ibiza with one girl.'

'I do not know. Ask Nasim.'

'When did you meet Makunda?'

'When I was around seventeen, he was my best friend at school.'

'What is his real name?'

'His christian name is Walter, I don't know his surname.'

'You do not know his name? You grow up with a person and you don't know his surname? I find that rather surprising.'

'Yes,' Mitchell quipped, 'when I think about it, it is perhaps a little surprising. Life is full of surprises.'

'When you lived in India, were you involved with drugs?'

'Absolutely not.'

'How long did you spend there?'

'Ten years.'

'What did you live on?'

'Money!'

'Yes, Mr Mitchell,' Placht sighed, 'but how did you make it?'

'I built houses, sold them and made a good profit; I ran a restaurant, sold good food and made good profits; I ran a disco, played good music and made a good profit; I worked as a physiotherapist, gave a good massage and made a good profit. Is that sufficient?' he asked coolly.

'Did you know Christopher Hayward in India?'

'No, he has only appeared recently in my life.'

'Was Makunda there?'

'Yes, he was always somewhere in the picture.'

'Mr Mitchell, the prosecutor has told the court that you have a clean record, but at your own trial you admitted to two previous drug convictions. Is that not so?'

'Yes, at one point in my life I was a dope smoking hippy and along with many millions of other people in the world, I enjoyed smoking cannabis. I was arrested once for possessing two grammes of hash, and on another occasion for four grammes. I have come up in the world since then, haven't I?'

'Are those your only previous convictions?'

'Yes.'

'Well, how about: 22/6/1967. Aberdeen Juvenile Court.

Seven counts of break-ins. Attempted break-in. Attempted theft. Two counts of theft. One of stealing a car. Is this all false?'

For once Mitchell was momentarily lost for words. 'Er, no . . . '

'Why did you not mention it earlier then?'

'Because nobody asked me.'

'I have just asked you, and you lied to me; but no matter. Perhaps you would now like to give the court an account of your other conviction?'

'I do not know what you are talking about.'

'Okay, let me expand. 22/6/1972. Aberdeen. Theft.'

What Placht was attempting to do, and to my mind clearly succeeding in doing, was not so much to highlight Mitchell's petty criminal record, but to prove him a liar.

'When did you meet Dook for the first time?'

'I was introduced to him by Chris in 1985. I have met him since on a few occasions, but as I told the prosecutor I do not in fact know him.'

'Would it surprise you therefore if I told you that Dook's attorney has telephoned me, and that he told me that his client knows you very well, and on the other hand hardly knows either of the Hayward brothers. He even asked for your address so that Dook could write to you.'

'Yes, that would surprise me, especially since about three months ago Inspector Bihlar asked me about a meeting that had taken place at the Royalty Café in Santa Eulalia between the Hayward brothers and an "aggressive Irishman", who I presume was this man Dook.'

My heart leapt when I heard him say 'Royalty Café'. I certainly had not remembered the name of the Santa Eulalia café, and had definitely not given it to Bihlar. Indeed when I had been questioned the previous week by the police no one had known it. Therefore neither could the police have mentioned it to Mitchell, which proved he had independent knowledge of the meeting with Dook. This was proof of a connection between the Irishman and Mitchell. Was it the break we had been looking for? I hurriedly held a whispered conference with Placht.

'You say,' continued Placht after several seconds, 'that you received information about this meeting at the Royalty Café?'

'That is correct. I was asked whether I knew what it was about.'

'What surprises me a little, Mr Mitchell, is that neither the police, nor my client knew the name of this café. Since you obviously do, it must mean that you know more about this meeting than you are willing to admit to!'

A flash of panic crossed Mitchell's eyes. Clearly he realized that he had blundered. His previous calm composure left him, he sat up in his seat and stammered out what must have been the best answer he could quickly come up with.

'Th-there are only t-two cafés in Santa Eulalia. I was given a description of the place, I therefore presumed . . . '

'Tom,' I whispered, 'I never gave a description of the café and there have to be dozens of bars and restaurants in Santa Eulalia, it's a major tourist resort.'

'According to my information,' Placht closed the trap, 'and some of us have actually been to Santa Eulalia Mr Mitchell, there are hundreds of cafés in the area.'

Mitchell was nothing if not a master of ambiguity, and very quick on the recovery. 'That may be, but the question was put to me a very long time ago – I m-might have m-made a m-mistake, but the point is not one of exactly which café it was, but the meeting that took place. And I knew nothing about it.'

'The point is that you know the name of the café when no one else does. That must mean you knew about the meeting, and yet you still claim otherwise and that you hardly know Dook!'

'I do not know him, I am only acquainted with him,' Mitchell repeated for the third time.

'I find that difficult to believe, not only in view of what his attorney has told me, but also because it has been established that Dook left Ibiza in extreme haste prior to the Easter holidays, which must have been around 15 April, and on 16 April you named Christopher Hayward as the 'Boss' for the first time.'

Ignoring the coincidence in timings Mitchell answered: 'Yes, the reason for this is that Chris is my friend, and I do not like squealing on my friends. Unfortunately the police had so much evidence against me, and one or a few of the others had already said that Chris was behind it, and the car was registered in his name, so I was forced in the end to admit that Chris was the boss.'

This in fact was another lie because none of the other witnesses had mentioned Christopher, or had admitted to knowing him. Presumably it was just an excuse to try to hide from his friends that he had turned Queen's evidence, or whatever it was called in Sweden. Placht let it pass and instead changed tacks.

'Mr Mitchell, at your trial you stated that you were only expecting twenty kilos from this run, at the most twenty-five, and therefore thought that half the hashish found in the Jaguar must have been for somebody else.'

'That is correct. I can assure you that we did not have a monopoly on hash dealing in Sweden.'

' Well,' continued Placht, 'let me tell you that Åsa Hoffman has told the police that from this shipment you were to give her 5 kilos, Nasim 20 kilos, and a person in Stockholm the remaining 30. Making a total of 55 kilos.'

'I cannot speak for Åsa, but the problem with unlawful activities is that when people are caught they always endeavour to minimise their own role. It is really a very logical process, and since I repeat that I was only expecting 25 kilos at the most, Åsa must be wrong.'

'That is a highly interesting theory – that everybody tries to make themselves seem as small as possible – because I believe that is precisely what you are doing. You claim to have made six shipments since 1984. Correct?'

'Yes, I believe it was seven including the one with the Jaguar.'

'Correct me if I am wrong, but you also claim to have sold each kilo for approximately 31,000 Krona; and you gave Christopher 27,500 Krona, leaving you with a profit of only 3,500 Krona per kilo which you shared equally with Makunda?'

'Yes, that sounds about right.'

'And on one trip in 1985 you lost 70,000 Krona, did you not?'

'Yes, Samdashi lost it.' This was another member of the

gang arrested in March.

'So, according to your own trial judgement you successfully smuggled a total of 112 kilos over a period of some thirty months. You earned 3,500 Krona per kilo, multiplied by 112 that equals 392,000 Krona. You say you lost 70,000 on the way, that leaves 322,000, which you shared equally with your partner, leaving you personally with 161,000 Krona. If we assume that the cost of each shipment was 5,000 Krona, we therefore come down to a net profit of 131,000 Krona. Distributed over 30 months this would only have given you a net income of 4,300 Krona a month. (About £430.) That is about one third of what an industrial worker earns, with the possible difference that you would not have paid any tax.'

Once again Mitchell was looking nervous. 'Yes,' he said, 'and I was spared working in a factory, plus the fact I only needed to put in a few hours to earn my money.'

'And at enormous risk,' Placht pointed out, 'you were risking up to ten years' imprisonment. Do you really think that we are going to believe you? To believe that you took part in a sophisticated drugs ring involving incredible risk for just £430 a month? That you only made £16,000 out of shipments worth approximately £350,000?'

'Well, as I have said, my actual involvement was in fact very small. I was Mr ten per cent.'

'If your role was so small, why did you not appeal against your sentence? Seven years is a very long time. It hardly seems fair if your involvement was so small. However you almost appear to be happy with it!'

For once Mitchell had no answer, not even a witty one. Placht squeezed him a little more.

'Mr Mitchell, you were visited by two police officers from England in June. Did you tell them that Simon Hayward was due to receive £20,000 for this shipment?'

'I did not tell them that directly. The question was put to me as to how much a courier who undertook such a run might receive. So I made a professional guess at around 200,000 Krona which is approximately £20,000, of course.'

This was an interesting revelation. It meant that the final paragraph on the Morgan and Moore Report was, to say the very least, inaccurate. Far from not prompting Mitchell, as the report claimed, it was now quite evident that the two detectives had done the exact opposite, asking him leading questions and to make guesses. Guesses which they later were to report as facts.

'200,000 Krona,' Placht repeated. 'That figure does not appear to tie in with what you have been earning in this business, which you claim was a mere 160,000 Krona. That is an enormous difference. What you are trying to make us believe is that Simon Hayward was going to earn more on one consignment playing a minor role than you made on six, playing a major role.'

Again Mitchell remained silent. It must have been obvious to everyone present that he was lying.

'I have a better theory Mitchell. One that makes a great deal more sense. Let's talk more realistic figures shall we? I have been told that cannabis costs about 10,000 Krona a kilo on Ibiza . . . '

'Yes, that sounds right, depending on the quality,' volunteered Mitchell.

'Then anybody who buys it on Ibiza and sells it for 31,000 Krona in Sweden will earn 21,000 per kilo. So why not cut out Christopher and do that yourself, it would not have involved any extra work or risk?'

Mitchell was looking extremely unhappy. He just shrugged his shoulders in response.

'If you had done that, and logically speaking it is what I believe you were doing, on 112 kilos you and Makunda would have made over 2.3 million Krona between you. On this final fifty kilos your personal earnings would have been somewhere in the region of one million and fifty thousand Krona. Is that not so, and on this occasion you did not even have to share your profits with Makunda?'

'Yes, but I repeat the hash was not mine; it belonged to Chris. I gave him 27,500 Krona per kilo!' insisted Mitchell. He had managed to regain some of his earlier composure. 'You sit there rattling off these large amounts. If you say they are exact, then okay I accept that. However, the hash trade is something akin to a small scale cottage industry. The growers in Morocco make their profit. Those who own the boats make their profit. Those who help crew the boats make their profit. The couriers make their profit. The distributors make their profit. Certainly there are large sums of money being transferred backwards and forwards, but once all the individuals concerned have received their portion, then it is not so much. No one becomes a millionaire overnight. Organizing a shipment is a large capital outlay and investment. There is the cost of the cannabis; the cost of the men who carry it down from the farms in Morocco to the beaches on their donkeys; the cost of the bribe for the police to look the other way; the cost of the boat and crew; the cost of the beach party on Ibiza who meet and unload the boat; the cost of the car, the packer and the courier. The overheads are high, no one gets rich quick.'

All this may well have been true, but it did not alter the fact that the creep was still asking the court to believe that although he and Makunda took all the risks and did all the work involved in smuggling the cannabis and selling it in Sweden, they still gave the lion's share of the profits to Christopher who did practically nothing, paying 27,500 Krona per kilo instead of 10,000. It was plainly too ridiculous for words, and must have been a very long way from the truth. I felt confident that Mitchell was losing all credibility as a witness in the eyes of the Bench.

'Only a couple more questions,' said Placht. 'Was Captain Hayward due to stay the night in Zinkgruvan?'

'I discussed this with Åsa and Viryo, and we decided to take things as they came. If Simon wished to depart that evening, then he could. If he wanted to stay, he was welcome.'

'Interesting that, because Åsa made it quite clear that you told her she was not to meet the courier. She was quite unambiguous on the point.'

Mitchell just sat there, making no attempt to comment. Placht fastened him with a profoundly menacing stare, his face was impassive, his eyes unblinking as he chewed on one of the arms of his spectacles.

'You see Mitchell, we are somewhat confused by all this contradictory evidence you insist on giving, and by the illogicality of it all!'

Still no comment from Mitchell.

'Why did you talk about the courier to your colleagues on this occasion. Åsa and Viryo have both said that it was the first time they learned who was behind the consignment. Again I see no logic in your actions.'

'The logic in it was that these people were receiving a shipment of drugs which was due to be unloaded in their garage, by a new courier, a man they knew nothing about. So of course they wanted me to tell them something about him.'

'But Mr Mitchell. It is precisely in such things that one is supposed to be professional. Åsa and Viryo were supposed to receive the cargo; they were not supposed to know a thing about the courier, still less who owns the consignment, or who was behind it. Indeed there was no need for them to know: it would only add to the security problems. They have both expressed surprise at you telling them so much. Therefore you must have had good reason for doing so?'

On receiving no reaction Placht went on. 'At your trial you said that at around the turn of the year, and I quote: "I had a feeling that time was running out in Sweden," and you advised Makunda not to drive on this occasion, because it was becoming too dangerous. Was Christopher informed of how you felt?'

'Not that I know of,' replied Mitchell.

'So, if we are to believe what you say, despite these feelings you allowed Christopher to put his brother inside this Jaguar and let him drive to Sweden carrying 50 kilos of hash?'

No comment from Mitchell.

'I would call that a "SET UP", Mr Mitchell. You see it is my opinion that this shipment was not only very different to the norm but also of great interest to you. Let me explain what I mean. For the first time you employ a completely new courier, whom you do not bother to brief despite having every opportunity to do so. You do not even inform your "good friend" Chris that Makunda has pulled out because it is too dangerous in Sweden and time is running out. There is twice as much hash as on previous occasions, and this time you are not going to have to share your profits. And finally, you go out of your way to tell your colleagues in Sweden all about this new courier when it was dangerous and unnecessary to do so.'

'Yes it is rather interesting, isn't it?' mocked Mitchell.

'To return to your own words: "If you can't do the time, don't do the crime" . . . Well it has obviously been worth seven years to you in any case.'

Round Six to the defence?

That evening the BBC Television News at 6.00pm showed a report by Mike Smart:

'Prosecutor Ulf Forsberg says that he is confident of a conviction in the Simon Hayward case, though he will not be demanding the maximum sentence of ten years in gaol.'

Forsberg, on screen in the same report: 'It is not normal to give the courier the maximum sentence. He has only done it once.'

DAY FOUR.   *Friday, 31 July 1987.*

Sitting in the holding cell the next morning waiting to be taken back to the courtroom, I heard the silence suddenly being shattered by Forsberg ranting and raving downstairs. Although I could not hear what he was shouting, the voice was unmistakably his. Hanna Pontein told me later that the kerfuffle had been a tremendous row between Forsberg and Christopher Murray, which almost prompted an exchange of blows and resulted in Forsberg stalking off screaming: 'I HATE THIS CASE, I HATE THIS CASE. I'M SO BLOODY TIRED OF IT!'

It transpired that the altercation had been over an article that had appeared that morning in *Svenska Dagbladet* which quoted Forsberg as expressing scepticism of the fact that evidence supporting the defence had only started to materialize once Kingsley Napley arrived on the scene. The inference was obvious; my lawyers were manufacturing evidence in my favour. Before driving to the Court Murray took the trouble to check these quotes with the *Svenska Dagbladet* reporter who confirmed that they had been taken directly from Forsberg the previous day. On arrival therefore he called Forsberg out of the courtroom and asked him to explain himself; the argument that followed became extremely heated.

Forsberg immediately claimed he had been misquoted, whereupon Murray expressed relief that he would no doubt point this out to the Court and thereby set the record straight. Forsberg refused, saying he could see no reason for doing so as he had been misquoted and therefore had nothing to retract, and stated that Murray obviously did not trust him. Murray in turn informed him that it was immaterial whether or not he trusted him, and as it happened he didn't, and insisted that the article be retracted. The exchange became more heated, with litigation being threatened and eventually resulted in Forsberg announcing in the courtroom at the outset of proceedings that the report appearing in the newspaper was inaccurate and that he had been misquoted.

Unfortunately the expression 'I have been misquoted' was one that we were to hear from the good Mr Forsberg on numerous occasions. Kingsley Napley subsequently established from a press source that throughout the pre-trial period Forsberg had been complaining that they were colluding with drug traffickers and were not to be trusted, and it was for this reason that he would not allow them access to their client. Once more Forsberg's impartiality was called into question.

Richard New, the private detective hired by Kingsley Napley to make enquiries on Ibiza, was the first witness that morning. The Court reconvened later than usual; he took the stand shortly before midday.

New was a vitally important defence witness. He had spent sixteen years in HM Customs and Excise, nine of them in the Central Investigation Division, the highest investigative body in British Customs directly involved in combating narcotic smuggling, before retiring to form his own company. Therefore he was not only able to lend some much needed independent expertise to the proceedings, but since most of the prosecution case was based on speculation he was able to supply alternative theories, using the same facts, based on hard experience.

During the following weeks leading up to my appeal he went on to supply sterling service, visiting Ibiza three more times and discovering a wealth of information which would have been readily available to the Swedish authorities had they but bothered to look for it. Sadly however, on this first occasion although his testimony was of value he had been poorly briefed on the facts of the case and in consequence some of his evidence was given out of context, was open to interpretation and therefore misconstrued by the Bench. Indeed in his judgement Hellbacher was to use some of his testimony against me. To supply the prosecution with additional ammunition is obviously not the purpose of a good defence witness.

New described the profile of a drugs courier as being one of life's failures, desperate for money, willing to take the most risk for the least reward. Through necessity he would have no connection with the principals involved in the organisation in case of arrest; he would also know as little as possible about the operation itself, his role being solely to drive from A to B, usually for a set fee. He would never be responsible for the packing or unpacking of the consignment from the vehicle, and indeed would probably not know the quantity being transported nor the exact place of concealment. He would always be extensively briefed on the dos and don'ts of the trade. For example, have a good cover story; never do anything en route that would attract attention, (like drive too fast); never have anything incriminating on him that might make a customs officer suspicious, (like a large sum of money); always leave ample time for the journey, drive carefully and take things easy. The car would always be low key and unlikely to attract attention, the courier and car should match, their papers should be in order; the route chosen to involve as few border crossings as possible; and finally the courier would never buy anything on the journey involved with the shipment (like a screwdriver).

New told the court that my character, behaviour and travel pattern, indeed everything about me, was entirely inconsistent with that of a drugs courier. In fact I had broken every rule in the book in my mad dash to Sweden, in a distinctive car with no papers, carrying £7,000 in cash not to mention an expensive military night sight, travelling through unnecessary borders. In his view, if I had known what was going on such an experienced and professional ring would never have allowed me to behave in this manner. He also found it inconceivable that I was to have been paid £20,000, an enormous and unnecessarily large sum of money, especially when there was a vast pool of down-and-outs on Ibiza who would have been more than willing to undertake the task for a quarter of that sum. As for Mitchell's alleged earnings? The figure of £16,000 was beyond belief.

When asked if he had ever heard of smugglers breaking a car window in order to concoct a story to safeguard the courier, New replied that he had not only never heard of such a ridiculous idea, but in his opinion to have deliberately done such a thing would have been like putting a sign on the roof of the car saying: 'Stop me, I am carrying drugs!'

When questioned on the Andorran border he answered that he had driven through it a couple of years previously and found it to be lax, with no passport control and normally no searching of cars. As for the main East coast route from Spain into France? He could not say with any accuracy but suspected it to be equally lax, with a good deal of tourist traffic.

Was the Jaguar a suitable car for smuggling drugs? Yes, for substantial quantities of narcotics a large car would be required. Therefore a Jaguar, Mercedes-Benz, or one of the bigger Volkswagens would be ideal. He was not asked to comment on the suitability of a Jaguar for a run to Sweden.

What do you know of the man known as Dook? Little, except that he disappeared from Ibiza with his family very suddenly in mid April.

I was encouraged by the overall tenor of this testimony but my heart sank when I heard New say that the Andorran customs checks were practically non-existent, which in any case was not how I had found them, and that the Jaguar was an ideal car for such a run. Having become used to the Swedish mentality I was very afraid that the prosecution would grab at such remarks. Time would prove me right. Round Seven – a draw?

It was an indication of Bihlar's control over Forsberg that the latter allowed him to cross-examine New, not uttering a word himself. What followed was a joke and only succeeded in making Bihlar look vaguely ridiculous. His questions were general and speculatory to the point that even this judge was stirred into action and eventually told him to stop.

The prosecution now unexpectedly called two Swedish police officers, I believe in an attempt to beef up Forsberg's case and to counteract some of New's testimony. Neither had anything to do with my case, and I had seen neither before. Both generalised about the drugs trade in Sweden. One testified that 70–80 per cent of the drug smuggling by car into Sweden passed through the customs post in Helsingborg; that foreign registered vehicles driven by foreigners were often used; that he knew of no cases in which couriers handed over the car to another courier once in Sweden to complete the journey, as Tervaniemi claimed was Makunda's role. The other supplied almost identical information, which made me wonder if both had not been carefully briefed beforehand. His evidence, like that of his colleague, was merely background material on Swedish police procedure and how narcotics arrived illegally in the country. As such it may have been interesting but was irrelevant to the proceedings in hand.

The final witness of the day was Bihlar himself, and perhaps surprisingly he was called by the defence. Placht wanted to question him about his telephone call with Prita that Forsberg had mentioned in his opening address. He proved to be a somewhat unwilling witness and became deliberately evasive, even obstructive when pushed to reveal the content of his conversation with her. This testimony was to assume great significance at a later date.

'Inspector Bihlar,' began Placht, 'I understand you have spoken with Mitchell's girlfriend, Prita, on the telephone. When exactly did this call take place, and how did you arrange it?'

'I think in June, and I arranged it via Ecko on Ibiza.'

'What questions did you put to her?'

'I had intended to meet her and obtain a statement.'

'Yes, but you were in contact, so what questions did you ask her?'

'I did my best to arrange an interview with her in order to take a statement,' insisted Bihlar.

'What questions PLEASE, Inspector?'

'I asked her if she would come forward but she replied that she was not involved and therefore not interested in doing so. I can understand how she felt, this case is a rather sensitive issue for those living on Ibiza.'

'What more did she say?'

'She refused to answer questions. What more could I do?'

'Okay, so please tell me what exactly you asked and what, if anything, she answered to these questions?'

'I think I asked her to come forward,' Bihlar repeated, 'and I told her it was important for her to do so, but she refused. In the end all I could do was thank her for talking to me.'

'I must repeat my question Inspector. What exactly were the questions she refused to answer?'

By this stage Bihlar was beginning to look extremely perturbed and Forsberg attempted to come to his rescue. 'This call took place a long time ago,' he interrupted.

Thus prompting Hellbacher into one of his rare interventions. 'If the Inspector does remember what this woman said, can we hear it please?'

'I did not get very far with her, nothing came of the call,' countered a very red faced Bihlar.

'I believe Advokat Placht is after something more concrete. What do you remember?' demanded the Judge.

I have to admit I was enjoying Bihlar's obvious embarrassment. After so many months of being at this man's mercy I would not have been human if I had not felt at least an iota of satisfaction at seeing our roles temporarily reversed. I could not help wondering why he was making such a meal out of what should have been a relatively simple matter. Surely it was just a question of reading from the notes that any policeman would have taken from an interview with a potential witness, not to mention from a potential defendant.

Bihlar continued to be evasive. 'I do not remember the call well, I could not get anything out of it at all.'

'Did you not make notes?' asked Placht.

'Why should I have done? Nothing came of it, so there was no information to be noted.'

Placht persisted. 'I have been asking the prosecution to interview this witness since April. Why was I not informed of this call?'

'Because, since I obtained nothing of value from it, I forgot all about it.'

'Yes, but if you had allowed me to be present during the call, together we might have learnt something.' Bihlar had no comment to make to this rhetorical question.

'Let me try to refresh your memory. The prosecutor has

informed the Court that Prita told you she did not want to come forward because she was afraid. Was he wrong in saying this?'

'She said she was afraid. Very afraid.'

'Then why did you not mention this fact earlier?'

No comment, just a hostile look.

'Did you not think to ask her what she was afraid of?'

'Look,' said Bihlar getting angry, 'I do not want to blow this out of proportion, it could have bad consequences for Prita. I think it is wrong if it is the counsel's intention to make her suffer through needless talk. If people are innocent and not involved then they should be left alone. I do not want to answer too many unnecessary questions.'

'But Inspector Bihlar, Mitchell himself has implicated Prita by saying she ran errands and took messages for this consignment. That makes her involved. We also have the testimony of another co-defendant who states that Prita handled money from drug sales, and may also be wanted by the German police. She ought to have been of some interest to you!'

'The information we have does not give us enough of a case against her.'

'But she helped to make this delivery to Sweden possible!'

'That is only your conclusion.' Bihlar was looking increasingly angry and defensive.

'But I am reading from one of Mitchell's statements. That makes it hardly "my conclusion".'

This was incredible. Bihlar was deliberately defending a suspect and had prevented Placht from talking to a potentially vital defence witness. However, Placht was obviously not going to get any further with him, so he changed the subject.

'You also had a telephone conversation with Christopher Hayward. Did you not? When did it take place?'

'On 23 March, ten days after the arrests. He introduced himself and told me that he knew his brother had been arrested. Shortly after that he asked: "Have you got Lokesh?" Realising why he was asking I refused to tell him.'

Bihlar was clearly having no problems in remembering the content of this call, despite the fact that it had taken place three months before his one with Prita. Christopher, he said, had been very shrewd and through general chit-chat had managed to establish that Mitchell had indeed been arrested.

'What exactly does "chit-chat" entail please,' asked Placht.

'I do not remember "exactly" what he said, it was just continuous talk. He did say he was calling from France, though.'

'Did you take notes?'

'No, I did not.'

'Inspector Bihlar, do you mean to tell me that you are the only person to have spoken to the one witness that everyone would like to interview, and you did not even bother to take notes!?' Placht raised his voice in mock surprise and anger.

Bihlar looked more embarrassed than ever and spluttered. 'I d-did not realise the significance at the time,' and then with a smirk he added, 'I do remember that I asked him if he would come forward to Sweden to help his brother and he answered that he was "too busy".'

'I have no further questions,' said Placht. Nor did the prosecutor.

The main issue to remember was that Bihlar had stated under oath that his only contact with Prita had been a telephone conversation in which she had stated that she was not involved and had refused to come forward to be questioned.

Bihlar's cross-examination came to an end shortly before 1500 hrs and was followed by the playing of an hour and a half's worth of totally irrelevant recordings of telephone calls tapped by the police. The conversations were between different members of the 'gang'; some in English, some in Swedish. In most cases the quality of the recording was appalling to the point of incomprehension, so much so that the interpreter got into difficulties and Placht was forced to challenge the translation.

The session became unbelievably laborious. I found myself wondering how they could accept this as evidence? More inconsequential conversations in Swedish followed. I had never telephoned anyone in Sweden, so my voice was not heard, and at no time was my name mentioned or the courier referred to. Had there been some kind of muddle? Were they playing the correct tapes? I exchanged glances of puzzlement with John Gorst, who like the rest of us was showing signs of bewilderment. I thought the Judge would intervene, again he sat back and did nothing. These calls might have been pertinent to Mitchell's trial, or to that of one of the other individuals talking or mentioned on the tapes but they had absolutely no bearing to mine whatsoever. At the very most one part of one tape proved that at one time Mitchell and Tervaniemi had been on friendly terms, but that was not in dispute; and in another instance Mitchell was heard to refer to his 'boss', which of course could have been anybody or even a cover to hide his true involvement from his Swedish contacts.

I lost concentration. My mind started to wander. Bored by these rambling tapes I glanced around the court. The Judge was sitting immobile, as if carved in granite. During the week's proceedings he had seldom intervened, other than to announce intervals or adjournments, or to swear in witnesses, so I had become accustomed to his quiescence. His pronouncements were, most memorably, for the sake of upholding the iniquities of Swedish law, viz. the admissibility of some outrageously irrelevant evidence – like these very tapes. This Judge, all Swedish judges I supposed, presided over proceedings that were more akin to a British tribunal of inquiry looking into, say a planning appeal – informal to the point of matter-of-factness. To me this neither looked nor felt like a court of law. If Hellbacher was ever to lose his judicial appointment, I thought, he would make a most forgettable and inconspicuous bank clerk or accountant.

The assessors looked very traditional dour Swedes. To date they had proved to be a narcoleptic bunch. On more than one occasion I had looked up to catch one or two, if not all of them taking a quiet snooze. They seemed blatantly unashamed of their somnolence. For my part, it was highly disconcerting to see the men and women who were going to have such a major say in my future, paying so little constant attention. I felt that was the least they could do, and I found it mildly annoying that Hellbacher seemed oblivious to their indifference. It is in fact a common complaint and one that periodically receives attention in the Swedish newspapers.

The last tape came to an almost inaudible conclusion.

Everybody, even the Judge I fancy, breathed a collective sigh of relief. Placht was asked if he had any questions.

'How many of these tapes has the prosecutor got?' he asked.

'Fourteen hours' worth,' answered Forsberg, 'but I did not think you would want to listen to them all.'

'No, no!' exclaimed Placht, with more than just a little hint of desperation in his voice, 'I just want to ask if my client's name is mentioned on any of them?'

'No, he is never mentioned,' Forsberg admitted reluctantly. If that was not a ready admission that this 'evidence' was irrelevant, nothing was!

The Court adjourned for the weekend. The next day was to be my thirty-second birthday.

That evening, in a discussion with some of the British reporters who had attended the trial throughout the week, John Gorst was told that they were now all of the view that I must be guilty. Buying a screwdriver when I arrived in Sweden had apparently clinched it for them. They had decided the Swedes would find me guilty because that was the way their system works. On the other hand, they also believed I would have been acquitted in a British court because all the evidence was so second-hand.

Gorst's comment when he subsequently related this to me was: 'God save us from a trial by the monsters of the British press!'

DAY FIVE. *Monday, 3 August 1987.*

During the week John Gorst had made frequent requests for permission to visit me one evening after the day's proceedings, to get confirmation of my confrontation with Morgan and Moore. Barring a few seconds during an interval however, just enough time to say hello, Bihlar had denied him access to me.

'There is no time. The guards are on overtime. The trial must be got through. I have no authority to grant your request. Ask Forsberg.' Excuses, excuses . . .

Gorst tried making a call to Ulf Juhlin, the Regional Prosecutor, for permission, only to be told that he was away 'on holiday'. This had prompted Forsberg to accuse him in press reports published on the Friday, of 'interfering in the case'.

Therefore, on arrival at the court on Monday morning, Gorst handed Forsberg a letter in which he again asked for permission to see me, explaining that he had to return to London that afternoon. Forsberg was obviously annoyed by this approach. 'I will read it later,' he said brusquely as he snatched it away.

During the first interval Bihlar went across to Gorst to deliver the reply. 'No, you cannot see Simon today. It is "no" because something, an event, is having to happen,' lapsing into worse English than usual. Bad English seemed to be his equivalent of having a diplomatic cold. 'Later in the week when the position – is that the right word I am to use? – is changed, or the "event" has transpired, then maybe a meeting is possible.' They knew of course from the letter that Gorst was leaving Sweden that day.

'Simon, you have told the Court that you were delayed on Ibiza because your brother wanted to ensure you were insured to drive the Jaguar. Is that correct?' asked Forsberg.

'Yes sir, it is.'

'Well, I have here a copy of Christopher's insurance policy which clearly states that it is valid for any driver!'

'I am afraid I do not understand. What are you getting at?'

'What I am getting at,' the note of triumph in his voice was unmistakable, I think he believed that at long last he had caught me out, 'is why should Christopher want to check if you were covered to drive his car when the policy is valid for all drivers?'

'But the problem, as I have already explained, was that he did not have a copy of the policy, only a cover note. Therefore he wasn't sure who was covered and wanted to check.'

For the umpteenth time Forsberg was blushing to the roots of his hair. Whether from embarrassment or anger I was not sure.

This was the final day of the trial. For over an hour the judge had been putting questions to me on various points of minutiae, clearing up outstanding queries, finishing with a report that a social worker had prepared on me:

'Good health. Neither alcohol nor drugs dependency ...
sport, travel, books, etc, etc ... No evidence to suggest a
normal sentence would not be suitable, if he is found guilty.
No reason for special treatment.'

Finally the floor had been handed over to Forsberg, and this
must have been one last effort on the latter's part to catch me
out before starting his summing up. If I had left Ibiza on the
date I had wanted to, instead of being delayed by the insurance
problem, I would have had five days skiing in Sweden, not just
two. He obviously thought it important to disprove this claim
in order to strengthen the case against me. His ploy had not
worked however.

If I had found many of the prosecutor's statements
exasperating during the trial, his summing up took the biscuit.
With mounting horror, annoyance and bewilderment I
listened for over ninety minutes as he reeled off a confusion
of misapprehensions, some of which could only be described
as a deliberate attempt to mislead the Bench. He started by
launching a stinging attack on the 'baseless criticism' in Britain
of his country's judicial system. There had been many
'unpleasant elements' in the mass media making deliberate
attacks on Sweden and Swedish justice.

'Some people have even said that Sweden is a police state
and that this trial has been the biggest scandal since World
War Two,' he observed with a glare at John Gorst. 'Well, I
hope it has emerged that Simon Hayward has been given a fair
trial, and has had as much time to make his case as we have.'
(That of course was very much open to debate.)

He was actually being very astute by bringing in a note of
xenophobia to the proceedings. The Swedes being excessively
nationalistic, nothing was better guaranteed to swing the
emotions of the Bench against me.

Then came the real shocker. 'Simon Hayward has given
three separate statements, two during the police investigation,
as I have already pointed out, and now he has provided a third
here in court to impress the Bench, once he had heard my
opening speech.'

What a load of bullshit! What third statement? If Forsberg
thought this he cannot have been attending the same trial as
me.

Before Forsberg could continue there was a knock at the door behind the Judge and an usher entered with a note for him. Hellbacher announced a short break whilst he took a telephone call. As it turned out, this was to be the first stage in Bihlar's 'event'.

'Simon Hayward,' Forsberg began once the Judge had returned, 'has lied repeatedly to this Court.' He then proceeded to give a long list of examples to prove his point; a list involving much speculation and many rhetorical questions. The car theft had been 'staged' to make it look as though Hayward was the Jaguar's owner (something I had never claimed); there had been no confusion over language when the theft had been reported to the Ibizan police (speculation); why had Christopher Hayward not taken his brother's luggage with him to the ferry (illogical)? was it not very convenient that all the car's registration documents had been stolen too?

'We cannot be expected to believe Simon Hayward's account of this theft. Mitchell's is more plausible. Such a theft would only arouse suspicion, therefore no one would steal a Jaguar.

'Christopher accompanied Simon as far as Narbonne, not to buy spare parts for his Lada but to help his brother.' (Just how he was supposed to help me was not explained.) 'They decided to travel via Andorra because it was an easy route for smugglers.' (Speculation.) 'Why hadn't he bought skis there?'

'What would have happened if Simon had missed Mitchell at Linkoping station?' (The same question would have arisen, of course, whether I had been smuggling drugs or not.)

'Why did he buy this special screwdriver? It has been shown conclusively that it was a practical impossibility for the driver's seat to rock. Why did he buy it only after arriving in Sweden? He must have had "hundreds" of opportunities to do so beforehand. Simon's claim that he stopped to find one en route is not true. The video film clearly shows that he did not know the position of the screws . . . so he could not have tightened them in Åstorp, and he obviously could not remember them from when the drugs were packed into the car, nor that one screw could not be reached without lifting the seat cushion.'

'Simon has also lied about staying the night at Zinkgruvan

– this has been amply proven by the testimonies of Mitchell, Hoffman and Viryo.' (Incorrect.)

'Simon cannot be believed when he claims to have come to Sweden to go skiing. He is not a keen skier and it is unreasonable to drive so far for just two days skiing.' (He had no idea how keen a skier I was.)

'The large sum of money he was carrying at the time of his arrest was not to buy a car in Germany.' (What was it for then? I had not spent it, and it had been proved that it had nothing to do with the drugs run.)

'The reason for not telling Sandra of his plan to drive to Sweden was solely because he did not want to involve her in narcotics smuggling.' (Speculation.)

Everyone was becoming restless. There were loud yawns from the public gallery. Nobody had to speak on their feet; perhaps Forsberg wouldn't rabbit on so much if he had to do it standing up? Bihlar, as ever, had his single finger on his lips, calling silently for silence. He kept looking at his watch.

'And now we come to Simon's third statement,' continued Forsberg, 'his specific lies to impress this Court.' He went on to list eleven points, some of them very minor ones, which he described not only as lies, but as new information invented by me during the week's proceedings in an attempt to sway the Judge and assessors, by making my story sound more plausible.

That Christopher needed to repair his Lada.

That I had thought Mitchell was either a Swede or someone who lived in Sweden.

That Christopher was short of money and consequently had needed to sell the Jaguar.

That I had never mentioned the Santa Eulalia meeting before.

That I had never mentioned Dook's name before.

That my departure from Ibiza had been postponed by the insurance problem.

That it had been my intention to buy secondhand skis in Andorra.

That I had asked Christopher for Mitchell's telephone number in Sweden.

That I had never before mentioned trying to buy or borrow the screwdriver en route to Sweden.

That I denied varying the number of seat screws I claimed to have tightened with it.

That Christopher had wanted to check the ferry on the morning we had left Ibiza, before discovering that the car had been recovered, possibly to ensure that whoever had stolen the Jaguar did not try to spirit it off the island before its loss was recovered.

I was infuriated by this monstrous attestation. All of these issues, apart from the last one which I had stated was only a theory while making it, had been mentioned time and again during the pre-trial investigation, some as early as March. Forsberg was either totally incompetent and did not know his brief; or incredibly idle and had not done his homework properly before starting his prosecution; or unbelievably crass and had misunderstood just about everything that had been going on around him since March; or finally, he was simply being devious by trying to strengthen the prosecution case by hoodwinking the Bench. I suspect it was a combination of all four possibilities.

Despite my irritation there was nothing I could do immediately as he ploughed ahead with his bid to damn me. I glanced at Tom Placht and took some comfort from the fact that he appeared untroubled by Forsberg's behaviour. Perhaps all prosecutors behaved in this manner in order to win convictions, and Placht was merely used to it. Looking back I now realise that I should not have hesitated to interrupt Forsberg and put him on the spot by challenging him to support these allegations. If only . . . ?

'We cannot believe anyone who gives three statements,' said Forsberg. 'Simon is lying and all his accounts can be, must be disregarded. HE WAS AWARE HE WAS SMUGGLING NARCOTICS.'

'He was the perfect courier. He and Christopher made the plan together in London in Autumn 1986. He knew exactly what he was doing before he left for Ibiza. He needed the money, he craved adventure, and he wanted to help his brother. The £20,000 was required to maintain him in proper style in his elite Regiment. His financial position was not stable. Sandra was invited to Ibiza as a cover. Simon was present when the drugs were packed into the Jaguar. The theft of the car was staged to make it appear that he was its owner. Christopher accompanied him as far as Narbonne to ensure all went well. He drove at breakneck speed to Sweden to ensure that he arrived on time for his meeting with Mitchell. The special screwdriver was purchased only after passing through the final customs check. Why did Simon buy only this one tool? Because it was the appropriate one to remove the front seats, and all the others required were available in Zinkgruvan. He carried £6,800 on him to avoid arousing suspicion en route.'

'Mitchell travelled to Sweden on 7 March to contact the ring and to tell everyone that the consignment was on its way. How would Mitchell have explained the situation to Viryo and Hoffman at the house if Simon had been innocent? Likewise a very interesting situation would have arisen in the garage where the cannabis was due to be unloaded, if Simon had in fact been innocent and Mitchell had thought him involved.

'Morgan and Moore were reliable, pleasant witnesses who, against their wills, had not been allowed to give their evidence. Assistant Commissioner Hewett had initially granted them permission to visit Sweden to interview Hayward, but had refused to allow them to testify at his trial. WHY? That was a travesty of justice!

'Kriminal Inspector Larsen had stated under oath that Mitchell had confirmed the Scotland Yard report and that the informant had always been 100% correct with his information in the past. Larsen had also confirmed that it was always the courier's job to unload a consignment.' (Not while I had been in court! Another figment of Forsberg's imagination.)

(Hoffman, Viryo and Andersen had given evidence that tallied in all important aspects with Mitchell's. Which was hardly surprising since they had only been able to repeat what he had told them about me.)

'Mitchell is a credible witness. He has given the same statements throughout the investigation. His evidence and arguments are logical and are to be believed.' (And because of Christopher's absence totally unverifiable.)

Forsberg wound up the case for the prosecution, by demanding that a ' . . . very long sentence to be passed.'

The Judge now adjourned the trial for lunch. During this interval Forsberg took the opportunity to hold yet another mini-press conference. Feedback to the defence team later, from 'sympathetic' journalists, was that he did not seem to be very confident; and that even the Swedish reporter from *Svenska Dagbladet* thought the prosecution evidence to be a bit thin. Forsberg had stated that if I was released after the trial today, 'on bail', it would be tantamount to a prospect that the ultimate verdict will be 'Not Proven'.

Tim Myles, of the *Daily Mail*, reported to John Gorst that Forsberg had been having a go at him for 'meddling' and 'interfering' in the case, and asked him for a comment:

'Yes,' Gorst told Myles, 'I have been "meddling". I was elected to Parliament to "meddle". I was elected to Parliament to interfere too. Seeing that the Convention of Human Rights is working is the duty of all MEDDLERS.'

'Do you think the trial has been fair?' asked Myles.

'No, even if the verdict is "Not Proven", the ends do not justify the means by which the Swedes have arrived at them. All this hearsay evidence puts an accused at greater risk of a wrong verdict. In that respect, the trial procedures are both unfair and a threat to arriving at a just result.'

It also did not accord with my sense of justice, to learn some weeks later that Hellbacher had circulated among British journalists during this same recess, and had made off-the-record, and derogatory comments about John Gorst, and how he hoped to evict him from the Court if the opportunity arose, and to charge him with contempt.

After lunch all those arriving back at the courthouse were met by an enormous security presence, greatly increased from the already substantial cover that had been evident all week, whereby everyone was carefully frisked and all bags thoroughly examined before being allowed to enter the courtroom. This turned out to be the second stage in Bihlar's 'event'.

In reply to Forsberg's summing-up, Tom Placht was dismissive of the main body of the 'trivial' evidence presented against his client. He twice read into the court record Hewett's letter giving his reasons for not allowing his officers to attend.

'The fact that drugs were discovered hidden in the Jaguar is not proof of guilt, the prosecution must prove that Captain Hayward was aware of their existence. This it has not been able to do . . . Not one prosecution witness has been able to give first-hand knowledge of my client's guilt.

'There is insufficient evidence for a conviction. There are three possible alternatives with variations here: that the drugs reached Sweden without Christopher or Simon knowing about them; that they did so without Simon's knowledge but with that of Christopher; or that they did so with Simon's knowledge as well. The police investigation has concentrated only on finding support for the third alternative.'

He continued by attacking the way the prosecutor and the police had handled the case, ' . . . with a blind conviction of Simon Hayward's guilt,' and with so many lines of enquiry left uninvestigated, and so many questions left unanswered.

The prosecution case was based on speculation about one possible theory pointing to Hayward's guilt. The defence had been able to supply other equally plausible theories which indicated his innocence. It should not be forgotten that in such cases it is almost always impossible for a defendant to positively prove his innocence, for the obvious reason that the true culprits who had tricked him into taking their risks for them were not about to come forward once he had been arrested. However, to prove innocence is not required, the law clearly states that it is up to the prosecutor to prove guilt.

'I repeat, this has not been done,' Placht said.

'It is better that 1,000 guilty men go free, than one innocent man goes to prison,' he reminded the Bench.

He ran through, one final time, the contradictions and confusions inherent in both Mitchell's testimony and the prosecution case as a whole, and challenged Forsberg to supply proof of some of the more outrageous allegations he had made during that morning.

'On what grounds do you state that the Hayward brothers

planned this run in London in 1986? That Simon Hayward knew what was going on before going to Ibiza? That he was present when the Jaguar was packed with cannabis? That Sandra went to Ibiza as cover? I have heard nothing to support these statements.'

Forsberg could give no answer. Again he was puce with embarrassment.

'As for this third statement? It does not exist, all those matters have been discussed during the preliminary investigation.'

The even tenor of Placht's voice began to disappear, he emphasised phrases, he raised his voice, peering across the tops of his spectacles – one of his mannerisms for stressing a point. All in all it was quite a performance, and totally outclassed the monologue presented by the prosecutor. Despite this, however, my attention was drawn to the British Consul who was asleep, or at least, he was relaxing his eyes by closing them against the daylight. Placht's delivery was back to a more subdued pitch:

'To add up circumstantial evidence and testimony from interested parties may work if a defendant has pleaded guilty to some extent. It does not work if the defendant completely denies all involvement . . . Mitchell's testimony must be regarded as things said in his own interest . . . Larsen's evidence is pathetically thin . . . The Court will have no difficulty in finding my client not guilty . . . There isn't the evidence to support any other verdict . . . It is not a question of beyond reasonable doubt, there can be no doubt.

'If there is any doubt in your minds, any doubt at all, Simon Hayward must go free. I demand that you release him immediately.'

His final words – 'Simon Hayward is not guilty!' He had spoken for exactly two hours.

Forsberg's face had dropped. He looked flushed and despondent; but that could just have been boredom now that his work was finished. I dare say that the past five months had not been that easy on him either, especially to have found himself so far out of his depth. He looked bleary-eyed and fondled his bushy moustache nervously. He had a very morose, glum face at the best of times, which apparently he only enlivened with a smile when talking to the press outside the courtroom. I certainly had never seen even a hint of a smile on his features.

In contrast I was wary of the self-satisfaction being displayed by Bihlar. It seemed to indicate a sense that nothing was going to stop him winning.

After a day of lengthy, often laborious, final submissions by the prosecution and defence, I decided to keep my own as short as possible; resisting the temptation to re-emphasize the improbity displayed by the prosecution and the many flaws in the case against me, and the manner in which it had been prepared and investigated. By way of a contrast I hoped that a short sharp statement from me would be crisply effective.

Just before I was about to open my mouth, Christopher Murray whipped away the few notes I had prepared.

'You don't need those. Speak from the heart,' he ordered. I gulped, my mind going temporarily blank.

'I had prepared a final speech,' I began, 'if indeed it can be called that. However almost everything necessary has been said by Mr Placht.' As Martin Naylor translated this, I winked at Placht – 'You've stolen all my thunder Tom,' I whispered, – he smiled at me encouragingly. 'It seems to me that a great deal boils down to whether or not you accept my word. I am in the lucky position of having a profession I thoroughly enjoy; a wonderful family and many fine friends. I was about to take over a new and very interesting job before my arrest, be promoted and, as a minor aspect with relevance to this case, with a greatly increased financial reward. I ask you,' I said looking straight at the Judge, 'would I have put all that at risk by stooping to the very depths and agreeing to become a drugs courier? I would have had to be mad, stupid or both! I realise I can still lose everything. The prosecutor claims I committed this crime to finance myself as a Life Guards officer, but I have been one for twelve years without needing to resort to crime to finance myself. Why should I do that now, by smuggling drugs? My financial position is getting better, not worse! And in any case, it has always been stable. I am, or rather was, very happy with my life as it is, thank you very much.

'I should point out that if I had decided to start smuggling drugs for a living, I certainly would not have done it in this manner. If I have learned anything from the Army, it is to weigh things up and to look hard before I leap. Would I really have put myself in the hands of a bunch of drug-smuggling hippies, reposing total trust in them? That would have been like putting my head in the lion's mouth. I would have been afraid of every knock on the front door from then on. Once I had completed this first run I could have been blackmailed into doing another and another and another. Would I have driven a smart looking car from Spain to Sweden, dressed in old sailing clothes; at breakneck speed; with a broken window; through more border posts than I needed to; with no fall-back plan in case I missed my rendezvous; with no proper documentation save for those papers that would have immediately shown that I had just left Spain, and would therefore have been guaranteed to raise the suspicions of every customs officer I came across; with almost £7,000 in cash in my pocket, not to mention an expensive military night sight in my suitcase? IT IS ALL TOO RIDICULOUS FOR WORDS!

'May I just remind you that the one time in my life that I have ever come across drugs, I went out of my way to find out who the dealer was, and then went straight to the police.

'I did not commit this crime! I did not know those drugs were in the car! I AM NOT A DRUGS SMUGGLER!'

John Gorst had this to say of my final plea: 'Simon finished abruptly. He spoke most effectively, with all the eloquence that comes from a combination of sincerity and simplicity. In more than a literal sense he was "fighting for his life", and for his liberty. I wonder whether, from his position in solitary confinement, he could appreciate what we all felt about the barbarisms of so-called Swedish "justice". I also wonder whether he was in blissful ignorance of the factors weighted against his receiving a fair verdict. I wonder how much he knows about what Forsberg has said of the case to the press, how much he has done to tip the scales of justice *outside* the court? Does Forsberg think the Bench are unaffected or influenced by those extramural activities? The spirit of the European Convention of Human Rights is looking rather thin after these five days in Stockholm.'

There was a moment's silence when I finished. The Judge stirred.

'The Court will now retire to consider the case in private.'

I caught my mother's eye, we exchanged smiles. I was taken back upstairs to the holding cell, feeling certain that I would soon be free – that the ordeal was finally over.

When I had gone, the courtroom scattered into expectant groups, everyone kept glancing at the heavy wood-panelled door through which, at some moment, the Judge and assessors would re-emerge. My mother was 'treating' her eyes, it was an agonising moment for her, my aunt was standing protectively at her shoulder. A Swedish journalist approached and asked for an interview with her and ' . . . your son when he is released'.

The British Consul was chatting to Bihlar. Reporters were mingling, trying for interviews. Amongst my supporters there was an apparent air of optimism. Tom Placht had out-shone Forsberg at every step, the prosecution case was looking weak, there was so much doubt about everything that the only reasonable, not to say fair, verdict had to be one of not guilty, or 'not proven', or whatever the Swedes cared to call it.

Sitting alone in my cell, I too was finding the waiting nerve racking. The butterflies were attacking my stomach for the first time. During the trial the sense of unreality had persisted, I had felt totally detached, as though watching the proceedings on television. Now the moment of truth had arrived – downstairs at that very moment six total strangers were debating whether or not to send me to prison. It was enough to give anyone the jitters.

The Judge returned, followed by his 'flock', I was brought back to the courtroom. (My fingers were crossed, I actually prayed.)

'The District Court will not announce its judgement today. It will do so on 10 August, in a week's time, at 2 pm. The judgement will be made available in the office of the District Court in Uppsala. Until it is issued, Simon Hayward is to remain in custody.'

That was it. The trial was over. No relief. No offer of prospects. Conjecture remained. So did the suspense; and a gnawing angst. I was allowed a few brief seconds to say goodbye to my mother, Myrtle, John Gorst and James Emson.

There were congratulations for Tom Placht and thanks for Christopher Murray. But congratulations for what? I did not know where I stood; I was still in custody. My mother inconspicuously held one of my fingers as I did the rounds. There were wishes of 'good luck'; finally I was led away.

For my mother there were microphones and TV cameras to face. She was brave, and smiling even. But inside . . . how must she have felt? All this had gone on for months. There had been disappointments, refusals of visits to me, threats, revelations, Chantal's death, Tarik's future and safety to worry about, the huge legal fees; and the emerging possibility of complicity on the part of her other son Christopher with the agony of the realisation that he might have condemned an innocent brother to prison. And even now the verdict hung in the balance. Where was Christopher? Why had he not come forward? What would happen to him when he was found? Was he alive? Had they got to him, as they had got to Chantal? Or was he being held somewhere under duress? Endless uncertainties, pressures, questions; and throughout it all my mother survived, tenaciously clinging to her sanity and her beliefs. Determined to get to the truth and to win for both her sons.

They had not quite finished with me. There was one surprise yet to come. It was not to be a pleasant one. My guards that day were two men and Pia, a striking blonde girl in her early twenties. It could only have happened in Sweden. It would almost have been worth making a break for it, only to be chased and captured by Pia.

We came to the end of the 'corridor of sighs'. Normally, as on previous evenings, they would have handcuffed me, marched me straight to the waiting car, and driven me back directly to my cell in Uppsala. But not on that evening. Instead of going straight ahead through the metal doors into the underground carpark, we did a smart right turn into a waiting lift which whisked us up to the ninth floor of the Kronoberg Building. A Häktet awaited me.

I was immediately aware of an unhealthy difference between the attitudes of the Kronoberg warders to those I had become used to in Uppsala. Two uniformed men were waiting for me, wearing rubber gloves.

'Empty your pockets,' one of them barked. I did as I was told. 'Go into that cell and strip. Pass me out your clothes.' I turned to Pia, who was standing hesitantly by, as one of her companions signed me over.

'What is going on? When are we leaving for Uppsala?' She just shrugged.

With a growing sense of dread, I entered the cell indicated and stripped. The two gloved guards stood in the doorway, searching each piece of clothing as I took it off. Reminiscences of that first night in custody came flooding back to me; with the memories came the old sense of uncertainty, the nagging fear. It is difficult to describe adequately the emotions one feels being so totally in someone else's power; of being forced into a situation with no explanation of what is happening and why it is happening; especially to have been on a high one moment, with great expectations, to find those hopes so utterly dashed the next.

I sat naked in the tiny search cell. A face appeared at the observation hatch, set into the door, which was opened with a jerk, my clothes returned to me in an untidy heap. I dressed, and sat back down. The cell was covered in graffiti and smelt of stale body odour. I felt incredibly depressed. The door opened again. Pia came in. She leant over and kissed me hurriedly on the cheek, an unexpected, touching gesture and one that obviously shocked my new warders.

'I can't tell you what is going on, but you will not be coming back to Uppsala tonight – if ever. I'm sorry. Goodbye.'

This was the third stage of Bihlar's 'event'.

Seven

The Häktet at Kronoberg is as clinical as it is enormous, totally impersonal. It is scoured of everything that is not absolutely necessary, a massive archive with a human being in each deposit-box. It is silent in the long corridors, despite the fact that hundreds of people are imprisoned there.

In each corridor there is a special punishment cell, devoid of all furnishings other than a metal bed fastened to the centre of the floor. To this bed difficult or noisy inmates are strapped naked for hours on end, without attention, until they decide to cooperate. The cell is soundproofed to dampen the clamour of its victim's screams.

On the roof, as with all other Häktets, are the exercise pens, built in this instance in a petal formation around a guardroom from where three warders keep watch over their charges. Kronoberg being on a hill, there should have been a good view from these pens over the surrounding roofs and streets, except that a high screen had been erected to prevent such a possibility. Any inmate attempting to climb up the side of his (or her) pen to catch a glimpse of the outside world is immediately returned to his cell. The same thing happens if he tries to communicate with his neighbour by calling out.

I was to spend five months in Kronoberg. An experience I will never forget.

As soon as reception formalities were completed they took me to a cell. I still did not have the faintest idea what was going on. The guards appeared to be equally in the dark.

'When am I going back to Uppsala?'

'We do not know. Maybe tomorrow, maybe never. Who cares!'

My new cell was almost identical to all the previous ones.

Same fitted pine furnishings; same low bunk with its thin mattress. A small black and white television, and radio. On the plus side the window blind was open, giving me an oblique view of a side-street T-junction with a shop that looked as though it sold some type of musical material, and a building site. On the down side the cell was filthy. It stank of its previous owner (and probably the hundred before him) – a powerful and foetid smell of stale urine and sweat – who judging from his hair, specimens of which he had left behind in copious quantities, must have been touched with a mighty big tarbrush. To make matters even worse blood had been smeared into a great patch on the wall directly above the bunk. I began to itch uncontrollably. There were clean sheets and a towel, but the mattress was foul. The itching increased.

I was exhausted after the day's 'adventures', not to say somewhat demoralised by the non-result of the trial and finding myself so unexpectedly in this terrible place. There was nothing else to do, so I undressed and climbed into bed. I dozed fitfully until it was time for the evening's TV News. The end of my trial was the main story – people leaving the court, a short interview with Forsberg. Everything, needless to say, was in Swedish, I could not understand a word. Then a new face appeared, an elderly man being interviewed outside the police station at Uppsala. He was obviously a senior police officer I caught my own name being mentioned and then the letters 'SAS' several times. The scene switched to show the massive security presence surrounding the trial. There was obviously some kind of major fuss. I wondered what on earth was going on.

I slept. The cell door suddenly swung open. A man in a white coat appeared above me. A doctor? Without a word he pulled back the bedclothes and jerked up first my left, then my right arm, and studied them both carefully. His manner was rough and discourteous – I was a nothing, deserving no sympathy and no explanation. Satisfied that I was not an intravenous drug abuser, he jotted some notes on a clipboard and then disappeared as abruptly as he had come; leaving me staring in surprise in his wake, not sure if I had not dreamt the entire episode.

The next couple of days were chaotic. Clearly nobody had the faintest idea what was going on. Initially I was told I would be returning to Uppsala immediately, then that the transfer had been postponed, and finally that I would be remaining at Kronoberg indefinitely. During this period I was refused permission to take a shower as the 'warders had no time to supervise me', nor was I allowed to change – my clothes, which had been delivered from Uppsala, were not passed onto me. I was still wearing the suit in which I had been dressed on the last day of the trial. No visits were permitted, although at the time my mother and Kingsley Napley were desperately trying to arrange one. When I was eventually allowed to telephone Tom Placht (by law detainees cannot be prevented from calling their lawyers) it was only to be told he had gone on a week's holiday with his family, something I did not begrudge him, despite my circumstances, because he had been working for me without a break for five months. However, having said that I still could not help feeling deserted. I did not know it at the time but Hanna Pontein was also being refused access to me, as were members of the British Embassy staff – indeed I was not even allowed to call the embassy, which again is every foreign prisoner's right.

Whereas I cannot claim to have enjoyed my stay in Uppsala, I had at least grown accustomed to the regime there and to the officials who had looked looked after me: the conditions I was now experiencing made it seem like a holiday camp. All I could do was grin and bear it. I consoled myself with the firm belief that none of it would matter in the long run because in a week's time I was going to be released. I would be free. I could put up with the very worst of conditions imaginable (which mine most certainly were not) until then.

The reason for my sudden transfer to Kronoberg became evident a week later when finally I was able to make contact with Placht, although it took somewhat longer for the combined efforts of my lawyers to get to the bottom of the affair.

When Judge Hellbacher had been called from the courtroom it had been to receive a telephone call from the Uppsala police. He was informed that there were four members of the Special Air Service on their way to Sweden to release me, and as a consequence it was decided not to risk driving me back to Uppsala but instead to move me to the top security facilities at Kronoberg.

The initial account given by both the Head of the Uppsala Police Force and Inspector Bihlar was that this information had been telexed to them by New Scotland Yard. An announcement to this effect was made on Swedish Television, which explained the hullabaloo I had witnessed on the box during my first evening at Kronoberg, and was widely reported in the national newspapers in both Sweden and Great Britain.

On hearing this Sir David Napley requested an immediate interview with the Metropolitan Police Commissioner, Sir Peter Imbert, and later the same day New Scotland Yard put out a press release categorically denying that it had either received or supplied any such information. A spokesman was quoted as saying:

'Checks have been made with all relevant squads (including the NDIU), and with Interpol, and no one has any knowledge of this reported plot.'

Similar enquiries were made of the SAS, and all members were accounted for.

Although Bihlar claimed the information had been received by telex he could not produce it when asked to do so, which forced him to climb down and change his account by stating that the tip-off had actually been received in a telephone call. Eventually he watered this down still further to the degree that he began to claim that this telephone call had not originated from Scotland Yard but from an off-duty junior officer in the Metropolitan Police, telephoning unofficially from outside New Scotland Yard. However this too received a categoric denial from the British Police.

Finally, in response to demands made by Tom Placht, the Uppsala Police Chief made an official statement in which he claimed that the information had come from, of all places, '. . . an informer in Northern Ireland', and that the plot to rescue me had not involved members of the SAS but four soldiers from The Life Guards. Since my Regiment had no connection with the Province at the time, this last pronouncement proved the lie.

The fact that Bihlar had told John Gorst that an 'event' was about to take place that would prevent him from visiting me, before the Judge received the telephone call also proves that Bihlar was involved in the plot. How else did he come to have prior warning of the call? If everything had been above board, why did he not inform Hellbacher immediately instead of waiting for the 'dramatic' telephone call? And why did the Uppsala police lie about the origins of their information?

Remembering Bihlar's obsession with the SAS throughout the investigation, there is absolutely no doubt in my mind that the entire episode was nothing more than a fabrication – made in conjunction with other police officers, designed to discredit me in the eyes of the Court which was about to consider its verdict. It would certainly have prejudiced my chances because, after all, innocent men do not need rescuing.

The consequences of this fictitious 'rescue' bid were to haunt me time and again in the months ahead, despite being exposed for the sham that it was.

On 6 August my circumstances started to improve. Once it had been established that I would be remaining in Kronoberg I was allowed a change of clothes, and a few personal possessions in my cell. I asked to be moved to a clean one, but the warder I was talking to just laughed and replied that all the cells were in the same state. Instead he supplied me with a mop and cleaning equipment, and told me to get on and disinfect my 'new home' myself.

On the same day my mother and Sandra, who had flown out to Stockholm with a friend to lend moral support, were able to visit me for half an hour, with the indomitable and ubiquitous Bihlar in attendance, needless to say. It was an unpleasant surprise seeing him because I had been led to believe that now the trial was over I would be allowed unguarded visits, which is usually the practice in Swedish prisons. Not a bit of it however, the same rules applied as before, and even though everything was now out in the open, we were not allowed to discuss the case in any way, shape or form. Despite Bihlar's presence it was wonderful to be with the 'girls' again and we all felt and could not help but to express great optimism about the pending verdict; due to be announced in just four days.

I spent those days analysing the trial and the evidence both for and against me as objectively as I could, from every conceivable angle, over and over again. I came to the conclusion, time and again, that the Court would have no difficulty, if it so wished, in finding me not guilty. There just was not the evidence to support any other verdict.

If I was found guilty, I would only be able to think that those sitting in judgement on me had been hearing an entirely different case from the one I had been listening to, and that they had been prepared to believe the implausible, the unverifiable, the unprovable, indeed the unbelievable. I would have to conjecture that there might have been some extraneous factor, not raised in court, that had influenced their judgement; and I would have no alternative but to conclude that considerations that should have played no part, such as speculation, hearsay, unsubstantiated testimony, and un-probed sources had been given weight without proof or even plausibility. That if there had been any doubt in the mind of the Bench, it had been exercised in favour of saving the face of the State's Bureaucracy and not for the benefit of the accused.

During their visit I had explained to Sandra and my mother what I could see from my window, and its exact location on the top floor of the building. Each day at set times for the rest of the week they would appear and stand on the corner by the shop; waving and transmitting 'positive thoughts' to me. By way of reply, because they could not see me, I would flash my cell light on and off repeatedly. Any contact with the outside world was a tremendous morale-booster.

The evening of the 9th was wet and windy, with a steady drizzle falling to discourage walkers from venturing out. At the allotted time, I seem to remember it was 1900 hrs, Sandra and her friend Bindy N arrived at 'our corner'. They stood side by side, under umbrellas, wrapped up in their coats, looking up at my window, waving and blowing kisses of encouragement. We all felt so sure of my pending release on the morrow. Then, stepping into the middle of the street, they broke out into a spontaneous and impromptu performance of 'Singing in the Rain', twirling their umbrellas and dancing in unison, kicking their legs high up into the air, and occasionally collapsing into each others arms in fits of laughter. I was laughing too – our spirits were high, the nightmare was almost over, tomorrow I would be flying back to England with them. No more Inspector Bihlar, no more mistrust, no more uncertainty. Back to my family, my brothers, my friends and my Regiment.

Time passed slowly the next morning. I agonised over every hour. At eleven o'clock I saw my mother outside, followed by a pack of reporters and cameramen. They filmed her as she stood on the corner and pointed to my window, making me feel certain that at any moment, just as in Uppsala, guards would burst in on me and close the blind; but nothing happened. A good omen?

At half past one I tidied up my cell, its next occupant would at least find it clean, and laid out my suit, clean shirt and tie, on the bunk ready for a quick getaway as soon as the verdict was announced. I surveyed my domain – this was the last occasion I would ever have to spend time in a place like this, or so I thought. The stomach butterflies were buzzing madly once again; I sat on the bunk, then on the chair, I couldn't keep still. I paced the floor – back and forwards, back and forwards.

Two o'clock came. Nothing! Five minutes past two – I could hear the sound of approaching footsteps in the otherwise silent corridor beyond the metal cell door. A jingle of keys, the door swung open. The adrenalin was pumping. I did not know who to expect – Tom Placht? The prison director? Forsberg? In the event it was only one of the warders, holding a memo slip in his hand. I jumped up to greet him. The hope, the anxiety, must have been all too evident to him on my face. He smiled at me, a half laugh. Another good sign? He held up his hands, I remember quite distinctly – the scene indelibly printed on my mind – his palms towards me.

'Steady, steady, be calm,' he ordered in strongly accented broken English. He read from the note, smiling as he did so.

'You have been found guilty. You are sentenced to five years, minus 149 days. To be followed by deportation for life.'

My first reaction was that I could not have heard properly. Why was this chap smiling? It was a joke. That was it, he was joking. It was a sick joke – he was playing with me.

'What,' I gasped, 'that cannot be. Tell me again please.'

He repeated the sentence, adding. 'Follow me, the Assistant wants to see you.'

I felt stunned. I don't know what it must be like to be hit by an express train, but the sensation could not have been that different to what I felt in the moments immediately following this grinning cretin's announcement. Total numbness. My legs felt like jelly, they refused to move under me. Unreality returned. THIS JUST COULD NOT BE HAPPENING TO ME!

The guard took me by the shoulder and led me out of the cell, leaning me against the corridor wall as he relocked the door after us. 'Guilty,' I kept repeating to myself, 'Guilty. FIVE YEARS! It cannot be? FIVE YEARS!' Perhaps this Assistant, whoever he was, would tell me the truth; tell me that the guard was just having a bit of fun at my expense. But it was not to be. Reality dawned; I had found guilty; I had been sentenced to five years' imprisonment; I would not be flying home that day. At least the Assistant, who turned out to be the man in charge of administration on the wing, had the grace to be sympathetic when he confirmed the bad news. He let me telephone Placht, who promised to drive over immediately.

The fact that I had been informed that I was going to have to spend the next five years of my life in prison by a sneering warder and not by the judge who had tried me only added to the sense of disbelief. It seemed a very odd way of passing sentence, and was I felt, taking egalitarianism to extremes. The entire process of announcing the verdict and sentence was handled impersonally to the point of cruelty. However, if it was harsh on me, it was far worse for my mother and Sandra. They were to hear the news in the worst possible fashion.

They were in my mother's hotel room shortly before two o'clock when a reporter, one of many who had gathered in the hotel lobby, telephoned.

'Mrs Hayward, why don't you and Miss Agar come downstairs to hear the good news with us? We have champagne on ice.'

For some reason they agreed, no doubt because like everyone they were brimming with confidence, and therefore took the bad tidings, via a telephone call from Placht, in public under the full glare of the media.

'Oh my God,' whispered my mother barely audibly, 'I'm afraid it's bad, they have found him guilty.' And then quickly regaining her composure as best she could, biting back the tears, she turned to the reporters, who were eagerly noting her every reaction, and told them: 'We will appeal straight away. My son is innocent. We must get him home. The fight starts now. This is unbelievable!'

Later in the day Tom Placht made a press statement confirming that an immediate appeal would be launched. In it he said:

'I have just spoken to Captain Hayward, and he is deeply shocked. We agreed immediately that we would fight on. I can tell you that my client is furious. He cannot believe that they could do something like this to an innocent person.'

He added that he had not yet had time to study the Court's detailed verdict in full but his initial reaction was that the 34 page judgement document seemed 'biased'. Indeed he was to tell me later, having examined it in detail, that as far as he was concerned it was not an appreciation to determine a verdict, but instead a justification of a foregone conclusion.

'This sentence is based on circumstantial and weak evidence,' he told the journalists, 'I can only conclude that the courts are more willing to accept circumstantial evidence in drug cases compared to other crimes. The Uppsala District Court has ignored all the many circumstances in Captain Hayward's favour. There was one assessor who wanted to acquit my client and has been critical of the evidence used to convict him. We agree with this gentleman.'

At the same time John Gorst was condemning the verdict, in the United Kingdom, branding it 'A very grave miscarriage of justice'. He went on to say:

'It is only one more in a long list of violations for which Sweden is now notorious in the eyes of civilised Europe. This case will go to the European Court of Human Rights, if Hayward is not acquitted on appeal ... Sweden is at a stage of constitutional developement which owes much to the fact that it is neighbours with the Russians ... The country has got to do a great deal to improve its judicial procedures if it wants to stay in the community of Europe ... The Swedish concept is that what is expedient for the State is more important than the rights of the individual ... It is a strange paradox that a country with an enlightened social policy should have a judicial system and treatment of suspects which stems from the "Dark Ages" ... '

Sir David Napley gave an expert legal view, describing Sweden's judicial system as 'deplorable'. 'By no stretch of the imagination could one describe as fair the system that has led to Captain Hayward's conviction.'

The day after my conviction I was allowed a visit from my mother, Sandra and Bindy. It was a difficult and tearful time for all of us, made even more trying by the presence of a totally unsympathetic and clearly delighted Inspector Bihlar. We were too shocked to say very much, just quiet words of encouragement to try and help each other, and determination to carry on the struggle to the bitter end, and ultimately to win.

'A press conference has been arranged,' they told me, 'you must speak to them. We must highlight this injustice.'

To be honest it was the very last thing I felt like doing but I accepted its importance, and when the reporteres filed in after our half hour visit was over, my sense of outrage took control. There were six of them, both Swedish and British, and together we filled the small visiting room. It was my first ever contact with journalists who wanted to interview me, and on the whole I found them sympathetic, and well practiced in their trade. Julian Isherwood, the *Daily Telegraph* correspondent for Scandinavia and someone I was to get to know fairly well, acted as spokcsman, with the occasional additional question being interjected by one of his colleagues.

He started, as far as I can recall, by consoling with me on the verdict and apologising for having to bother me at such a time. I in turn tried to sound as cheerful as possible, cheerful being anything but what I felt, and to appear as strong and as optimistic about the immediate future as possible. I wanted to show them that I had taken the bad news on the chin and was not going to let it prevent me from continuing the fight.

'Now that you have been found guilty, do you still profess to be innocent?'

'Yes I most certainly do, more so now than ever. I was totally convinced that I would be walking free on Monday, and I was stunned when I heard I had been given five years.'

'What do you think of the sentence?'

That was a stupid question, of course I thought it was

terrible. Did he think I was looking forward to being sent to prison? I wanted to curse, to scream and shout out that it stunk, but . . .

'I think that in anyone's book it is a very heavy sentence, but for an innocent man it is a totally devastating one.'

'You have been in solitary now for five months. How are you coping? Are you going to crack?'

'No way. What good would that do? I hope to be free in another month or two. I sat through that trial and I did not hear one scrap of real evidence against me. I have been convicted on hearsay, and hearsay alone; and that, if nothing else, gives me hope and strength for the future. If there is any justice to be had in this country, I will win on appeal. I have coped, I think, fairly well since my arrest. I am just going to have to carry on coping for a while longer, that's all.'

'Do you suffer from depression?'

'Yes, of course. But I get over those periods.'

'How are you going to feel when Sandra and your mother return to England?'

'It's just going to be a little more lonely.'

'What do you miss most, being in prison?'

What did I miss? I missed everything. All the things we all take so much for granted. I paused to consider:

'Long walks, freedom, and a good glass of whisky,' I smiled at the thought, and then turning to Sands, 'and Sandra of course.'

'How are you feeling? What's your physical condition like?'

'Not as strong as normal, but good enough. I have lost about one and a half stone, and I get the odd severe headache. I have been seen by a doctor, or so they say; a man in a white coat walks into my cell and asks – "How are you feeling?" I say "well", and out he walks again. No examination at all.'

'How about your future with the Army?'

This was a difficult one, I had to think for a moment. 'As far as I know I am still in the Army. I hope one day to be able to rejoin my Regiment and start again. However I can understand why they have now stopped my pay.'

'Do you think your conviction has resulted in a blemish on the reputation of The Life Guards?'

'No I don't think so. I certainly hope not. Probably on me,

yes. I think it is something I am just going to have to live with.'

'Surely you are going to have to consider your future as an officer?'

'Yes, of course. I have already offered my resignation, but it was turned down. I am going to have to think about my position and future once I am over the next hurdle.'

'What has your treatment been like so far?'

'I have no real complaints to make about the treatment I have received at the hands of the Prison Service, apart, that is, from the solitary confinement. However it is another matter when you consider the attitude of the police and public prosecutor.' I looked straight at Bihlar, whose eyes were blazing with anger. 'Certain officers,' everyone in the room knew exactly whom I meant, 'have been completely blind to any avenue of investigation that even hinted at my innocence. They have been interested in establishing guilt and nothing else; and have followed avidly any course that could have led to that conclusion. For instance why have they not conducted any enquiries on Ibiza, and why have they not interviewed important witnesses?'

'What do you think about the actions of those two NDIU detectives?'

'I believe they overstepped the mark, and acted beyond their authority. I would criticise them in the same way I would criticise two of my own soldiers who overstepped the mark. I think that their behaviour was unprofessional and beneath contempt. I must emphasize that I have nothing whatsoever against the British police in general, indeed I have the utmost regard for them. Their reputation speaks for itself, and I have worked with them in both England and Northern Ireland, and I have always been highly impressed.'

Finally the questioning turned to Christopher. It was apparent they wanted a condemnation of him from my lips. They were going to be disappointed.

'The prosecution believe your brother is heavily involved in this affair. He is perhaps the one person who could clear your name and yet he has remained silent and has failed to come forward. What are your feelings towards him? Do you know where he is?'

'I have yet to be convinced that he is behind all of this. There are just too many facts that point to the contrary, or cannot be properly explained. However I don't now why he has not come forward yet. I think it may be because he is afraid to; maybe he is being threatened. I just do not know, and I do not know where he is.

'This interview will be broadcast worldwide. Perhaps he will hear it. Have you any message for him?'

'No, I have no message. It is up to him. He knows what he must do.'

The final question. 'What hopes for the future?'

'I am innocent and therefore I am hopeful. I have to be.'

The interview was written up on the front page of almost every national newspaper in Britain, and broadcast on both television and radio. Not that I was allowed to read any of it at the time.

The old game started anew. The endless waiting; the long silent hours; the loneliness; the psychological pressure. The regime at Kronoberg was much harsher than at Uppsala, probably because the warders had hundreds more prisoners to cope with. Apart from the daily ration of an hour in the exercise pens, and one visit a week to the prison gym, I remained in my cell. There was no Inger to take me out of my solitude for the occasional chat over a cup of coffee. There was no manual work to keep me busy when I needed a break from reading. On the whole, initially at any rate, the guards were off-hand, uncaring and grumpy. I was just a number to them – 9.1.24. (pronounced – nio ett shugo-furrer), never a name, I suspect not a person. I had to concentrate hard to remain mentally active, but once again sleep became my safety valve.

Being so far from Uppsala, Tom Placht was unable to visit me as frequently as he had before my transfer, with no question of purely social calls. Indeed visits in general became a problem. Sandra was allowed to see me briefly ten days after the verdict but after that a total ban was imposed, on what turned out to be a fictitious excuse. Once again, every ounce of flesh was extracted from the 'game', with me being told that a visit had been agreed upon, only to have it cancelled at the last moment.

The initial date for the appeal was set for 9 September,

but with some reluctance my lawyers decided that they had no alternative but to ask for a postponement, to allow the defence time to gather more evidence. In the end the appeal did not commence for a further seven weeks; but they were fruitful weeks and the delay was worth it.

During the trial the defence had been operating under a severe disadvantage, namely we had no real idea what the prosecution case against me would entail. Clearly the ability to prepare a proper defence, and thereby be in a position to cross-examine prosecution witnesses, counter prosecution arguments, and indeed to call effective defence evidence had been severely curtailed by having had only six days in which to study the extremely lengthy and complicated prosecution case papers. The possibility of calling evidence in rebuttal had been virtually non-existent. Considering these odds Placht had nonetheless put on a very impressive performance.

Now, armed with a comprehensive knowledge of the prosecution case, and the weight the Bench had attached to various parts of it, my lawyers immediately set about making enquiries and gathering evidence. Enquiries which, had there been advance notice of the evidence against me, and sufficient time in which to make them, would have been made prior to my trial.

To this end Richard New was despatched for a second time to Ibiza by Kingsley Napley, and returned with a considerable amount of information, all of which pointed to my innocence and cast severe doubt on the accuracy of the testimony given by Mitchell. In six days on Ibiza New was able to establish more factual information about the case than the police had done in their four and a half months' investigation. In so doing he verified many of the aspects of my statement which Forsberg, having made no attempt to corroborate or disprove them himself, had dismissed, and publicly labelled, as lies.

On his first visit to Ibiza New had discovered that a continual stumbling block to his enquiries was the fact that the expatriate community had the 'Three Monkeys' attitude of 'Hear No Evil, See No Evil, Speak No Evil'. He thought this was because most appeared to be escaping from one thing or another – mostly themselves. Some were probably fugitives from justice, and others were probably dabbling in the drug business. In addition, many were working without the necessary permits and were, of course, paying no taxes. The result was a community that tended not to ask personal questions, and people genuinely had little idea of each others backgrounds or sources of income. There was a general paranoia of being associated with anything that may have turned the police or press spotlight on themselves. Members of the Bhagwan Sect were even more self-protective and wary of outsiders. The Swedish Affair, together with the death of Chantal, had further heightened these feelings of paranoia. In short, few people, if anyone, had been willing to speak to him. The situation had obviously been further exacerbated by the probings of the press. As a consequence it was decided that on this second occasion my mother would accompany him with the intention of establishing his bona fides, and hopefully putting some of this widespread paranoia to rest. They travelled to the island together on 1 September.

These are the significant points from the report submitted by New on his return to England:

1. GENERAL ENQUIRIES CONDUCTED.

The enquiries conducted included a meeting with the Ibizan police drug squad officer in charge of the Hayward case – Inspector Rogelio. In addition, a number of persons were located and interviewed who knew Christopher Hayward well, or who had some knowledge of Mitchell and Dook. Some of these persons were only prepared to talk with us on the understanding that we would not reveal their identities or addresses. We located, and photographed, the house in Santa Gertrudis where Simon stayed and Christopher's house in San Juan. We also interviewed the manager and staff of a garage identified by Simon.

2. MEETING WITH THE POLICE.

This was held at the National Police Headquarters in Ibiza Town, on Wednesday 2 September. Inspector Rogelio stated that he was the officer in charge of the Hayward Case, and frequently referred to a file of papers on his desk.

New questioned him but the circumstances surrounding the recovery of the Jaguar on 10 March, following the earlier report of its theft by Simon Hayward. He confirmed that Simon had reported it stolen the previous day, from the port area. Of more importance, he stated that details of the car had been circulated to the police patrols, and that it had been one of these normal patrols that had later located the car, in another area of the port, without any kind of 'tip off'.

Whilst generally unwilling to provide us with information, in answer to our questions Rogelio did provide valuable information in relation to various matters.

Re Christopher:

a)　The Swedish police were arriving the following week in connection with their investigation.

b)　It was not until *June* that the Ibizan police had been requested by the Swedes to look for, or make enquiries about, Christopher.

c)　They were satisfied that Christopher was no longer on Ibiza, and believed that he may be in Gibraltar.

Re DOOK:

a)　He would not state when the Swedish authorities had first notified them about DOOK.

b)　They knew DOOK's identity, but he would not tell us. He was popularly thought on Ibiza to be Dutch. However, they had reason to believe he was in fact Irish.

c)　They knew the name of DOOK's boat, but would not tell us.

d)　They had reason to believe that DOOK had a number of false passports, including an American one.

e)　DOOK was no longer on Ibiza, and they thought he may be in the United States.

Re Mitchell/ Prita/ Makunda:

a)　They had never been informed by the Swedish

authorities of anyone called Mitchell, Lokesh or Prita, neither were the names familiar to him.

b) New described Mitchell's confessed role to the officer, the fact that Mitchell's home was on Ibiza, and that Prita was still living on Ibiza. He expressed surprise that this information had not been supplied to the Ibizan police by the Swedes.

c) Similarly, he had never heard of, or been informed about, Makunda.

3. REPAIRS TO CHRISTOPHER'S LADA JEEP.

The garage described by Simon was located on the outskirts of Ibiza town. The manager and the mechanic who had worked on the Lada, were interviewed. They provided evidence which confirmed Simon's testimony, which in turn provided credibility to support the view that Christopher took the Lada to mainland Spain, or even France, in order to obtain the necessary spares.

New also interviewed a Bhagwan member, known by the name of BAM BOO, at the bar in San Juan. He stated that the Lada had previously been his, and that he had sold it to Christopher in November 1986. BAM BOO is German, and he said that he sold the car as he was returning to Germany at the time, and needed the money. Christopher had got the car very cheaply. New asked him whether there had been anything wrong with it when he had sold it, and he volunteered the fact that there was an unidentified vibration problem.

4. CHRISTOPHER'S HOUSES.

Both houses were visited. The Santa Gertrudis landlord was interviewed and he confirmed the reason why Christopher had rented two houses and that he had tried to cancel the contract for the one in Santa Gertrudis in November, 1986.

5. THE UNSUITABILITY OF THE JAGUAR FOR SAN JUAN.

We understand that Simon has stated that Christopher considered the Jaguar to be unsuitable for the road to his house near San Juan, and that it was for this reason that Christopher no longer needed the Jaguar, and wished to dispose of it. We further understand that Simon also supported that view, and that there was therefore no reason for him to be suspicious when Christopher suggested that he take the car to England or Sweden and sell it.

Generally, the roads between the main towns, and holiday resorts, on Ibiza are of reasonable tarmac construction, and the Jaguar would be suitable. This would certainly apply to Santa Gertrudis, and to the house there. However there is an extensive network of dirt tracks leading off these main roads, usually of poor quality, where the Jaguar would often be unsuitable. (Especially in winter.) It is in houses down such tracks that most of Christopher's and Mitchell's circles appear to live.

In relation to the mountain road to Christopher's house near San Juan, in our opinion the use of such a car would result in it being wrecked. We consider it would be madness, even if possible, to use a Jaguar on that track.

It was clearly for this reason that Christopher purchased the Lada from Bam Boo, at the time he rented the San Juan shack. The Lada would be highly suitable for the road conditions.

The facts therefore entirely support Simon's statements. We consider this to be of crucial importance as it provides complete credibility to the reasons given for why the Jaguar was taken off the island, and why Simon should not have been suspicious in any way. Following Christopher's move to San Juan, the car was clearly superfluous. Neither is it likely, from our enquiries, that the car could have been sold to others in his circles. They would neither want such a vehicle, nor would it be suitable for where most of them lived. It is also highly unlikely that a Spaniard would have been interested in buying it.

It is therefore perfectly feasible that, if a suitable situation arose, Christopher might suggest to a friend, or relative, that they drive it to England or, in this case, Sweden. Certainly, given the facts, there would have been no reason for Simon to have been suspicious, or to have been put on his guard, with such a suggestion.

6.   CHRISTOPHER HAYWARD.

Sources that we were able to locate, and who said that they knew Christopher well, stated that:

a)   Christopher remained on Ibiza during April, and possibly later. There was, in fact, a 'whip round' to provide funds to enable him to leave. No one would admit to having heard from him since, or to having any knowledge as to his current whereabouts.

b)   He was not a serious follower of the Bhagwan, but had merely flirted with the subject. He had, in fact, only been introduced to the sect in about 1981, by a German girlfriend called Panna, following his split from Chantal. It was Panna who was a very devoted follower and, since his split with her his interest had been minimal. However, he had made friends, and aquaintances in the Bhagwan circle as a result.

c)   He was generally very popular, although there were some (unnamed) people who did not like him.

d)   It was generally believed that he earned his living by chartering his boat in the summer. It was known that he had charters in the summer of 1986.

e)   Christopher never exhibited any visible signs of wealth.

f)   Not surprisingly, nobody would confirm his involvement in the Swedish matter. The standard response was that no one knew, one way or another. However, without exception, the suggestion that he was 'The Boss' or 'Mr Big' was dismissed as absurd. The popular view was that if he was involved, it was not in such a role, as he was considered to be a bit of a bum, and far too lazy, laid back disorganised to be capable of such a role.

g)   Christopher knew Mitchell and Prita, but they were not close friends.

h)   Christopher had been, however, good friends with DOOK. It was understood that they had met several years ago, as a result of them both being in the boating community, and both having catamarans. However, at some time towards the end of 1986, they had had a substantial disagreement and had ceased to be friends. Early in 1987, subsequent to Christopher moving to the house in San Juan, DOOK had apparently been asking questions in the village, trying to locate Christopher's house. His manner was clearly unfriendly, therefore no one would tell him.

Nobody could, or would, tell us the exact cause of the disagreement between them. Several sources believed it related to a financial matter. One source said it was possibly something to do with Christopher's boat. However, whatever it was, it was certainly serious.

7. MITCHELL/PRITA.

From our enquiries, we understand that Mitchell is closely involved in the Bhagwan movement, and is high up in the Bhagwan pecking order on Ibiza. He is known by his Bhagwan name, LOKESH, and has been on the island for many years. However, nobody professed to have any idea what Mitchell did for a living.

We were unable to locate his house, but we were told that it was somewhere between San Juan and Santa Eulalia, and that it was a substantial dwelling.

We were also unsuccessful in our attempts to locate and interview Prita. We were told that she had certainly been around earlier in the week but despite leaving messages with her friends, and with the ECO message service in San Juan she refused to contact us.

We were told by friends of hers that she regularly travels to Sweden to visit Mitchell, and had very recently spent five days there with him. During the week previous to our visit, she had been telling everyone that the Swedish police would be coming to Ibiza within a few weeks.

On Thursday 3 September, we met two Bhagwan friends of Mitchell's in the bar in San Juan. They disbelieved that he had implicated others following his arrest. From the conversation it was clear that they knew, or accepted that Mitchell was guilty. They stated it was Simon who had been naming people whom he had met, but that Mitchell had kept quiet. We told them that Mitchell, far from keeping quiet had sung like a canary, and had even stated that Christopher was the 'Boss' and that he had also implicated Simon and the people in Sweden. They refused to believe that Mitchell had talked, and stated that he would not have implicated either Christopher or Simon. We therefore showed them Mitchell's testimony at Simon's trial. Having read it they were visibly shaken. They stated that, regardless of either Christopher or Simon's innocence or guilt (they would not offer an opinion either way) it had been totally unnecessary for Mitchell to implicate them. They said that they knew Mitchell well, and that the only explanation was that the Swedish police must have some extremely powerful hold over him.

We believe that Prita deliberately avoided us, and established that she has been conducting a deliberate campaign of disinformation on Ibiza – anti Simon and pro Mitchell.

8. POSSIBLE MOTIVES FOR MITCHELL'S TESTIMONY.

In the opinion of Mitchell's friends, they clearly now consider that the Swedish police have 'the arm on' him in some manner, and that that is the reason for his implicating Makunda, Christopher and Simon.

It is difficult to see how a seven year sentence was an inducement to Mitchell. The maximum was only ten years, leaving a difference, after likely remission, of only a year and a half.

However, it is easy to see how they could pressure him in relation to Prita. In Mr Placht's opinion, the Swedes have sufficient evidence to arrest and charge her. Yet they have not done so, despite the fact that she appears to regularly travel to Sweden, with impunity, and has even stayed with Mitchell. One can easily imagine a deal with Mitchell, whereby he was invited to implicate others, in return for which Prita would not be arrested, neither would she be hassled on Ibiza. She would also be allowed to visit Mitchell freely.

We believe that this would have been a powerful and

attractive inducement for Mitchell to implicate others, even falsely, in order for him to achieve his personal objectives. This would also explain the bizzare situation whereby the Swedes have asked the Ibizan police to investigate Christopher and possibly DOOK, but have apparently kept quiet about the other three key players – Mitchell, Prita and his partner Makunda. Especially given that Prita, and almost certainly Makunda, are currently living on Ibiza.

9. DOOK.

Few people professed to know much about DOOK. Sources state that he was something of a loner, who was not part of either Christopher's or the Bhagwan circles. However, in addition to him having previously been a friend of Christopher, he is said also to know Mitchell. It is believed that he has only been on Ibiza for three or four years, having previously come from Majorca. He had no visible sourcc of income.

He lived on Ibiza with his common-law wife Gitta, and their two children. Gitta is said to be Danish. They have an apartment in Santa Eulalia and in 1986 purchased an expensive house in the Santa Gertrudis area.

DOOK was clearly in a different class, in having the money to purchase a house, which are extremely expensive on Ibiza. Various sources stated that he obviously had money, and that the house was substantial, with a large pool. Dook had also initiated extensive, and expensive, reconstruction work on the building.

At some date during the week commencing 13 April, DOOK abruptly removed his six year old son, Alvie, from the English school in San Carlos, and left the island. The house is understood to have been subsequently sold.

DOOK is described as being outwardly pleasant, but with an occasional visible nasty streak under the surface. His relationship with Gitta is said to have deteriorated this year, and that he had physically abused her on several occasions.

10. OTHER MATTERS.

We now understand that the Jaguar is registered in

Christopher's name. To have therefore then, used that car for a drugs run appears unnecessary, and suicidal, to say the least. It would not have been difficult to obtain a suitable car, untraceable to Christopher. If Simon was involved, they could then have easily concocted a suitable story to cover Simon driving that vehicle. However, if Christopher was involved, but Simon not, then the former may well have been forced to use the Jaguar in order for the trip to appear logical to Simon, and not to arouse Simon's suspicions. If Christopher was desperate enough to use his own car, we consider that he may well have been desperate enough to dupe his own brother.

We have provided British Airways in London with details of Simon's one-way London to Gibraltar ticket on 18 February. They state that it was purchased in London on the 17 February, and was paid for with an American Express card, the number of which is shown on the ticket. The ticket was a special low-cost economy fare, only valid on that flight on that day. Furthermore, the reservation can only be made within the preceding 24 hours. In effect, it is like a standby fare, with the difference that it can be booked and confirmed the previous day, subject to seat availability. The normal one-way economy price would have been in the region of £150; this ticket cost just £49.

In our opinion, for Simon to have purchased such a ticket is far more consistent with a person trying to economise on holiday expenses, rather than the action of an all-expenses paid drugs courier.

Richard New,
Managing Director,
Veritas Management Services Ltd,
London.

9 September 1987.

In addition to instructing New, my lawyers were still keen on encouraging Forsberg to broaden the scope of his investigation. After all, they had seen the suspicion with which the prosecution and the courts looked upon evidence gathered and presented by the defence. With this in mind Tom Placht made yet another official request, via the Appellant Court that was to eventually hear my case, for the police to conduct their own enquiries on Ibiza and specifically to question Prita. Greatly influenced, I believe, by the fact that Richard New had already visited the island in July and would be doing so again in September, and to pre-empt a court order, Forsberg finally agreed to this request. I will resist the temptation to comment upon the usefulness of a trip to Ibiza some six months too late, but in any event the manner in which he conducted his enquiries proved to be nothing short of scandalous.

In order to represent my interests and to lend assistance to the police investigation, Placht sought, and was granted, permission from the Appellant Court to accompany the prosecution team, which comprised Forsberg, Bihlar and Nilsson, on the trip. When Forsberg was made aware of this he also, personally, agreed that Placht could go along.

As it turned out, Placht flew to Ibiza a day early, on 5 September, to liaise with Richard New who had remained on the island specifically to brief him, after my mother had left for London, and to offer his information and services to the Swedish police due to arrive the next day. Needless to say, this offer was turned down by Forsberg, and New returned to London on the 6th.

Having been briefed by New on his discoveries and shown the relevant sights, Placht booked into the hotel where he and the other Swedes would be staying. Already waiting there was the Drugs Liaison Police Officer attached to the Norwegian Embassy in Madrid – Thor Bjornevog, who had helped arrange the visit with the Ibizan authorities. He and Placht had a long and detailed discussion about the case while waiting for the rest of the party to arrive. Immediately they did so however, it became evident that Bihlar was extremely upset about Placht's presence. Angrily he took Bjornevog aside, and from then on the Norwegian refused to have anything further to do with the lawyer – a somewhat remarkable change in attitude.

In fact, Placht was to be ignored from that moment on, and was consequently excluded from all enquiries. He stuck this ostracism out for two days, waiting in vain for the ridiculous situation to change; becoming angrier and more frustrated by the hour, especially so since he was on Ibiza with the official blessing of the Swedish Courts, not to mention Forsberg's prior agreement. Eventually a note signed by Bihlar, who was obviously running the show, exerting his usual dominance over the weak charactered prosecutor, was slipped quietly under his bedroom door. Curtly it informed him that he was being left out of the proceedings because the Ibizan police were refusing to allow him to take part. This was a demonstrable lie, since only days beforehand they had quite readily spoken to Richard New and my mother. Besides which, they were so laid back and out to lunch that I very much doubt that they would have taken exception to, or for that matter noticed, the presence of every lawyer in Sweden.

There was however little point in arguing, and realising that his continued presence on the island had become superfluous, Placht made arrangements to fly home the next day.

No doubt believing his own propaganda, that it was dangerous for the police to investigate on Ibiza, Forsberg had arranged around the clock protection for his party before agreeing to the visit. By deliberately denying Placht access to his programme, he must therefore have been aware that he was also denying a fellow Swede the protection that he had so fervently sought for himself, and was now in the act of enjoying – as it turned out, with almost disastrous results.

When he left the hotel early the following morning to drive to the airport, Placht found that his hire car had been tampered with and purposefully immobilised. The battery cables had been cut through. As he closed the car's bonnet, he noticed two ominously large bruisers approaching him from across the street, and he was left in no doubt that they had no intention of merely wishing him a 'Good morning. Can we be of any assistance?' A clear desire for blood was written across their faces. The streets were deadly quiet, with not another soul in sight – the perfect time for a mugging. Not wishing to see his worst suspicions confirmed, Placht grabbed his suitcase and scuttled back into the hotel lobby, where he asked the sleepy and disinterested concierge to call for a taxi. The heavies retired to their previous positions opposite the hotel entrance, waiting conspicuously; ready to pounce. When the taxi arrived they jumped into a waiting car and followed

Placht to the airport. Inside the terminal safety was still not at hand, for they started to jostle my, by this stage highly nervous, lawyer. Satisfied that their 'message' had been delivered they then proceeded generally to hang around in a menacingly provocative and aggressive manner, only taking their leave when, with a monumental sigh of relief, Placht passed into the departure lounge.

So who were these men? The answer to that question was never resolved but the first and natural option was that they had been members of the local drug smuggling fraternity who had taken exception to Placht poking around on the island. However he hadn't been poking around; he had been sitting in his hotel room for two days waiting to be allowed to join in the 'poking around'. In addition no one from the local community knew that he was even on Ibiza; nor which hotel he was staying at; nor that he had decided to return to Sweden early; nor which flight he would be catching. Under these circumstances therefore, this first possibility can be safely discounted.

Despite spending five days on Ibiza, the prosecution established next to nothing with their enquiries, which were in any case, as we were to ultimately discover, carried out with the sole intention of proving guilt. Once again all avenues indicating innocence were left untouched. No attempt was made to verify those parts of my statement that Forsberg was so ready to condemn as lies. No attempt was made to interview those witnesses who New had spoken to. No attempt was made to locate Dook or Makunda. As far as we could make out, they only investigated the circumstances of the Jaguar's theft; visited Christopher's houses; and went to Mitchell's home, where, needless to say, they were unsuccessful in finding Prita.

If they did more, it was never admitted to, and one can only speculate that the reason for this was because, if indeed other evidence was collected, it must have corroborated my testimony. What can definitely be said, is that they returned home with precious little to show for their five days of 'work', except that is for deeper suntans.

To add insult to injury, a press statement was released, when back in Sweden, claiming that the police had found new evidence, whilst on Ibiza, that proved my guilt – a blatant lie. Nilsson was quoted as saying: 'We found a lot of material that will allow us to present an even stronger case against Simon Hayward,' and adding that several interesting finds were made during a search of the villa in Santa Gertrudis.

If indeed anything was discovered, I for one cannot imagine what it could have been, and since 'it' was never produced, I can only assume this claim was also untrue, and a further attempt to publicly discredit me.

I, of course, remained in blissful ignorance of these events as they progressed. That is to say I knew that Richard New and the police were making visits to Ibiza but not what was being achieved. In fact the security restrictions applied by Forsberg were tightened and more rigorously enforced.

As I have already mentioned, in the middle of August a total ban on all further private visits was imposed; initially on the grounds that Inspector Bihlar was not available to drive up to Stockholm to sit in. However, when my wing Assistant, a likeable man by the name of Frembeck who was proving to be very sympathetic to my plight, reminded Forsberg that other prisoners with the same restrictions were permitted to receive visits supervised only by warders, and offered an English-speaking warder to supervise me, permission was again refused. One wonders why a distinction had to be made in my case?

On this occasion the risk of collusion was given as an added excuse, which was strange because my trial was over, it had received blanket publicity, all facts surrounding the affair were consequently out in the open, and if I was to have changed my story between trial and appeal it would have been to court disaster.

Perhaps Forsberg too realised the illogicality of the situation because latterly he stated that the ban had been imposed in order to prevent news of his pending visit to Ibiza from leaking out. This was ironic, considering the fact that details of his trip were published in newspaper reports the day before he left; and especially so since Richard New established that Prita had been given prior warning weeks beforehand. One could perhaps be excused for drawing the conclusion that this ban was imposed simply to make life more difficult and unpleasant for me, my family and friends.

To make matters worse, on the day the ban came into force, while cancelling an arranged visit at very short notice from Sandra and her father, on 'security grounds', Forsberg allowed a British journalist to interview me without the presence of a police officer. On the face of it therefore, it appeared that some distinction was being made between family and friends, and the press.

There is a story behind this interview, which was published in a well known Sunday rag. Worried by some adverse publicity, especially articles relating to my conditions at Kronoberg, but encouraged by a couple of anti Life Guard stories, the Press Attache at the Swedish Embassy in London invited the journalist concerned to Sweden 'all expenses paid' in an attempt to conduct an exercise in damage limitation. The brief was to write an article that would diffuse much of the criticism being levelled at the Swedish system.

On hearing of this visit, further efforts to see me were made by both the Agars and my mother, but to no avail. The excuse this time, and again published in leading newspapers, was that the journalist had spoken to me just prior to the ban being imposed – the visit by Sandra and her father had 'sadly come too late'.

I was not complaining that Forsberg had decided to prevent me from receiving visits; indeed I had little right to do so, after all I was in custody and, on the face of it, had been convicted of a crime, albeit waiting an appeal. It was within the prosecutor's power, under the country's law, to do whatever he liked. What I, and for that matter everyone else, was complaining about however, was the underhand manner in which he chose to conduct himself. Why resort to subterfuge? Why provide weak excuses? When all he had to say was – 'I have decided that for the time being Simon Hayward cannot have visitors', end of story. Or for that matter, why could he not uphold the law in a proper manner, and treat me like any other prisoner on remand?

As one can imagine, life was not particularly easy during this period. Although I tried to remain optimistic of being acquitted at the forthcoming appeal, I found it quite impossible not to dwell on my circumstances, and on my future prospects. Even if I was released on appeal, to have been caught up in such a sordid business was bad enough; to have been convicted of a serious crime, even if that conviction was later overturned, did not bear thinking about. To many, some doubt would remain, and it was bound to affect my career in the army; the stigma of this affair was going to prove exceedingly difficult to live down. The strongest feeling remained one of intense, deep, embarrassment.

I settled down to life back in solitary confinement – the trial had been a welcome break from that at least. I tried hard to forget about my imminent future, and instead to continue my existence on a day by day basis. Two people greatly helped to lift my spirits. One was Mr Frembeck, who went out of his way to make me as comfortable as possible; apart from trying to arrange private visits, he arranged for me to watch the occasional video film, to have more time on the roof in the fresh air, and even spent the odd half-hour himself chatting with me. He also advised me to see a representative from the Red Cross, whose members visited inmates on a daily basis, to help pass the time. At first I refused, perhaps out of shyness, perhaps because I had become unused to seeing people, but also because I had never before considered it necessary to seek help from any kind of social worker. With hindsight, this was a rather arrogant point of view, and I must admit out of sheer boredom I eventually relented and hence met the second of my helpers – Miss Ulla Barkman.

She was a thin, very upright spinster in her early seventies, with as warm, understanding, and loving a character as one would ever hope to find. We were to spend many an enjoyable hour together discussing a wide variety of topics, including the one very obvious one, and she managed to return some spark of normality into my life, and thereby helped me through a very difficult time. I always looked forward to her visits eagerly each week. She spoke good English, amongst a variety of other languages, and was exceptionally well-read with the wide experience that comes from having to fend for oneself. I was only one of her 'patients', some of whom, she once admitted to me shyly, quite literally terrified her; she also spent three nights a week sitting beside a telephone working for the Samaritans. Where would the world be without the like of Ulla Barkman?

Like Inger Jonsson, Ulla has become a good and valued friend, and I owe both ladies a great debt of gratitude.

The only other 'friendly faces' I was permitted to see during this period, apart from Tom Placht, were members of the British Embassy staff. Jenny Cummings, Colonel Russel Wright (the Military Attache), and another Consul – John White, were all kind enough to visit on a fairly regular basis. It was during a conversation with White that a strong point of supportive evidence cropped up that would have counteracted one of the prosecution allegations made against me. I say 'would have' because sadly we were never able to use it.

One seeming piece of trivia had been exaggerated, the defence thought out of all proportion, by the prosecutor into a major piece of evidence. Evidence, at least in the way Forsberg described it in court, that was presented as yet another example of my mendacity. It concerned my stated belief, as the prosecution would have it, that Mitchell was a Swede.

Ignoring the fact that I had only ever said that I had been told that Mitchell was either a Swede or someone who lived in Sweden, three witnesses, Larsen, Morgan and Moore, were quoted as saying that Mitchell's accent was unmistakably Scottish, and for me to state otherwise was merely a smokescreen and a lie. To me the point seemed so trivial as to be hardly worth a mention.

John White was Scottish. When I related this story to him as a specimen of the type of evidence Forsberg had to resort to in order to build his case against me, he immediately exclaimed that when he had first met Mitchell he too had not realised that he was a Scot. Indeed, he thought the man's accent was negligible.

Sadly, when I requested that he appear at the forthcoming appeal as a defence witness, to make this point, White refused on the grounds that as a British diplomat he could not be seen to be taking sides!

The visiting ban was eventually lifted in the third week of September, allowing Sandra and her father to fly out to me. However Christopher Murray, who had also travelled to Sweden at the same time, to discuss strategy with Tom Placht was once again denied access to me. Indeed the ban was reimposed after the Agar visit and remained in force until my appeal commenced.

As I had done at Uppsala, I once again began to get to know my warders, and they me. I made a point, sometimes against severe provocation, of always being polite, and even cheerful, when dealing with them. Since it is part of human nature to respond to such treatment, they did so in kind. They must have realised that I was not like their customary 'retards' and whereas our relationship could never have been described as warm, at least it became fairly cordial, and based on some degree of mutual respect. Even Anders, the guard who had taken such obvious pleasure in delivering the verdict to me (a great slob of a man) softened his attitude as the weeks passed. It became not unusual for two or three of them to come to my cell of an evening to pass some time with me, occasionally going so far as to bring me a cup of coffee, biscuits, or a tub of ice-cream. As I have said, when spending so much time alone in a tiny cell for months on end, any human contact became a real bonus, and I used to relish these infrequent visits.

Towards the end of August the defence received information that Prita, far from being unwilling to come forward, had actually travelled to Sweden to see Mitchell. Since all prison visitors have to be checked out by the police, it seemed inconceivable that the Uppsala Drug Squad had not been made aware of this visit. If confirmation was needed, it was received in a telephone conversation with Prita on 2 September. No doubt because of the public criticisms levelled at them for not interviewing her properly, the police had arranged this call to speak to her on Ibiza, and they allowed Hanna Pontein to be present to put questions to her.

The caller, if indeed it was Prita, gave information of a fairly inconsequential nature. She replied to Bihlar's questions by reaffirming that she was not involved, other than having once passed a message from Mitchell to Christopher; that she had never received money from Nasim, nor did she know exactly what Mitchell's business involved except that it was not 'totally correct'; that she was afraid but she would not say of whom; and that she wished people would leave her alone because she did not want to become involved. Of greater significance she said that on the day Mitchell had talked to me at Santa Gertrudis he had gone to the villa with the sole intention of seeing Christopher, only to find that he was out. This, of course, directly contradicted Mitchell, who had testified that he had driven to the villa with the sole intention of meeting me, so that I would be able to recognise him at a later date. As for her visit to Sweden? In reply to Hanna asking when was the last time she had seen Mitchell, she said: 'I saw him before he travelled with my son to Berlin.' (En route to Sweden before his arrest.)

'But we have obtained information that you have visited him since that date in his prison here in Sweden?'

'Yes, that is correct, that is correct,' said Prita, quickly changing her story.

'When was that, and how long did you stay in Sweden?'

'It was shortly after his trial and I stayed for about a week.'

Prita admitted to knowing Chantal was dead, and added that she had been extremely anxious about something before her death.

This conversation raised the question why the police had not known of Prita's visit to Sweden? Or, more sinisterly, if they had known, why had they not interviewed her, and why had the defence not been informed? Since Bihlar had testified under oath at my trial that when he had spoken to Prita in June, she had refused to come to Sweden, one could only assume that he had not known of her actual visit. Somehow she must have managed to deceive everyone, and slip through the net.

For someone who was 'not involved' this woman continued to behave in a very odd manner. A month later she was to telephone my mother to threaten that if private detectives continued to make enquiries she was prepared to go to Sweden and 'make things worse for Simon'.

Clearly the authorities believed Christopher to be deeply implicated in running drugs to Sweden and it was equally clear that they looked upon his disappearance not only as an indication of his guilt, but also of mine. In addition, judging from the District Court verdict, little weight had been placed on my mother's testimony during the trial. It was considered vital therefore that Christopher was either found, persuaded to come forward, or at the very least to make a statement. Consequently a press conference was held in London on 10th September, during which my mother made an impassioned plea for him to come forward.

'I expect Christopher to come forward like a man and face his accusers, with any evidence he has to support his brother, or at least to make contact with his lawyers.'

Speaking of the threats made against Tarik, she told the assembled journalists: 'Christopher has told me that if he had to weigh up the life of his son against Simon going to prison, Tarik's safety had to come first. Now Tarik is safe and in no position to be harmed, so I appeal to Christopher to come forward.'

However, two weeks later she was once again approached outside her house by a man who threatened her and her grandson. The threat was along the same lines as on the previous occasion but this time it was even more terrifying because the little boy was asleep in the house not ten feet away.

Christopher did make contact, and gave a brief verbal statement, as I was to discover during the appeal.

A somewhat bizarre, not to mention incredible, event took place on 18th September. Mitchell was allowed to give an interview over the telephone to a *Sunday Times* reporter called Max Prangnell, in which he made new and incriminating accusations against me. It was a glaring indictment of the way in which Forsberg had conducted his case that he allowed prosecution witnesses to make damning press statements from inside prison, whilst at the same time I was being denied access to my lawyers. It was true that I had been interviewed by reporters, but I had never been permitted to go into any detail about the case.

The main theme of what Mitchell had to say in this interview, a transcript of which was given to Kingsley Napley, was that I had taken a far more active role in the ring than had to date been thought, and that I had intended to sell half the cannabis found in the Jaguar myself for £250,000 and pass the money on to Christopher.

MP: 'What do you think of Simon?'

FM: 'To me he was just an officer in the army. That's what other people thought of him too. When I met him I wasn't interested in him, and neither was anyone else.'

MP: 'And Chris?'

FM: 'He's a better man than his brother, I can tell you. He's a very kind and gentle person. He's very sensitive. He wasn't in Ireland popping out paddies.'

MP: 'So who is Dook?'

FM: 'Ha ha, come on you know better than that. I can tell you he's a family man and he's got absolutely nothing to do with this.'

MP: 'So where is Chris?'

FM: 'I've no idea. I hope he is safe. I should think he is.'

MP: 'What do you think of Mrs Hayward?'

FM: 'She's a cow! Ask her how many times she's been to Ibiza, she says she's never met me. Ask her about that. I know she's been on Ibiza asking questions about me. I know they've had private detectives over there . . . When I first came in here I didn't mention Chris's name for two months but within a week Simon had said everything. He told his story like he was on holiday. When I heard he had been naming all of Chris's friends and associates, I got word out to Ibiza for everyone to get off the island . . . Then Mrs Hayward went to Ibiza and told people it was me who'd named everyone, that really gets me.
If I get bothered too much I can let a lot be known. Placht tries to make me look a fool! Prita has got out of the way, right? But there's a point that I may reach where I can be very nasty. I don't think what I know would help Simon at all . . .
I haven't said everything I know, right? I want Simon to be in a neutral standpoint in his trial . . . I can tell you if the defence go too far I can reveal things that can damage him. Although I told the truth at Simon's hearing, I did not elaborate on it . . .'

MP: 'Isn't it odd that the Swedish police haven't interviewed Prita?'

FM: 'I haven't received pressure from the police, but if Prita is interviewed then trouble will start!'

MP: 'There have been allegations that you made a deal with the police to keep Prita out of it. That's why she has not been questioned?'

FM: 'That's crazy. I got seven years by my own work. I mean, those guys really wanted me.'

MP: 'What about the screwdriver?

FM: 'Yeah, what about it? He could not have bought it for the seat, it was an old screwdriver.' (Untrue.) 'Of course he was going to use it to get the dope out, it's obvious.'

MP: 'Really?'

FM: 'Yeah, right. Why did he drive from Ibiza in three days? He knew damn well what he was doing. He changed his story three times on that one. Look, I know that it's easier on the Andorran border. All this bullshit about him going there to buy skis. It's all wrong, man! I mean, where were the skis when he was arrested?'

MP: 'What about selling the car?'

FM: 'That's complete rubbish! How can you sell a ten-year old Jag in Sweden?' (It was actually only five.) 'There weren't any papers in the car, where was the log book? It had summer tyres on it. Who in Sweden would buy that?'

MP: 'But you were going to sell it for him.'

FM: 'Come on man. How was I going to sell it? When I was arrested I had a confirmed ticket back to Ibiza in my pocket for the next day.' (In reality of course, I doubt whether the ring had any intention of selling the car. That was just an excuse to trick me into driving it to Sweden.)

MP: 'So you are saying he's right in it?'

FM: 'Sure. I didn't say it in the trial but, I was only told to expect 15 kilos. I thought if I was really lucky I'd get 25. That guy was carrying 50, man. I can only think he was selling the rest privately for Chris.'

MP: 'Are you saying he was going to sell that separately? He didn't have any contacts?'

FM: 'Oh, how long does it take to get rid of dope. He only needed to see one person.'

MP: 'So you are saying he was going to get rid of half the dope he was carrying directly for his brother. The rest was for you to sell?'

FM: 'You got it. You're a smart guy. That's what the police think . . . no they know that.'

MP: 'Really?'

FM: 'Yeah, they got this whole thing sewn up. I'm the only person in Sweden who knows the whole truth about this, apart from Simon. I could really drop him in it. We're only small fish. If the normal driver had done the job the whole thing would be over and done with by now.'

The contents of this interview were not only a load of tommyrot, but they showed up Mitchell to be the thoroughly vindictive character that he truly was. The interview was also to supply the defence with one or two questions that Mitchell was to have a great deal of trouble answering during the appeal and, perhaps more importantly, the first hint we received of his true motive for framing me.

Prangnell also asked Forsberg for his comments:

'I know Simon is guilty. We already have enough evidence to get him convicted for six or seven years. But I want to know why Mitchell has started saying these things now.' He went on to explain how he was planning to call three expert witnesses at the appeal in an attempt to secure an extended sentence:

(a) A Swedish policeman to tell the court how I had apparently tried to speed up when the police had moved in to arrest me.

(b) A Spanish policeman to explain that there were more than 100 Jaguars on Ibiza, which made my claim that the car was unsuitable for the island's rough roads and had to be sold totally unbelievable.

(c) A Norwegian customs expert to confirm that border controls in Andorra were less stringent than on alternative routes.

At about this time Dook's name began to reappear. All enquiries into who he was and what part, if any, he might have played in the run to Sweden had drawn a blank. The police were obviously not interested in him and the defence did not have the resources to pursue the matter. It was therefore entirely his own doing that he became re-involved. On this occasion, his lawyer H K ter Brake, who had last spoken to Placht in July, sent a copy of a letter Dook had supposedly written to my mother to a Swedish lawyer called Sjernender, who he mistakenly thought represented Mitchell, but who in fact worked for Nasim Tervaniemi, asking him to pass it on to his client. Instead Sjernender passed it on to Placht.

It was four pages of highly emotional, quasi-religious, rambling typed claptrap. In his covering letter ter Brake explained that he had changed the original handwritten script into type to protect his client. Its theme was an unequivocal statement that Dook had nothing to do with smuggling drugs, and that Christopher had not only duped me, but also my mother and the Swedish Courts. It began:

Mrs Hayward, I pray to God each night to help you. I pray he grant you the vision to see the truth. I have nothing to do with Captain Hayward's case. I was not involved in any way with the Jaguar. I have duped no one and not your Simon. I have not threatened you, or Christopher, or the child Tarik – whom I cherish. I was not connected in any way with the death of Chantal. Please stop making me into a scapegoat for your sons.

And continued with an effusive, often incoherent, arbitrary hate-filled scrawl:

The truth will eventually come out and prove me wronged. I believe RIGHTS will ultimately transform and protect this case ... Mrs Hayward you have fallen into Christopher's evil plan to throw a smoke screen while he escapes and you and Simon carry the pain and the shame ... This evil must be cured at its roots. My heart bleeds for you ... Christopher is a weak, wicked child ... You pursue and slander me and all the while he laughs. Laughs at you. Laughs at me. Laughs at his brother whom he has led to harm ...

If you have been threatened alone at night – it was by one of Christopher's criminal colleagues ... not by me! Mrs Hayward, almost everything Christopher has said about me are lies. Oh yes, he was right when he said I am small ... the smallest, little-ist man in the whole world. And is that not always the way of wicked children when the big blame the small because they cannot face up to the truth ... of course it suits his sick mind to make the villain of the piece an Irishman. He exploits the unnatural friction between our peoples. Jingoism of the lowest form. Christopher rabble-rouses the rats. Christopher's sin now is not just against you, Simon and me, but against humanity ... he treads on the dead, mocks armies, insults governments, despoils Nobel Prize winners. While they work towards bringing peace and harmony, this leech tries to stir up hatred between our peoples, so as to cover his own nefarious acts ... Christopher has deceived you, fed you Lucifer's lie. He has duped you, and from reading the newspaper reports, I suspect he has duped those others into believing Simon agreed to do this.

Mrs Hayward, you must respond to the will of Heaven and replace cowardice and concealment by courage and common sense ... You must stop the darkness about this case ... you must spread the light, the truth. The truth is that your son Christopher stands and lies behind this case, and him alone. He is the Chief, the Boss, the Mastermind. He is not running from any other threat other than the authorities. He is a liar fleeing from his detestable deeds. He is a 36-year-old child afraid to tell his 'mummy' the truth. This pernicious person has pawned you and Simon.

The letter ended with: 'May God in his infinite mercy bless you Mrs Hayward.'

At first no one could make head or tail of this letter, although it came as no surprise to find it presented by the prosecution as evidence against me at the appeal. It just appeared to be an insane carry on, a justification of a stand. However on closer analysis a definite method could be perceived amongst the madness. It was addressed to my mother but was clearly intended for Mitchell's eyes as well. But why should Dook want to write to Mitchell in such a strange manner? Especially since Mitchell was trying to maintain that they hardly knew each other. The only possible answer was that it contained a message, in fact to be more precise instructions. Since the letter was anti Christopher, but pro me and sympathetic towards my mother, claiming that Christopher had duped us all, the message must have read: 'Stop implicating Simon Hayward, you are creating too much publicity and raising too many awkward questions. Continue blaming Christopher, but leave it at that.'

Dook must have realised that Mitchell could easily have cleared me, a course of action that would certainly have resulted in the end of the investigation; and he had to get instructions to Mitchell without associating too closely with him. In any event, if Mitchell ever saw a copy of the letter, he chose to ignore its contents, either because he failed to understand them or perhaps because he had an ulterior motive of his own?

Tom Placht was obliged to pass a copy of this letter to the prosecutor, and in so doing requested that H K ter Brake be questioned about it. To his surprise Forsberg not only agreed but together with Nilsson travelled to Hoorn, north of Amsterdam, to conduct the interview personally. He achieved little by his visit however, except to arrange for ter Brake to appear at my appeal as a prosecution witness. It also became evident that during their time with ter Brake a telephone conversation took place with Dook in which Nilsson told the Irishman to 'lie low' and not to come forward to be questioned. An incredible 'piece of police work', considering Nilsson knew only too well that the defence was extremely keen on interviewing Dook, and that there was a better than good chance that he could help the police with their enquiries. This action meant that for the umpteenth time my lawyers were frustrated in their attempts to call evidence.

There was an amusingly ironic sequel to this visit. On his return Nilsson came to Kronoberg to question me, by which time Placht had already shown me a transcript of what appeared to be a telephone conversation between Dook and Nilsson, signed by Nilsson, in which the 'lie low' order was given. When I asked him why he had prevented the defence from speaking to a potentially vital witness Nilsson denied that he had done so.

'But Mr Nilsson, you have signed a document which clearly states you did precisely that.'

'If it contained this information, there must have been some mistake.'

It was now my turn to ask a question put to me at the trial, and being only human, I must admit that I enjoyed doing so: 'You signed it, Mr Nilsson. Don't you read documents before putting your signature to them?'

He blushed to the roots of his hair and immediately called a stop to the interview.

On 25 September Richard New was sent again to Ibiza merely to locate and photograph, if at all possible, the houses owned by Dook and Forbes Mitchell. He established that they both lived in substantial and beautiful mansions, with extensive grounds. Neither bore any comparison to the shack in which Christopher lived outside San Juan, and it was clear that he was not in their league financially. By going through the rubbish bins at both houses, New made some interesting discoveries. In Dook's he found a receipt for a new bathroom, part of the extensive repairs being carried out, the cost of which was more than a year's full rent on Christopher's villa in Santa Gertrudis. In Mitchell's, he found an invoice from a travel agents in Ibiza Town for an air ticket with a confirmed booking in the name of Marylyn J Waterfield, to travel Ibiza/Barcelona/Stockholm on 28 August, returning on 8 September. The significance of this invoice was to become apparent during my appeal.

A second private investigator, Larry Gilmurray – an ex Metropolitan police officer, was also hired by the defence at this time. His task was to drive the route I had taken – Barcelona/Andorra/Narbonne – to check on the vigilance, or otherwise, of the customs posts at the national boundaries; and to compare them with those on the direct coastal route. In an extremely thorough report, eventually given as evidence at the appeal, he established that while none of the customs checks were very stringent, those on the Andorran borders were, if anything, more effective and thorough. This nullified one of the arguments used by Forsberg against me.

On 28 September, the day before the appeal finally got under way, help arrived from a most unexpected quarter. Help that provided the defence with potentially its strongest evidence to date. Tom Placht received a telephone call from a fellow inmate of Mitchell, a man called Per Philipsson, who said that he was ringing on his own behalf and that of another inmate, Michael Sundin. He stated that they had information concerning Mitchell that they felt certain would have a bearing on the case. In the course of the next two days Placht spoke to both men on the telephone and Hanna Pontein interviewed them in prison. Conversations with Philipsson were taped with his consent, however Sandin refused to allow this because he was loath to jeopardise a forthcoming weekend release on parole.

The gist of their information was that Mitchell was boasting that he had 'done a deal' with the police; and that he was walking around telling everyone that he was going to 'get Simon Hayward' by saying that I had received money for acting as a courier and that I had known exactly what was going on. The deal involved the police not charging Mitchell with a further 80 kilos of cannabis they knew he had smuggled, and a promise that they would not arrest or bother Prita, nor make enquiries on Ibiza, if he stuck to his story implicating me.

According to Philipsson, Mitchell had told him that he was not sure if I was involved or not; that he was very afraid of getting a longer sentence and he had sought the advice of other convicts as to what would happen if he talked. It was the general view that he had received a short sentence for what he had done, especially since he openly admitted that there were 'hundreds more kilos involved'. The police knew about some of these but not all, and consequently he was terrified of further investigations being instigated. He was also very worried in case the police should arrest Prita, because she was heavily involved and could make things much worse for him. When she had visited him in June she had travelled to Sweden on a false passport. Mitchell had also said that he was afraid of someone on the outside, and that there were big things involved, 'the IRA and other things'.

Sandin was able to confirm much of what Philipsson had to say, with two vital additions. Mitchell had told him that he knew I was definitely not involved; and had only agreed to testify against me after frequent visits from the police, who had provided him, before he testified, with copies of all the relevant statements from other important witnesses.

Both men said that they had taken the unusual step of deciding to come forward because Mitchell was breaking the 'criminal's code' and that they did not like people using a court of law for their own purposes. They thought Mitchell was going too far, adding that he had been in a dreadful state during the past week.

This development was dramatic in the extreme and my hopes soared when Placht came to see me on the evening before the appeal and told me, without naming the two inmates, what was going on. We both realised that the men could be lying for some reason, but there seemed little motive for them to do so, indeed they had nothing to gain and possibly much to lose by speaking up. Their information also provided answers to so many of the strange anomalies surrounding the case. For example: Why the police had not arrested, or even interviewed Prita; and why they had not conducted proper enquiries on Ibiza.

My last question to Placht before he left me that evening was: 'What do you think Forsberg will say in his opening address tomorrow?'

Tom chuckled. 'Well, he is a very lazy man, so I have no doubts that he will use exactly the same text as at the trial.'

Eight

'That proves his guilt,' said the Queen.
   'It proves nothing of the sort!' said Alice.
   'He denies it,' said the King: 'leave out that part!'

Lewis Carroll

'I haven't said anything to anyone!' Mitchell was shouting.

'It's okay, it's okay,' said Bihlar, trying to calm him down, 'don't worry, I will come and discuss it with you this afternoon.'

It was Thursday 1 October and the appeal was into its third day. For some as yet unexplained reason there was a delay on this particular morning and I had been sitting alone in a holding cell above the courtroom for two hours waiting for the proceedings to start.

Through the observation portal set into the door I had seen Bihlar walk past a few seconds earlier, and now I could hear him as he stood in the corridor talking to Mitchell through the open door of his cell.

The previous two days had been rather repetitive, for as I had been told to expect the appeal was in fact a complete re-trial, and as such had so far taken the form of an almost exact replica of the first hearing. To date it was all proving to be rather tedious. It was being held in the same courtroom, with the same heavy police presence, and a similar swarm of bored looking journalists. Indeed the only noticeable difference was the composition of the Bench itself. This time there were three judges – two men and a woman – and only two assessors, both middle aged women. I felt happier in my assumption that on this occasion the judges would be able to approach their task with open minds since, unlike Judge Hellbacher, they had not been heavily involved with the case from its conception.

The presiding judge, Mr Lars Wilhelmson, sat in the centre of the Bench flanked by his colleagues, Mrs Anna Espmark on the right and Mr Anders Frohling to the left. Beyond them, one on each side, sat the two lady assessors. Even in this, the High Court, informality was the name of the game. Although smartly dressed none of the judges wore any symbol or badge of office. Indeed they made a somewhat odd looking trio.

Forsberg's opening speech had been exactly as Tom Placht had predicted it would be – an almost word for word copy of the one he had made at the trial, the only real change being the inclusion of his third statement allegation. He had also informed the Court that the prosecution would be calling three new witnesses whose evidence 'would prove Simon Hayward's guilt'. He had concluded by appealing for reasons known only to himself against the 'too lenient sentence' awarded by the District Court, demanding a stiffer but unspecified penalty.

In response Placht had once again highlighted the irregularities in the police investigation and the gross inconsistencies in the so-called evidence being presented against his client. 'The prosecutor's case is based on speculation and unsubstantiated hearsay,' he told the Court, 'even the main prosecution witness cannot directly implicate Simon Hayward.' He had continued by emphasising all of the evidence, much of it newly collected, that stood in my favour, running through all the salient factors that had emerged during the trial and in the subsequent defence investigations. He had ended by reminding the Bench that it was the prosecutor's job to prove guilt, not the defence's job to prove innocence. In his view this had not been established at the trial and as far as he was aware the prosecution was still not in a position to prove it at the appeal. 'There are obviously very strong, and as yet undetected, forces at play behind this affair. I suspect a great deal of the truth remains untold, and this must stand against my client's chances of receiving a fair hearing.'

If his second opening speech had been identical to his first, so too had been Forsberg's cross-examination of me, allowing me to make the same interruptions and asking me all the same old questions. Letting my bitterness and anger surface, I had responded in kind, going into as much detail as possible, hoping to avoid the accusation of deliberately omitting anything or of changing my statement for a 'fourth time'. Clearly it had all proved just a little too boring for the judges who had obviously read all there was to read about the case, both from official documents, from which they had been won't to quote at regular intervals, and I suspect from the wide media coverage, to the point where Mr Wilhelmson had felt inclined to intervene to enquire as to whether the topics being discussed were absolutely relevant. Whereupon I had had to explain my motives and he had permitted me to continue.

I had decided to make a strong rebuttal of the third statement nonsense, because with all due respect to Tom Placht I had felt it had been an accusation he had not countered forcibly enough. As I had found each so-called 'newly invented lie' in my police statements, giving the exact date of the statement, the page number and paragraph, effectively destroying his argument, Forsberg's face had fallen afresh. As had happened so often at the trial, his features had taken on the deep crimson colour of anger and embarrassment.

'Yes, yes,' he would say, 'so you may have mentioned that Christopher's Lada jeep needed repair, but how about trying to borrow or buy a screwdriver en route to Sweden?'

'Well sir, if you would care to look at statement number . . .' and so the banter had continued until I had felt certain that the subject had been killed off once and for all, and for good.

The other seemingly trivial allegation that I had felt needed clarifying was the issue of Mitchell's nationality, or to be more accurate, the nationality I had believed him to be. Once again Forsberg had made a meal out of it, and even Judge Hellbacher had mentioned it in justifying his decision to convict me. Since John White was unwilling to help I had had to resort to other tactics when Forsberg had broached the topic. I had explained for about the twentieth time that I had never actually personally deduced from his accent that Mitchell was a Swede, but only had been told that he was Swedish, or someone who lived in Sweden.

'. . . and one cannot always tell these days what nationality a person is just by listening to his or her accent. Take your own daughter as an example Mr Bihlar,' I said looking across at the

man, 'she speaks English without a trace of a Swedish accent,'
this brought a wry smile to the policeman's lips, 'and there's
a girl who brings the food trolley around in the Häktet. She is
Swedish, born and bred, and yet when she opens her mouth
she speaks English like a true Cockney. No one would ever
believe she is Swedish.' This comment had met with laughter
from the public gallery, and looks of dejection from the
prosecution bench.

Åsa Hoffman, Lennart Viryo and Joachim Anderson had
put in a second appearance. Nothing of any great importance
had come from their testimony, which had remained to all
intents and purposes the same, except for an admission by
Viryo that women had indeed been used as couriers by
Mitchell.

The Jaguar videos had also been shown, but on this occasion
and much to Forsberg's obvious consternation, the Bench had
cut them short. I had taken this to be a good sign.

During those first two days Hanna Pontein had been busy
interviewing the two inmates from Österåker, Mitchell's
prison. Philipsson confirmed all that he had told Placht on the
telephone and had supplied a fully taped statement. Sandin,
albeit being open and cooperative, had still refused to allow
himself to be recorded until after his pending weekend leave.

Consequently, although Placht would have preferred to wait
until the following Monday, to enable a comprehensive
statement to be taken from Sandin, before disclosing this new
evidence to the Court, he had decided that he was under an
obligation to do so sooner. This he had done on the Thursday
morning, and was of course the reason behind the unscheduled
delay in the proceedings, for his decision had prompted more
than a little confusion and the cancellation of the morning's
session as the Bench considered the problem.

Placht presented his evidence to an *in camera* session of the
Court, during which Philipsson's recorded statement was
played and Sandin's given verbally. Apart from the judges, the
only people permitted inside the courtroom were Placht,
Forsberg, and Pontein. There was a policeman standing sentry
at the door but he was out of earshot of the proceedings.

As soon as the presentation was over, Judge Wilhelmson
ordered that an inquiry be set up forthwith into the allegations.

It was to be led by the senior prosecutor for the District, Alf Juhlin. Furthermore, all parties were expressly forbidden from identifying the two inmates, or indeed from giving any indication as to the background of the *in camera* hearing.

In spite of this directive, in what must have been only minutes after the hearing broke up, Bihlar was up briefing Mitchell, who had been waiting to give evidence in the cell adjacent to my own. No prizes for guessing who in turn must have told Bihlar what had taken place behind the closed doors of the courtroom that morning.

'What's going on? Why the delay?' Mitchell sounded nervous, a tremble of panic in his voice.

'It is nothing to worry about, the defence have produced two new witnesses, inmates from your prison, who are making certain allegations about a deal between us.'

By this time I had an ear pressed firmly against my cell door, but their conversation remained muffled. However I was able to hear Bihlar asking Mitchell if the names 'Philipsson and . . .' I could not quite catch the second one, meant anything to him. The result from Mitchell was close to hysteria, and it was at this point that I heard him screaming:

'I haven't said anything to anyone!' Shortly afterwards Bihlar left him with the promise that he would come to see him again that afternoon.

Placht came up to my cell some time later to explain the course of action he had decided upon.

'Tom, is one of the inmates called Philipsson?' I asked when he had finished speaking.

'Yes, but how do you know that?' he looked nonplussed.

I explained what had taken place. We then made a mistake, we should have gone straight back to the Court to lodge a complaint against Bihlar, and more importantly to demand that he be prevented from further contact with Mitchell and that the latter be isolated from Philipsson and Sandin. That is easy to say with the benefit of hindsight; at the time however Placht counselled against it on the grounds that such a course of action ran the risk of antagonising the Bench by appearing as though we were attempting to strengthen our stand by deceit.

Again with hindsight, I would guess that the true reason was because he realised that in a situation where the the police are paramount, where a policeman's word is taken before all others, it would have been pointless to make further allegations that could not have been conclusively proven.

We could not afford to do anything that might have jeopardised the new evidence. As I say, later I thought we had made a mistake; we should have tried.

The Court reconvened shortly afterwards with Judge Wilhelmson announcing that a 'Supplementary Investigation into certain aspects of the case had been instigated.' He ruled that my appeal would continue to run in parallel with it for as long as was necessary, with only that evidence being called which had no connection with the new investigation. There would then have to be an adjournment until Wednesday 21 October. Mitchell, Tervaniemi and certain new defence witnesses would not be heard until that date.

Mitchell, who had been brought into the courtroom to listen to this announcement, was led away, smirking at me as he went. In contrast, Bihlar, Nilsson and Forsberg were looking highly dejected.

In the following days a repetition of witnesses came and went; Brigadier James Emson and Inspector Gunnar Larsen. The Jaguar was inspected with Olsson giving the same rather one-sided demonstration. This time each judge and assessor actually sat in the driver's seat, and I took the opportunity to physically rock the seat on its foundations as they did so. There could be no denying that it moved in exactly the way I had described.

My mother gave a recapitulation of her previous testimony, adding that she had received further threats since the trial:

'Shut your mouth or we will kill you and your family!'

And: 'Christopher telephoned me again in September. I begged him to come forward to give himself up.'

'I cannot. If I do they will kill Tarik, I am being threatened over him the same as you . . . I will do all I can to help Simon but I cannot come forward. He will understand, he loves Tarik as much as I do . . . I will send a taped statement . . . for God's sake be careful of Dook, he would kill us like stamping on a fly.' My mother explained that Christopher had sounded under great stress and had been crying throughout the call.

'Did your son not also tell you something about the IRA,' asked Placht.

'Yes, he told me that Dook was involved with them, and with gun running.'

This latest revelation may well have been true but it sounded far-fetched and therefore did not add weight to my mother's testimony. I could not help feeling that since we had no way of proving it, that it would have been better left unsaid. Too many people already looked upon me as some kind of spy, and this only added confusion to an already confused situation.

My mother continued by explaining that Christopher had been unable to send a tape but instead had telephoned her again a few days later and had made a statement which she had recorded. Whereupon she held a cassette up in one hand and offered it as evidence to the Court. The defence had been expecting this but it was clearly an unpleasant surprise for Forsberg. He sat bolt upright in his chair and demanded to be allowed to hear it first. The courtroom was cleared to allow him to do so, after which the Bench decided to accept the tape as evidence. What weight would be attached to its contents remained to be seen.

There was a hush as the voice of the one person who everyone thought could clear me rang out in the panelled chamber. In precise English I heard the voice of my brother announce:

My name is Christopher David Hayward. Today's date is September 25. I am the owner of a Jaguar car, metallic green, registration number HMH 959X. In March this year, at the beginning of March, I asked my brother Simon if he would deliver the car to Sweden to a man known to me as Lokesh.

I told Simon that Lokesh would sell the car after converting it to left hand drive. I also told him that I did not want to drive the car myself, as I wanted to spend some time with a girlfriend in France.

As Simon was due back in England very soon, I told him he should just leave the car with Lokesh and fly home.

At no time did I mention anything to Simon about drugs and I never told him there were drugs in the car.

Under these conditions, Simon agreed to drive the car for me.

I telephoned an Inspector Bihlar last March and during our conversation he asked where I was. I told him I was in France. He then asked me what the weather was like in France. I told him I had not telephoned to talk about the weather. I hope that's enough to prove who I am.

The voice stopped, the tape crackled on for a few seconds. Then there was silence. All eyes instinctively turned towards Bihlar, who nodded sheepishly, then shrugged his shoulders. The first thing that struck me was that the voice had definitely been Christopher's; of that there was no doubt. The second was that he had got the car's registration number wrong; but there again how many people remember their car's number plate?

At any rate, no matter. At last we had heard from Christopher. The evidential value of the tape was probably weak, but it had to count for something.

There had been some disagreement, not to say a certain amount of speculation, over what Christopher had meant by 'set up' ... 'The set up was meant for me ...' Some, Dook included in his letter to my mother, had taken it to mean 'frame up'. In other words that the entire case had been concocted to frame Christopher, and/or me. Logically, it was being stressed that no one in their right mind would be willing to fork out the cost of fifty kilos of cannabis just to frame a layabout boat owner and his soldier brother. On Mitchell's part, it would have meant that he had also been willing to sacrifice his freedom. So, it was being argued that Christopher's claim was nothing more than a smokescreen, and was therefore proof of his mendacity. Unless there were significantly stronger forces at work, they had a point. Stronger forces? As my lawyers pointed out, the IRA, if indeed Dook was involved with them, would be quite willing to lay out a great deal more to frame an army officer. In return, I pointed out that a simple bullet would have been a much quicker and cheaper remedy for them.

In fact the answer was a simple one, as my mother revealed under cross-examination. She had understood Christopher to mean the event, the goings on, the entire scenario. '. . . by set up he meant that he should have been driving the car, not Simon.' No one had been framing anyone. Originally Christopher was to have driven the Jaguar, and he was implying that he was to have been the person being tricked.

My mother had given a second plucky performance in the witness box, and I believe everyone felt sympathy for the position she was in. However Forsberg managed to unnerve her towards the end of her testimony. It was ironic that he did so on an issue over which he was more than a little muddled himself. Perhaps that was the reason for his success?

'Where is your son Mrs Hayward?'

'I do not know. He would not tell me.'

'We heard earlier about a telephone call on 30 June during which a threat is alleged to have been made. Did you receive this call in your own home or elsewhere?'

'The call from Christopher? Not in my house, no.'

'And the subsequent calls you received; were they to your own home?'

'None were to my house. They were made to several different addresses.'

Forsberg was looking pleased with himself, and beside him Bihlar's face had taken on a self satisfied, smug expression.

'I would naturally like to know how your son knew where you would be?' It was not a question, it was an accusation.

'He would ring a particular number, one of several in a circle of family and friends, and ask the people concerned if they would in turn telephone me and invite me around. He would then call back some time later.'

'Did this procedure involve different people on each occasion?'

'Not always. If I remember correctly, one person twice, the others different.'

'Why did you not receive these phone calls at home?'

'Because I believe my telephone to be tapped.'

This was clearly an answer Forsberg had been waiting for. He was now looking extremely pleased with himself.

'But Mrs Hayward, a threat was made on 30 June in the first call. Would it not have been appropriate to agree with Christopher that he should telephone to your home so that the calls could be tapped?'

'Why should I do that? He is my son.'

'To get a better picture of the threats that were being made. Through having your phone tapped.'

This line of questioning was obviously confusing my mother. She paused for a few seconds before replying: 'I do not agree.'

My mother was looking puzzled. Of course she was, and she was not alone. What was Forsberg on about? There had been no threats made over the telephone, least of all by my brother. The threats had all been made verbally, by men who had approached my mother in the street. Unfortunately however, for the defence, Forsberg's line of questioning, albeit confusing, had made it look as though my mother was hiding Christopher's whereabouts. In fact, and this should have been better explained in court, she had no control over where and when Christopher telephoned; and I am sure that even if she had insisted on him ringing the home number, he would not have done so. It would have been logical for him to presume that since there was an Interpol warrant out for his arrest, that this line, if no other, would be tapped. Furthermore it had been the police who had warned my mother that her phone was in all probability being listened into, not by the authorities – they had bigger fish to fry – but illegally by unscrupulous journalists. It was just a pity that in the heat of the moment, and with the red-herring of threats being made over telephones, the true situation was not properly explained in court.

My younger brother Justin took the stand in order to clarify any doubts concerning the Jaguar's insurance policy. He explained that he had helped Christopher to arrange cover and presented documents as verification. There had been a problem over the no claims bonus and a consequent delay while the insurance company had sorted it out. A problem not helped by the difficult postal system on Ibiza. Christopher had only been given cover notes and had never received his actual policy document. Therefore, although he had asked for any driver and all European countries to be included, he had never received confirmation of this request. He had telephoned Justin from Ibiza in early March to establish whether I was indeed covered.

Justin was asked several questions regarding the complexities of British motor insurance, and he answered them all knowledgeably and confidently. It may seem a trivial subject but in reality his testimony added tremendous weight to mine, because it constituted independent verification of my reasons for having delayed my departure from Ibiza. It was a simple matter and as it turned out one that the Court took lightly.

Placht introduced Richard New and explained why he had been called as a witness.

'This testimony will show that a transport of fifty kilos of cannabis involving Captain Hayward would not have been carried out in the manner alleged; that there was no reason to be suspicious when Christopher Hayward told his brother that he wanted to sell his Jaguar; that information given by Mitchell cannot be correct; that it cannot be the case that Christopher is the organiser behind this shipment rather than Mitchell; that my client's claim that Christopher needed to repair his jeep and to buy spare parts for it in France is correct; that Mitchell, possibly with others, is the man behind this shipment, at least more involved than Christopher Hayward; that the theft of the Jaguar cannot have anything to do with any attempt to conceal knowledge about the drugs being hidden inside it; that Christopher is not a dangerous, highly qualified gangster as the prosecutor will try and make out; and that Mitchell must have known that Simon Hayward had no knowledge of the drugs' existence.'

New's evidence was of vital importance to the defence case, and expertly delivered with an air of confidence based on years of experience in combating drug smugglers. This time he left no room for misinterpretation or misunderstanding. He was the master of his brief, and under cross-examination drew attention to the fact that the District Court Judgement had totally misrepresented aspects of his previous testimony.

He expanded upon the information he had given at the trial, decribing his investigations on Ibiza, and detailing the inconsistencies in my behaviour with that of a person knowingly smuggling drugs, once again profiling the character of the usual type of courier.

'If Simon Hayward had been aware of what he was doing,'

he stated, 'I find it inconceivable that he did not bother to discuss the run in detail with Mitchell . . . with his background he would certainly have planned it better . . . In my opinion there are so many features about this trip, and so many things that happened before and during it, that would not be consistent with the behaviour of any knowing courier, let alone with someone of Mr Hayward's experience.'

· As to the theft of the Jaguar, having spoken to the Ibizan police regarding the way in which it was recovered . . . 'I am satisfied that the theft was genuine . . . no one would leave a vehicle unattended in Ibiza Town with 50 kilos of cannabis hidden inside it.'

'. . . it would have been unnecessary to drive via Andorra because the route is very much more difficult and dangerous than the coast road at that time of the year.'

'Aren't the customs posts in Andorra less effective?' asked Placht. The District Court had accepted that Andorra represented an easy route for smugglers.

'That is not correct. I've travelled both routes in the past. As far as I am aware there is no effective difference between either of them. At the trial I testified that customs checks were lax on both, however in the District Court Judgement the only aspect recorded are my views on the Andorran controls. The Judgement totally misrepresents what I actually said, in that it suggests that I support the view that Mr Hayward went that way to avoid more stringent customs checks on the direct coast road. I repeat that they are lax on both routes . . . Skiing equipment is considerably cheaper in Andorra. I have been skiing there.'

Judge Frohling was nodding off during this exchange. Could it have been because he didn't find this evidence helpful to his preconceptions?

'Can you describe what sort of character Christopher Hayward is?' asked Placht.

'Popular. There was a whip-round to enable him to leave Ibiza . . . a lazy bum. People just laughed at the idea that he was the boss behind this drugs ring. He was commonly viewed as being just too lazy, and totally incapable of organising anything on that scale . . . His source of income was generally known to have come from chartering his yacht.'

'Did you visit where he lived?'

'. . . I talked to the owner . . .' New continued by describing the villa in Santa Gertrudis. He had established that the rent for the property was approximately £2,500 a year. The house above San Juan he described as '. . . a shack.'

'Have you seen Mitchell's and Dook's houses?'

'Yes, Mitchell's is beautiful, with electricity, running water, swimming pool, ornamental ponds and a large landscaped garden. There is a main house and separate accommodation in outhouses. I went inside the house and it was very well furnished. By Ibizan standards it is a very expensive place. At Dook's there was considerable construction work going on. When completed it will be as expensive and as beautiful as Mitchell's, if not more so. It has all modern conveniences, and a very large swimming pool. It was very impressive.'

'How did you gain entry into Mitchell's house?'

'I was invited in by a 6ft 8in German "gentleman". I wanted to leave my telephone number for Prita in the hope that she would contact me. She did not.' There was laughter at the description of Prita's minder.

'Did you ask the Spanish police about Christopher, Dook and Mitchell?'

'They were not very forthcoming about Dook, except to say that he was known to have several passports . . . They were not asked to look for Christopher until June, by which time he had left the island. They had never heard of Mitchell, Prita or Makunda.'

When New said this there were sheepish looks on the prosecuting team's faces. It was little wonder they were embarrassed.

'You are used to interviewing suspects in drugs cases. In your experience do innocent people lie to protect close relatives. Do they often change their stories?'

'It is not at all uncommon. In fact it happens all the time, especially when close relatives are involved.' When New said this, there was an open sneer on Bihlar's face.

'Have you ever experienced, or heard of situations where a courier has been totally unaware that drugs were hidden in his car?'

'It is difficult to give an accurate answer, because of course one never hears of successful cases; but I do know of instances where couriers have carried not only narcotics but also other types of contraband without realising it. I can quote one recent and well known example of the woman who was given a case by her Arab boyfriend, containing explosives, to take on board an El Al Jumbo jet. She had no idea what she was being asked to do, and in fact would have gone down with the plane if the explosives had not been discovered.'

'. . . I would like to say a couple of things about the Jaguar, if I may?' Judge Frohling nodded his approval. 'I now understand it to be registered in Christopher Hayward's name. I find it inconceivable that someone who is supposed to be a principal in a professional drugs ring would use his own car for a run. To do so would be both unnecessary and suicidal. Likewise with using a relative to drive it. He might just as well have driven the thing himself . . . During the trial I was asked whether I thought a Jaguar was a suitable car for transporting large quantities of cannabis. I replied that for such purposes a large car, like a Jaguar, would be needed. However, it is needless to say not suitable for running drugs to Sweden where it would stand out, especially with British number plates. Clearly a Volvo or a SAAB would have been a better choice.'

'. . . I was able to verify many aspects of Simon Hayward's statements during my enquiries on Ibiza. In contrast, nothing I found in any way indicated that he was knowingly involved in this affair.'

New concluded his testimony by presenting photographs and a video of the various relevant sights on Ibiza. Part of the video showed the camino leading up to the house above San Juan. From it, it must have been clear to everyone in the courtroom that it would not have been possible to drive the Jaguar along it.

I felt greatly encouraged by New's testimony. It destroyed so much of the speculation being presented by the prosecution as evidence against me. What made me feel even better was that if appearances were anything to go by, Forsberg thought likewise.

Referring to notes throughout, Lawrence Gilmurray carefully detailed the contrasting road conditions and customs checks between the route I had driven from Spain into France via Andorra, and the direct coast road. It was a highly professional performance, complete with photographs in support of his claims, which was so methodical it risked becoming pedantic. Under the circumstances it was just what was needed.

He described the direct route as a fast and easy drive on motorway. The customs post was on the motorway itself, and when he had passed through it the 30 or 40 cars with him had all been waved through without 'challenge, question, or visual inspection'. All officials had looked bored and indifferent.

On the other hand, the drive to Andorra was on congested inland routes and small mountain roads, which were difficult especially in the winter, and would have been dangerous to an experienced driver. The Spanish customs going into the Principality and the French coming out had been 'smart, alert and vigilant'. When he had been there, cars were being stopped in random checks and thoroughly searched.

'Which of these two routes would be more suitable for a drugs courier to use?' asked Placht.

'In my view, there is no comparison whatsoever. My personal experience has convinced me that a courier would not entertain taking the Andorran route. Such people usually rely on the shortest route with regard to time and distance. Furthermore if for some reason the direct route could not be used, there are other much easier ones in existence through the Pyrenees than via Andorra.' He produced photographs of a couple of examples. 'Some with no customs at all . . . In my professional opinion for a courier to drive through Andorra would only be to enhance his chances of detection. Not only because he would have to pass through two border posts instead of one, but also if he needed to pass through quickly, as in the case with Captain Hayward, he would have drawn unnecessary attention to himself. To my mind it would not make sense.'

'So, to be absolutely clear, which customs post is the most efficient?' asked Placht.

'Those on the Andorran route.'

The three prosecution witnesses, whose testimony Forsberg had so optimistically declared would positively prove my guilt, actually provided nothing of the sort. Indeed they did not even come close to the mark.

Inspector Bjornevog, whom Placht had met on Ibiza, had been asked by the prosecutor to check on the border crossing points between Spain, Andorra and France; but in so doing, and this fact quickly became apparent from his testimony, he had not only driven totally different routes to my own but had also passed through each border in the opposite direction, and in consequence met with different customs checks. In effect he could not comment with any degree of authority on the issues in question, and although he tried hard to slant his evidence in favour of the prosecution, his testimony was at best neutral and at worst irrelevant. Compared to Gilmurray his performance was vague and unconvincing.

When his cross-examination was complete, he, Forsberg, Placht and I had to approach the Bench to explain with the use of a map exactly which roads we had driven along. During the ensuing discussion I was amused to see, when I stole a glance at the courtroom over one shoulder, that a rather eager young *Times* reporter was creeping forward, notebook in hand, craning to catch what was being said. I wondered how far he would get before one of the heavily armed guards 'arrested' him. To my surprise he safely reached the defence table. No one stopped him. He continued by edging along it, and finally sat on it, looking pleased with himself, having virtually arrived at the judge's Bench. From there he made his notes. It was only a pity we could not reward him with the 'scoop' his efforts had so richly deserved.

If this episode had been an indication of the relaxed easy going nature of Swedish courts, proof positive of this informality was to arrive a few minutes later when the Bench were putting some questions to the next witness.

'Could you speak up, Judge, we can't hear you back here,' a man shouted from the rear of the public gallery.

Without raising an eyebrow, and before one could say 'Contempt of Court', the amiable Judge Wilhelmson asked for a microphone to be switched on.

'Is that any better?' he asked.

'Ya, thanks very much.'

Having assured himself that he was now heard by all, the case continued. Christopher Murray looked visibly taken aback.

'In an English court,' he whispered to me, 'that chap's feet wouldn't have touched the ground before he was done for contempt.'

If Inspector Roger Sales Traver, Head of the Ibizan Drug Squad, was anything to go by, it was little wonder that the island had become a haven for drug smugglers.

His testimony became so confusing and so speculative that as it turned out it did not even warrant analysis in the Court Judgement. All it received was the smallest of mentions explaining the reason why he had been called as a prosecution witness, which was to prove that no theft of the Jaguar had taken place – an aim he failed to achieve.

To confuse the situation still further, he spoke only Spanish. (Not his fault of course.) Consequently a woman interpreter sat beside him in the witness box translating his Spanish into Swedish. Beside me, Martin Naylor, the usual court interpreter translated the Swedish interpretation into English. The opportunities for semantic errors were endless – a translation of a translation.

It very quickly became apparent that Traver had been the police officer whom Richard New had interviewed with my mother on Ibiza. On that occasion he had been called Inspector Rogelio, so either he had decided for some reason to give them a false name or there had been a genuine misunderstanding somewhere along the line. Such factors only served to further complicate the situation. He had also been, on his own admission, the duty officer who countersigned the reports of the Jaguar's theft; although he 'forgot' to tell the Court that he had to be woken up to do so.

He stated that in his opinion the theft had been faked but could not properly justify his conclusion. He stated that there should have been no language problem when I had reported the car stolen, but in so doing not only did he fail to admit that he had been fast asleep at the time but it also became evident that he was not at all sure if the officers who had been on duty that night could speak English or not, nor of the exact procedures they had followed. He stated that the car had been recovered less than 500 metres from where it had supposedly been stolen – 'no robber would do that' – but on examining a map of the area it was quite clear that the actual distance between both points was in fact closer to a kilometre and a half. Whilst agreeing that the car had been recovered by a roving patrol without any kind of tip-off, he claimed that it had been abandoned in an obvious position beside a popular discotheque where it was common local knowledge that the police made frequent checks. What he failed to mention was that in March the discotheque would have been closed, and therefore presumably these checks would not normally have been carried out.

He agreed that he had spoken to Richard New but denied that he had informed him that Dook had a number of false passports, indeed he told the Court that he still did not know if this was the case. Since New had taped the original conversation and there had been other witnesses to it, my mother and the Spanish interpreter who had been hired for the interview, the defence could have proved this statement was blatantly untrue and a breach of the oath he had taken before giving evidence. However Placht decided to let the issue pass on the grounds that the testimony was already so discredited that it would have made little difference.

To cap it all, from the way the police had written up the documents recording the theft it appeared as though the car had been recovered before it had been stolen, a discrepancy that Traver was at a loss to explain.

In addition, far from saying that there were more than a hundred Jaguars on Ibiza, as Forsberg had claimed he would, he said instead that there were never more than five, all owned by tourists and none by locals. Thus unwittingly he further weakened the prosecutor's contention that the island roads were quite suitable for such vehicles.

I took it as an indictment of the way the entire investigation had been conducted that this same man had told New and my mother that in his opinion I had nothing to do with the smuggling ring, and yet after a visit from his Swedish counterparts here he was trying to prove the exact opposite at my trial.

Kriminal Inspector Åke Swan had been the officer in charge of the police surveillance team which had ambushed and arrested me. At the time I thought little of his testimony if anything it seemed to support defence points of view, but as it was to turn out the Bench clearly saw things differently and used it as one of their strongest arguments against me.

The gist of his evidence was that I had been checking my tail on the drive from Linköping railway station, and therefore by implication must have known what was hidden in the car.

He explained that he had had six car loads of policemen in position around the station on the evening of 13 March. He had been alone in the lead car when Mitchell and I had left on the drive towards Motala but a few kilometres further on had surrendered the lead and had taken up second place in the team. Several kilometres after that the leading police driver had reported over the radio that both Saab and Jaguar had suddenly turned off right into a smaller road, and that he had overshot the turning and was unable to follow.

Swan described how he had been so close behind that he had only just managed to make the turn himself, drifting widely as he did so. He had then seen the Jaguar completely stationary in the middle of the side road about 100 metres away, and had been able to drive slowly up behind it before it in turn had begun to roll slowly forwards before gathering speed to catch up with the Saab.

He explained that this manoeuvre was a text book example of a counter surveillance measure, and that he had therefore come to the conclusion that his team had been rumbled and had consequently ordered a strike.

I was astonished by this evidence. I was certain I had neither stopped the car in the middle of the road, nor had I slowly driven forward when another car had approached close behind, nor had I positively realised I was being followed; indeed I had known of no reason why anyone should want to follow me. None of Swan's testimony made any sense to me, and I was equally certain that this police officer was genuinely mistaken, with a sketchy recollection of events – a belief strengthened when under cross-examination he could not even remember what type of car he had been driving on the night.

In any case, his evidence was more than a little illogical, because he continued by saying that having carried out this supposed 'cops and robbers' manoeuvre to see if I was being followed, and having established that I was, I had then driven on normally for a further five kilometres as if nothing had happened, until the police had finally sprung their ambush. My behaviour he claimed was proof that I knew what was hidden in the Jaguar.

He must have realised that his theory was weak, and sounded implausible, because he attempted to strengthen it by adding that in his view the driver of the Jaguar would have had only two options once he had established he was being followed. Namely to continue to drive smoothly with the risk (if not certainty) of being arrested; or of trying to drive away and escape, something which for an Englishman would not have been easy, if at all possible, on Sweden's narrow roads.

With his admitted amateur driving antics, anyone knowing that they were committing a crime and therefore on the lookout for the police, could not have failed to notice Swan's fast and erratic entry into the narrow side road, to say nothing of his supposedly suspiciously slow approach to the supposedly stationary Jaguar.

Once anyone realises he is being followed the adrenalin starts to pump, especially I would venture a criminal with something to hide. Had I known that I was sitting on fifty kilos of cannabis, and then discovered or even suspected that I was about to be arrested, my veins would have been full of the stuff. My immediate concern would have been survival. To avoid arrest at all costs and the inevitable consequences of conviction. For me, such consequences would have been totally unthinkable. In short, I would have found it hard not to panic, I would have done anything to get away.

Anticipating the content of Swan's testimony, Placht had asked Gilmurray and Brigadier Emson what in their view my reaction to such a situation would have been. Gilmurray had testified that the immediate reaction of any miscreant would be to try and place as much distance between himself and his pursuers as possible, to enable him either to lose them completely, or temporarily while he abandoned his car and escaped on foot to safety. In the event that this course of action proves impossible then the very least anyone could do would be to abandon the vehicle immediately and attempt to decamp on foot. The brigadier explained that soldiers using civilian cars in Northern Ireland are trained to drive out of an ambush and go immediately to the nearest Security Force base.

I had done none of these things. Albeit I had been in unknown territory, and the Jaguar had not been equipped with snow tyres, the narrow Swedish roads would have presented no more difficulty than those in Northern Ireland; and I am an experienced and well-trained driver. In addition, I had been at the wheel of a large and powerful car, if nothing else if I had known what was going down, I could have, indeed I would have, made a jolly good attempt at getting away. I would have had nothing to lose, and a lot to gain, by trying. At the very least, at the next T-junction, I could have turned left instead of following Mitchell to the right towards Zinkgruvan.

The fact remained that I had continued to drive normally for a further five kilometres before being stopped and detained. The least reasonable behaviour for a drugs courier, once he establishes that he is about to be arrested would be to drive on as if nothing had happened. Only a complete madman, or alternatively an innocent man, would do that.

If anything, Swahn's evidence was an indication of my innocence, not my guilt.

Of all the witnesses, without a doubt the most extraordinary was H K ter Brake, Dook's Dutch lawyer, who had been called by Forsberg in an attempt to counteract the defence argument that Dook was involved in the case and that Mitchell was lying in order to protect him.

He was a thin, effeminate man in his early thirties, with a spurious relaxation in his manner that made him seem rather tense – a contradiction that conveyed an impression of neurosis. During the time he delivered his evidence, which he did in reasonable but heavily accented English, his manner and general appearance undermine what little credibility he might otherwise have had, which was virtually nil. To me, he seemed to incriminate rather than vindicate his client.

'The main reason I am here,' he stated, 'is not to testify against Simon Hayward, but to clear the name of Dook ... Dook is not involved in this crime, he is innocent. If he could prove Simon's innocence he would, but he knows nothing and cannot help.'

He said Dook had come to see him on 27 April in Holland to ask for help, explaining that he had fled from Ibiza because 'Hayward has been arrested and they are going to blame me for that.' He had asked ter Brake to make contact with the lawyers in Sweden to find out if his name had been mentioned.

This was very interesting news. Christopher had not revealed Dook's identity, or his alleged role in the affair, until the end of June. So why was it that Dook had gone to a lawyer in April saying that he was going to be implicated? How could he possibly have known that? Of course, the only logical answer lay in the fact that he was very much involved and realising that there was a strong possibility of his name cropping up sooner or later in the investigation, had decided to hedge his bets. And why, if he had nothing to hide, had he found it necessary to uproot his family by 'fleeing' from Ibiza, leaving behind a beautiful house and a comfortable way of life?

'Dook came to see me in August,' ter Brake was saying, 'after the trial of Simon Hayward and he showed me press-cuttings "MY SEARCH FOR DOOK THE DRUGS BARON". He said to me: "What shall we do about this? I am an innocent man." He wanted to write to Mrs Hayward ... so that she could see that Dook is innocent and Chris Hayward is a liar ... The reason for sending this letter to Mitchell was because he knows him from Ibiza, they are not close friends, and Dook said Mitchell must be informed about this ... I typed out Dook's letter to ensure his handwriting could not be identified.'

'The defence is blaming Dook more and more; WHY, WHY, WHY ...? to begin with he thought Simon was innocent but after he saw the trial judgement he realised that Simon is framing him too.'

This misconception was obviously based on a mistake in the District Court Judgement document, in which it was stated I had testified that Dook and Christopher had left the table together during the meeting at Santa Eulalia and had been away for 'about an hour'. I had never said any such thing, and I have not the least idea why the mistake was made, but under the circumstances Dook could be forgiven for thinking that I had been lying about him.

In fact many such seemingly irrelevant errors can be found in the judgement documents from both the trial and appeal. Perhaps because the court officials were more often than not sound asleep.

Ter Brake continued with his testimony: 'Dook was sending me articles from English newspapers. They became worse, and worse, and worse. Mrs Hayward keeps blaming Dook! WHY, WHY, WHY? . . . He is suffering a lot. He is travelling around the world. He believes his life is in danger because of his being in the British press. There is so much hatred against this little, little Irishman. They are going to murder him.'

'Who are going to murder him?' asked Placht.

'Uncontrollable elements in the British Army. It fits the picture to blame an Irishman. A small Irishman!' While he made this idiotic claim ter Brake held his arm out, the palm of his hand downwards, to emphasise just what a pigmy this Dook fellow really was. The situation was becoming more ludicrous by the second. 'The British people and the British Army believe that a little Irishman can bring down a big captain, that is why he is so afraid.'

'Dook phoned me last night . . . I told him that Richard New had shown video films of a big house with a swimming pool. 'That is not my house,' he told me, 'Lies, lies, lies!' I said that the defence were claiming he is in the IRA. 'More lies, more lies,' he told me. I tried to convince him to come forward as a witness but he says his life in in danger. 'They will murder me . . . You cannot trust these lawyers, you cannot trust these Haywards'.'

'You spoke to Dook yesterday?' asked Placht.

'Yes, with Mr Forsberg and Inspectors Nilsson and Bihlar at the police station.

'Why was I not informed of this call before it was made?' Placht demanded of Forsberg.

'Because Dook will not speak with the defence,' Forsberg replied. So once again the prosecutor had denied my lawyers access to a witness. The list seemed never-ending. At the very least he could have allowed Placht to sit in on the call as a silent observer, and to have put defence questions for him.

Ter Brake went on to confirm that Nilsson had indeed told Dook to 'lie low at an unknown place' and not to come forward to testify. 'Inspector Nilsson said to me: "We are not interested in Dook at all, we believe Mitchell when he says book is not involved".'

'What is your client's real name?' Placht asked.

'I cannot answer that question. He is afraid of anything that will reveal his identity. He is afraid of the British Army.'

'Isn't it unusual for innocent people to have false names? Isn't it unusual for them not to come forward to put themselves at the disposal of the investigating authorities? Isn't it unusual for them not even to want to show their handwriting?'

'Yes,' agreed ter Brake, 'very unusual, and Dook is my first client to behave like this; but I am convinced he is innocent. I feel it. He is not a liar. He is a quiet family man.'

'A quiet family man.' That was exactly the same way Mitchell had described Dook. It made me wonder if he and this strange lawyer had not been swapping notes with one another?

'You and I are both lawyers,' continued Placht, 'Wouldn't you say it was unusual for lawyers to make up their minds so positively about their client's innocence or guilt?'

'Yes, very unusual,' agreed ter Brake for the second time, before going on to make himself look even more inane, 'but Dook is my first client who really is innocent. He is not involved. I never say such things normally. It is the first time in my life!'

'You can say that on the basis of two or three meetings?'

'Yes, but they were long ones.' (Very long, one had lasted for at least two hours.)

By this stage everyone was looking at the Dutchman with incredulity. When he finished, I was left feeling that his testimony was nothing more than a complete red herring and had no relevance, from the prosecutions point of view. I must confess that I never understood the basis on which he gave his evidence, nor for that matter what he was really talking about. I suspect the Bench felt likewise.

In fact, by going overboard, Dook and his lawyer seemed not only to be protesting too much but also, by becoming involved at all, to be incurring a lot of suspicion and gaining precious little exoneration. Indeed, from a defence point of view, ter Brake had supplied some valuable tit-bits of information.

Richard New returned to the stand immediately after ter Brake for re-examination. He produced proof that the house he had filmed was in fact Dook's, despite the Irishman's claims to the contrary. Not only had local people directed him to it, but once there he had found items in the rubbish bins that belonged to Dook and his family: A letter addressed to Dook's common-law-wife, which ended 'give my regards to Dook'; a school report for one of his children; and invitations to his son Alvi's birthday party, incorporating not only Dook's name but also a detailed map of how to find the house. Dook's decision to deny ownership only incriminated him still further.

After a short break the Court resumed with Judge Frohling reciting the evidence of witnesses who attended the District Court but were not being called to appear at the appeal – Basil Hadrell, Simon Falkner and the two Swedish police officers. He also read out two letters from Dook, the one that had been sent to my mother and another posted to Forsberg. The second was in the same rambling, semi-religious style as the first but in this instance, far from hinting at my innocence, Dook was taking a swing at me, Christopher, and my mother; whom he accused of personally organising Christopher's escape and of terrorising everyone on Ibiza with 'hired henchmen'.

I am not involved. Christopher Hayward has 'framed' me. The Haywards are using me as a scapegoat. They have fabricated this cloud of confusion so Christopher could escape. He is more than an embarrassment to them. They know that if Christopher was to talk directly to the authorities his lies would be quickly exposed. They have created another Lord Lucan saga. They have master-minded and financed his escape and have fed the British media the lie – leaving it howling for the blood of an Irishman.

In this time of struggle I must persevere in my claim that I am not involved in any way with Captain Simon Hayward. I have nothing to do with it. But this struggle will have its reward . . . the truth will come out. These lies, cast in the face of God, will not float. They will sink with the liars.

The letter continued in this vein for another four pages. At the time I was surprised that the Bench had accepted either script as evidence, I believed in doing so it had only weakened the Court's image and prestige. In the following months when additional evidence did finally come to light, I was to remember Dook's words '... the truth will come out ... the lies will not float' – with a smile. They were to rebound firmly back onto him.

On Wednesday 7 October, at the end of seven days of often laborious cross examination, Judge Wilhelmson adjourned the Court pending the result of the Juhlin investigation.

Giving a press conference outside the courthouse, Forsberg stated: 'It's getting repetitive. One feels a bit disconsolate. I've been at it for seven months now. I'm tired.' He even admitted to a British journalist that he did not feel sure of himself in court unless Bihlar was present to support him, and that he was thinking of giving up law to become an insurance salesman. Good riddance to him!

Tom Placht gave an interview of his own: 'This case is such a hell of a mess. The police are determined that Captain Hayward is guilty, determined to nail him, and have only looked at evidence that will help them do that.'

When Bihlar was asked to comment about the supplementary investigation, he said: 'That does not bother us, the conviction will still be upheld.'

Whilst I was returned to languish in the cells of Kronoberg, my lawyers continued to work on my behalf. One major problem that had arisen was the interpretation being attached to Assistant Commissioner Hewett's letter explaining his decision not to allow Morgan and Moore to give evidence. Although he had written that neither officer could 'vouch for the truth and accuracy' of their report, and 'all the information within their knowledge would amount to hearsay evidence' – inadmissible in an English court; the District Court had taken this to mean that the information could not be vouched for only because it was hearsay. Hearsay is of course admissible in Swedish courts.

Mr Hewett had retired before the appeal had started but in reply to a summons issued against Morgan and Moore by Forsberg to attend as prosecution witnesses, a Detective Chief Superintendent David Stockley (NDIU) had written to the Court to explain that the criteria behind Hewett's original letter still stood, and once again refused to allow the two officers to testify.

However, Kingsley Napley were concerned that the Appeal

Court would draw the same conclusion as the District Court and therefore took advantage of the adjournment to seek an unequivocal interpretation of the facts. The following answer was received from the NDIU, signed by a Detective Superintendent C Flint, on 16 October:

Mr Hewett, in his response to a request by Mr Forsberg for the two NDIU officers to attend the hearing, made it clear that neither officer was able to vouch for the truthfulness or accuracy of the information contained in the report given by them to the Swedish Police and, further, that the information within their knowledge amounted to hearsay evidence. In any similar proceedings in this country it would be held to be inadmissible. For *both* these reasons he regretted that he was unable to accede to the request.

It was felt that this clarification, and reiteration, of Mr Hewett's motives would put the informer issue to rest for good. Surely no court, not even a Swedish one, could attach any weight to information that had been so totally discredited, despite Gunnar Larsen's testimony. In fact there was an interesting sequel to the matter which served to highlight an inconsistency in Larsen's behaviour.

By coincidence there was a second drugs case going on at the same time in Norway involving two English brothers called Harward, who had been held in a similar manner to my own. Towards the end of October Nicholas Rossiter, a British journalist who had been following their plight, telephoned Christopher Murray to inform him that Larsen had also featured at the Harward trial at which he had once again supplied information originating from an informer. The difference on this occasion was that he had quite happily revealed his informant's name. His refusal to do the same at my trial and appeal, for given reasons that should have applied in both cases, added further weight to the contention that there was something very fishy about the Morgan and Moore Report.

I found this period waiting for the appeal to restart incredibly frustrating, not to say nerve-racking. A sentiment that was not helped by the ink-slinging accomplishments of the press.

As if the situation was not already complicated enough, yet another red herring was produced by elements of the media to further confuse matters. An article appeared in the satirical magazine *The Digger* on 8 October identifying Dook as a well known Irish terrorist-cum-conman by the name of James 'The Fox' Mcann, a theme which other publications picked up and expanded upon. Although it seemed unlikely that there was any truth behind the story, it prompted further investigations during which Bihlar and Nilson visited me with photographs of Mcann to see if I could identify him as Dook. In fact they did not show me photographs but poor quality photocopies of equally poor quality photographs from which it would have been difficult to identify one's own father. However, I was fairly certain that whoever was in the blurred prints I was shown, it was not Dook.

Mr Juhlin produced his report on 15 October. Tom Placht brought a copy of it to Kronoberg to discuss its more salient points with me. It was a 105 page document consisting of a covering letter, signed by the two police officers who had conducted most of the legwork involved; several extracts from Österåker prison records referring to Mitchell's visits and telephone calls; and statements taken from Forsberg, Nilsson, Bihlar, Philipsson, Sandin and Mitchell.

Juhlin came to two basic conclusions. The first and most surprising was that there was no proof that Rita and a woman calling herself Marylyn J Waterfield, who had visited Mitchell at Österåker in June, were one and the same person. This was a quite extraordinary assertion and all that is really needed to show that the inquiry report was indeed a deception. To quote from the official findings drawn up on page one of the covering letter:

'The visit has been recorded but investigations have not been able to show that Mitchell's common-law-wife "Prita" is identical with the woman who visited him at the prison during 21-27 June 1987.'

And yet on page eight of the report it clearly states, and again I quote:

Concerning Prita, Mitchell's common-law wife.

Sometime during the middle of June Mitchell requested

(to the prison authorities) that his common-law-wife Prita should be allowed to visit him. Mitchell provided an uncompleted civic registration number (5205) for his visitor. The reason for this could be that he had forgotten or did not want to leave the correct number. Upon arrival at Österåker Prita had to present her passport, a British one, from which it was evident that her name is Waterfield Marylyn J, 530504. On the visiting card the name Prita has been signed beside the above mentioned name.

From the visiting records it is clear that Waterfield has had an unguarded visit with Mitchell in accordance with the prosecutor's wishes.

One can only marvel at this clear contradiction and speculate that as with so many prolix bureaucratic reports, the authors were banking that the reader would only refer to its covering letter.

Even ignoring the comments on page eight there was a great deal of evidence to prove that Prita was using a passport in the name of Waterfield, all of which was available to the inquiry. The most significant perhaps was the receipt that Richard New had found in Prita's rubbish bins on Ibiza, which had been presented to the Appellant Court as an exhibit. Both Mitchell and Philipsson had told the inquiry that Prita had visited Mitchell in June, shortly after his trial; and had not Prita herself grudgingly admitted the same in her telephone conversation with Bihlar and Pontein. Bihlar had also told the investigators that he had seen Prita at Österåker in June. (An admission that stunned Placht and was going to lead to some awkward questioning for Bihlar when the appeal reconvened.) Finally, the prison records noted Waterfield as Mitchell's common-law-wife – how many was the man supposed to have?

The only logical answer, and one that any open-minded investigator would have come to, was that Prita, a German National, was using a false British passport.

Juhlin's second conclusion was that there was no evidence of a deal between the prosecution and Mitchell. To quote from the covering letter once more:

Prosecutor Forsberg and Kriminalinspektor's Jan-Erik

Nilsson and Jan Bihlar have all contested the claims that they gave promises to Mitchell with the intention of persuading him to testify against Simon Hayward. It is also contested that they refused to investigate suspicions concerning 'Prita' for the same reasons.

During questioning with Philipsson it has been evident that some of his statements made to the lawyer (Placht) in general contain information that Mitchell claims to have given to other people. (In other words – hearsay.)

In effect Juhlin was stating that there was no evidence of a deal simply because the prosecution refused to admit to one. However, while there may have been no concrete proof of any 'arrangement,' there were, for anyone willing to look beyond the end of his nose, very strong indications that one had occurred. Presumably in its blind conviction that a public official would never dream of telling a lie, the inquiry did not believe they were worth even a mention. For example:

1. Philipsson and Sandin had nothing to gain by coming forward, nor had they an axe to grind. This fact should have strengthened their evidence and yet, despite being corroborated from other independent sources, it was brushed aside and labelled as unsubstantiated hearsay.

2. Again significant, and not questioned by Juhlin, was Sandin's sudden refusal to testify. When interviewed by the investigators his entire attitude had undergone an extraordinary change from his earlier discussions with Placht and Pontein. On this occasion he apparently went wild, literally bellowing that he had nothing to say. It was evident that Bihlar's deliberate act of sabotage in tipping off Mitchell had contributed to Sandin's change of heart and unwillingness to co-operate. There was little doubt that Mitchell had put his newly acquired information to good use by intimidating the man, who lived in the same prison wing as himself, into silence. Philipsson would have been more difficult to 'discourage' because he was on a different wing.

Bihlar, needless to say, denied telling Mitchell anything,

saying that he had only learnt the inmates' identities himself from a journalist later on the same day that Placht had presented their statements to the Court. This was yet another lie, and demonstrably so, because not only had I been able to give Philipsson's name to Placht right out of the blue, but no reporter had been able to glean the details of the supplementary investigation until the following day. Indeed questions should have been asked as to how Mitchell had been able to rubbish the allegations in an LBC broadcast before he himself had been interviewed by the inquiry and officially informed of the inmates names.

3. Viryo and Anderson had testified that there had been at least nine runs to Sweden, yet Mitchell had only been charged with six. A fact that lent weight to the allegations of a deal.

4. Prita was neither officially interviewed, nor arrested. Neither were any other of Mitchell's accomplices on Ibiza. Nor were enquiries carried out on the island until September. If these facts do not point to a deal, nothing does.

5. It is unusual, to say the very least, for an arrested member of a drugs ring to talk openly about his superiors, as Mitchell had done. There was a possibility therefore that he had been given a strong inducement to do so.

6. Mitchell told the investigators that while in the Häktet he had been able to pass messages out to Ibiza, warning his accomplices to flee. The ability to evade the strict restrictions supposedly placed upon him by Forsberg could only lend support to the probability of a deal, especially since he must have passed his messages by telephone.

7. If Tervaniemi's testimony was anything to go by, Prita was herself a fugitive from the German authorities. She had been living together with Mitchell during the time the Jaguar's run to Sweden had been planned. She had been in practically daily contact with Mitchell when he had been in Sweden before his arrest. Mitchell had told the police she had passed

messages between him and Christopher concerning the run.
And finally she had met Mitchell's Swedish accomplices.
Despite all of this the police had refused to interview her and
had allowed her to visit Mitchell in Sweden on a false British
passport. It was clear also that she was living on Ibiza on
these false papers, and if inquiries had commenced on the
island resulting in her true identity being discovered she
would have had to have left. As a German citizen she would
probably have found herself in custody, and deported back
to Germany. It must have been obvious to anyone, even
Juhlin's investigators, that it was clearly in Mitchell's
interests to protect her. An aim he had quite evidently
succeeded in; and yet they still persisted in their claim that
there was no evidence of a deal.

8. Österåker Prison records revealed that Prita's visit had been
   authorised by Forsberg, and that Bihlar had also called on
   Mitchell on 25 June – one of the days Prita had been with
   him. It should be remembered that when Placht had asked,
   during the District Court hearing, why no attempt had been
   made to question Prita, Forsberg had replied that Bihlar had
   in fact spoken to her on the telephone. Furthermore, Bihlar
   had in turn testified under oath that he had asked Prita to
   come forward to be interviewed but that she had refused to
   comply. Clearly that had been a lie, and Forsberg must have
   been aware that Bihlar was lying. It was now quite evident
   that Prita had been in Sweden only six weeks previously and
   neither man had mentioned this. Since both had known of
   her visit, this omission could only be interpreted as a
   deliberate attempt to mislead the Court, and to my mind
   was a clear case of perjury.

Despite these serious misgivings about the results of the
Supplementary Investigation; misgivings only strengthened by
the knowledge that the person charged with carrying it out, far
from being a wholly independent and neutral investigator, was
in fact Forsberg's direct superior; needless to say the Appellant
Court accepted its findings in full and without question. In
turn an indication of its own bias and lack of impartiality.
When it was accepted, I realised that I was going to be

convicted. It was obvious that nothing the defence put forward was going to make the slightest difference – I was going to be convicted.

When the inquiry results were made public the prosecution tried to push home its advantage.

'The inquiry has found no substance to the defence claims. If anything, it is the other way around and Mitchell has in fact been harshly treated.'

Bihlar said he was dismayed at what he called 'the undercover activity and smoke screen tactics' of the defence team, led jointly by the Swedish advokat Tom Placht and the London firm of solicitors, Kingsley Napley. 'Look at Hitler,' he said. 'They blamed the Jews for everything when it was in fact the SS going around smashing windows. Tom Placht should know better than to try to get at me. He knows I'm honest.'

I was never able to fathom how Bihlar's mind worked. This ridiculous statement did not help.

Mitchell was the first witness to be called when the Court reconvened. His examination followed exactly the same lines as on the previous occasion. Once again he said just enough to damn me without actually condemning me outright, giving his evidence with the same laid-back self confidence, choosing his words carefully but effortlessly – as if they had been well rehearsed. Once again he gave a convincing performance but just as before Placht succeeded in tying him up in knots and in highlighting the inherent contradictions and discrepancies in his testimony.

'Objectively one should say I never spoke to Simon Hayward about drugs and he may not have known that there was cannabis hidden in the Jaguar. Subjectively I have my own opinions on the matter, but considering my position I feel it's wisest to keep them to myself . . . It is actually possible that Chris lied to me. I can scarcely imagine why he should lie, but it is in any case a possibility. He had never lied to me previously . . . On both occasions I met Simon, it appeared to me that he was aware of what he was doing, but of course I might have been mistaken . . . I can assure you that if I had been met by someone who had the impression that he was to deliver a car to me so that I could sell it, rather than the drugs

that were hidden inside it, a very confusing situation would
have arisen.'

'What can you tell us about the person known as Dook?'

'Not very much. I was introduced to him by Chris in 1985.
I am sure he does not have anything to do with this matter.
The idea that he is the dangerous man in the background is,
I consider, totally unfounded and totally ridiculous. He is a
quiet family man.'

He spoke with bitterness about what he said was harassment
by agents employed by 'Haywards mother' of his girlfriend,
whom he repeated had nothing to do with the affair,
emphasising that these agents had tried to persuade people on
Ibiza that he had been spilling the beans when in reality it was
'Simon who had been doing all the talking.'

'My girlfriend and her son have been harassed by some men
employed by Mrs Hayward who go under the ambiguous
description of private detectives,' he said. 'This came to a head
a few weeks ago when one of them actually entered my house
by force, claiming to be looking for some papers.'

Now that he had had time to think and knowing what
arguments the defence were employing, Mitchell was able to
limit some of the damage he had committed at the trial. For
example, when re-questioned about the 'Royalty Cafe' he
replied simply that Christopher had told him of the meeting.
Sadly the importance of this point would have been lost on the
Judges without having seen his earlier confusion.

'Has Prita been to visit you?' asked Placht.

'Yes, she came after my trial. She was here in Sweden for a
week, and I think she came and visited me on five occasions.'

'Were there any contacts between you and the police
concerning her visit?'

'No, the police were not interested in her.'

'Did they tell you that?'

'Yes, she has nothing to do with this affair.'

'What type of citizenship does she hold?'

'I do not wish to discuss my girlfriend's nationality or her
name.' Mitchell was looking shifty.

'In your interview with the police officers conducting the
supplementary investigation you said, and I quote:
Simon told his story as if he were on holiday. So I sent down

a message to Ibiza in order to get everybody off the island.'

'Who received this message?'

'I cannot discuss that?'

'Well then, perhaps you will tell us how you got the messages out?'

'I can't talk about that either.' Not won't, but can't.

'Do I understand that it was possible to send and also to receive messages during the period when you were sitting in an isolation cell?' demanded Placht.

'Yes, of the simplest kind.'

As for Philipsson's and Sandin's allegations? Mitchell rubbished them, saying there was not a word of truth in anything that had been said. 'I have been given seven years,' he said, 'I wouldn't call that a very good deal!' Sandin had not wanted to become involved but Philipsson had forced him. And then, as is so often the case when a person is trying to hide something, Mitchell went too far, trying to be too clever, and in any impartial hearing would have destroyed much of his credibility.

He denounced Philipsson as an AIDS carrier, a rather malicious, totally irrelevant and unnecessary revelation, saying that he was confined in the prison psychiatric wing, thus implying that the man was also a lunatic. He declared that he had come forward only because he bore a personal grudge against Forsberg, an allegation that the prosecutor reluctantly had to disagree with because neither man had come across the other before. And finally he stated that Philipsson had been paid to testify against him.

As for Nasim Tervaniemi, Mitchell declared that even her own lawyer had told him that he could not believe a word the woman said; and that far from being her 'boss', she had once asked Prita and him to carry seven kilos of cannabis in a suitcase from India to Central Europe, a request they had both turned down. And just for good measure he mounted a personal attack by saying Tervaniemi had been a brothel keeper in Bombay. He was obviously conducting a mud-slinging exercise, hoping that if he threw enough some of it would stick.

Before Mitchell stood down Judge Frohling asked him some questions:

'Do you know when the car was loaded?'

'Yes, more or less. Some time between 2 or 3 March and the 7 or 8 March.'

I doubt Mitchell realised it but he had just destroyed his own argument that I, as the courier, would have been present when the drugs were loaded, so that I would know how to unload them in Sweden. During this period I had not even been on Ibiza, I had been on Gibraltar.

'Do you know who Poonananda is?'

'Yes, that was Chris's Bhagwan name.'

Per Philipsson followed Mitchell to the stand, and for both his testimony and Tervaniemi's, who testified on the following day, Mitchell was allowed to remain in the courtroom, sitting conspicuously in the front row of he public gallery, in order that he could comment on the evidence after each witness had finished. If anything was designed to be intimidating for a witness, this was. On Philipsson especially it had a noticeable effect.

Sadly he was not a convincing witness. He was obviously unwell, and looked it. A man of about forty and above average height, wearing jeans and a khaki shirt. He had longish, somewhat unkept hair. The overall impression he gave was one of dissipation and depravity. As Mitchell had so unkindly revealed, he was a heroin addict suffering from AIDS.

'Yes, I am housed in the Psychiatric Wing of the prison,' he admitted when Placht questioned him, 'but only because I have an illness in my body, not because I am mentally sick.'

He was clearly under a good deal of pressure, especially, as he stated, in the prison where his willingness to testify had made life very difficult for him. Unfortunately for the defence, this obviously had an efect on his testimony since he was less forthcoming in court than he had been in private to Pontein.

The gist of what he would say was that Mitchell had been worried about receiving a larger sentence, was very satisfied with only seven years' and that he had struck a deal with the police in which he would stick to his statements about me in return for the police not involving Prita in the investigation; and that they would help him to get half remission on his sentence.

He added that Sandin had been subjected to 'a lot of trouble' which was why he was refusing to co-operate.

'Have you a personal grudge against Mr. Forsberg?'

'No, why should I have? I have never met him or these policemen before.'

Mitchell's response to this was once again to deny all the allegations: 'The only deals I discussed with the police were hash deals!'

In direct contrast to Philipsson, Nasim Tervaniemi proved to be even more loquacious than on her previous appearance. She explained in as much detail as she could about the structure of the drugs ring, repeating that Mitchell owned the consignments and employed someone called 'Poonananda' to transport them from Morocco to Ibiza. On the island a mechanic would conceal the cannabis in cars and then women were used as couriers to Sweden, where Makunda, who was Mitchell's right-hand-man, would meet them and deliver the consignments personally to Mitchell.

As for Prita? She was heavily involved. She had even introduced Mitchell to the right contacts to enable him to set up the first drug run from Ibiza, from which he had made enough money to invest in Morocco himself. The two of them had been working together for years:

'Mitchell and Prita were smuggling hash in Germany in the early 1980s. Prita was arrested but managed to escape to Ibiza, where she is still living on a false passport . . . I have never asked Mitchell or her to smuggle drugs for me in Central Europe . . . I have never run a brothel in Bombay.'

She went on to describe Mitchell as a rich man, with a Swiss bank account, who had boasted to her that he need never work again.

'Do you know who this Poonananda is?' asked Placht.

'No, I don't know his real name.'

Her most significant disclosure, and one that came almost as an after-thought, was that Mitchell had an Irish partner on Ibiza. She did not recognise the name 'Dook' but remained adamant that Mitchell and this Irishman were 'a team on Ibiza.' The Irishman figured prominently in the sale of drugs from the island to Sweden. He had not been involved in Mitchell's first shipment, but he had in all subsequent ones. Together they had also sold drugs in Norway.

'Do you think that this is the person Mitchell wants to protect?' asked Placht.'

'Yes, but also Makunda and Prita.'

'Are you certain that Prita is involved in Mitchell's smuggling activities?'

'Oh yes. I have handed money to Prita on Ibiza, and I was in contact with her generally over business matters. She was the go-between between Mitchell and Poonananda, because they did not keep in close contact with one another.'

'Do you know who Makunda is?'

'No, but I do know that he was due back in Sweden in April.'

Throughout her testimony Tervaniemi refused to be intimidated by Mitchell, who was sitting right behind her, often turning defiantly to face him as she spoke. On one occasion Judge Frohling stopped her to ask if Mitchell, who was slouched deep in his chair, head down, feigning total disinterest, could hear the witness properly?

'Not really,' he replied, looking up nonchalantly, 'but I am not that interested.' A few minutes later he re-took the stand.

'What have you to say about this?' asked Judge Wilhelmson.

'I have one general, overall comment to make on what Nasim has just said. By enrolling in drama school she has in fact found her vocation in life. I have to give it to the woman, she is a first class actress.'

'Is anything she has said correct?'

'Well, it is quite a potpourri. There is a smattering of fact in what she says, but basically it is outrageous lies.'

'Do you wish to change any of your previous statements?'

'No, I do not.'

We then had to go through the rigmarole of listening to Forsberg's telephone tapes again. The second time around was more excruciating than the first, but on this occasion Mitchell and Tervaniemi were asked for their comments at the end of each tape, and some valuable titbits of additional information emerged as each vied with the other over the exact meaning of the codes being used.

'In this call on 24 February, when Mitchell is asking Viryo If he wants to come down to Ibiza for a holiday, what he is really asking is if Viryo will do the couriers job. For which the sum of 50,000 Krona was going to be paid regardless of the amount being transported.'

This was highly relevant because not only did it confirm that the ring had been having difficulty finding a courier, but also, contrary to his testimony, it showed that Mitchell did indeed involve himself in organizing the Ibiza end of the runs. In addition it discredited the £20,000 fee I was supposed to have been paid.

Another tape showed that Mitchell had been intending to return to Sweden in April which would coincide with Makunda's next trip. Yet another further incriminated Prita, at Mitchell's hand:

'What did you mean by – 'She has not met her friends yet' – ?' one of the judges asked him.

'It means,' replied Mitchell, 'that the secretary, that's my girlfriend on Ibiza, had not yet given my messages to the others.'

And the prosecution claimed that Prita was not involved!?

When you referred to 'the boss' on the telephone, who were you actually talking about?'

'Chris. Christopher Hayward was the boss,' Mitchell insisted.

Bihlar was to have been the final witness before the summing up speeches but it turned out that he was 'unavailable'. He had decided to take a 'holiday.' I believe he had deliberately absented himself, or perhaps had even been sent away, to avoid having to face up to some extremely awkward questioning, under oath, regarding Prita's visit and his testimony at my trial. In the event, and to Forsbergs obvious dismay, the Bench ordered a second adjournment, this time for a week until 28th, to allow time for him to return.

Before the adjournment two letters were submitted to the Court as evidence. The one from Superintendent Flint, and another containing a statement from a woman calling herself Heather Weissand, which had been passed on to Forsberg by none other than H K ter Brake.

11 October 1987

Dear Sirs,

Re: Captain Simon Hayward.

I am writing to confirm my telephone conversation with Mr Brake on 10 October.

I was present at the meeting between Christopher, Simon Hayward and Dook in Santa Eulalia, Ibiza, earlier this year. The subject of the meeting was an amount of money that Christopher owed to Dook.

Captain Hayward's claim that Christopher and Dook left the meeting for a period of time for a private discussion is absolutely untrue.

When the meeting broke up, I left with Dook. We walked in the same direction as our cars were parked in the same street.

I was present throughout the meeting, none of us left the table.

The claim that Christopher Hayward and Dook were conspiring together is ridiculous as the atmosphere between them was 'frosty' to say the least.

I am working on a charter sailing yacht at the present and do not have a permanent contact address. Any correspondence should be directed to Mr Brake.

I look forward to hearing from you in due course.

Yours faithfully,

Heather Weissand.

'This letter,' Forsberg claimed, 'confirms that Dook and Christopher Hayward did not leave the table together and that Simon is therefore lying. It is also important because it shows that no threat was made against Christopher.'

He went on to explain that Weissand had initially been prepared to attend the appeal as a witness '. . . or that is what she told ter Brake' but subsequently when she had spoken to Forsberg on the telephone she had refused to come forward because she was afraid to do so '. . . she was not prepared to go into detail why she was afraid.'

'Do you recognize the name Heather Weissand?' he asked me.

'No sir, I do not. I have never heard it before. And may I add that there was only one woman present at that meeting and she I am almost certain, was Dook's wife Gita.'

Turning to face the Bench, I continued: 'So, unless this letter is from Dook's wife; unless she, like Dook, has a false name; and unless Mr. Forsberg can say who she actually is, I do not see how it confirms or proves anything.'

Tom Placht now took up the challenge: 'Do you know who this person is?' he asked Forsberg.

'No, I know nothing about her except her name.'

'Do you know where she lives?'

'No, I don't.'

'Where was she when she telephoned you?'

'I don't know.'

'Well, do you know where her letter was posted from?'

'No. I am not sure, I think it came from ter Brake in Holland.'

'Do you know if she actually exists?'

'I have spoken to her on the telephone.' Forsberg was beginning to look pained.

'Yes,' replied Placht, 'but that could have been anybody.'

No comment from the prosecutor.

My turn again. 'Even if we accept for a moment that this woman was actually at the meeting, despite not knowing who she is, or indeed if she exists at all, most of what she claims would still be untrue. Christopher and Dook did leave together, not as the District Court Judgement states for over an hour, but for a few minutes into the cafe itself. And when she says that ". . . none of us left the table," that is also nonsense because I left it, to go and buy a newspaper. However the one thing the letter does do, is confirm my statement that there was bad feeling between my brother and Dook.'

Forsberg was looking extremely embarrassed by this stage, and so he should have been. By submitting this letter he had made himself look a complete idiot. The fact that it ever got near the Court as evidence was quite astonishing. It was valueless, it might just as well have been from an anonymous source. Weissand's refusal to corroborate it in person spoke for itself. It proved nothing except how desperate the prosecutor was. Once again I had to pinch myself to make myself believe I was in court of law in a civilised country.

There was a noticeable change in the attitude of the Bench when the Court reconvened on Wednesday 28 October. Whereas the judges, especially Mrs Espark and Mr Frohling, had previously been assiduous, now they seemed almost disinterested, even bored. It was as if they had already reached a decision. Espark contented herself throughout the day by filling in what looked like appointments into her diary, Frohling sat with his head in his hands, staring at the ceiling for long periods at a time with a resigned look on his face. There was little change in Judge Wilhelmson, he dozed as usual.

Bihlar's testimony was staggering. He readily admitted to knowing about Prita's visit – at this stage, of course, he had had to, he had no choice. In fact he said that he had arranged it himself with the prison at Mitchell's behest, and agreed that he had spoken with Prita at Osteraker on 25 June, although she had refused to be interviewed officially.

This was tantamount to an open admission of perjury because he had definitely stated, under oath in the District Court, that he had asked Prita over the telephone to come forward to be questioned but that she had refused to do so.

There was now no escaping the fact that that statement had been a lie because when making it Bihlar had known that in truth he had been speaking to her in Sweden only six weeks previously.

Neither was Forsberg blameless. Bihlar went on to say that he had discussed the visit with the prosecutor before arranging it. Forsberg immediately denied this, saying that he had only been told of it after Prita had returned to Ibiza. Clearly one of them was incorrect, and since the prison records stated that the visit had been authorised by the prosecutor, it was obvious that in this instance it was Forsberg. And to add insult to injury, it was equally obvious that he had allowed Mitchell an unguarded visit with Prita, thus giving them the opportunity to compare notes and effectively destroying the value of any evidence Prita might have given, before Mitchell's restrictions had been lifted and before his sentence had become non-appealable.

In any case it was clear that Forsberg had known of the visit when Bihlar had testified in the District Court, and he had sat back and listened to the police officer's statement without a word of protest.

Bihlar's was not quite over yet. 'What nationality is Prita?' Placht asked him.

'I believe she is German.'

'Do you know her full name?'

'No.'

'Did you not check her identity before arranging her visit?'

'No.'

This had to be untrue. Before someone can visit a Swedish prison their name has to be registered along with all personal details. For security reasons they are then checked out by the police. If when the visitor arrives at the prison his or her identity does not match the one registered, they are denied entry. The reasons for this are obvious.

It would have been quite impossible for Bihlar to have arranged Prita's visit therefore, without knowing her full identity. Consequently he must have realised that she was travelling on a false British passport, especially, as he had now admitted, he knew she was a German.

'Why did you not mention this visit while testifying in the District Court?' Placht asked.

'Because you did not ask me.' That was no excuse.

'But you stated that Prita had refused to come forward!'

No comment, just a very red, sheepish face. Now that the lie had been exposed Bihlar was wriggling like mad. I felt confident that the Court was about to indict him. But why should he and the prosecutor have gone to such lengths to conceal Prita's visit? The only possible answer was that they had indeed struck a deal with Mitchell.

Leaving aside the highly questionable actions of the prosecution in allowing an accomplice to visit their main witness without being interviewed, under a false name and carrying a false passport, Forsberg had once again displayed the most scant regard for the impartiality it was his duty to observe. Without this impartiality, under the Swedish legal system where the prosecutor is charged with producing all evidence both for and against a suspect, it becomes impossible for a defendant to receive a fair trial. In this case the defence had been in effect prevented from interviewing potentially the most important witness available.

And this was not all. Now that it had been established beyond any doubt that Prita was using a passport in the name of Waterfield, the real significance of the travel receipt that New had found on Ibiza became apparent. It indicated that Waterfield had travelled to Sweden for a second time between

28 August and 8 September. Mitchell denied the visit ever took place, and unfortunately we were not able to confirm with the airline that Prita had taken the flight, nor would the prison allow us access to its visit records for that period.

However, confirmation did come from Mitchell's prison telephone register, which for some reason had been included in the Juhlin Report. It showed that he had received regular calls from Prita until 29 August, when they had ceased entirely until 7 September. These dates coincide exactly with the apparent dates of the journey, and the absence of telephone calls would be explained by the fact that a personal visit was taking place. It would also explain why Prita had not been available for interview by either New or the Swedish police when they had visited Ibiza in September.

Of greater concern, it should be remembered that Bihlar had invited Hanna Pontein to his office on 2 September supposedly to take part in a telephone conversation with Prita, whom he claimed was speaking from Ibiza. It was now a distinct probability that she had actually been in Sweden at the time, presumably with Bihlar's knowledge.

I stared at Mr Wilhelmson in total disbelief as he did nothing more than thank Bihlar and allow him to stand down. Far from investigating Forsberg for committing a breach of duty or investigating Bihlar for perjury, it was quite plain that the High Court felt able to disregard the whole sorry issue. Indeed, rather than upholding the law, the Bench was condoning malversation and malpractice, to say nothing of blatant dishonesty.

'Surely Tom,' I whispered, turning to face Placht, 'these are grounds for a mistrial?'

He looked somewhat taken aback at the very suggestion.

'Not in Sweden. It is not the Swedish way!'

It is a thoroughly depressing experience to have to sit quietly and listen as someone tries his level best to pillory you, to brand you a liar and a drug smuggler, and to have you sent to prison for a crime you know you took no part in. It is even worse when the onslaught comes from a man who has been less than totally honest in his own conduct, and for whom you hold nothing but disrespect.

It came as no surprise to hear Forsberg repeat the same

summing up speech as he had used in the District Court, contenting himself with merely incorporating into it any new and relevant points he thought necessary, which was everything and anything. I would not have minded if he had at the same time edited out those issues which had been disproven or discredited. He did nothing of the sort however; he stuck rigidly to his original theme. It was almost as though he had not been in Court when any of the defence evidence had been presented. Even points that had been destroyed as evidence, such as his third statement allegation, were re-submitted as if he had concrete proof of their validity. If his summing up had been his opening address one could have understood his logic.

'. . . it is quite natural for a Guards Captain to carry £7,000,' he said, '. . . New was briefed as a defence witness, his testimony can therefore be disregarded . . . No credence can be given to Nasim, her evidence must be seen in the light that she has a vested interest in discrediting Mitchell, because she has yet to stand trial . . . Why was Chef-Superintendent Haddrell given permission to attend by Scotland Yard but not Morgan and Moore? . . . Christopher Hayward's tape is further evidence that Simon is lying, Mitchell would have had no time to convert the Jaguar to left-hand drive. In any case the tape may have been a forgery, even the registration number was incorrect . . . the threats to Mrs. Hayward have nothing to do with Simon's awareness of the presence of the drugs . . . Heather Weissand sounded credible to me on the telephone, HK ter Brake thought the same . . . Dook is not involved in this affair . . . that is nothing but a smokescreen put forward by the defence to cloud the issue . . . Mitchell is a credible and trustworthy witness . . . The Juhlin Inquiry has cleared the police on all points . . . Philipsson's evidence was nothing more than prison gossip . . .'

And so he went on, and on, and on, for over two hours. His argument was based on plausible theories, nothing else. His case against me was totally unsupported by fact, indeed almost all of it was unverifiable. I could not believe, I did not want to believe, that this Court, indeed any Court in the Western World, would accept it as a basis on which to send a person to gaol. Forsberg finished by saying:

'The evidence put forward during this hearing makes it very clear to us that Simon Hayward smuggled 50.5 kilos of cannabis into Sweden for his brother Chris. In various ways he has tried to explain the fact that he was more or less sitting on the cannabis. He has not succeeded.

'Simon Hayward is guilty, and should be given a longer prison sentence than five years. He should be deported. He has cynically put in jeopardy the lives and health of Swedish young people, in order to earn £20,000. Thank you.'

After Forsberg, Tom Placht had a chance to speak. Calmly, logically, and in great detail he once again went through the prosecution's 'case', revealing it as the farrago of perjury, half-truth and prejudice it was.

As in the District Court, he concluded by saying:

'The Court will have no difficulty in finding my client not guilty. There just is not the evidence to support any other verdict . . . It is not a question of beyond reasonable doubt, there can be no doubt. Simon Hayward is innocent. I demand that you release him immediately. Thank you.'

I decided that if I was going down, I would go down fighting every inch of the way. For almost eight months I had been at the mercy of the impropriety of the men sitting opposite me. I had not said much at the end of the District Court trial, and it had found me guilty. This was going to my last chance to put my own case, to speak for myself, I had nothing to lose by stating my mind.

I started. My voice trembling with anger, with an acrimony that until that moment I had managed to suppress.

'Mr Forsberg, I believe you have a duty to investigate all evidence, both on behalf of the defence as well as the for prosecution. You have a duty, under Swedish law, to present all the facts, not just those that support your viewpoint. And above all you have a duty to remain strictly impartial, to observe a principle of objectivity, until the end of the investigation and until, and if, you decide to prefer charges against a suspect. How can you possibly justify, therefore, conducting such a narrow and partial investigation? How can you justify not questioning important witnesses? How can you justify misleading the District Court? And above all how can you justify declaring your total belief in my guilt at a press conference in March, four months before you charged me? That does not say much for your impartiality, nor your objectivity! And you cannot deny this accusation because we have a video tape of the interview . . . '

Forsberg was looking a little upset at my comments. I turned to the Bench:

'I believe the investigation into my alleged role in this affair has been totally inadequate . . . the only place to properly establish the truth about me was on Ibiza but the police made no attempt to go there until September, six months too late . . . The prosecutor has made no real effort to confirm details given in my statements, prefering instead to believe other information gathered from unknown informers and from people who have a great deal to gain from hiding as much as possible . . . Why should my family have to spend many thousands of pounds in hiring solicitors and private investigators to do the work the police should have done?

'If I had been Mitchell's courier, part of his gang, isn't it reasonable to expect him to want to protect me, to clear me if he could? He could easily have done so . . . Mitchell says that I was the perfect courier. Is that why he set me up, and used me instead of Makunda or a local from Ibiza?

'How can the prosecution claim that Prita is not involved, at the very least, why has she not been properly interviewed? It has been shown conclusively that she must have information relevant to this case . . . innocent people do not need false passports . . . Why did Inspector Bihlar lie to the District Court . . . why did the prosecutor let him do so? . . . How can you claim that Mitchell is a trustworthy witness?

'In presenting his case against me, Mr Forsberg has been unable to refute one single aspect, not one part, of my testimony. Instead all he has done is provide his own theories for what might have happened based on nothing more than capricious speculation . . . his investigation has been conducted with a blind conviction of my guilt with no consideration whatsoever of the possibility of my innocence. Every avenue of inquiry that even hinted of innocence has been ignored . . . I have been accused of lying continually, yet the specific points brought up have been checked by the defence and on each of them it has been proved I told the truth . . .

'I am not a drug smuggler. I have been unfairly caught up in this business. I have been very badly treated by the people who put those drugs in the car in the first place, but I have also been given a bum deal by the Swedish authorities. There is no other way to describe it.

'I have spent seven and a half months listening to people, some of whom hold positions of authority and should have known better, lie about me, ignore information that could prove my innocence, and distort facts, blowing them out of all proportion. I believe the Swedish expression is "making a hen out of a feather". After a while one tends to get just a little fed up.

'Some of my behaviour, some of my actions, may seem strange to you, but if we all went through life thinking that we would have to justify all of our actions, however small, before a court of law, then none of us would ever dare do anything . . .'

I continued for over an hour, reiterating all the facts surrounding the case, emphasizing time and again the appalling way in which the investigation had been conducted. Placht had been diplomatic in his summing-up, I was anything but diplomatic. I did not pull my punches, and I called a spade, a spade.

'There are so many loose ends to this case . . . so many unanswered questions . . . that it is quite impossible to come to a firm conclusion about anything . . . One day hopefully the truth will come out.

'I AM NOT A DRUGS SMUGGLER! I AM TOTALLY INNOCENT OF THESE CHARGES! THERE IS NO EVIDENCE AGAINST ME!'

I finished abruptly. By raising my voice, being forceful, by letting my anger, frustration and indignation show, I hoped to have got my message across. Some newspapers later remarked that I had 'stolen the show,' but I had not, I just wanted to have my say after so long. Most importantly, by referring to the judges and looking them in the eyes as I spoke, I had succeeded in holding their attention. I felt certain that at last they had taken everything in; even Mr Wilhelmson had remained alert.

Forsberg asked to make a comment: 'If I stated my belief in Simon's guilt as early as March all I can say is that I am sorry.' He must have felt very vulnerable to be forced into such an apology, but there was no point in making one at this stage. The damage had been done. Who knows? – If he had done his job properly, to the letter of the law from day one, the case might never have got into court. I could feel nothing but contempt for the man. He could keep his apologies.

The Court went into recess while the Bench considered Placht's demand for my immediate release. I was taken back upstairs to the holding cells where Simon Falkner, who had flown out that day to represent The Life Guards and to lend moral support, was allowed to wait out what we all hoped would be the dying moments of the nightmare with me. My mother, Sandra and her father remained downstairs.

To have hope is one thing, reality is quite another and I fully expected the judges to return immediately, as had been the case with the District Court, to send me back to the Häktet while they took a week to deliberate. However Simon and I were still chatting nervously together an hour later. After an hour and a half we were speculating optimistically that the verdict was about to go my way. It had to be a good sign, we thought. There was still no proof of any wrong doing, nothing had changed since the original trial, there was no real new evidence. Despite appearances, in spite of the judges' behaviour, we could not help feeling optimistic. This was after all, we kept telling ourselves, a High Court in a Western democratic nation. It was bound to overturn the District Court's verdict.

I did not know it at the time, but Forsberg was having similar thoughts. He was telling journalists that he thought he had lost, and if that proved to be the case he was not going to bother appealing against the verdict.

Of course, it was not to be. When the judges returned it was only for Mr Wilhelmson to proclaim that the verdict would be announced in, not one but, two weeks time. Once again I said my goodbyes, the 'girls' biting back their tears. The handcuffs were snapped back into place, and with a feeling of dread I was escorted along the 'corridor of sighs' to Kronoberg. I had been in custody for 230 days. A mere 32 weeks and six days. My last thought as I left the courtroom was 'how many more?'

Nine

The guilty verdict was announced at 11 o'clock on 11 November – Armistice Day. I wonder if the Swedes realised the significance of the coincidence? I think almost certainly not.

I was told the bad news quietly by Fremback in his office. No leering warder this time. The High Court had made a unanimous decision to uphold the five year sentence; I suppose I should have been thankful that the judges had resisted the temptation to increase it.

I found myself consumed with a burning sense of anger and injustice, hatred even. The sense of embarrassment that had been so acute since my arrest now took second place to one of deep resentment. At that moment, as I sat without a word in front of Frembäck, if I could have got my hands around Forsberg's neck I would have done something to earn those five unjust years. The one small consolation was that on this occasion the verdict was not such a shock; having not been released early I had been expecting the worst, but I had never felt so bitterly angry before in my life.

Christopher Murray, Tom Placht and my mother came to see me later that afternoon. After talking things through we were allowed to hold a press conference in which we announced the immediate intention to appeal to the Supreme Court and if that failed, to take the case to the European Court of Human Rights.

My sense of outrage was not diminished either when I eventually received translations of the Trial and Appeal Judgements from Kingsley Napley. Both were masterpieces of ambiguity and bias. Although based on nothing more than hearsay, speculation and, it must be said, blatant misrepresentation of the little factual evidence available, to the casual reader, with little or no detailed knowledge of the case, both documents would have appeared to be fair and impartial appraisals, leaving room for no conclusion other than a guilty verdict. As such they served well as an exercise in public relations.

However, to anyone who had followed events closely they were nothing but a transparent confidence trick. The only surprise in them was the poor quality of the argument that had gone into establishing what had clearly been a forgone conclusion. One would have thought that a judiciary would have had access to more talent; at least, to present the wider world a bad judgement in a plausible fashion. The fact seemed to be that they had so softened the pliable Swedish public that anything would do.

Obviously, scant attention had been paid to the defence case. Protests about inconsistencies in the hearsay evidence presented had been overruled, more often than not without even a mention. Valid defence explanations had been discounted for no apparent reason. It would appear that 'trivial' matters such as a total lack of motive had been ignored, and had played no part in the reaching of a verdict.

I had been found guilty on the grounds of beyond reasonable doubt. However the judgements were consistently peppered with such phrases as: 'a high degree of probability that Hayward had knowledge'; 'the circumstances . . . appear to be peculiar'; 'somewhat unlikely'; 'appear rather unlikely'; 'a strong chance'; 'barely credible'; 'somewhat remarkable'; 'most peculiar'; 'this does not actually rule out the possibility'; 'it can be thought'; 'but he thinks'; 'in his view' and 'a reasonable explanation may instead be'. These are phrases that indicate possibility, or at the very most some degree of probability, certainly not 'Beyond all reasonable doubt'. Indeed there was hardly a concrete factual statement to be found in either document.

Clearly, the case against me had been built around Mitchell's testimony. Without it, as a cement to bind the chain of circumstantial evidence together, the prosecution's arguments did not hold water. Incredibly, both Courts, in declaring him a credible witness, had chosen to believe a self-confessed drug smuggler with a previous criminal record, who had given conflicting, unverifiable second-hand evidence, the truth of which even he had cast aspersions upon, and who had obvious interests in playing down his own role by making others responsible.

There was no escaping the fact that the relevant sections of his testimony had been entirely hearsay, and furthermore, neither had any attempt been made to have them properly verified. Indeed there remained only his word concerning what, if anything, had been said between himself and Christopher. He stood uncontradicted – allowed to formulate himself in a manner that had furthered his own cause. Making no mention of this, the District Court had concluded:

'Nothing has emerged to suggest that Mitchell would not tell the truth.'

And that his statements: ' . . . are to be trusted . . . and as having serious implications for Simon Hayward.'

Placht had proved beyond a shadow of a doubt that Mitchell's evidence had been confused, contradictory, and in areas blatantly untrue and yet the Court still felt able to declare it to be: '. . . not in itself improbable or contradictory.'

The Appeal Court found Mitchell to be credible only in that part of his testimony which referred to the 'Hayward brothers'. In other words, the only part that could not be substantiated, and it justified this by saying:

'The information which Mitchell provided about Christopher and Simon Hayward does not appear to have the purpose of diminishing his own involvement or of shifting the responsibility for the drug dealing onto the two brothers.'

And yet:

'Mitchell does not feel directly able to say that Simon Hayward was aware that there was a consignment of cannabis hidden in the Jaguar, but *he thinks* that Hayward acted as if he knew.'

By far its most damning statement could only have been made with a blind conviction in Mitchell's veracity:

'Mitchell had not been told by Christopher Hayward that his brother should be kept uninformed. It can therefore be taken as read that the purpose of the journey would sooner or later be revealed to Simon Hayward with all the consequences that this would entail. For this reason alone, the Court of Appeal finds that there is a high degree of probability that Simon had knowledge of the drugs consignment hidden in the car.'

Without a total belief in Mitchell's word this statement was meaningless. In believing him both courts questioned why he should choose to do anything other than to tell the truth. The naivety of that remark defies analysis. The question that should have been posed was why he should have chosen to do anything other than lie, both to protect his colleagues still at large and, by reducing his responsibility, to minimise the punishment he was likely to receive himself. In fact, as I was subsequently to learn from inmates at the prison I was sent to, it is a golden rule among the criminal fraternity that whenever possible one must take the opportunity to exculpate a partner or for that matter any other suspect. A simple statement from Mitchell could have cleared me, regardless of what he thought or knew to be the truth. He had chosen not to. He must have had very good reason for his actions.

Unable to disprove my testimony, the judges had contented themselves by speculating upon it. Again no mention was made of the fact that the police had made little or no effort to verify my statements, other than to compare them to Mitchell's.

'The reason why Simon Hayward changed his story may actually have been the one he gave but . . . It cannot be ruled out that from the outset he supplied false information to protect his brother but this does not appear to be likely . . . It may be noted that the latter version is more consistent with Mitchell's statements.' (District Court)

Under the circumstances it was ludicrous to suggest that I had altered my story to make it agree with Mitchell's. The Court of Appeal was, for once, more impartial on the subject and simply stated that the alteration had detracted from my credibility, which was fair enough.

During the Appeal, the Bench had made a point of considering Christopher's culpability as well as my own, and then used their views on his guilt as evidence against me. To quote:

'In examining this case, it is important to determine the extent to which Christopher Hayward has been involved in drug dealing . . . The Court of Appeal considers Mitchell's testimony to be credible. In view of this and of other facts that have emerged, it is of the opinion that Christopher Hayward, who owned the Jaguar, intentionally sent the car from Ibiza to Sweden with its consignment of drugs, driven by his brother. According to Simon, Christopher never told him that drugs were hidden in the car. NO EXPLANATION FOR SUCH A COURSE OF ACTION HAS EMERGED.'

If that is not a biased, narrow statement, nothing is. It meant that the Court had accepted one prosecution theory, whilst dismissing all defence counter arguments out of turn. No proof existed to support it only Mitchell's word. Even if it were true, would Christopher's guilt necessarily have been indicative of mine? Drug smugglers are not known for their moral principles. It proved nothing except an overriding desire to convict me.

If 'masterpieces of ambiguity and bias' sounds a subjective accusation, one substantial omission alone justifies it. While both courts relied on Larsen's evidence and the Morgan and Moore Report, especially so in the District Court where it had formed as major part of the evidence against me as Mitchell's testimony, neither made any mention of Assistant Commissioner Hewett's letter, or the supporting correspondence from Stockley and Flint. This fact, if nothing else, must raise serious doubts about the impartiality and integrity of the judges.

In depending on Larsen's testimony, Judge Hellbacher had this to say of the informer's character:

'. . . there is no cause to assume other than that this person is in fact reliable.'

An incredible, stupefying statement considering the identity of the informer was unknown, he had not been available for cross-examination, he was known to have a criminal record, and finally Hewett had described his information as unreliable.

Another equally substantial omission was any mention of, let alone rebuke for, Forsberg's breaches of his Codes of Conduct and Bihlar's mendacity both in and out of the courtroom. Clearly they were considered to be above the law, and the fact that their actions had reduced my chances of receiving a fair trial had counted for nothing.

Both judgements had relied on a string of circumstantial evidence to further justify and add weight to their verdicts:

... it is hardly likely that Simon, against the background of training that he has had, would accept to drive the long distance up to Sweden to deliver the car under the circumstances indicated ...

Generally speaking, it must be regarded as somewhat unlikely that a courier driving more than 2,200 kms in two days would be unaware of there being drugs in the car ... If during the journey the Jaguar had in any way become unusable, there must have been a strong chance that Hayward, if he was unaware of the consignment, would abandon the car, which was insured, and proceed directly to England. The drugs could then easily have been lost ... It would also appear rather unlikely that Hayward would undertake such a rapid and testing journey through Europe simply in order to spend some time delivering the car for sale in Sweden.

Hayward's claim that he was delivering the car for sale is barely credible ... he did not declare it as an import at Swedish customs, he knew nothing of the details of the sale, the car registration documents were missing, and Mitchell, who was due to leave Sweden two days later, categorically denied all knowledge of any purchase.

Hayward's stated reason for driving via Andorra ... is not deserving of credence ... A reasonable explanation may instead be that there are no actual checks at Andorra's borders with Spain and France.

The District Court gives no credence to the assertion that Simon understood Mitchell to be Swedish ... this does not rule out the possibility that he believed Mitchell was resident in Sweden, but weakens his credibility ...

Nor does the information provided for buying a special screwdriver bear the stamp of probability ... the possibility that the screws came loose in the seat cannot be ruled out ... Tests (in the District Court) showed that no movement could be noted with the car stationary, (The High Court failed to comment on whether it had noted movement or not) ... it is possible to tighten the screws with any normal

screwdriver . . . The fact that Hayward went to great lengths
to obtain this tool substantially supports the view that he
was aware . . .

. . . the circumstances surrounding the declared theft of
the Jaguar appear to be peculiar.

. . . Hayward drove his car in such a manner that a police
officer following him had the definite impression that he was
checking whether he was being followed. The only possible
explanation is that Simon Hayward was aware that there
were drugs in the car.

Taken individually these statements had next to no
evidential value. They were based on speculation, opinion and
interpretation, and had clearly been reached with a blatant
disregard for any aspect of available evidence favourable to the
defence. For the Appeal Court to start speculating on notions
that had not even been discussed during the hearing – such as
what might have happened in the (highly unlikely) event that
I had suddenly decided to abandon the car for some reason en
route to Sweden; or why I had not known the details of the car
sale (a question that had in fact been answered) – was
unjustifiable in the extreme.

Even taken collectively, their cumulative value only
amounted to theory, nothing more. To use theory as evidence
to support Mitchell's already weak testimony was little short
of iniquitous. Obviously Forsberg had been allowed to
produce a likely scenario, without actually proving anything,
– indeed the defence had comprehensively demonstrated that
the component parts of his case were either incorrect,
unreliable, or capable of alternative, and innocent, explanation – and the Courts had accepted it without a word of
protest. That could not possibly be described as 'justice' by any
stretch of the imagination.

Had I received a fair trial? No – of that I was absolutely
convinced. To start with, it was certain that the prosecutor and
police, while conducting their preliminary investigations
behind closed doors, had been quite unable in the course of
their duties to give any thought to the 'presumption of
innocence' as a counterbalance to their own professional
desire to make the charges stick. Furthermore, it had been a

novel experience to behold a judge prepared to interrupt court proceedings in order to take telephone calls and to exchange gossip with the press during intervals in the proceedings. It had been novel to see judges and assessors dozing in court when they held a defendant's future in their hands. It had also been novel to see a prosecutor enliven luncheon breaks with press conferences for the purpose of disseminating his views on the progress of the trial.

But most disturbing had been the use of uncorroborated hearsay evidence. There was Larsen who had given damaging testimony, while at the same time claiming immunity from the need to substantiate it because of the nature of his work. There was Mitchell with his unverifiable second-hand opinions. Worst of all there were the untested written allegations, supplied by Morgan and Moore, which the head of their organisation had sought to have withdrawn because of unreliability.

All of this would have been torn to shreds in five minutes in a British court – but not so in Stockholm.

An open-minded observer would conclude that there was definitely no degree of proof against me, and that I had been convicted, not on the grounds of beyond reasonable doubt but on the grounds of possibility. Perhaps he would also agree that I had not received a fair trial? A trial which, despite claims to the contrary, had shown clearly that in a country which likes to be known as the world's moral superpower a defendant is still considered to be guilty until proven innocent.

The case was a difficult one, there can be no denying that, but even the most cynical observer would agree that there was profound doubt as to my guilt, or for that matter my innocence. Only one man, from the eleven judges and assessors who tried me, had been prepared to give me the benefit of that considerable doubt, acknowledging the extreme difficulty that any unwitting courier would have in proving his innocence. Mr Gunnar Thorson alone was prepared to stand up and be counted, I salute his objectivity and moral courage. His argument highlighted the level of subjectivity in the trial and appeal verdicts:

... the Scotland Yard informant ... this is second or third-hand information from a source that has not been identified. It is therefore impossible to make a satisfactory assessment of its reliability . . . It was supplied so late in the investigation that essential details would have been generally known in Great Britain owing to the level of publicity . . . It is not possible to attribute the full force of evidence and the importance which the prosecutor would wish to Larsen's testimony.

Mitchell states that he has not, directly or indirectly, discussed any drug deals with Hayward. There are well founded reasons for believing that Mitchell has not told the Court everything he knows on this case. The possibility cannot be ruled out that he has an interest in concealing or obscuring certain facts. It is therefore necessary to exercise care with his statements. . . It is not possible to attribute the: full force of evidence to Mitchell's testimony.

The fact that Hayward changed his statements on a few points does not alter his story as a whole. It cannot be disregarded that he initially supplied an incorrect version with the sole aim of protecting his brother . . .

The circumstances of the meeting in Lingköping . . . do not point to anything in particular . . . the same problems of making contact with Mitchell if they had missed each other at the station would have been the same whether Simon had known there were drugs in the car or not . . .

With regard to the short time which Hayward would have had to go skiing . . . if he had left Ibiza as originally planned, he would have had a perfectly reasonable amount of time . . .

The motive for Hayward to smuggle drugs appears to be very unclear. It is unreasonable that he did so for the sake of excitement, since presumably his duty in Northern Ireland supplied him with ample . . . nor does the money motive appear reasonable, since he was not in financial difficulties . . . It does not seem credible that his motive was to help his brother in view of what is known of his character. There is no motive which stands out and points against him.

The prosecution evidence may be strong but it is not convincing, and cannot alone be taken as the basis for a conviction. Simon Hayward's statements contain some peculiarities, to which there are, however, plausible explanations. Peculiarities cannot be accumulated in order to reach an unreasonable verdict.

Dissenting from the majority, I find for the defendant.

If further corroboration was needed to show that the Appeal Court had been trying a foregone conclusion it came from a contact within the courthouse bureaucracy who informed us that a draft copy of the judgement had been submitted for typing on the final day of the appeal. This meant that the verdict must have been reached long before the hearing had come to an end.

The disappointment of being returned to Kronoberg was tempered by the news that I had now become the direct responsibility of the prison service; no longer could the Uppsala authorities exert any influence on the conditions of my incarceration. Forsberg's restrictions, in place since 13 March, were lifted with immediate effect. Although I remained in solitary confinement, despite public assertions by Forsberg to the contrary, it felt like a new beginning. The atmosphere became more relaxed, I was allowed to receive the occasional telephone call, uncensored mail and newspapers; and best of all, unguarded visits – the usual practice in Swedish prisons.

The last time I saw Bihlar was a few days after the verdict was announced, when he came to Kronoberg to deliver the remaining items from my personal effects that he had kept as 'evidence'. I was in the exercise pens at the time and he spoke to me through the guards' window. To my astonishment he greeted me like a long lost friend, happy and smiling, with a proffered hand, as if to say 'Let's let bygones be bygones, we can still be mates'. I did not reciprocate. I could not. The very sight of him was loathsome. I have to say that such was the depth of my feeling that if I could have reached him I would almost certainly have lost my self control and given him something to remember me by.

Instead, keeping my hands firmly in my pockets, I contented myself by staring at the creature for a few moments of stony silence, before making it perfectly clear how I felt in my most icily menacing but quiet voice. He looked quite taken aback, even upset at my animosity. That at least was some consolation, albeit a rather petty one.

If anything summed up Bihlar's unreasonable, I would even go so far as to say emotionally childish, attitude towards me it was a ridiculous statement he made during an interview with a reporter in mid November. He was asked why, unlike most suspects held on remand in solitary confinement for long periods of time, I had not confessed? And rhetorically, was this not an indication of innocence?

'No,' Bihlar had answered, 'Hayward cannot let England down. If he was to confess, he would be failing his family, the British Queen, Margaret Thatcher, the Queen's Guards, the majors, the brigadiers – yes the whole British Empire.'

Need I say more?

Unguarded visits – for the first time in eight months I was able to spend some time alone with Sandra, my mother and other friends. It was a real delight, despite the gloom that hung over all of us, to be able to hold a proper conversation, without continuous interruptions reminding us not to venture close to any topic that could possibly be construed as having the slightest relevance to my predicament. To be able to discuss openly the trials and tribulations of the past months, and to catch up on news from home was an experience that took me a while to become accustomed to. As one would expect, these visits were emotional times for all of us.

I was determined to carry on the fight, and not to give up hope. I was not about to spend the next five years of my life in prison, to say nothing of accepting the opprobrium of being branded a drug smuggler, without one hell of a struggle. Even if it took for ever, I was determined to clear my name.

There were two legal avenues remaining to me. An appeal to the Swedish Supreme Court, and if that failed, a petition to the European Court of Human Rights. Despite the realisation that only prejudice, not justice, was on offer to me, I was compelled to try the first before I could become eligible for the second. The European Court will only accept a petition once every local remedy has been exhausted.

However, if one of the remand centre sub-governors, known as inspectors, had had his way I would have been disqualified from all further appeals, no matter to which court. Under Swedish law, once convicted a defendant has to be offered the chance to sign acceptance of the verdict. If he, or she, refuses to do so, or does not lodge an appeal, the verdict becomes enforceable in any event after 21 days. More importantly, by signing the individual gives up all rights to future appeals unless on the grounds of new evidence. Why sign, one might ask? – Because it gets you out of solitary confinement straight away. The Inspector in question visited me on the morning of 12th with a Swedish copy of the Appellant Court judgement, which he asked me to sign for. Tom Placht had advised me not to sign anything, and in any case my suspicions were aroused because the man was asking me to sign at the bottom of another copy of the judgement. I refused.

'But you must sign,' he instructed me in bad English, 'it is the law of Sweden. If you will not sign, I cannot give you the judgement.'

He handed me a pen, and pointed angrily to the dotted line where I had to sign. Once again I refused. Whereupon he looked at me knowingly and with a smile dropped the copy of the judgement on my bunk and walked out of the cell.

The chances of the Supreme Court accepting my case were minimal. The problem was that it does not consider evidence, unless new facts of a highly significant nature are involved, but will only hear an appeal on strict legal criteria – in order to set precedent; in the event of procedural error, when it becomes necessary to give guidance to the lower courts; or where it is decided that a case did not receive a fair hearing in the lower courts. In practice, regardless of the circumstances, next to no cases are heard.

Throughout the summer Placht had sought help and advice from one of Sweden's leading legal experts, Professor Per-Olof Ekelöf, who was described to me as the 'Father of the Modern Swedish Code of Procedure'. It was the professor who had been responsible for re-codifying and amending the criminal code after the war, in which he had laid down guidelines for the courts to follow when evaluating evidence. He was showing an interest in my case, not because it involved a British Guards officer, but because he considered that both the District and Appellant Courts had acted quite wrongly in attaching too much weight to the prosecution evidence. He now offered his services in helping to draw up my appeal to the Supreme Court. His participation obviously added enormous weight to the defence arguments, as well as giving us some grounds for optimism.

We had no new evidence and it was, at best, extremely unlikely that the Supreme Court would judge that I had not received a fair trial; we had therefore, in any case, no option but to base the appeal on a need for guidance to be given to the lower courts.

Placht contributed the main body of the appeal, reiterating the theme he had employed in his summing up in court, and arguing that the evidence against me had been weak, or in his words 'the proof requirements have not been fulfilled'. Ekelöf added an 'Opinion' – an eleven page document propounding from a purely legal point of view the need for the Supreme Court to accept the appeal because 'it is extremely important that the Court provide guidance relating to the proof requirement in serious criminal cases'; and when faced with a chain of circumstantial evidence, guidance on the dangers of allowing the proof value of one piece of evidence to reinforce the value of another.

While not giving an opinion on my innocence or guilt, in support of his arguments the professor effectively, and easily, destroyed every aspect of prosecution evidence:

MITCHELL – The Court of Appeal's pronouncement seems to me to be far too superficial. Mitchell's situation means that his statement has a rather limited value as evidence.

Like the District Court, the Court of Appeal does not believe that Chris deceived Simon. An important experienced-based principle in the evaluation of this, is how likely it is that drug dealers should use couriers without notifying them of the contents of the car. A lawyer with a great deal of experience in drugs cases has told me that, in his experience, this is certainly not unusual.

As to the likelihood that Chris could have deceived his brother? Drug dealers are not usually distinguished by their high morals.

Presumably it was Chris who placed the drugs in the car. Yet it is also conceivable that someone else did so and that Chris was unaware of the fact. A cross-examination of Chris might have supported the view that Simon is innocent . . .

the Court of Appeal should, under these circumstances, have taken into account, in Simon's favour, the fact that Chris could not be heard in this case.

The judgement also contains other items of circumstantial evidence which is quoted in support of Simon's awareness of the drugs . . . each and every one of them, in my view, has only a low value as evidence and in certain cases even that is lacking:

SKIING: Presumably the Court attached no credence to this . . . (Initially) this was also true of me but . . . the cross examination of the English officers revealed to me that strange leisure habits prevail amongst the English upper classes . . . We have here one more example of the danger of relying upon one's own life experience . . .

CAR SALE: According to Simon, he had not undertaken to sell the Jaguar but only to hand it over to Mitchell. If this is correct, then it is not that strange that he did not give further thought to the problems which might have arisen over the sale.

CHANGE OF STORY: Simon's explanation of this does not appear unreasonable. Moreover, it is not rare for even innocent persons to lie under police interrogation . . .

As far as the fact that Simon did not tell his girlfriend that he was intending to drive to Sweden, it is my view that this has no value whatsoever as evidence to suggest that he is lying with regard to his awareness of drugs in the car.

SCREWDRIVER: The question is what Simon was intending to do with this purchase? . . . the Court of Appeal failed to mention . . . the evidence which was presented to show that the seat 'rocked' . . . I myself feel that the reasons for and against are in this case quite well balanced.

DRIVING: . . . I do not believe that this item of circumstantial evidence can have notable proof value. Even if Simon did not have any idea that he had cannabis in the car, he might still have gained the impression that a car was following him and have become irritated by this.

'To conclude,' the professor stated, 'I would like to point out that the Supreme Court has maintained in previous cases that "Even in drugs cases, for a guilty verdict to be found, it must be established beyond reasonable doubt that the accused committed the offence . . ." The fact that the evidence in such cases is difficult to assess should not result in a downgrading of the proof requirement. The only area of dispute in the present case however is the subjective requisite: Was Simon Hayward aware of the fact that cannabis had been hidden in the car? If he lacked such knowledge, then no blame whatsoever can be directed against him.'

Although he defended the judicial system as a whole, the very fact that such an eminent legal figure could feel justified in becoming personally involved in a case, especially one that had attracted so much notoriety, and in so doing publicly criticise the lower courts not only, in his view, for judging the issue improperly but in the case of the Appellant Court for not providing a detailed enough judgement, had to add substantially to the already considerable doubt that surrounded my conviction.

Like most people I have lived, and enjoyed living, an anonymous and private life. Never have I envied public figures their notability, indeed I have often felt sympathy for them; the problems of constantly being recognized must become excessively tedious. Despite the solitary confinement I was aware that my arrest had received a certain amount of publicity, if nothing else the number of reporters at my trials had been an indication of the level of interest, but I had no means of knowing just how much. Therefore it came as something of an unpleasant surprise when, in November, I was permitted to read the backlog of articles written about me during the previous eight months.

There were literally dozens of them, and it was not only the sheer volume of the material but also the content of many articles that was so shocking and cause for concern. It was not fame, it was infamy. I had become notorious as a drug smuggler, and it hurt.

For the first time in my life I was able to read stories in newspapers about which I already knew the background information. To be critical, I would have to say that the coverage was often paraphrased and inaccurate, and sometimes imbued with ill-informed comment. Everyone knows that sensationalism sells, and to that very obvious end the most sensational aspects of my predicament were repeated time and again, in every paper. To be more critical, this was done at the expense of the broad picture.

Of the mass publicity I had received, I suppose 50% was more or less true, 25% was speculation, and the remaining 25% total absurdity. I was not sure whether to be amused or upset at some of the lunatic absurdities that the popular press printed as accepted fact. They labelled me as a 'Daredevil Guardsman' and an 'SAS Hero' who had organised ambushes in Northern Ireland responsible for the deaths of numerous terrorists; apparently I had been on a 'secret mission' to Sweden, and had claimed as much to the police when arrested; Sandra was not my girlfriend but my 'controller'; I was a constant escort to The Queen, and to Mrs Thatcher; and so the list of pure invention went on. They made me out to be a cross between James Bond and a royal bodyguard.

Some wag writing for the *News of the World* had worked out that my army salary was £15,000 (another inaccuracy) added on the £20,000 I was supposed to have earned from the drugs run, and then published an article claiming that this mythical figure of £35,000 was the sum needed by Guards Officers to lead the 'high life' in their 'uppercrust' regiments. He even produced the following list of ridiculous expenses to prove his point:

Club membership	£ 750
Restaurant bills, dinner parties	£4,320
Mess Bills	£8,254
Hunting and polo	£6,700
Riding boots	£ 800
Holidays (winter and summer)	£5,000
Running Golf GTi or BMW	£4,800
Suits, shoes, brolly, bowler	£1,675
Regimental overcoat, breeches	£ 720
Guards Wine Club subscription	£ 500
Gambling	£ 600
Incidentals	£2,250
	———
TOTAL	£35,250

Well, nice try Weatherup, but oh so wrong. If the truth be known, the vast majority of my fellow officers survive, and survive quite comfortably, on their army pay. Gone are the days when a large private income was a prerequisite before taking a commission in The Household Division. Sadly the myth lives on, and by acting as a deterrence it prevents many suitable candidates from applying to join us. In this instance it was being proffered as a motive for me to resort to drug smuggling, and was just the sort of ammunition the Swedes were looking for.

Some weeks later I was to ask a journalist, whom I had come to know quite well, how his colleagues or for that matter their editors could justify printing such nonsense.

'Oh,' he said, looking surprised as well as amused, 'they can't. They make these stories up, or at least grossly exaggerate a snippet of information that some reporter has caught a whiff of. Sensationalism sells newspapers.'

'Aren't they afraid of being sued?'

'Not really, most of the "victims" don't bother. The papers can afford the legal costs that arise from those that do, and in any case it is all good publicity and only helps to sell even more copies.'

In spite of the speculation and the inaccuracies, I must say that on the whole I had little cause for complaint. In many cases the reports were fair and objective, indeed most could have been construed as sympathetic to my plight. Considering the justified antagonism with which society regards the illegal use of drugs, and those that deal in them, and the responsible position I had held in the community, the media could have had a field day in nailing me to the cross. With few exceptions they had chosen not to, and for that I am grateful. Even when the *Guardian*, alone amongst the quality daily newspapers in its absence from the appeal, printed what could only be described as a sarcastically inaccurate and anti-Leader Comment on the case, the editor kindly printed letters in rebuttal by myself, Christopher Murray, and a charity called the National Council for the Welfare of Prisoners Abroad.

Having said that, not one article in any newspaper related the complete story. Even taken collectively vast gaps were apparent to anyone in a position to know the difference. If a member of the public had read avidly every available inch in every available column he would still not have received a true and complete account of what had actually taken place. In addition, and regardless of which newspaper, I will only ever be able to look cynically at any quote pertaining to come from an unnamed source, such as a 'government spokesman', a 'senior officer in the Ministry of Defence', a 'Trade Union official', etc, etc. In my experience the journalist will invariably be indulging in his own make-believe, not protecting the origins of his information

I am not trying to say that the only good articles were those written with a bias in my favour, indeed I am surprised more were not published criticising my behaviour, but what I do believe is that no matter what the bias any article should be factually correct. I did find it mildly annoying, not to say incredibly frustrating, that after two trials and months of publicity, the facts of my case were still being widely misrepresented. One common distortion was that my brother had duped me, and even worse, quotes allegedly coming from me claiming that he had done so. Christopher is my brother regardless of anything he may or may not have done, and I was not about to condemn him out of turn. Certainly, it was a possibility that he had tricked me, but there again it was also possible that he had not. I was then, and I still am going to reserve judgement on the issue.

With this in mind, and in an attempt to provide a wider picture, I wrote an article myself which the *Daily Mail* eventually published in early 1988. Hopefully it did some good. I also, on advice from my lawyers, gave numerous press interviews, which surprisingly the prison authorities seemed more than happy to allow me to do. It was not something I enjoyed, indeed it was rather like being interrogated all over again, but I believe I gave a good account of myself and it had the added attraction of relieving the isolation of solitary confinement. Not all the results were as I expected or what I would have hoped for. I could give an interview but I could never control what the reporter would write, of course. One such example was a young chap from a Stockholm evening paper called *Expressen*. He quizzed me in great detail for three hours, taking copious quantities of notes. It was just before

Christmas and just as he was leaving, almost as a throw away remark, he asked me if I had received any presents from home. I admitted that I had been allowed a tinned fruit cake from my mother. His article, when it came out the next evening, did not mention one specific issue involved with the case, and was titled 'ENGLISH FRUIT CAKE'. To this day I do not know whether he was referring to me or my present.

If I had fallen victim to a certain amount of sensationalism, I still would not want to trespass on the freedom of the press. Freedom of speech, and with it the freedom of the press, is a fundamental right in any democracy. Any legislation to curb its excesses would be to pick at the very fabric of the liberty that all of us cherish. That is not to say I agree with the ability of the 'gutter' press to invade an individual's privacy with impunity, but the media should put its own house in order, and should not be forced into doing so with legislation, the abuse of which would be infinitely worse than the problem it was designed to solve. Sadly, freedom can only flourish if we recognise that freedom must include the right to abuse it, however much accepting that principle hurts.

Freedom of speech, freedom of expression, and a free press are the only real safeguards against the excesses of those who would wish to abuse power. The results of which are only too evident in totalitarian states where such freedoms do not exist. Even in countries like Sweden, true democracy suffers from the effects of a tame press.

By appealing to the Supreme Court I prolonged my stay in solitary confinement awaiting its decision. Without the restrictions life improved but still the routine that was Kronoberg dragged on in its ghastliness. I continued to spend the long, lonely, silent, claustrophobic hours alone in my cell, clinging to the last, desperate hope that somewhere, somehow, someone would come to his senses and acquit me.

It was just a question of biting one's lip, sitting it out and waiting. I was now allowed to mix with other inmates on the weekly visit to the gymnasium or when I was taken to watch a video. In fact Frembäck offered me the chance to double up with another prisoner during the day, but in the same breath advised against it.

'I cannot guarantee that he will be able to speak English, and we get some very strange people in here. He could be a violent murderer, he could be a drug addict, he could even have AIDS. It is up to you.'

The cells were small enough, I was used to my own company, and under those pre-conditions I took his advice and refused the offer.

As at Uppsala I occasionally heard people go bananas in the cells around me. One moment all would be quiet, the next someone would start to scream and shout, and weep hysterically. Invariably it would be a member of one of the ethnic minorities in Sweden. I listened for hours one afternoon as an Arab begged not to be returned to his cell, each time he quietened down sufficiently to be put back inside it, the screams would start again. Eventually they just left him to it. On another occasion I was woken up early in the morning, at about three o'clock, by the sounds of someone being dragged down the corridor outside my cell. He was a negro and he was pleading in English:

'Why are you doing this to me? Why . . . why . . . why? PLEASE!' It was a rather spooky experience because none of the warders, who were obviously doing the dragging, uttered a word. I could hear only the grunts and heaves of their exertions. The punishment cell was adjacent to mine and I listened fascinated as the poor wretch was thrown inside, stripped and tied to the iron bed. The next morning the warder who took me for my exercise boasted of their feat. He said that the man was huge and it had taken eight guards to tie him down. When I asked what he had done to deserve such treatment, he simply smiled and shrugged his shoulders.

I met an American in the gymnasium one week. His T-shirt was covered in blood, and he kept muttering 'Gulag . . . effing gulag . . .' under his breath. I asked him where the blood had come from. He rolled his eyes at me and showed me a heavily bandaged wrist.

'I can't effing take this place,' he said, 'so I cut myself.'

'How long have you been here?'

'Three effing weeks! Three effing weeks, and it's all her fault.' He then launched into a lurid tale about arguments and fights with his Swedish wife. I could see the wisdom in Frembäck's advice, and began to wish I had never engaged this madman in conversation.

'How long have you been in this hell-hole?'

'Nine months,' I told him.

'Jesus! Effing gulag . . . effing Gestapo . . .' and, thankfully, with that he wandered off.

His cell was opposite mine. Later in the day I came out for a shower to see his door open and a large pool of congealing blood on his floor. I thought he had succeeded in doing away with himself the second time around, but he was back a couple of hours later, I heard him telling his escort that the place was 'an effing Gulag'. They even made him clean up the blood.

The days passed. Looking at the diary I kept at the time I see that I slept for hours on end. My despair grew and I slowly gave up hope. My friends in England continued to fight, writing letters and going to see anyone who could possibly help, but really it was only a rearguard action; there was very little, if any chance of their efforts having an immediate effect on my circumstances. The one high point was that the Army had not yet sacked me, or asked me to resign. That was a comfort but I realised that if my appeal failed it could only be a matter of time before it did so.

At five to eleven on the morning of Tuesday 22 December Frembäck came to see me.

'I have some bad news for you,' he told me, 'I'm sorry, but the Supreme Court have refused to hear your case.'

Well, that was it. It came as no real surprise, I could show no emotion one way or the other, I just felt extremely negative. It was the end of the appeal road. I was now officially branded a convicted criminal. However I did not feel like a criminal. The newspapers had described me as 'shamed' and the 'Disgraced Captain', but you are only what you feel and I did not feel shamed or disgraced; I knew I had done nothing to deserve such labels. But the truth and reality of the situation sank slowly in, soon they would transfer me to a prison, I would be a convict. My life as I had known it was gone for ever, or at the very least, the boats were burning fiercely.

It was ironic that in refusing my appeal the Supreme Court Judges had obviously chosen not to heed the advice of Professor Ekelöf, the man who had originally laid down the guidelines they were supposed now to be following. Perhaps the professor had chosen not to involve himself in the politics of the matter, but had looked at it from a purely legal point of view? Even more surprising was that the highest court in the country had also felt able to condone Forsberg's actions in breaching his Codes, not to mention a police officer committing perjury.

The news was received stoically at home. The general feeling was that it was no bad thing, even a good thing that the appeal had been turned down. If it had been accepted, the case retried for a third time, and a guilty verdict handed down for the third time, which would almost certainly have been the outcome, my position would have been weakened still further. As it was, work could go ahead more quickly on a petition to the European Court of Human Rights. There, at least, I had a chance of receiving some proper justice.

Christmas came and went almost unnoticed, it was just like any other day spent alone in my box. I was allowed to receive a couple of telephone calls, and Ulla Barkman visited me on Christmas Eve for an hour, which was unbelievably kind of her. Otherwise it was just me and the BBC World Service, I began to look upon people like Paddy Pheeney, the sports commentator, as close friends. Thank God for the Beeb, it made the English way of life seem that much closer; something else we take for granted until it suddenly is not there any more.

On the Monday after Christmas I went before a Board which was to decide which prison I would be sent to. Frembäck had explained to me that I was entitled to list my first three choices and if possible I would be sent to one of them. Not knowing the first thing about Swedish or any type of gaols I had sought Ulla's advice and together we had shortlisted the ones she thought most suitable. The Board was informed of my choice before interviewing me.

It was not what I had expected. In typically Swedish style it was informal to the point of familiarity. I was ushered into one of the television rooms and asked to sit on an easy chair among a group of five men and women, all of whom were sipping cups of coffee. There was no discussion, they had made up their minds long before I arrived on the scene. All my choices had been turned down, in fact they told me that in my case the decision had been made by the Prison Authorities at the main Headquarters in Norrköping, a town south of Stockholm. I was still given a choice of three, but for institutions that had been chosen for me, KUMLA, TIDAHOLM, or NORRTÄLJE. They said Norrtälje would be best, and not knowing any different I accepted their advice. I was to be transferred as soon as possible, maybe the next day.

Frembäck had something close to a fit when he heard the news. 'Those places aren't for you,' he told me, 'they are three of the worst maximum security prisons in Sweden, for the most difficult prisoners with long sentences.'

He promised to speak to the Criminal Board in Norrköping to see if I could not be sent somewhere else, adding that if he failed and I was sent to Norrtälje I would almost certainly emerge a hardened criminal, even if in his view I was not going in as one.

Luckily he succeeded, and the next day told me that I would be going to the gaol in Malmö, a town right in the south of the country, on the coast opposite Denmark. He said it was still a maximum security prison, I could expect nothing else, but it was one of the better ones and being in the south, much easier and cheaper for my family to visit. The date of the transfer had been set for 7 January. I thanked him, he had done his best for me.

My final memories of Kronoberg are: of the man in the cell next to mine who would thump out a 'goodnight' on the wall late each evening which I would return. When alone it felt good to have that little piece of human contact. Of a warder I had not seen before taking me for exercise one morning:

'So you are the "captain", are you?'

'Yes, I am.'

'Did you do it?'

'Since you ask. No, I did not.'

'Ha, that is what they all say in here. Everyone is innocent!'

He made me realise what a totally hopeless situation I was in, and that nothing I said would be taken at face value. I had lost that cloak of respectability and trust.

And lastly, of 30 December when all the cells on the wing bar mine were cleared, and re-filled with a planeload of Vietnamese boat people, who had flown in that day in search of the promised land. Some welcome, to spend their first New Years Day in 'freedom', not with their families but in solitary confinement. They must have wondered if they had come to the right country after all. Their cries of anguish were worse than all the others.

Ten

The seventh of January had arrived. The last morning at Kronoberg, and my 300th spent in solitary confinement. The past two weeks had been more than usually difficult, I had never spent a more unhappy festive season. I packed my personal belongings and gave the cell one final look over. It had been my home for just under twenty-three weeks, in it I had passed some of the blackest days of my life and I was not in the least bit sad to see the back of it. However I had nothing to feel pleased about, there was another one, probably just like it, waiting for me in Malmö.

The seven hundred kilometre journey took all day, with a pit-stop at a police station in Jönköping for lunch and a change of escorts. I was driven, handcuffed, in a prison mini-bus under the personal supervision of four guards, one of whom told me that it would have been normal to fly such long distances but the authorities did not want me to be seen by anyone, nor to double up with other prisoners being taken south. The newspapers later reported that I had been spirited out of Stockholm, and that is exactly how it felt. Like a very bad dream.

I was feeling gloomy and despondent, deeply depressed at my prospects and took little interest in the passing scenery. In any case, for much of the time it snowed heavily and visibility was poor. They were taking the same route south as I had used coming north ten months previously and it was with a sense of profound regret that I noticed the signs for Linköping – I wished I had never heard of the infernal place. It was late in the afternoon and dark when we arrived in Malmö.

I had a fleeting impression of a housing estate, then football fields, then high walls and spotlights before the van pulled up with a lurch in front of a set of large bleak gates which shone green in the arc of the headlights. The guard in the front passenger seat climbed out and spoke into an intercom box, someone on the inside must have pushed a button, for the gates started to slide open automatically to reveal a small courtyard. We drove in, the gates closing behind us. I turned to look at them over one shoulder, my attention riveted to the diminishing gap between both halves and what I thought would be my last view of the outside world for years was shut off with a clunk as they came together.

The sense of being in a dream prevailed. I was taken out of the van and into the building. The yellow glow of lights. A warder in a blue uniform waiting. Down some narrow stone steps into a cellar. The handcuffs were removed. Into yet another graffiti-covered holding cell. A metal bowl of mashed potato and a slice of sausage. The place had a strange musky smell. It was quiet except for muffled voices coming from far away. Two hours passed.

Finally they came for me. Two warders, one elderly with grey hair, balding, a goatee beard, a round man with a large gut who looked as though he enjoyed his whiskey. The other was a child in comparison, very young – about twenty, tall, with a bewildered expression and enormous 'Joe 90' glasses.

'Come with us.'

Through a metal gate into an office. My bags were piled in the centre of the floor. I had to sign some forms, handing them over for safe keeping to the prison.

'Follow him,' the old guard ordered me, once I had signed.

Across the corridor into another room. Shelves stocked with bundles of bedclothes and green uniforms. Boxes full of odd shoes. A shower in one corner.

'What size are you?'

'I am six foot, one inch. About a 34-inch waist.'

'What is that in centimetres?'

'I don't know.'

'Take this bundle, it will do. Now strip. Put all your clothes in this sack, and put on the uniform.'

I did as I was bid. The uniform was very second hand. Threadbare trousers that reached only as far as half way down my shins. A thin cotton shirt with hardly any buttons. Old grey, once-white Y-Fronts, heavily stained – with holes in them. A tatty T-shirt. Heavy woollen socks. An unmatching pair of tired, rather smelly leather slippers. It reminded me of *Papillon*, when Steve McQueen arrived on Devil's Island. I was feeling very miserable.

'What now?' I asked the young guard.

'I don't know. I am new here myself.'

His partner came in. He told me to pick up what remained of the clothing bundle and to follow him. Along a well lit concrete floored corridor, through metal doors that were relocked behind us. I noticed the warder was using the same key for all of them. Up several flights of wide stone stairs. Another office. More warders. I was sure I would wake up at any moment. This could only be a dream.

'Hayward,' one of them was speaking to me, 'Hayward!'

'Yes, that's me.'

'You are number 405. You are on Wing A II. Come with me.'

Three warders this time, escorted me up another flight of stairs to a large landing, then onto a long, quiet corridor with rows of wooden cell doors on either side. This was the Wing. I followed the men past a small snooker table, then a table tennis table. A door was opened halfway down on the left.

'This is for you. Go inside.' He continued to speak to me from the open doorway. 'You will be woken by the bell in the morning at half past six. Have breakfast, then you will be taken to work. All convicts in Swedish gaols must work, it is the law. Goodnight.'

The door closed. The lock turned. Once again I was alone. The cell was similar to those in the Häktets, but much older with wooden fitments, a metal framed chair, and a low wooden bunk with the usual thin foam mattress. There was no wash basin. Underneath the fitments was a small cupboard set into the wall which contained a plastic jerry.

Without thinking I made the bed and put the spare clothes they had given me on a shelf. I was moving in a trance, not wanting to believe what was happening to me, or where I was. I lay down and tried to sleep, but it would not come. I could hear the sound of a television coming from the adjacent cell, mine did not have one. I felt heavy, the atmosphere of the little cell pressing in on me. Before, in the Häktets, I had always had the hope of being acquitted to keep me going, now that hope was gone. Unless something dramatic occurred in the form of new evidence or a quick result from the European Court, I was going to have to spend several years of my life in this place. My mind was reeling, the very thought of being in prison was humiliating enough. I had reached the end of the line, rock bottom. Tears of anger, frustration, disillusionment, trickled down my face. The hours slipped by. Finally I slept.

A bell was ringing, far away but coming closer, growing louder. I came to, opened my eyes, blinking at the unfamiliar surroundings, not recognising where I was. The bell with its constant shrill electric ring, actually unmoving right outside my door, came to an abrupt stop. A few seconds of silence. I sat up with a jolt, memories of the previous day came flooding back to me, and with them the deep-felt bitterness. I lay back not wanting to move, to accept the situation. I could now hear the sound of doors banging and shouted 'God Morgons' working its way down the corridor. My door opened, a warder poked his head into the cell:

'Good morning 405. Time to get up.'

I emerged rather sheepishly, not knowing what to expect, to find my new 'colleagues' busy with the morning's business. Men, still bleary-eyed and in various states of undress, were wandering around, slopping out, washing, taking their breakfasts from a trolley in the corridor before sitting at one of a number of dining tables. No one took the least notice of me.

I had breakfast. There was porridge and smorgasbord – bread with slices of processed cheese and fatty sausage. At seven-fifteen the bell gave another five-second burst and soon afterwards men started to drift off the wing, obviously going to the work that the warder had mentioned to me the evening before.

I was assigned to the 'Plastics Factory', a large open-plan workshop where several machines belched out a variety of plastic office folders by the thousand which had to be sorted, stacked, counted and boxed by the convicts. Other jobs involved glueing cardboard boxes together or counting out piles of waxed cooking paper and packaging them into plastic bags. I was put to work on this last option. Within half an hour I was bored silly and the unceasing background noise of the machines as they sucked, wheezed and burped on the compressed air that ran them was already driving me to distraction. I had not been at it for an hour and I was going nuts. What, I wondered, would it feel like after a year? It did not bear thinking about.

That first day, and those immediately subsequent to it, passed in a daze as the system accepted and processed me with interviews with the Governor, Wing Administrative Officer and Head Warder, as well as medical and dental checks. However, as with any new routine, one becomes accustomed to it and I found myself slowly settling down. It was much easier if I did not dwell on the situation but lived each day as it came. The very worst thing was to look too far ahead, at the seemingly endless drudgery of the cycle, each day the same, day in day out. To do so achieved nothing and only served to plunge me into the very depths of depression, especially if I compared my present existence to what I should have been doing on the outside.

Malmö Prison was the oldest maximum-security institution in the country, built in 1913, and was situated in a residential suburb of the town. Its main structure consisted of a long four-storey building housing the various wings, each leading off from the central staircase I had climbed on the first evening. There was another smaller two-storey block crossing its centre at right-angles incorporating the main entrance, guardroom, reception hall, visiting rooms, administration, the hospital and kitchens. From the air it would have looked like an elongated cross. There were also several outhouses and exercise yards, and the entire complex was surrounded, needless to say, by a high wall. Every surface was painted a dirty cream except for the roofs and window frames which were lime green.

Sweden is renowned for its liberal, humane and relaxed penal system, and although I have no yardstick I expect the regime at Malmö would compare favourably to the equivalent category A or B prisons in the United Kingdom; or for that matter most other countries in the world.

Some one hundred and fifty inmates, of different categories, were locked up in the place. The regular prisoners in three wings numbered A I – III, twenty-five on each. There were two Häktet wings, another fifty men on those; and finally a psychiatric wing holding approximately twenty-five. Quite how a man qualified as a psychiatric case I was never to find out because in my opinion many of the so called 'normal' prisoners were certainly crazy enough to make the grade.

Each A Wing was a self contained unit with its own shower room, lavatories and small kitchen equipped with a refrigerator, toaster, and boiling water geyser. Although meals were brought up from the main kitchens on a hotplate, there was always a constant supply of milk, yoghurt, cereal, bread, margarine, jams, sugar, tea and coffee available. The quality of the food was surprisingly good, it usually ranged from mediocre to bad; rarely disgusting and never inedible. The wing corridor doubled as the dining and association area; there were snooker and table tennis tables; and perhaps most important of all, a coin-operated telephone box for which each inmate was entitled to have three numbers logged into an automatic dialer, controlled by the warders, two of whom were on duty at all times sitting at a desk by the wing entrance. Every man had a cell of his own, equipped with a prison radio and a colour television if he was able to supply one himself. During the daytime there was free association on the wing itself, but as a rule prisoners from the other wings were not allowed to visit.

A weekday at Malmö looked like this:

0630 hrs: Reveille
0630–0715 hrs: Slop out/wash/breakfast
0715–1130 hrs: Work/school
1145–1200 hrs: Lunch
1200–1325 hrs: Exercise/free time
1330–1615 hrs: Work/school
1630–1645 hrs: Dinner
1700–1800 hrs: Exercise (summer only) Sports/free time
1800–1930 hrs: Sports/free time
1930 hrs. Lock-up

Saturday:
   0800 hrs: Reveille
   0900–1100 hrs: Clean laundry issue/sauna
   1200 hrs: Lunch
   1300–1600 hrs: Exercise/sport/free time
   1700 hrs: Dinner
   1930 hrs: Lock-up

Sunday:
   0800 hrs: Reveille
   1100 hrs: Lunch
   1145 hrs: Film show (Usually recently released and English spoken)
   1400–1600 hrs: Exercise/sport/free time
   1700 hrs: Dinner
   1930 hrs: Lock-up

On weekends there was no work and inmates were allowed free association on their own wings. The 'clean' laundry issued on a Saturday morning took some getting used to. Clothes were washed universally and then re-issued according to size only. One did not own one's own uniform. It did not do to look around and try and guess who had been wearing your 'clean' clothes the week before. The resulting itching fits were unbearable, for many of the prisoners had strange standards of personal hygiene. During the week there was an administrative officer assigned to each wing who was, in theory at least, always available to sort out personal problems, arrange for extra telephone calls, visits and the like.

Exercise was taken in a yard, fifty metres long by twenty-five wide, which just allowed for a rather stunted game of football; or a circular walk, hugging the walls, that made one dizzy. During the summer months when exercise periods were extended a small garden was also used allowing prisoners to sunbathe on a patch of what could loosely be described as lawn. Because the prison was so old, sporting facilities compared to other Swedish gaols were minimal: apart from the football, for two hours each evening a maximum of fifteen men could weight train in a small but well equipped gymnasium, and another four could play badminton or a form of indoor hockey called Bandy. Wanting to take part entailed a mad dash first thing each morning to sign one's name on a list. Due to the lack of space there were invariably disappointed faces on those who arrived just too late, to find the list already full. I would weight-train occasionally, more as a therapy than a sport, but 'pumping iron' has to rate as one of the most boring pastimes available. I played badminton more often; the prison game of doubles was fast and furious and a good way of retaining a degree of fitness. However, when playing against a murderer and a bank-robber, it was not always a good idea to win.

In addition to the plastics factory there was a mechanical workshop where prisoners produced an assortment of metal goods on lathes and milling machines. Those wishing to, and indeed some that did not, could attend educational classes in a modern school block with civilian teachers. Courses were associated to outside colleges, and with the right motivation an inmate could, in theory, work for qualifications up to and including a degree in a wide range of subjects. Since many prisoners lacked a proper education the school was well attended and courses usually oversubscribed. The fact that work in the factories was so monotonous probably had something to do with the school's popularity. Some inmates were able to become full-time students but the majority had to work in the factories and at best attend school part time.

Trustee prisoners worked in the clothing store, the laundry, as gardeners, in the prison maintenance department, or as cleaners. These were the best jobs because of the added freedom that went with them, and were eagerly sought after.

Everyone received a salary regardless, even full-time students, and wages were surprisingly high – converted into sterling, between thirty and forty pounds a week. By contrast in the United Kingdom a convict earns a maximum of £2.40 per week, and a single person claiming unemployment benefit only £31.00. Many of the foreign prisoners in Malmö, coming from Third World countries, were earning more in prison than they had done in full-time employment at home. Convicts were forced to save 850 Krona which was kept in a special account for exeats and their release date; most accumulated considerably more, especially those serving long sentences.

Money was needed within the prison to buy things from a small shop, known as the 'Kiosk'. It was a little like the tuck shop at school, selling a wide variety of 'goodies' from fruit to sweets; soft drinks to tobacco. No alcohol was available, nor anything that needed cooking. It was open four days a week and the only limit on the quantity one could buy was the amount of money one had available. Prices are high in Sweden in any event but at this shop they were painful; 100 Krona (approximately £10) bought next to nothing and one could easily have spent twice one's weekly salary without being in the least extravagant.

There was a well-equipped library, catering for all languages, open four days a week and associated with the municipal library in the town. Just about any book published anywhere in the world was on offer, and no inmate could possibly complain that he did not have sufficient reading material to keep him interested. Recent copies of international newspapers and magazines were also provided.

Visiting hours and conditions were generous. Every man was entitled to a two-hour visit, conjugal if he so wished, each week. They were unguarded, the prisoner being left alone in a small room, furnished with a bed, table and chairs, with his visitor(s) for the allotted time. Space permitting, extra time was available, and the system was relaxed and friendly. Foreigners, whose families had to travel to Sweden from abroad, were allowed to bank their hours to enable them to save enough to have visits lasting for several days, seven hours a day.

The routine was not difficult to adapt to. The thing that struck me most was the artificiality of it all. Just a few locked doors away was freedom and an entirely different world; a world that was impossible to reach. I would spend much of my free time staring out of the window. In fact staring out of my cell window will be one of my lasting memories of being in prison.

For Swedish nationals the penal system appeared to work on the basis of re-education, reform and gradual rehabilitation for the outside world. After serving one quarter of his sentence, and depending on his individual circumstances, a Swedish prisoner, (and I stress the 'Swedish') could qualify for a programme of exeats called 'permissions', eventually being given up to seventy-two hours off on his own recognisance every two months. There was also a Prison Service holiday camp in the wilds of Northern Sweden, where inmates lucky enough to be given the chance, from gaols all over the country, could spend up to eleven days on trust, living with their families in chalets, enjoying the open air. Under normal conditions, six months before his release date a convict would be transferred to an open prison, ultimately working normally in the community and only returning to be locked up in the evenings.

Foreign prisoners were treated differently for the understandable reason that if given permissions 95 per cent of them would never have been seen again. They would have disappeared in a cloud of dust the moment the gates closed behind them. However they were allowed four hours on the outside under heavy guard every six months. On two occasions during my sentence when Sandra and my mother visited me, we were able to spend four consecutive days together as well as being taken out for lunch to a local restaurant, followed by a walk along the Malmö sea front. I cannot think of another system in the world where such privileges would be on offer.

The system was certainly enlightened – even men serving life sentences were granted permissions – but it was justified by the fact that it was rarely abused. Very infrequently did prisoners fail to return, none that I know of from Malmö during my sojourn, and usually the examples one did hear of involved short-term inmates from open prisons. There are always exceptions to the rule of course – the most notorious case of a convict taking advantage of his temporary freedom and betraying the trust put in him, while I was in Sweden, was that of a spy called Stig Berling. His disappearance was a great embarrassment to the government and eventually resulted in the resignation of the Justice Minister. The policy of granting criminals exeats continued however.

In my opinion the penal system could on occasion become too enlightened. Situated at one end of the prison, just beyond its walls, were three houses occupied by prison staff and their families and surrounded by a large wooded garden. Just the other side of the garden was a local school attended by children as young as seven. I was to watch with horror and amazement from my window as a convicted child molester, who had committed the most foul perversions against his own children, was allowed to work unsupervised in these gardens. To make matters even worse, when the weather was fine a toddler from one of the houses would play naked on the lawns, right in front of the lecherous eyes of this man. It must be said that the decision to give him the job as gardener would have been made internally at the prison and therefore the system as a whole cannot be blamed, but I fail to understand how anyone could put children so blatantly at risk. The prison Governor would have had a lot to answer for if the convict had taken the opportunity to re-offend.

The general relationship between warders and inmates, indeed internal discipline as a whole, was also relaxed and easygoing, sometimes even familiar and friendly. As a rule warders were addressed by their surnames, never the Swedish equivalent of 'sir' or 'mister', but it was not at all uncommon for them to be called by nicknames or even their Christian names. In fact the head warder, known as the 'Overtill-sysman', was always addressed by his Christian name by staff and prisoners alike. Exactly the same applied when warders spoke to inmates. Being used to the military system of rank it took me some time to get used to this very familiar arrangement, when I initially addressed the Governor and his Deputy Director as 'Sir', or called warders Mr So-en-So, they looked so surprised and uncomfortable that I soon gave up trying and adopted the policy of 'When in Rome . . .'

Familiarity can breed contempt, of course, and a certain amount of what prisoners in the last World War called 'Goon-bating' went on, not all of it by any means good-natured, but outbursts were normally ignored. Indeed some of the guards, especially the younger ones, appeared at a total loss to know how to react and what to do about it.

There were some two hundred warders, easily outnumbering the inmates, most of whom were in their twenties and many of whom were women – although it was not always easy to tell the difference. They were supported by an administrative staff of about forty. There was a very high turnover, with a constant stream of new faces appearing as the 'old timers' left for greener pastures. In the summer months an influx of students, earning their holiday money, swelled their ranks and the fact that these 'instant' guards were put in charge of dangerous criminals after only two weeks probation was an indication of the very casual atmosphere within the prison.

The warders imposed little obvious discipline and practically no deterrence against bad behaviour. One third remission, the carrot that keeps British prisoners in hand, was not a privilege that had to be earned but a right granted to all, regardless of behaviour and record. Half remission was on offer but seemingly a good record was not a prerequisite. In fact I sometimes wondered if the exact opposite was not a requirement when badly behaved men were given half time and well behaved men serving similar sentences for similar crimes were not. A warder who had been in the service for years described the system of half remission as a game of bingo. He said it was like a lottery with the most unexpected prisoners winning the prizes.

There was little a warder could do to enforce his authority against an unruly prisoner. The first step was threaten to, then actually write a report against the man. A report constituted nothing more than a slapped wrist and not surprisingly most prisoners simply laughed at that. The next stage was to place him in an isolation cell for a few days, but this meant nothing to men who had all spent months in solitary confinement before coming to gaol, indeed it was looked upon as a welcome break from the prison routine. Next, visiting and permission rights would be temporarily withdrawn, and finally extra days to a man's sentence could be awarded, in groups of three to five, up to a maximum total of forty-five. It is not difficult to understand that for a determined individual all of this had little or no effect. Some men intentionally worked up the extra forty-five days as quickly as possible, giving them an almost free hand from then on. As a last resort the most difficult cases would be transferred to another prison but that solved nothing, it only passed the problem on. It was a credit to the guards' personal discipline that, often in the face of extreme provocation, they very rarely took matters into their own hands by resorting to physical intimidation and violence against inmates.

There is invariably one exception to the rule. In this case it was a guard called Rengbrandt, who was the prison 'bully'. He was a great hulk of a man with a hatred of prisoners in general and foreign ones in particular. His size was matched only by his ignorance. As with all bullies, he would pick on the smaller inmates and those he knew would not 'bite' back. He never gave me any problem. One 'mean' guard out of two hundred was acceptable.

The obvious solution of a system whereby a convict had to earn his remission by good behaviour had for some reason not been adopted. In an attempt to enforce order all prisoners were invited to go before a board called a 'Kollegium', made up of the prison heads of departments, every three months, to be told how they were progressing and what was officially thought of them. Since this was voluntary most refused to attend. As far as I could see the prison ran on little more than the goodwill of its prisoners; an opinion openly shared by members of the staff.

To a British convict serving his sentence in a prison like Wandsworth or Wormwood Scrubs, which by all reports are a national disgrace, shut up in a cell with two or even three other men for twenty-three hours a day, with no proper sanitation, only allowed one shower a week, given appalling food, and subjected to a regime of harsh discipline, I would imagine the routine I have just described at Malmö must make the place sound like a three-star hotel.

The Criminal Board justified its philanthropic attitude in saying that by giving convicts normal contacts with the outside world it made it easier for them to rejoin the community when released. Allowing conjugal visits and facilities like telephones and televisions helped release tensions in the prisons. The statistics support this view. For example, the incidence of bad behaviour and suicide attempts plummeted when televisions were first allowed in the 1970s.

My 'fellow' convicts were a rum bunch. All kinds of criminals were mixed in together – from murderers serving life sentences, to drug smugglers, bank robbers, rapists, child molesters, to petty thieves serving short sentences. However, as a rule sex offenders were housed on Wing AI, or segregated in the Psychiatric Wing, because nobody liked them. There was also a wide range of nationalities and it made me realise how very bad the British are at learning foreign languages when I heard Continental inmates chopping and changing with apparent ease mid-conversation from Dutch to German to Italian, Spanish, French, Swedish and English. Luckily most spoke some English, even the warders, so I had little difficulty in making myself understood.

After only a week on AII I was transferred to Wing AIII where the majority of long-term prisoners were kept. It was known as the mature wing and was much quieter than the other two. It also had the added bonus of having larger cells, the extra space making all the difference. I had to get used to living with criminals, some of whom had committed the most ghastly crimes imaginable, some of whom were the very dregs of society, and none of whom I had anything in common with. In fact it felt far easier to identify with the guards, who in many respects reminded me of the soldiers I had once led.

It was a novelty, when sitting with a group of men around one of the wing tables drinking coffee, to be told that the quiet, inoffensive, slightly-built and balding little fellow beside me had actually murdered a man in cold blood by stabbing him seventeen times in the throat whilst in a mad frenzy. Or that the middle-aged, heavily tattooed man opposite, with the resigned look and quick sense of humour, was one of Sweden's most notorious bank robbers who had spent a total of more than twenty-five years behind bars for a string of presumably unsuccessful hold-ups. Or that this chap had suffocated his wife, or that one had shot a policeman when seventeen years old and out of his mind on amphetamines.

'I'm serving seven years for smuggling heroin,' a long-haired Albanian would add, 'I was arrested at the border when customs officers discovered four kilos of amphetamines in my car's petrol tank, someone else would say.' And so the list went on.

I did not relish the prospect of living at close quarters for a prolonged period with such unsavoury people, but what struck me very quickly, perhaps surprisingly, was just how ordinary they seemed. One had to forget what they had done and simply accept them at face value. I also had to accept that I had one thing in common with them if nothing else, I was in prison with them.

However, I made a promise to myself. Accepting my new companions for who they were was one thing, but I was not going to let myself be influenced by them.

To begin with the other prisoners treated me with a good deal of suspicion – I was not one of them, I was an establishment figure, I was not admitting to any guilt. I found myself in a kind of limbo, ostracised by one side and not fully welcomed by the other. Conversations would dry up abruptly when I approached and resume when I had passed. There was interest in me because of the notoriety of my arrest and trial, but nothing more. For my part I was happy just to be with people again after the months spent in solitary confinement, and it did not matter too much who they were. Everything felt new, it was an experience to be able to move around relatively freely, to talk with people, to get some proper exercise. However, once the novelty of my new-found, albeit limited, freedom had worn off I started to spend an increasing amount of time alone in my cell. To be frank I preferred my own company.

It is almost impossible to describe what being in gaol is really like; one needs to experience it. Initially I suppose it felt a little like being back in my first term at prep school. That long-forgotten sensation of being a new boy; the unfamiliar surroundings, the smell of the place, the strange uniform, the strange people, being self-conscious, not knowing what to do, what to say, where to go.

Three weeks after my arrival at Malmö my brother David, just twenty-three years old, was killed in a road accident in Scotland with two friends. It happened shortly after eight o'clock on the morning of Sunday 31 January. He had been an undergraduate at St. Andrews, reading history, one of his great passions in life. Another of his passions was fencing and had captained the university team. That morning he and his companions had been driving to Aberdeen to represent St. Andrews in the Scottish Universities Fencing Championships when, just outside Forfar, their car hit sheet ice and skidded head-on into the front of an on-coming gritting lorry. They died instantly, that much at least was a blessing, for seconds after impact the car exploded into flames. The thought of them being trapped alive in a burning car is too horrible to contemplate. The twist was that if they had passed by two minutes, or even one minute, later the road would have been salted. Such is fate. A terrible waste of three young lives.

It was a dreadful blow to the whole family, particularly for my mother who was visiting me in Sweden when the accident occurred. She broke the news quietly to me on the Monday morning. I knew something was wrong the moment I walked into the visiting room to see that my aunt, who had flown out immediately, was with her. That awful dark empty void, last experienced with my father's death, came rushing back with a vengeance. With it, the self-recriminations – why could it not have been me, instead of him? If I had been there it would have been different, the accident would not have happened, I could have saved him. Of course it does no good, in fact if anything it makes it worse. I suppose it is all part of the process of coming to terms with losing someone you love. Slowly the numbness wears off; one has to accept reality, however painful, and then get on with life.

The sense of disbelief and loss was intensified by the inevitable decision not to allow me to return home for the funeral. The Swedes, perhaps understandably, were convinced that once in England I would refuse to come back. No amount of persuasion would make them change their minds. My aunt even offered to remain in Sweden as a 'hostage' to guarantee my quick return; Kingsley Napley, John Gorst, and Brigadier Emson tried to work miracles in the corridors of power to provide similar guarantees, such as an escort of Army Officers, but all to no avail.

Soon after the Supreme Court had turned down my appeal the authorities had tried to persuade me to return to Britain to serve my sentence, even going so far as to draw up the necessary paperwork without my or Tom Placht's knowledge. At the time I had refused, not, as was widely put about, because Swedish prisons are so much better than British ones, though that was admittedly one consideration. The main reason was that it was felt that once out of their jurisdiction the Swedish authorities would be extremely loathe to re-open my case, regardless of what new evidence we managed to unearth. I had to stick it out in Sweden as a means of applying pressure and I did so knowing that my decision might well have been prolonging my incarceration, since in Britain I would have been eligible for parole after one third of the sentence, in November 1988, (in Sweden the best I could hope for was half remission, with just one third being more probable). It was much more important to increase my chances of clearing my name than to reduce the time spent behind bars.

When I was told that I would not be allowed to return temporarily I immediately offered to let them repatriate me permanently, if the authorities could get me home in time for David's funeral. However the bureaucratic processes on both sides of the North Sea were not geared to making speedy decisions, and finally I had to accept defeat. I don't think I will ever be able to forgive those people who deprived me of the opportunity of saying a proper farewell to a young brother who meant the world to me. An indication of the hypocrisy that not infrequently rises to the surface in Sweden was the news item proclaiming that I had in fact been offered the opportunity of returning to England to attend the funeral, but that I had callously turned it down because of the comforts I was enjoying in my Swedish prison. At a time when I would have given my right arm to be with my family this sort of thing filled me with a bitterness and hatred towards Sweden that quite shocked me when I thought about it more rationally later. It is actually very typical of the Swedish mentality to seek to justify what could be construed as an insensitive decision by passing the responsibility for it onto someone else.

As a gesture I wrote to Mr Björn Wejbo, Head of the Criminal Board, and The Justice Minister, Mrs Anna-Greta Leijon. Wejbo never bothered to reply; Mrs Leijon did weeks later with a non-committal answer that totally ducked the issue. I also sent a letter to Mitchell, explaining what had happened and appealing to the better side of his nature to take the opportunity to come clean and tell the truth. I pointed out to him that his testimony had convicted me, and by telling the truth he could easily clear me. I hated to ask the man for any favours, but I literally begged him to speak up quickly to enable me to be released in time for the funeral. His reply was nothing if not predictable, and was clearly written with the censor in mind. While having the good grace to commiserate on the accident, he otherwise stuck rigidly to his guns, even accusing me of talking to the police about other members of the gang, mentioning names like Basil, whom I had never heard of. The letter was littered with such phrases as 'You want the truth, well the truth always hurts, man' and 'you were caught red-handed', and 'we both know the truth, don't we?' I was both saddened and disgusted by his stand.

My mother had left Sweden for home on that same Monday; by the Wednesday I knew positively that I would not be allowed to follow her. It was a very miserable time for all of us, and Sandra flew out to be with me on the Thursday and Friday. Once again she was standing by me during a difficult period. I could not have wished for a better friend.

They cremated David on Saturday 6 February in Scotland and it was decided to hold a Thanksgiving Service for his life in the Henry VIII Chapel at Westminster Abbey the following Tuesday. He had been educated at Westminster School. All I was able to do was send a recorded reading to be played during the service; I chose Dryden's poem used at the front of this book, along with a short extract from the Bible. Otherwise I remained alone in my cell, trying to come to terms with the reality of his death. When this entire Swedish nightmare is over and long forgotten, David's passing will be the only enduring wrong that cannot ever be put right.

There was an epilogue to the issue that highlighted the depths to which elements of the British press are prepared to sink in their search for a story. A reporter (I do not know from which tabloid) circulated among the students at St. Andrews, offering a cash reward of five thousand pounds to anyone who would come forward with the information that David had been pushing drugs at the University. The idea was totally without foundation and it was an exercise in nothing more than mud-slinging. It was a measure of the University, its students, my brother's friends and David himself (who by all accounts was immensely popular) that the offer was never accepted, despite the fact that five thousand pounds to an impoverished student must have been an enormous inducement.

Something similar happened to me in Sweden when I received an extraordinary letter from a woman calling herself Marianne H. The gist of it was that she had seen me on television, fancied me something rotten and wanted to visit me in prison to strike up a 'relationship'. She included photographs of herself and asked me to respond in kind. I thought it must have been somebody having a joke, although I have since learnt that it is far from unusual for convicts to be contacted by 'lonely' girls. In any event I sent back an equally outrageous letter declining her 'kind' offer but passing her on to an Italian prisoner who wanted to try his luck. Angelo had the morals of an alley cat and I portrayed him as a young 'Latin Adonis' in my letter, never imagining that his advances would be accepted, and half expecting a highly irate response to come my way from Miss H. Not a bit of it; the hungry lady was visiting Angelo within the week. The strange thing, he told me, was that she kept asking him questions about me. When I pressed him further he refused to elaborate.

To cut a long story short, I was eventually warned by a journalist who kept in regular touch with me and who had higher moral scruples than some of his colleagues, that Marianne H. had been hired by a well known British newspaper to befriend me, to seduce me in one of the visiting rooms and to try and establish if I knew where Christopher was. One can just imagine the sordid headlines that would have ensued. As it was, faced with my refusal to meet her, she had taken second best by attempting to acquire her information via Angelo. My journalist friend described the woman as a sad figure who had once been a successful model, but who would now do anything for money. When I faced up to Angelo he rather sheepishly told me that she had indeed tried to recruit him as her accomplice but that he had been playing for time whilst having his fun with her. He admitted that he had been tempted to go along with her plans (there was quite a large sum of money involved) but that the prisoners' code of ethics had prevented him from doing so. Since he had never asked me a single question referring to Christopher or the case in general, I had no reason to disbelieve him, although I remained on my guard from that moment on.

The possibility of making money by selling scandalous

stories to the press was one that had obviously not escaped the notice of my new companions. The very thought filled me with dread and would start me off on a spiral of paranoia. The reason for my concern was quite simply that I had no defence against it. Nothing was more certain to have me running for the hills than some slippery character sliding up to me with thoughts of a 'nice little earner' on his mind.

Sid, another English prisoner, had the most imaginative scheme, to invent a story along the lines of a 'prison confession' based on a pang of conscience, and then to sell it to the highest bidder. Once it had been published, the idea was to sue the newspaper for defamation. We would then split the profits fifty-fifty. But if I refused to participate he promised to resort to plan B: I will say you're the wing queen, that is sure to sell.' With the benefit of hindsight I do not think there was much to worry about, he may even have been joking, but at the time it struck a raw nerve. It was an additional problem that on top of everything else I did not need. My only insurance policy against him, and others like him, was to point out that two could play at his little game and to let Tom Placht know the exact date and time of every occasion the subject came up. The whole thing was a confounded nuisance, but to date as far as I am aware nothing has ever come of it.

The months passed slowly by and with them my hopes of an early release. My petition to the European Court was lodged but I was warned not to expect a quick result, indeed it was probable that I would be released long before hearing anything. The search for new evidence continued but progress was frustratingly slow. I resigned myself to the reality of being in prison.

The shock of losing my liberty never wore off. Never a day went by when I did not kick myself for not realising what had been going on around me on Ibiza. As each day passed the frustrations of being confined became more difficult to bear. I could not see the end of my sentence; I could not imagine what it would be like to be free again. It was as if life behind the bars was all I had to look forward to.

I relived the past. The circumstances of my arrest, trials and conviction became an obsession. I lived, breathed and even slept them, often waking up in the middle of the night bathed in sweat to find that my mind had been working overtime. I could think of nothing else, despite the depression these memories brought with them. I would run through the facts of the case continually, usually ending up going around in circles because I did not have all the pieces of the puzzle. They read more like the plot of a fictional thriller than something that I had actually lived through.

Apart from my freedom, the aspects of life I missed the most were common trust, respect and responsibility. I was classified Category 7:3, a security tag reserved for the most dangerous criminals most likely to escape. In fact the authorities seemed convinced I would try to abscond, Carselid even referred to the 'SAS rescue bid' on the first occasion he interviewed me.

It was clear that nothing I could do or say would make them change their minds. I tried explaining to Carselid and in letters to the Criminal Board that I had no intention of escaping. That for me escape was the very worst option, that it would solve nothing, only create more problems. That if I was to escape I would be giving up any chance of clearing my name and of being able to return to some semblance of a normal life because it would put an end to my petition to the European Court of Human Rights and of any future appeal to a Swedish court. That it would also result in my certain dismissal from the Army; that even if I succeeded in escaping I could never return to the United Kingdom, to my family and a way of life I enjoyed because, quite rightly, the British authorities would immediately send me back to Sweden. I had nothing to gain and everything to lose by running away, for I would have to keep running for the rest of my life instead of spending a maximum of another two and a half years in prison before being allowed to return home as a free man. It was pointless. My arguments fell on deaf ears, it was obvious that they had heard it all countless times before. I was looked upon with the utmost suspicion and distrust, and there was absolutely nothing I could do about it except keep quiet and accept the situation. It was as if they were looking for an ulterior motive in all that I did or asked for, however insignificant. For example, I was refused permission to work in the mechanical workshop because I was 'too dangerous'. Apparently it was feared I would put my 'military knowledge' to good use by manufacturing a weapon on one of the lathes; and besides, the last escape had taken place from there. When the time came for my first four-hour permission I was given a nine-man escort, four of them armed police officers, when even murderers serving life sentences only qualified for three.

As with any enforced routine one gets used to it, and I suppose I became temporarily institutionalised. I began to fit in, to accept the unacceptable. Gradually the other prisoners drew me into their midst, we got to know one another, developed a mutual understanding, I became one of them. Day to day relations were friendly, although I doubt whether I will ever consider holding any 'Year of '88' Malmö reunion parties. Living at very close quarters to twenty-four criminals, with whom I shared no common interests, was not always easy. Only once did one of them overstep the mark with me; if I remember correctly he did not like my 'attitude'. The law of the jungle took over, and I invited the man into the kitchen, out of sight of the guards, where I could explain matters to him. When he picked himself up off the floor, I believe he understood.

Not knowing what to expect, I had originally thought there would be certain unwritten rules amongst the convicts; subjects one could broach, subjects one could never mention; things one could do, things one could not. (For instance, I had assumed a man's crime would have been his business and never talked about, but in fact it was always one of the first questions asked of any newcomer.) I soon learnt there was only one rule – to mind one's own business; to never see anything never hear anything never interfere, and above all never to talk about anything to a member of the staff.

I also learnt quickly that life in prison was incredibly petty, with the most insignificant things taking on exaggerated importance. It was like being in another world with a different set of values. It was all too easy to lose touch with reality, to lose one's sense of objectivity and become introverted. I craved contact with the outside world. Sadly prison red tape prevented me from keeping my short-wave radio, so I was unable to continue listening to the BBC World Service, but towards the end of my sentence an exception was made for a German inmate and he would occasionally let me use his. In the meantime I would avidly read any newspapers I could lay my hands on. Visits were also important. An hour's chat with someone from the real world brought one down to earth and helped to put one's views back into perspective.

For many of the prisoners, conversation revolved around the topic of drugs. There were no dangerous big-time, Mafia-style smugglers in the gaol. Most were men in their twenties or early thirties who had tried to make an easy living by selling a few kilos here and there. I am not trying to condone their activities – there is no way one can justify the sheer misery, the crime and the mayhem that goes hand in glove with the illegal drugs trade – but strictly on prison terms these people were the most normal of the inmates. They looked upon themselves as nothing more than amoral businessmen; they were criminals but they were not violent or personally dangerous, they had not murdered or carried out armed robberies. Being caught and locked up was all part of their chosen way of life, nothing more than an inconvenience. They were serving time for an error of judgement on their part. They did not enjoy it, for many it was their first offence or at least the first time they had been caught, but imprisonment was obviously not going to reform them. Most were planning their next deal, due to take place the moment they were released; some even continued with the business whilst confined, planning with their colleagues still at large. Others acted as dealers within the prison.

At least while in Malmö these characters had the chance to see the results of their trade because there was a constant stream of addicts passing through, serving short sentences. Many had been arrested whilst committing crimes to finance their habits. For these sad individuals the prison served as a health and rehabilitation centre. Some came and went half a dozen times during my sojourn. Most of them were amphetamine users, or 'speed freaks'. Amphetamines dull the appetite and force the body to use its energy and resources without replenishing them. They would consequently arrive looking thoroughly spent, thin and lethargic. Not an ounce of fat on their frames, the skin stretched tight over gaunt features. In prison they would be deprived of their daily fix, or at least of the dosage they would have been using on the outside. They would be given three square meals a day, clean clothes, a clean bed to sleep in. Most were young men who would weight-train and play football, now that they had the opportunity. The results were apparent almost immediately. After a couple of months they would put on weight and look fit and healthy once more. Eventually they would be released, they would return to their old habits and the gutter, and the cycle would start afresh.

If the plight of their customers touched the consciences of the imprisoned smugglers it didn't show. The planning and dealing continued unabated.

Drug abuse was endemic within the prison. Cannabis was readily available, but to my surprise most hard drugs were also on offer. One day in the factory, while talking to a Colombian, I expressed disbelief that this could be the case. He responded by pointing out four men who regularly injected themselves with heroin. I was having my eyes opened to a different side of life, one that I had never expected to encounter.

Carselid hated drugs and took a very harsh attitude towards any inmate caught with them. Quite rightly he and his staff did their best to stem the flood, but it was obviously a losing battle. It was known that visitors and men returning from permissions would smuggle them in, and consequently all inmates were strip-searched after visits and exeats. It did not solve the problem because there were always methods of circumventing the checks. Packets of drugs wrapped in durexes could be swallowed and retrieved later when nature had taken its course, or simply hidden in an orifice. Suspected dealers would often be searched intimately or kept under observation for a number of days, having to go to the lavatory in a special bucket. Some were caught, but I suspect they represented only the tip of the iceberg. In any case, it was an open secret among the inmates that two of the warders would supply any kind of narcotic required.

All cells were searched every day and occasionally prisoners had to give urine samples for analysis. The process of extracting them was a humiliating one. There were ways of cheating the tests and the warders knew it. A tiny amount of chlorine or ground salt secreted in a sample would render a negative result, even for a regular drug-user. Because of this, when supplying a sample the donor was forced to strip in one room, walk naked into another and pee into a flask under the close scrutiny of two guards. It was a thoroughly unpleasant procedure for all concerned. Thankfully I was only asked to do it once, and luckily my system did not freeze on me. Needless to say the result was negative and I was never required to repeat the process.

I was offered cannabis on numerous occasions, but I never accepted. I had not found it necessary to smoke it on the outside and I saw no reason to start doing so just because I was now in prison. In any case I realised that if I was caught trying cannabis all my credibility, or what little I had remaining, would be destroyed. Whenever I knew inmates were using the stuff I would ensure I stayed well clear. Occasionally when clouds of 'herbal' smoke were permeating across the wing it was obvious that the warders were adopting a laissez faire attitude, for it would have taken a complete idiot not to have recognized what was going on. I believe they let it pass 'unnoticed' because cannabis helped to reduce the tensions within the prison. It was a different matter with hard drugs, of course.

In its constant battle against the use of narcotics the Prison Authority employed a roving team of inspectors known as the Black Gang, because they had once dressed in black overalls, to descend on a prison unannounced to staff and convicts alike to conduct snap searches.

One evening after lock-up, not long after my arrival in Malmö, my cell door swung open without warning to reveal three very large men in green jump-suits. Without a word they grabbed me and searched me thoroughly, before handing me over to a warder who frog-marched me downstairs to wait in a häktet cell whilst my own was torn apart. Of course there was nothing for the 'hit team' to find and I was allowed to return half an hour or so later to a chaotic mess that took me another half hour to clean up.

Others were not so fortunate, as the number of cells that remained locked and empty the next morning showed. The culprits, who had been placed on the isolation wing, came back in dribs and drabs over the following days with stories of how they had been caught redhanded in mid 'puff' and what punishments they had received – normally an extra three days to their sentences if the amounts involved were small; a court appearance if not.

These searches could become quite violent affairs, and often men returned to the wing with the bruises to prove it.

I had a lucky escape of my own when a group of inmates on my wing decided it would be a great joke to hide something that looked like amphetamine in my cell for the daily search to find. They crushed up some sugar and put it in a small envelope of folded paper marked 'Amphetamine 400 Kr' before hiding it in a tracksuit hanging in my wardrobe. Fortunately for me the warders missed it and Sid, having dropped his plans of selling wicked stories to the newpapers, came and warned me that it was there. It was meant as a joke, not a malicious act, but it could nonetheless have proved incredibly damaging to me, for there would have been no telling how the Director would have reacted to the find. It didn't matter that the substance was only sugar because I could still have been accused, in the ever-suspicious world in which I now lived, of possessing amphetamine. I could just hear Carselid saying 'The fact that the inmate who must have sold this powder to you has clearly tricked you into buying sugar is neither here nor there. The intent to buy drugs was still present.'

I continued to work in the plastics factory, progressing on to counting folders from waxed paper; hating every second of it. What redeemed the situation was the chance to go to school. I grabbed the opportunity of getting out of the factory by studying Swedish and French. All foreign inmates were strongly encouraged to learn Swedish and an excellent tutor came in on two afternoons each week for this purpose. French classes were held but once a week and I decided to enrol to brush up on my schoolboy grasp of the language.

I hit an immediate snag with the Swedish lessons. As soon as I opened the first text book I met a complete psychological block to the learning progress. With hindsight I am ashamed to say that I allowed myself to blame Sweden for all my problems, indeed I went through a stage of despising anything and everything Swedish. It was an all too natural but nonetheless xenophobic reaction to my predicament. To be asked to learn Swedish after all the injustices I had received at Swedish hands was like adding insult to injury. I just could not do it. The lessons became a focus for all the wrong that had been done to me, they revived the bitter feelings of anger and bewilderment to the degree that learning became next to impossible and I would often find myself leaving a period in a filthy temper. I persevered, but my heart was never in it. In any case, I reminded myself, since I was ultimately to be deported from Sweden for life, a prospect that at the time I was more than happy about, there was no incentive to learn a language that would clearly never be of any use to me. Eventually I gave up trying and left the school. It boiled down to learning Swedish or writing this book; it might sound strange, but I did not have time for both. Swedish lost.

To my surprise I was taken out of the factory in June and made the wing cleaner. It was a surprise because this was a trustee's position and it was quite obvious that they did not altogether trust me, but in actual fact the job provided me with little extra freedom and as before I was never left unguarded. Now instead of going to work in the factory I remained on the wing all day. Both the warders and prisoners thought it a great joke, and initially there were frequent cries of 'From captain to cleaner' and 'Hey you, Captain Cleaner . . . ' but I did not care; the job was just what I needed. I felt there was no disgrace in mopping floors or cleaning lavatories, especially when compared to the stigma of being in prison, and it was something I was quite used to from my early days in the army. With the job came the great benefit of being left alone for most of the day, I was no longer continually surrounded by other inmates. When everyone else was at work in the factories the wing was quiet and peaceful. My chores were easy and took me no more than a few hours each morning, leaving me ample time for my own devices. Without this extra free time, for example, it would have taken me far longer to write this book. Above all else the new job took me out of that awful factory. I would have done almost anything to achieve that.

I also found it surprising that as part of a society that professed care as a priority for all its citizens, the prison service medical policy left so much to be desired. It was a subject that almost every warder I ever talked to expressed dissatisfaction over. A doctor held surgery twice a week at Malmö; if one fell ill in between visits, unless it was an obvious emergency it was tough luck. The general treatment for all ailments, handed out by a totally untrained warder in a white coat acting the part of a medical orderly, was a couple of aspirins and wait for the doctor's next call.

I have no personal complaints, but I believe that if Piet Van Uden, a Dutch prisoner, was in a position to do so he would have a few words to say on the matter. Piet started to experience paralysis in one of his legs in the summer of 1987. He reported sick but the doctor refused to believe him, called him a skiver, and sent him packing. The paralysis did not remedy itself, in fact it became progressively worse, but despite repeated complaints that something was badly amiss the doctor still refused to make a diagnosis, other than to label him a malingerer even sending him to the prison psychiatrist. Eventually, over a year later, and only after Piet had refused to continue working, an appointment was made for him to be seen by a specialist who initially diagnosed multiple sclerosis. However a body scan revealed a malignant tumour on the spinal cord in his neck. He was discharged on medical grounds in November 1988 and repatriated to the Netherlands, where doctors established that the tumour was twenty centimetres long and inoperable. Piet died three months later. It is impossible to be sure, but if he had received prompt medical treatment in 1987 he might still be alive today.

In fact Van Uden was only one of two Malmö prisoners to die during my time in Sweden. The other was a Swede who one day complained of feeling terribly unwell, but unfortunately for him had chosen to fall sick in between doctor's visits. He was given the mandatory two aspirins and told to wait. They even made him return to the factory for work. When the doctor did eventually see him the man was immediately hospitalised. He died of liver failure the next day.

I found it a further surprise that for an otherwise enlightened regime in a supposedly progressive society, the penal system so blatantly discriminated against foreigners. Foreign prisoners, as I have already mentioned, were not eligible for permissions. (This was understandable, but in Denmark, for instance, days that should have been spent on exeats would be knocked off a foreigner's sentence in lieu.) It was also extremely unusual for foreign inmates to receive half remission, especially if their sentence was longer than four years. Carselid made it very clear to me when I arrived that I would definitely not be given it. For Swedish nationals the opposite was the case. Nor were foreigners granted the rehabilitation procedure of graduating to an open prison; of gradually working their way back to normality. A Dutchman on my wing worked out that although he and his Swedish partner had been given exactly the same sentence for drug-smuggling, in effect he could end up serving five hundred and fifty-six days more.

The same kind of prejudices operated internally within the prison itself. The wide range of educational courses available in the school were for Swedes only. Foreigners could only study Swedish and very rarely a basic computer course. Even the French lessons were cancelled when no Swedish inmates showed an interest. There was a second mechanical workshop for instruction in metalwork with good qualifications on offer, but once again only for Swedes. It was clear that the authorities did not wish to waste financial resources on prisoners who were never going to be of use to their community.

1989 arrived. The beginning of my third year in prison. If the worst came to the worst, I would definitely be released in July 1990 after serving two-thirds of my five-year sentence, so at least I was on the downhill slope, if not yet on the home run. However, in spite of Carselid's warning, part of me never gave up hoping that they would grant me half remission. Hope is all one has in prison. My head was telling me one thing, my heart was hoping for another. I reassured myself that Carselid had only been trying to do the right thing by playing devil's advocate.

In April these hopes were given a boost when I was called to a Kollegium to be told by the Deputy Governor (Carselid was away on holiday) that it had been decided by a majority vote to recommend me for half remission to the parole board in Stockholm. He explained what he meant by a majority decision. It was policy for each of the seven members of the Kollegium, representing all the departments within the prison, to cast a vote on the issue. I had scraped through with four votes in favour, two abstentions, and one against. He continued by stressing that in effect this recommendation meant very little; the final and totally independent decision rested with the parole board. He considered that my ultimate chances were still slim, but at least it was a step in the right direction.

Needless to say, I was extremely pleased with the news, but also somewhat bewildered by the illogicality of the system. The decision had been made on the basis of my 'exemplary behaviour,' I was described as a 'model prisoner,' and more importantly, it was thought to be exceedingly unlikely that I would ever reoffend. However, not two months previously, these very same people had recommended to the Criminal Board in Norrköping that I should remain classified Category 7:3, thus continuing to label me a dangerous criminal, because as a 'vital link in the organisation of an international drugs ring' they thought it highly likely not only that would I reoffend, even while I was still behind bars, but that I would also attempt to escape if given half a chance.

Not wishing to press my luck, I refrained from drawing attention to this clear contradiction.

Nor could I help being amused by the reasons given by the one dissenting voice for his no vote. It was made by Mr Markku Roitto, the man in charge of the school. He stated in writing that although he agreed it was unlikely I would reoffend, he believed I was guilty of the crime and should therefore be made to serve the full sentence. This was strange logic indeed. Did he think that only 'innocent prisoners' should receive half remission?

I decided that the best attitude would be to avoid becoming too excited, and not to start counting my chickens; but if the parole board accepted the recommendation I would be released on 12 September, only five months away. However, as everyone kept telling me, even Tom Placht, my chances remained minimal. For this reason I also decided not to tell anyone at home. It would only make the situation more unbearable for them to raise their hopes, only to have to dash them at a later date. It was best to bank on 1990 and look upon September as a possible bonus.

Eleven

I never gave up hope, and nor did my family and friends in England, that one day the truth would emerge and I would be vindicated. The hope of finding fresh evidence and of winning a new appeal was the one thing that kept me going when everything I held dear seemed to be crumbling around me.

It was obvious that Swedish enquiries into Mitchell's drugs ring had uncovered only the very tip of the iceberg, and yet apart from the warrant out for Christopher's arrest the case file had been closed. If further evidence was to be forthcoming we were going to have to do the searching. Therefore Christopher Murray and Tom Placht continued to explore all avenues that might provide the necessary proof of my innocence.

Progress was frustratingly slow for everyone concerned. Information came to light in a gradual manner over a period of many months, slowly crystallising into sufficiently strong fresh evidence upon which to endeavour to launch further appeal proceedings. The new evidence came in three parts: two of which I deal with in this chapter. The third aspect, which relates to Inspector Larsen's evidence about an 'informer', and includes a significant re-examination of the role played by the two Scotland Yard officers, Morgan and Moore, needs some ends to be tied up immediately after my return to London, so I cannot deal with it here. But it is no less important and plays a significant part in the appeal proceedings in Sweden.

1.

As is so often the case, the first breakthrough came quickly and right out of the blue, when in February 1988 the British Embassy telephoned Tom Placht to say that a man in police custody had come forward with important information.

On 29 December, after a lengthy police surveillance operation, four men had been arrested in Stockholm on drug-smuggling charges. One of them was a 27-year-old Anglo-Indian named Jason Gregory.

In two long interviews with Placht, Gregory supplied the first totally independent evidence of the fact that I had not known cannabis was hidden in the Jaguar:

'I know Simon Hayward is innocent. The hash that went into that car came from the people I was working for, and I was definitely told he was being tricked. He is innocent, it is as simple as that.'

Gregory stated that during the early months of 1987 he had been employed by a Dutch-controlled drugs ring operating out of Spain. He refused to identify other members of the ring, none of whom had been involved with the affair over which he had been arrested in Sweden. They had been staying at a villa in Altea, near Benidorm, when a call came through for help.

'We knew Mitchell, or rather my company did. He was not an associate of ours, rather someone we could do business with if we wanted to. We were asked to contact him on Ibiza . . .'

Gregory went along to a local telephone centre with one of the Dutchmen who telephoned Mitchell's organisation. He was not told who was actually spoken to, he only knew that there was a piece of paper with Mitchell's name and number written on it. The Dutchmen were asked for help with a drugs delivery to Sweden. Apparently a courier was needed.

'They also wanted to buy some hash from us. This was quite a common procedure, if one firm is short and has a deadline to meet then they buy it from another firm's bank. It was not the first time they had come to us.'

A deal was struck, and between fifty and eighty kilos of cannabis, packed into four Samsonite suitcases, were collected from Altea by two Englishmen on 8 March. These men asked Gregory if he would be prepared to deliver the drugs to Sweden for them. A Jaguar was mentioned as an incentive 'because a luxury car is not only comfortable, it is also relatively easy to drive through borders without any hassles because people think its occupants are respectable. You know, not villains or anything.'

Not knowing how to drive, Gregory had to refuse. Whereupon he was asked if he would accompany another courier on the run to ensure the hash was delivered, or failing that, would he travel to Sweden independently to take delivery of the car once it arrived. This second courier was described as a British Army officer, 'a captain of something' who was in a 'good regiment in England', and was 'clean and everything'. The name Hayward was mentioned.

'They said he was a dead cert to get through. 'Nice car, British Captain. He is bound to get through.' However, if he was used he would be unaware of what he was carrying, and they needed someone to travel with him as a passenger who did.'

The Dutch warned Gregory to have nothing to do with it; but he told Placht he did not need any warning. 'Of course I refused. It is the last thing anybody should do – to use a blind donkey. In other words, a courier who does not know what he is doing.

'We were suspicious of this particular trip . . . It was pretty obvious there was pressure involved, and a tight time factor, because of the way they came rushing over for the hash. When someone rushes around like that it puts people off . . . There was something very fishy about this business, the way the whole thing was set up. From my experience of the drug trade it was all wrong.'

Initially Gregory described the Ibizan organisation as the 'Mitchell/Christopher Hayward Ring' but during the interviews he added that he was only positive about Mitchell's involvement. 'To me, Mitchell means the lot of them, all of them . . . he was very high up.'

'How do you know that Chris Hayward was a member of the ring?'

'He must have been. In retrospect he must have been.'

'That is only a conclusion,' Placht pointed out.

'Yes, I know. I think I drew it from the newspaper reports.'

'Therefore, at the time you knew nothing about the direct involvement of Chris Hayward?'

'No, there was nothing to say he was involved.'

'How about the Jaguar. Did they tell you who owned it?'

'No of course not. They were not going to tell me anything unnecessary. You are only ever informed on a need to know basis.'

Gregory explained his motives for coming forward. When the story had broken in the newspapers he had known immediately that I was innocent of the allegations being made against me and that for some reason Mitchell was not telling the truth, but at that stage there had been nothing he could do about it. To have volunteered information would have resulted in his own arrest; no one could have reasonably expected him to risk that. He had therefore been forced to look on helplessly while a man was sent to prison for a crime he had not committed. However, once he had found himself in police custody on charges he had no hope of avoiding, it was a different matter. He realised that for him the game was up, he would be going to prison, and that he now had nothing to lose by speaking up.

He also described how the authorities had done their best to ignore him, even to silence him. He had told his story to the police in December and again in January, but they had refused to listen, telling him that they knew I was guilty, and in any case I had been convicted and that was that. He claimed they had tried to persuade him to keep quiet, threatening that by talking he was making his own situation worse. However, he had persevered by trying to tell the prosecutor, but the man had simply lost his temper, saying he did not want to discuss the Hayward case. As far as he was concerned the file was closed and there was nothing more to be done about it. He wrote to *The Times* but received no reply, later realising that his letter had not been posted. In desperation he telephoned the British Embassy, and through it had made contact with Tom Placht.

True to form, the Swedish authorities had attempted to suppress evidence that stood in my favour. They went further still, when after his eventual conviction Gregory was sent to the same prison as me in Malmö, in circumstances that permitted no other interpretation than that the transfer was made for the sole purpose of fabricating an appearance that we had been colluding together. But since we had never met, and since Gregory had already supplied a factually correct statement to Placht incorporating details that had never been made public, collusion was going to be a very difficult allegation to prove. Nevertheless, as soon as he heard of the transfer, Placht travelled to Malmö to interview him for the second time, just to minimise the risks.

The same logic for Gregory not wanting to come forward in 1987 would apply to any accusation that his evidence was being planted, or that an inducement had been given to him to supply information. No one in their right mind would allow himself to be apprehended on serious drug charges simply in order to testify in an unrelated case. If nothing else, the planning and execution of such a scheme would have been well-nigh impossible, especially since Gregory had been arrested with three other men. The strength of his statement lay in the fact that it would never have been made if he had not himself been arrested; that he had given it while in solitary confinement, isolated from the rest of the world; that he had no axe to grind, indeed no personal interest in saying anything; and that we had never met before his arrival in Malmö.

Gregory went on to add that in his opinion the informant referred to by the NDIU in their statement to the Swedish police, which he had read about, must 'be lying' when, as the police claimed, he told them that I was to have been paid £20,000 to act as a courier:

'For an informer to turn up in London when the hash had come from Spain, and the deal set up on Ibiza,' he said, 'is very suspicious. What is even more suspicious is that the informer knows the exact amount of money involved, details like that are kept very close to the chest. I did not even know that and I was there . . . If they don't tell the people who supply the hash nor the person they want to drive the car how much the courier is being paid or any other details, they certainly are not going to tell anyone else. So how the hell does some informer in London know . . . ? If I go to work for someone, he does not tell others how much I am getting. It's not normal.'

'So why do you think the informant came forward?' asked Placht.

'That depends on how much he was paid.'

'By whom?'

'Whoever was going to pay him. A grass never does

something for nothing, so the only reason one would come forward with information that is not true is if he was paid to do it, unless he had a personal grudge, or had some kind of pressure put on him. That is how it always works.'

Another factor that made Gregory suspicious of the informant's evidence was the figure of £20,000 itself. 'That is a ridiculous figure. No courier would earn that much. The normal rate for a job like this would be something around five thousand pounds, at the very most ten thousand.'

These were conclusions based on opinion and experience but it was interesting to note that they coincided exactly with those of my lawyers and the likes of Richard New. The more we pondered the question of this mystery informer, and the information he or she had supplied, the more illogical it all seemed.

Gregory's evidence was indeed an exciting breakthrough. At last we had an independent witness to my innocence. A witness who had been told just two days before I left Ibiza that I was being tricked into running drugs. The dilemma now facing us was how best to use it. The first impulse was to try for an immediate appeal but on consideration it was decided to wait. Although I had been convicted on circumstantial evidence, it was clear that the Supreme Court was going to require something as close to 100 per cent proof of my innocence as possible before it would consider granting me an appeal. While Gregory's evidence was strong it might not be looked upon by the Swedes as conclusive. We decided to wait, and see what else our investigations turned up. Little did we know at the time, but it would be a further eighteen months before we would finally be ready.

2.

If there was one man available to be questioned who held all the answers, that man was Forbes Mitchell. His testimony had convicted me, if he had told the truth I would not have been found guilty and sent to prison. That he had lied and thereby misled the courts was beyond doubt, but if his letter to me after David's accident was anything to go by he was sticking rigidly to his guns. Knowing he had lied was one thing, proving his mendacity was going to be quite another; but if I was going to have any chance of winning a new appeal, we had to prove it.

There was one clear chink in his armour and that was Prita's false passport. As far as we knew nothing was being done officially to retrieve it. The Swedish authorities were obviously not interested, indeed they allowed Prita to visit Mitchell, using the same passport, on at least two occasions after my appeal had failed when there could have been no possible excuse for them not to have known she was travelling on it. If we could discover where she had obtained it, we might be able to find out more about Mitchell's criminal activities. As it turned out, the passport proved to be the key to the whole affair.

It was a British passport, recovering it was therefore a British problem, and here I can only express a measure of surprise that our Embassy in Stockholm, whose diplomats had attended every day of my trial and appeal, did not take the first steps to ensure it was recovered. It was as though they did not want to believe it existed, nor that the Swedes could have been so blatant in ignoring its use. Consequently John Gorst tabled a question to the Home Secretary in October 1987 asking for the matter to be investigated. As a result enquiries were instigated, initially by Special Branch but later by the Regional Crime Squad. Apparently it quickly became evident that the police were not simply investigating the relatively minor crime of forged travel documents but something much more sinister. They began to uncover traces of a highly professional drugs ring, controlled by none other than the mysterious Irishman 'Dook'.

Operation Kaleidoscope went into action, led by Detective Inspector Terry Anslow of No. 4 Regional Crime Squad's drugs wing based in Telford, Shropshire.

The police dug up the application forms for the passport and the attached photograph was identified as Prita's. The real Marylyn J Waterfield was interviewed and revealed that the false passport had been obtained by her brother, William John Waterfield, using her birth certificate, for another man called Patrick Flynn. Both these men were arrested along with several other people, including Flynn's 23-year-old brother-in-law, Stuart Bryer. It turned out that Flynn's real name was Ian Patrick Harvey, a man who used a string of different identities – Flynn, Ryan, O'Rourke. Under interrogation Harvey admitted that he had supplied numerous passports for a friend of his called Dook. Prita's had been just one of them.

In April 1988 Inspector Anslow travelled to Sweden accompanied by a colleague from the South West Regional Crime Squad, Inspector David Warren. Together with Jan Bihlar they interviewed Mitchell at his prison just outside Stockholm. The information he gave them was dynamite, both in building their case against Dook, Harvey and co, and, as far as my lawyers were concerned, in their efforts to prove my innocence.

Willingly he supplied the officers with written statements about the passport, and general background information regarding Ibiza, Dook, Makunda and Christopher. When these had been completed and signed a further discussion took place during which Mitchell went into much greater detail about Dook's activities, taking great pains to ensure that none of this additional material was recorded or any written notes taken down. Before he would say anything he even asked to check inside the officer's briefcases for hidden tape-recorders.

Kingsley Napley were able subsequently to obtain copies of Mitchell's statements, along with statements taken from Anslow and Warren about what he had told them verbally, from the Attorney General's Chambers in the Royal Courts of Justice in London. In addition the Inspectors could not have been more helpful.

Mitchell supplied the following information:

PRITA

She is a German national called Lisa Freutag. They had met in India in the late seventies. They set up home together on Ibiza in 1983 or '84, with Prita's seventeen-year-old son, Tim. Prita did not have a valid passport and was unable to get one because of something that had happened to her in Germany. He refused to say what this something was, except that it had nothing to do with his situation in Sweden.

'However, she wanted to travel out of Spain so I went to a *friend* of mine who I knew only as Dook, an Irishman living in Ibiza, and asked him if he could get Prita a passport.'

Dook agreed, saying it would cost £500. Instead of the

money Mitchell gave him an old white Mercedes. About six months later the Marylyn J Waterfield passport was handed over. 'Later I found out indirectly that it had been obtained through a friend of Dook's called "Pat".'

Mitchell stated that Prita had been living under this name ever since, but she had never used the passport for anything involved with narcotics. He added that he would now tell her to hand it in to the authorities. (The passport was eventually delivered anonymously to the British Embassy in Paris. On the basis of Mitchell's information Prita was ultimately arrested and sentenced in Germany for the smuggling of a kilo of cannabis).

DOOK

Mitchell explained that there were two separate 'Drug Organisations' centred on Ibiza which were closely associated with one another. He was a member of one and was responsible for the distribution of drugs in Scandinavia. His Bagwhan friend, Christopher Hayward, was responsible for obtaining the drugs, mainly from Morocco. A second friend, whom he was only prepared to name as Makunda, acted as the courier.

He alleged that Christopher had reliable contacts in Morocco and because of these contacts he met and became involved with the second group of smugglers which was led by the Irishman 'Dook'. Dook's syndicate was made up of 'criminal types' as opposed to 'redundant hippies' as Mitchell described himself. They were far more professional, using professional packers and various couriers who were known to be prepared to take all the risks. This syndicate also imported larger consignments of cannabis.

Mitchell believed that Dook and Christopher had a mutual agreement that on occasion Christopher would use Dook's packers in exchange for Makunda acting as Dook's courier. Dook and Christopher had eventually fallen out over money.

He described two runs that Dook and Makunda had organised to Scandinavia. The first was in 1985 involving a camper van which was brought to Ibiza from England to be 'packed'. A Belgian mechanic was flown in to hide the consignment professionally. The van was bound for

Copenhagen with various drops en route in Europe.

He gave greater detail about the second run:

'In the summer of 1986 I saw a light coloured Talbot camper van at Dook's house . . . I knew that a run was being arranged from the island . . . Makunda had a lot to do with Dook's guests.'

Mitchell was shown a series of photographs, some of which he identified. One was of William John Waterfield, whom he called 'J.R.' Another was the Talbot camper van he had seen in Dook's driveway.

The Belgian mechanic was again used to conceal two hundred kilos of cannabis in the sides of the camper van. Dook then employed 'J.R.', another man and two women to drive it to Sweden where it was met and unloaded by Makunda. Mitchell claimed that he never actually met the occupants of the van, and yet he was able to identify 'J.R.' from a photograph. He described this as just a normal 'dummy run'.

Anslow asked him what he meant by a 'dummy run'. Mitchell replied that Dook's team always used the term to indicate the person driving was a dummy for taking the risks for so little money. He was emphatic that Waterfield knew the purpose of the run, where the drugs were hidden and who he had to hand the van over to in Sweden. Makunda even told Waterfield that he was not being paid enough.

'Shortly after this, around August time 1986, I travelled to Sweden with my family . . . I met and spoke with Makunda. I never saw the camper van in Sweden during my stay.'

Mitchell also identified someone called Paul 'who would crew a boat if required'; and another man called Keith from a photograph, who was an 'odd job man'.

'Christopher Hayward owned an eleven meter catamaran called *True Love*, the main colour was white, it was an ocean-going vessel. Dook also owns a catamaran, the *Sabel Fleur de Lys*. I have been shown a photograph album marked Staffordshire Police. Photograph 'R' I identify as . . . Dook's boat.

The *True Love* is in my opinion a very good boat and capable of an Atlantic crossing. Comparing it with Dook's boat, there is no comparison. The engine on the *Fleur de Lys* was useless and it was hard to handle.

The *True Love* was Christopher Hayward's pride and joy, he spent a lot of money on it . . . I can also say Christopher was a first class sailor and could manage the *True Love* excellently.'

Mitchell felt that it was obvious from the amount of cannabis found in the Jaguar that Simon Hayward knew exactly what he was doing at the time of his arrest, because he had only been expecting twenty-five kilos. He inferred that he could implicate Hayward further but did not wish to do so for fear of involving other people.

Once again Mitchell was being extremely clever with these statements, mixing half the truth with a pack of lies. At first glance what he claimed seemed plausible enough but by reading in between the lines one could tell that he was indeed mixing fact with fiction to diminish his own responbility.

He told the police that in the summer of 1986 Dook had been renting the small villa called 'Campunta' which Christopher took over in November. (Dook also owned a luxury flat in Santa Eulalia, and the large house that Richard New found in 1987.) It was outside 'Campunta' that the camper van had been packed with the two hundred kilos of cannabis. Since this villa is in a very isolated position, well off the beaten track at the end of a tortuous eight-kilometre path, Mitchell had obviously not seen the camper van by chance as he happened to be driving by. He must have been going to the place for a specific purpose.

Drug smugglers keep their activities very close to their chests, as secret as possible. For obvious reasons they do not advertise what they are doing by telling people who do not need to know what is going on. That Mitchell knew about the Waterfield run to Sweden at all, let alone the detail that he was able to give to Anslow, reveals that he was very much involved himself.

It seems more than odd that Dook would use Makunda, a member of a different group, either as a courier or to unload consignments in Sweden. If he normally used 'dummies' who were paid next to nothing, as Mitchell claimed, why bother to use someone whom he would have to pay more? To use Makunda in Sweden would be to reveal his contacts to a rival organisation, a risk Dook would certainly not have been prepared to take. The only logical answer is that Dook, Mitchell and Makunda were all members of the same ring; Makunda did not act as a courier, instead his job was to meet consignments, as Mitchell said he had done with Waterfield in Sweden, and pass them on for distribution.

It can be no coincidence that Mitchell travelled to Sweden himself at the same time as the camper van, and once there met up with Makunda. As a matter of interest so did Prita. Just as Nasim Tervaniemi testified, Makunda would rendezvous with the consignments to unload them, acting as a cut-off to prevent the courier, a low paid 'dummy', from learning the identities of any of the ring in Sweden, and thus ensuring its security. He would then deliver the drugs to Mitchell.

Mitchell was being exceedingly devious by stating that there were two separate drug rings operating on Ibiza, because by doing so he successfully distanced himself from what he believed the police were on the verge of finding out about Dook. One might ask why he admitted that Makunda was involved with Dook and the camper van run to Sweden, when by doing so he established a closer connection with himself? The answer was that he had no choice because he would have realised that Waterfield would probably name Makunda as the man he had met. By getting in first and co-operating with the police, by claiming that there were two rings and that Makunda was only working for Dook at the time, he was clearly hoping to avoid being charged with smuggling another two hundred kilos of cannabis; which one should remember was more than he had been convicted and sentenced to seven years imprisonment for in the first place.

By sticking to his statements concerning my participation, by claiming that Christopher was the connection between the 'two rings', he was not only retaining credibility with the Swedish police, but also reducing his own culpability. By giving information to the British police he was hedging his bets in case his name was to come up during their investigations.

This new information not only proved that Mitchell had been lying at my trial, but that the courts had been quite wrong in rejecting evidence given by other witnesses.

Nasim Tervaniemi had been telling the truth when she testified that an Irishman was involved with Mitchell, a man who figured prominently in the sale of drugs to Sweden and who, with Mitchell, formed a team on Ibiza; that Prita held a false passport, was involved in drug-smuggling and was wanted by the German police; that Mitchell used various couriers, and Makunda to meet them in Sweden.

Lennart Viryo and Joakim Andersen had been telling the truth in stating that there had been more than just seven runs to Sweden.

Per Philipsson had also been telling the truth. It should be remembered that he had not only testified that Mitchell had 'done a deal' with the police, but that there were 'hundreds more kilos' involved and that Mitchell was terrified of further investigations being instigated.

All of these statements from all of these witnesses that the prosecutor, the police and not least of all the courts had seen fit to disregard, had proved to be correct.

Operation Kaleidoscope had uncovered a highly sophisticated drugs ring smuggling millions of pounds' worth of cannabis on a Europe-wide scale. Patrick Harvey was central to the organisation and William Waterfield was his right-hand man. Dook ran the entire network from Ibiza. What part Mitchell played was not investigated, or at least was not made public. Harvey, helped by Waterfield, would supply vehicles, in the main caravanettes, recruit couriers and obtain false passports on Dook's instructions. The quantity of drugs involved was revealed by the seizure of half a ton of cannabis on 19 September 1985 from a sailing yacht, the *Jasmine Francisca*, in St Peter Port in Guernsey just after it arrived from Spain. The crew, one of them a South African called Graham Rooke, held false passports obtained by Harvey for Dook. Stuart Bryer, Harvey's brother-in-law was also deeply involved. Eventually he was to plead guilty to conspiring to smuggle drugs into Britain, Sweden, Holland and Italy. He was sentenced to three years imprisonment.

Harvey and Waterfield were put on trial in 1989. In June they were found guilty and sentenced to twelve and nine years respectively. During the proceedings the prosecutor, Mr Anthony Barker, QC, told the jury: 'The collapse of the drugs conspiracy from Ibiza northwards began with the arrest in Sweden of a man called Forbes Mitchell and a name with which you will be familiar – Captain Simon Hayward . . . You are not inquiring whether Captain Hayward was innocent or not.'

We already knew that Dook had left Ibiza without warning in considerable haste in early April 1987. He had left behind a substantial villa, a large yacht and a luxury flat. His child had been removed from school without notice. We were aware that Mitchell had, in his own words, 'got a message out to Ibiza' warning those involved. Bryer told the police that in April 1989 Harvey had sent him to Spain in a Bedford camper van to 'rescue' Dook and his family, and to spirit them off to Amsterdam. Everything was done in a great hurry. Bryer travelled out with his girlfriend, Sussane Barlow, and her baby daughter; they met up with Dook in a campsite on mainland Spain. Dook had changed his name, he was now calling himself Tayo, and his common law wife Gitte, Taya. There was some hanging around for two or three days and talk of waiting for money. Before leaving for Holland, Dook gave away his white Peugot car to a travelling circus they happened to pass. They journeyed north on the tourist routes; approaching customs at one of the border crossings 'Taya' was seen to take out a handful of passports from her bag and shuffle through them, apparently choosing the right ones to use.

Dook told Bryer that he had lost his house and boat because of Hayward; he needed to move in this way under a new identity for the same reason. In other words, and just as ter Brake had said in court, Dook was running away from something. This was proof positive, beyond any shadow of a doubt, that he was involved with my predicament in Sweden. If he had not been responsible with Mitchell for those drugs found in Christopher's Jaguar, why was he running? It also proved that he had received Mitchell's message; there would have been no other way for him to have known what was going on, Christopher did not mention his name until the end of June, two and a half months later.

As a side issue, Bryer admitted at his trial that he had told the police a pack of lies about me. He had made up a story involving me, Waterfield and Dook: ' . . . I read in the papers that Mrs Hayward had been warned about an Irishman named Dook . . . I made it up about Captain Hayward to get me off the charges.' There is no real significance to this except that it may have formed part of the corroborative information, mentioned by Thompson, to the NDIU report.

As it turned out, I must also admit to having met Harvey, or so I am told. Apparently he was the gold medallion festooned 'spiv' I had met at the barbecue on Ibiza in 1984. No wonder he had had kittens when I told him I was a police officer!

According to evidence given at the Harvey/Waterfield trial, Dook was known to be on the run in Holland, travelling in the name of Kelvin J. James, a passport purloined for him by Harvey, and one of at least a dozen identities he had acquired in different nationalities. Another was an Irish Republic passport in the name of Ciaran Carte. However, at the time his real identity was thought to be Timothy Behan, born in Dublin in 1956. Harvey told the police that he had found a birth certificate bearing this name in Dook's boats one day when he had been 'sniffing around'. As far as I am concerned being born in 1956 would make Dook too young, so I doubt they have reached his true origins yet, making Behan just another alias. In any event an international warrant has been issued for his arrest.

The real significance of all this was that it proved Mitchell a liar. It could now be shown that he had deceived both Courts in the evidence he gave about his knowledge of and dealings with Dook. Such a deception placed his credibility in question on all aspects, as well as strengthening the credibility of other witnesses. The statements he had given to Anslow and Warren contradicted the evidence he gave in court which, as both Judgements confirm, was relied on so heavily.

Mitchell had sought to protect Dook at all costs and had taken great pains to distance himself from him, describing him as someone whom he did not really know, not his friend but a friend of Christopher Hayward's, and not someone involved in drugs: 'I do not know him, I am acquainted with him . . . he is not involved in this matter . . . He is a quiet family man.'

As we now knew, the exact opposite was the truth. By his own admission Mitchell and Dook were friends; Dook had supplied Prita's passport; Dook controlled a drugs ring; Dook was heavily involved with Makunda, Mitchells partner;

Mitchell knew a great deal about Dook's activities, which he would certainly not have done if he had not been involved himself; Makunda was not a courier, he was a security cut-off. Operation Kaleidoscope had revealed that the ring had collapsed after my arrest; Dook had told Bryer that he was having to run because of 'Captain Hayward'. Mitchell's entire testimony in court was valueless.

Dook's involvement made fools of Forsberg, Bihlar, Nilsson and ter Brake. Forsberg had stated at my appeal that Dook was definitely not 'involved in this affair. . .that is nothing but a smokescreen put forward by the defence to cloud the issue . . . Mitchell is a credible and trustworthy witness'. Nilsson had even instructed Dook to 'lie low' and not to come forward. Ter Brake's testimony at the time sounded strange to everyone – he was a crackpot and this new evidence proved it. Worst of all, Bihlar had been present when Mitchell was interviewed by Anslow, he had even counter-signed Mitchell's statements; but did he step forward immediately to say that Mitchell was changing his story? No, true to form he had remained silent. Once again, and I have lost count of how many times it happened, the Swedish police were trying to conceal evidence that stood in my favour. By contrast, Anslow and Warren could not have been more helpful and honest in their conduct, and in their dealings with Christopher Murray.

The prosecutions case against me had been based on three main 'Pillars': a) The cannabis in the car; b) Larsen's testimony supported by the NDIU report; c) Mitchell's evidence, supported by a string of circumstantial evidence. This new evidence effectively destroyed every argument put forward by Forsberg. Without Mitchell to bind it together, his case collapsed.

Twelve

Despite the progress, many questions remain completely unanswered. For instance: where is Christopher, and what sort of life is he leading? What motivated his disappearance? What connection did he have with the ring?

These questions remain a dilemma for me personally, but I must make one thing perfectly clear. If I thought Christopher had played a significant role, like the one described by Mitchell, I would have no hesitation in saying so; family loyalties only go so far. But I do not, and I believe the known facts support this belief.

Christopher lived a very simple existence on Ibiza, and nothing has emerged to refute the claim that he usually made a living from chartering his yacht. Certainly his lifestyle did not compare with that of either Mitchell or Dook, and yet he was supposed to have been the 'Boss'. But the 'Boss' surely does not live in a shack without running water or even electricity while his employees live in luxury villas. I witnessed at first hand that he was short of money, even having to pay for his travelling expenses between Gibraltar and Ibiza myself. Richard New independently corroborated this by establishing that before Christopher could leave the island the 'hat' had to be passed around to fund him. Indeed everything New discovered pointed to the fact that Christopher could only have played a small part in the 'ring'.

Time has proved Nasim Tervaniemi a credible witness. She testified that a man called Poonananda, identified by Mitchell as Christopher, was only a boatman employed by Mitchell when the need arose - he was not Mitchell's partner, nor his 'Boss'. Christopher came close to admitting this to my mother during one of his 1987 telephone calls: 'I may have been involved with some things in the past, but I am not involved with this business . . . ' He told her that he had been on the periphery of drug-smuggling. Being someone occasionally employed by the ring to act as a sea courier between Morocco and Ibiza would explain this.

If Christopher had been the principle behind 'my run' he would not have used his own car, nor his own brother to drive it, as this would have guaranteed his own detection if something went wrong. As I have said before, he might just as well have saved on expenses and acted as the courier himself. If he was the 'Boss', to take such suicidal risks made no sense. Another interesting factor is that as far as we have been able to deduce nothing incriminating about Christopher was established during the very thorough investigations conducted during Operation Kaleidoscope. This must stand strongly in his favour.

Mitchell went out of his way to protect Dook, at the same time naming Christopher as the 'Mr Big' behind the entire network. If anything proves that the exact opposite was the truth, this does. If Christopher had been the 'Boss' Mitchell would never have dared identify him, just as he never dared talk about Dook publicly.

Finally, and the one fact that stands out strongest in his favour, is that everything Christopher testified to over the telephone about Dook and Mitchell, and their relationship, has turned out to be the truth.

It must be remembered that the only people to have claimed that Christopher played a major role in this affair have been Mitchell and Dook. Both have been shown to have ulterior motives for doing so; both have been proved to be liars.

The fact of the matter is that Christopher Hayward made his living from chartering his yacht. Sadly for him he succumbed to the temptations of life on Ibiza by occasionally chartering it to the wrong sort of people for the wrong purposes. I am not trying to make excuses for him, nor to condone his actions, but there has to be a world of difference between supplementing one's income by doing the occasional 'midnight run' for a drugs gang, to being its principal figure.

What part did Christopher play in the events that led to my arrest? I have to accept the possibility that if nothing else he may have been a willing participant in the plan to trick me. This would provide the simplest answer to why he asked me to drive the Jaguar. However, one cannot dismiss out of hand other factors that may have influenced him.

Mitchell described the Waterfield consignment as a 'dummy run'. I asked experienced smugglers in prison with me what they took the term to mean. They all gave the same answer: that either the driver did not know what he was transporting and was therefore a dummy; or that the run was a trial to check out a proposed drugs route. They said that both instances were fairly common practice.

As an example given of the first, if a drugs ring wanted to smuggle from Spain to the United Kingdom, it was an old ploy to find a suitable British family holidaying on the Costa del Sol. While one member of the ring befriends the family, keeping it occupied, eventually swapping addresses and promising to 'get in touch back home', as people are wont to do on holiday, other members are stealing their car and stashing drugs inside it, before returning it as if nothing had happened. The family drive home, none the wiser for what they are 'smuggling'. In England, the ring simply steals the car from outside the given address, and they have their drugs at the market place, at no risk to themselves and with the minimum of expense.

Trial 'dummy' runs, or dry runs, are apparently a normal procedure to test out a new route, new couriers or new methods; to establish what customs checks are like for example, and to iron out any unforeseen problems. The double dummy is when a courier is told that he is not actually carrying anything when the reverse is true. Again according to my 'inmate sources' this ploy is all too common, especially with new untried couriers who will obviously act normally if they believe themselves to be 'clean'.

There is no doubt that Christopher was coming under some kind of pressure from Dook at the time of my visit to Ibiza. An amount of money was given as the reason, but I believe there was more to it than that. Christopher may have owed Dook something, how much and for what reason I have no idea, but I believe he was being pressurised into becoming a courier himself, driving his Jaguar to Sweden. There are several possibilities here: perhaps the money was being used as leverage? Perhaps he was being threatened? – 'You do it, or we will hurt your son!' Similar threats were made after my arrest, after all. Perhaps he was being told it would be a dummy run. Another alternative is that he too was being tricked by being told that Mitchell would buy his Jaguar, for a handsome figure, if he would deliver it to Sweden. Dook applying the pressure to get his money back, knowing Christopher did not have it, then supplying an 'out' through Mitchell making the offer to buy the car too good to ignore. Christopher would probably have been aware that this was a ruse but if he was desperate for cash, he might just have been desperate enough, and frightened enough, to ignore the risks involved. This is conjecture, but two things are certain. My brother was being backed into a corner, and he was resisting as best he could. There is no evidence to suggest that he had acted as a land courier before, with all the enormous risks the job entailed; and I saw the animosity between him and Dook that day at Santa Eulalia. I had also seen that Christopher was scared.

In any event my arrival on the scene changed everything. Dook and Mitchell recognised a golden opportunity when they saw one. They decided to take advantage of the situation by tricking me into running their drugs, and they forced Christopher into helping them. I believe they managed to persuade him that there was nothing to worry about, probably with the dummy run story, backed up with a deal to buy the car, and the odd threat thrown in for good measure. My brother is not a strong character and he was desperate enough to accept; he knew there could be no possible risk to me if there was nothing hidden in the Jaguar. Perhaps he thought the risks involved were minimal either way, it would be unlikely that a Guards officer would be suspected of being a drug smuggler. Perhaps he wanted to believe that everything would be okay.

Drug-smuggling is a dirty business and those that participate in it are not known for their high moral standards, but I remain convinced, and call me naive if you like, that Christopher would not have allowed me near that car if he had definitely known what was hidden inside it; and more to the point I believe that Dook and Mitchell would have realised this.

Therefore they could not take the chance of telling him. My brother would have warned me, and I would have been off like a shot, straight to the police, dragging him behind me. If Christopher knew what was going on at all, he was only aware of part of the conspiracy. His spontaneous outburst on the telephone indicates this strongly: 'Oh my God. The set up was meant for me, and I've passed it on to Simon.' There is one final possibility. If the threats against his son were dire enough, Christopher would have been prepared to do anything to protect him, even if that meant tricking me. I could not blame him for that.

So what is the real story behind the events of 1987? Perhaps the full truth will never emerge, but from what considerable efforts over a period lasting more than two years have been able to uncover, the following must be something close to the truth. Inevitably some of it is pure conjecture on my part.

I do not know how many drug rings operated from Ibiza, but certainly one of them was a partnership between Forbes Mitchell and Dook. Makunda, whoever he is, was an employee or at best a junior partner. People like Christopher were small fry used if and when the need arose. Mitchell ran the 'Scandinavian Department', Dook the 'United Kingdom and Holland Department'. Drugs were smuggled to other countries as well but that is not relevant to this story.

The cannabis was procured from Morocco and brought across to Ibiza on yachts, where it was packed into a variety of motor vehicles by professional mechanics. Couriers were recruited in Britain as well as locally. As the *Jasmine Francisca* incident proved, larger consignments went all the way by boat.

After the successful Waterfield run in August 1986, the next was planned for April 1987. Both Tervaniemi and Mitchell testified in court that Makunda was due back in Sweden at that time. The telephone tapes also proved that Mitchell was planning a visit to coincide with Makunda's, and that feelers were being put out for a courier – Mitchell asked Viryo in February if he would do it for a fee of 50,000 Krona. That sum, the equivalent to £5,000, appears to be the going rate for a courier. But Viryo refused.

They tried to get Christopher to drive for them but he was being difficult, and then I showed up. It was too good an opportunity to miss and they decided to trick me. This new plan entailed bringing the dates of the run forward, hence the mad dash over to Lehal's Dutch 'company' to buy cannabis, instead of waiting for it to arrive from Morocco in the normal manner. Lehal was asked if he wanted to be the courier as a back-up just in case I had changed my holiday plans without warning and flown home early. Christopher was told that I would be driving the Jaguar simply as a rehearsal for the real thing in April.

To be on the safe side Christopher guarded the car jealously, forcing Dook to steal it in order to load the drugs. Three of the gang were told to keep me busy and to get me drunk while it was being stolen. The break-in at Santa Gertrudis was a failed attempt to get the keys of the car.

When the drugs were safely packed into the Jaguar's sills it was left somewhere easy for the local police to find. A spare set of keys was hidden behind the back bumper, where the Swedish police eventually found them, as a contingency in the event of me doing something unforeseen.

On the morning we left Ibiza, when I told Christopher that the car had been stolen, he went to find Dook because he suspected something was 'up'. Dook must have reassured him, and our travel arrangements went ahead. The rest, as they say, is history.

That Mitchell was in on the decision to trick me is beyond all reasonable doubt. He was Dook's partner; he knew about the Santa Eulalia meeting; he refused to see me himself, having as little to do with me as possible, even when I arrived in Sweden. The fact that Prita was involved in drug-running, as her passport and arrest in Germany prove, blows an enormous hole in his excuse for not having me to his house to be briefed. His reasons for Makunda not acting as courier on this occasion were also nonsense, not only because it was not Makunda's job but because he was due back in Sweden in April in any case. The reason Makunda was not involved was because there was no requirement for a security cut-off on this run. The courier did not know what was going on, therefore it did not matter whom he met in Sweden.

Once Mitchell found himself in custody, he realised that he was facing a long sentence in prison; if the full extent of his activities became known, the maximum sentence of twelve years. His only chance lay in minimising his own responsibility and ensuring that the investigation was kept as superficial as possible. To achieve this he had to be seen to be co-operating with the police, and he had to give them what they wanted to know. He needed to strike a deal, both to reduce his own sentence and to protect his family.

The police would obviously want to know where the drugs came from. He could not talk about Dook, that would have been like signing his own death warrant, so he chose a suitable scapegoat. Someone who would not be able to fight back – a lazy boat-bum: Christopher Hayward. In order to strengthen his case against Christopher he had no choice but to implicate me, because people would find it difficult to believe that one brother could treat another so badly. To reduce his own role Mitchell had a stong interest in saying he worked for someone else – the 'Boss'. If he had told the police that I was not involved he would inevitably have faced a long drawn-out investigation, and Prita, perhaps even other members of the ring on Ibiza, would have been dragged in.

At the same time he could not afford to let his friends and colleagues on Ibiza know that he was talking, so he chose another, indeed the only suitable scapegoat available: me. People on the island would not have known if I was involved or not. Mitchell tried to persuade them that I was doing the talking, not him. He was highly irritated by Richard New's visit when he showed people an English translation of his trial Judgement proving the opposite was in fact the case. Until then, and helped by the rumours spread around by Prita that I was singing like a bird, everyone had thought Mitchell would keep quiet all the way to the prison gates, and beyond. Dook would have known differently, he would have realised I had nothing to tell, but he did not care. He was the one being protected.

Mitchell is not stupid. He had a week to think things through before being questioned. Time to spy out the lie of the land. He had every opportunity to see what the police were after. I had been arrested and the prosecutor was saying I was guilty. For the Uppsala Drugs Squad the arrest of a British Army officer was a real coup and they were highly pleased with themselves. This would have been obvious to Mitchell from the way he was questioned. By implicating me he was therefore doing what was wanted of him; by admitting to what was already known about himself, he was seen to be co-operating with the police; nothing more is demanded of him, no further information is needed. Prita is left alone.

The final question is why did Christopher not come forward to help me more positively? Why has he run away, why has he disappeared? Only he knows the answer. But initially I believe he thought I would be released. After all, he knew I had done nothing wrong, and he was afraid to come forward in person. An understandable reaction, if not acceptable. He had been involved in smuggling drugs, if not directly on this particular run. To have come forward would have meant arrest. By the time he realised that I was going to be convicted, it was too late, no one would have believed him. The only result would have been two Haywards in a Swedish prison.

I am not trying to excuse Christopher's actions. I believed then, and I still believe now, that he should have given himself up and 'faced the music'. Surely anything is preferable to running for the rest of one's life? Having said that, I also believe he would never receive a fair trial in Sweden; there are too many preconceptions as to his role in this affair for that. I cannot and will not condemn him out of hand as I have been condemned, because regardless of what he may or may not have done, he is still my brother. If by defending him as a person, not his actions; by stating what I feel to be right, I weaken my own case and perhaps make people wonder if I have not got something to hide after all, that is a risk I am prepared to take.

One other factor must be considered. None of us knows what pressures he was under at the time. What threats were being issued. Chantal volunteered to come forward with the truth, and two days later she was dead. This is obviously a highly dangerous game. No one has heard from Christopher since October 1987. He broke the 'rules' by giving information about Dook to help me. Perhaps he has paid the price?

There have been two false alarms concerning his capture, since my conviction. The first was when my mother travelled to San Francisco to spend some time with my sister, the week after David's death. Somehow the Swedish police got wind of her intentions, put two and two together, came up with five and told the FBI that she was meeting Christopher. The FBI in turn mounted a surveillance operation, but of course nothing came of it. When my mother had left for England, they interviewed my sister and her husband, and were apparently furious when they were told of the circumstances surrounding my mother's visit. They had also been asked by the Swedes, via Interpol, to be on the look-out for a dangerous drugs 'baron' not a laid back half-a-hippy wanted for questioning over a mere fifty kilos of cannabis. 'The FBI does not deal in such petty matters'.

The second occasion involved the arrest of a man in Canada on minor charges with the same name as Christopher. After a great deal of Swedish excitement, including premature media reports in Uppsala along the lines of 'We have got our man', it turned out to be a different Christopher Hayward.

Thirteen

The refusal by the Supreme Court to hear my appeal opened the way for a Petition to the European Court of Human Rights. The procedure is a long drawn-out one that takes several years to see a result, if a petition is found admissible in the first place. Therefore it was not going to provide a quick solution to my problems.

Initially a petition is examined by the European Commission which decides if it is admissable or not. Evidence is not considered, only possible breaches of the Convention. Some 95 per cent of complaints are found, for one reason or another, to be inadmissible. Once a petition is declared admissible the Commission tries to reach a friendly settlement between the parties. If it fails, it draws up an official report on the case and states a view on possible violation of the Convention. The report is then sent to the Committee of Ministers of the Council of Europe, opening a three-month period when either party can ask for the case to be sent to the European Court of Human Rights. If neither does the Committee will make a finding. Only a small proportion of petitions make it all the way to the Court. The procedure can take as long as five years.

Three of the United Kingdom's leading experts on European Law volunteered to prepare my petition: Anthony Lester QC, Monica Carss-Frisk, and Philippe Sands. I cannot go into details as the case is still pending and therefore *sub judice*. However, it has been described as a strong one with not just one, but eight possible violations identified. As an example of a typical violation – not necessarily appearing in my petition – in November 1988 the results of a case where the United Kingdom lost against four applicants from Northern Ireland was published: the applicants, all men, had been arrested under the Prevention of Terrorism Act and held in custody without being placed before a court for periods varying between four days and six hours to six days and sixteen and a half hours. All were eventually released without charge.

The European Court found that '. . . detention for four days and six hours in police custody without appearance before a judge or other judicial officer impaired the *very essence* to the right to prompt judicial control protected by Article 5 (3) of the European Convention on Human Rights'.

Well, I was kept in police custody for eleven days and some thirteen hours before being put in front of Judge Hellbacher. My petition could not have been drawn up in a more professional manner and I must be in with a good chance. Only time will tell.

In November 1988 the Army Board took the inevitable, and in my view absolutely correct, decision to ask me to resign my commission. It is one of my most profound regrets that I had not re-tendered my resignation in late 1987 when the final appeal failed, and insisted on it being accepted. My reason for not doing so was simple. With hopes of a new appeal still strong I could not risk taking any course of action that could have been in any way misinterpreted by the Swedish authorities as an admission of guilt. My lawyers considered that a voluntary resignation would have been one such course of action. The likes of Forsberg would never have understood a decision taken on the grounds of honour, obligation or sense of duty.

There is a paragraph in Queen's Regulations for the Army (6.178b(2) (b)) that states when the Defence Council addresses itself to the case of an officer convicted by a court outside the United Kingdom it should first consider: '. . . whether the proceedings and concepts of justice generally in the country concerned were in basic accord with standards prevailing in the United Kingdom'. Force of circumstance, the belief and hope that the ends would justify the means, took me down the dishonourable path of invoking this clause as a means of delaying the inevitable.

There can be no doubt that Swedish law is totally different to British law; indeed their concepts of justice could not be more different. It was Kingsley Napley's considered opinion that I would not have been convicted in a British Court. To some, therefore, it was difficult to reconcile this fact with the decision to call on me to resign. It seemed that by following this course of action, the Generals had demonstrated implicitly – some in Sweden might think explicitly – that in their view I had received a trial that was 'in accord with circumstances prevailing in the United Kingdom' or, in plain English, one that matched up to British standards of justice, and the verdict of 'guilty' was consequently a fair one.

This may have been one point of view, but there were wider issues at stake. Officers do not lead by divine right, simply because they wear badges of rank on their shoulders. They have to lead by example, they have to command the respect, and earn the loyalty and confidence of their men. The Sandhurst motto says it all – 'Serve to Lead'. An officer with a criminal conviction, especially one for drug-smuggling, no matter how dubious the decision to convict, could have no hope of retaining that respect. Consequently there could be no question of him remaining in uniform. The Army Board's decision was therefore totally correct.

The Army Board did not sack me; I was asked to resign, with the proviso that should the European Court find in my favour the matter would be reviewed. For that I am very grateful. In any case, even if I had not been asked to do so, I would have felt it necessary to resign before returning to Great Britain, and I would not ask nor expect to be reinstated until I manage to clear my name. I would like nothing more than to be able to return to my Regiment, but only under those circumstances. If any doubt remains, my presence would only be an embarrassment to all concerned.

The two and a half years between March 1987 and September 1989 were a nightmare experience, not just for me but for those I love and care for. I have heard it said that it is always easier for the inmate than for those he leaves behind on the outside, and I would go along with that. Being in prison was a thoroughly unpleasant experience, but it was like being in another world and one is therefore cocooned from the realities and everyday problems of life. I was able to retreat into that cocoon when the going got tough, and live each day as it came. My family and close friends could not.

My mother in particular has been made to suffer. Her youngest son is dead; her oldest has disappeared off the face of the Earth; she has seen another ruined and imprisoned. Her daughter-in-law has been murdered. On top of all that, she has had to endure the worry, the expense and the threats. No one deserves such treatment.

As for me? I have many regrets, but above all my Swedish experience has taught me never to trust. There are very few people to whom I would extend that privilege today. My confidence in a system I have been brought up to believe in and to support has received an almighty dent.

I have been critical of elements of the British police, I can make no apologies for that. I would not have done so if I did not believe my stand to be justified. As a rule I have the utmost regard for the police and the job they do. When one hears of unarmed officers going up against dangerous gunmen; or going into the King's Cross Underground Station to rescue passengers from a fire; or venturing into a blazing football stadium to pull members of the public free; and all too often losing their own lives in the process, one can only be filled with total admiration and respect. However, I have now experienced what happens when that same police officer perceives one to have crossed the line between the law-abiding and the law-breaking. He ceases to be a 'friend' but an all too devious adversary.

I was brought up to look upon the policeman as my friend, not my enemy. In other words I am one of those who instinctively side with the police, but if our trust is to be maintained, the police have got to justify it because once it is lost it will very likely never be regained.

I was unhappy at the way the matter was handled by the two British police officers to say the least. Policemen should not be allowed to supply hearsay on hearsay intelligence, emanating from unvouchable criminal sources which would never get near a British court, to foreign authorities who will use it in any way they see fit to convict British citizens.

It is a sad indictment, but I will never again allow myself to be interviewed by a police officer of any nationality (I have seen at first hand how they all stick together) without a lawyer's presence. In any case I will not utter a single word unless the entire proceedings are recorded and my lawyer walks away with a copy of the tape. I would advise everybody to do likewise.

I do not know whether people would consider me justified

if I confessed to a feeling of dismay, even frustration, at the lack of assistance I received from the British Embassy, and through it the Foreign Office. Granted the situation was very complicated. I am not for a moment suggesting that I deserved special treatment simply because I was an army officer. I had managed to get myself mixed up in a very dirty business. No one likes drugs, and for all anyone knew I could have been guilty. I accept without question that it is not open to the British government to intervene, whenever it feels the desire, in the normal judicial process of another sovereign state. However, when the degree of improbity and impropriety became evident, and it was evident to anyone attending my blatantly unfair trials, then I believe any British citizen could have expected better, not least a serving army officer.

In any case, when it suits their purposes politicians seldom hesitate to air their views, regardless of whether their comments could be seen as interference in the internal affairs of another sovereign state. The Swedes in particular are very adept at it, in spite of their so-called neutrality. I would often listen with increasing fury on the radio in my solitary cell in the häktet during the months of isolation – to a series of Swedish government ministers as they criticized the human rights records of other countries.

I remember admiring the robust and courageous behaviour of Mr David Mellor, a Foreign Office Minister, when on a visit to the occupied territories, I think it was in early 1988, he intervened to prevent Israeli soldiers from arresting a young Palestinian demonstrator. His action apparently supported by the government, was clearly a protest, if not interference, and engendered world-wide publicity and comment.

There was enough evidence of malpractice by Swedish officials against me to justify a protest; certainly as much as an Israeli colonel arresting a boy. If the government supported such a protest against the Israeli treatment of Palestinian refugees, why could it not take some measure of action over Swedish treatment of a British soldier?

On a personal level the embassy staff were charming, very sympathetic, and as helpful as possible. On an official level it was a different story – one diplomat described the attitude towards me as one of 'official disinterest', another tried to justify this stance by telling me that if they were to help me on an official level, then they would have to help all British citizens in similar positions. Perhaps I am labouring under a misapprehension, but is that not their proper function?

Based on our new evidence, Tom Placht lodged a further appeal to the Supreme Court in August 1989. The Court's answer is still pending. We are still not in a position to prove my innocence positively, and until Mitchell decides to tell the full truth or until someone else with first-hand knowledge of what exactly took place on Ibiza in March 1987 comes forward, there remains little prospect that we will be able to. However, I do not have to prove my innocence; it is for the State to prove my guilt, and in spite of my conviction this has not been done. If there is any justice to be had the appeal will be granted. The defence position is very strong because the evidence we can now provide effectively destroys every argument and theory used by the prosecution to achieve the guilty verdict. In short, Forsberg's case against me has collapsed.

As a consequence I ought to be feeling optimistic, but if anything I feel pessimistic, and the reason for my pessimism is my belief in the unwillingness of the judges to conceive that the entire apparatus of their law may have gone hideously wrong. Unfortunately, I suspect they will behave as though upholding the system is more important than justice for the individual. Again, only time will tell.

I am fully aware that the one question that nags in everybody's mind, is why I was not even slightly suspicious when asked to drive the Jaguar to Sweden. Even some of my staunchest allies ask – 'how could you have been so naive?' Others take an opposite view, a view expressed to me by a journalist who interviewed me soon after my appeal had failed in 1987. He said: 'I sat through both your trial and appeal and I don't believe there was sufficient evidence to convict you. But I also saw how you performed and I don't think you're naive. I don't think anyone could have tricked you into driving that car; therefore despite the lack of evidence I believe you are guilty. If the judges thought the same, in this country that is enough to convict you. I'm sorry, but to be honest, that's how I feel.'

Well, I do not believe I am naive, or no more so than the next man. And it is such an easy accusation to make with the benefit of hindsight. My answer is this, and it comes in the form of a question. Why should I have been suspicious? I was on holiday, and I did not go on holiday expecting to have to be on the look-out for drugs or drug-smugglers. The subject never crossed my mind. True, if a total stranger had approached me in the street and said: 'Pssst, drive my car to Sweden for me,' then like anyone, I would have been more than merely suspicious; I would have told the man exactly what he could do with himself, and then gone straight to the nearest police station. However, I was not asked by a stranger; the request was put to me by a sibling whom I had no reason to distrust. Furthermore I knew that Christopher had good reasons for wanting to sell his Jaguar and he had been trying to do so for months. It never occurred to me to ask him whether there was cannabis hidden inside it. Indeed I do not believe the thought would have occurred to anybody under such circumstances.

Against all the odds I was granted half remission. The good news was given to me in May; I would be released on Tuesday 12 September 1989. It was a real surprise, a bolt out of the blue, made more unexpected by the fact that all the 'experts' had told me I had no chance of receiving it. Indeed, it was extremely unusual; almost unheard of. The reason the parole board gave for its magnanimous gesture? It was considered most unlikely that I would re-offend – I had received so much publicity, I could not possibly be of any further use to a drugs ring. That comment proved that someone had a dry sense of humour, if nothing else.

To be freed early was indeed good news. It was a step forward but it was only half the battle I would never feel truly free until I succeeded in clearing my name.

As the countdown started and the twelfth drew closer I experienced the reawakening of a long-dormant memory from prep-school. That end-of-term feeling – of the final morning before the holidays; the air of expectancy; the final bell; the shouted goodbyes; the sense of release.

The door opened. I stepped out into freedom. The waiting was over. As I looked back at the walls and the daunting buildings behind them I made a silent vow to myself: no man would ever put me behind bars again for something I had not done.

Afterword

I have written this book because the story needed to be told.
Too many misconceptions and half-truths have been allowed
to circulate. Too much improbity has been allowed to pass
unnoticed. In the telling some might question how I have been
able to provide such detailed descriptions of lengthy police
interviews and court sessions. They might wonder if I have not
allowed poetic licence to fill in the gaps to make the story a
better one. Nothing could be further from the truth. One of the
many admirable things about Sweden is the public right of
access to information: I have had at my disposal extensive
documentation, including police statements and court
transcripts. Occasionally I have had to work from private
notes and tape-recordings made at the time. When I have had
to rely on memory I have always endeavoured to corroborate
the facts before committing them to paper.

Inevitably the amount of researched documentation was
vast, and I have had to paraphrase and, on occasion, especially
during the trial proceedings, alter the sequence of events for
the sake of continuity and to allow the story to flow. However,
I have never intentionally changed the meaning of the
account, and I have supportive documentation to prove it; as
when I made specific accusations against individuals.

Appendix

Report produced by Richard New, Managing Director of Veritas Management, for Kingsley Napley

REPORT CONCERNING SIMON HAYWARD'S CONVICTION IN SWEDEN

1. OVERVIEW

1.1 Following Simon Hayward's conviction by the Swedish courts, I have been asked to provide a report detailing my professional opinion as to his guilt or innocence. The qualifications that enable me to competently provide such an opinion are:

- I am an independent expert in matters relating to drug-smuggling;

- I have attended many drugs trials in the UK where the charges have been of a similar nature;

- I have assessed, and am familiar with, the evidence presented at the District and Appeal Courts; and

- I have conducted my own extensive enquiries in this case.

1.2 It must be appreciated that it is frequently impossible for the defendant to prove his innocence in such cases. That requires proving a negative, with all the attendant difficulties, and it is therefore rare that the defence is able to produce some magic 'rabbit out of a hat' that conclusively proves innocence.

However, quite rightly, in civilized countries the onus is placed on the prosecution to prove its case. The role of the defence is therefore primarily to test the evidence, and attempt to

demonstrate that it is incorrect, unreliable, inadequate or capable
of alternative, innocent, interpretation.

Unlike civil cases, where the less stringent 'balance of
probability' criteria is applied, in criminal cases the members (or
at least a given majority) of a jury, or where appropriate, a court,
are required to be sure 'beyond all reasonable doubt' before
returning a guilty verdict. Conversely, where any doubt exists,
they should acquit.

1.3   In my professional opinion, based on the known facts, Simon
Hayward should have been acquitted at the Appeal Court. In my
opinion, he would undoubtedly have been acquitted had the trial
been conducted before a court in this country.

2.   QUALIFICATIONS AS AN EXPERT WITNESS

2.1   My qualifications as an expert witness were unreservedly accepted
by both the Swedish prosecution and courts.

2.2   I served for some sixteen years in Her Majesty's Customs and
Excise. Unlike most countries, where drugs matters are handed
over to the police, the U.K. Customs service is solely responsible
for all matters relating to the importation and exportation of
drugs. It conducts its own investigations, which include the
interviewing of suspects and witnesses, arrests, intelligence work,
and extensive surveillance operations. It also has its own legal
branch, responsible for the subsequent prosecution of cases.

2.3   My initial five to six years service was spent in the Preventive
branch – the uniform side – based at major UK airports and
ports, where I was employed on anti-smuggling duties, including
drugs. I was then recruited into the Central Investigation
Division, the highest investigative body of the Customs. In
relation to Customs matters, it is responsible for the investigation
of only the most major criminal activities, including organised
crime. Much of the Division's work, in terms of manpower and
resources, was, and is, related to drug-smuggling. During my nine
years with the Division, I spent some four years on one of the
principal operational drug sections, and a further year on drugs
intelligence work. Together with my fellow section colleagues, I
specialised in the detection and investigation of professional
cannabis smuggling organisations. Many of these operated
between Morocco and the UK using vehicles for the
transportation.

2.4 The Swedish case is typical of the operations conducted by my section. During my period of service, I was intimately involved in dozens of such cases, although most involved greater quantities of drugs.

2.5 I left the Customs service in 1981, to join a leading private consultancy company specialising, *inter alia*, in international investigations, primarily of a commercial nature. I subsequently became a director of the company, responsible for investigation matters, and left in 1985 to form Veritas, a similar company.

3. QUALITY OF THE SWEDISH POLICE INVESTIGATION

During the Appeal, I had the opportunity to assess the background and experience of the professional prosecution witnesses – assorted police officers – and to assess the investigation that was (or perhaps more accurately, was not) conducted.

It was clear to me that my experience in the field of drug, and other, smuggling cases was considerably superior to that of the police officers and public prosecutor. It was clear that the police had little previous experience in the investigation of such major cases, and it is my opinion that they were 'out of their depth' with the Hayward case, and that this resulted in an unprofessional investigation, lacking in both quality and integrity. They failed to conduct many important basic enquiries, the results of which were clearly of crucial importance to the defence.

4. EXPERIENCE OF THE APPEAL COURT

I cannot comment on the experience of the Appeal court members, although I understand that major, multi-defendant, international drug-smuggling cases are not common in Sweden.

5. THE DEFENCE CASE

During the Appeal hearing, in my opinion the defence comprehensively demonstrated that the component parts of the prosecution's case (many of which were, in effect, theories) were either incorrect, unreliable or capable of alternative, and innocent, explanation.

6. THE JUDGEMENT

6.1 In my considerable experience I have never seen a verdict reached with such apparent blatant disregard for the facts – primarily those aspects of the evidence favourable to the defence.

6.2 By the conclusion of the hearing, even the general view of independent observers – such as journalists – was that Simon should have been acquitted. On the basis of the evidence, the prosecution had not conclusively proved its case, and there was profound doubt as to Simon Hayward's guilt or innocence.

6.3 In the circumstances, the benefit of the (considerable) doubt should clearly have been applied by the court in Simon Hayward's favour, with a resulting acquittal. In my opinion, and by UK standards, the body of the Judgement, when compared to its conclusion, is totally contradictory.

7. SIMON HAYWARD – EVIDENCE INCONSISTENT WITH HIM HAVING BEEN A KNOWING DRUGS COURIER

7.1 There are numerous aspects of the case, in relation to the organisation of the 'run' to Sweden, Simon Hayward's background and behaviour, and other significant matters, that are totally inconsistent with him having been a knowing courier. These are detailed below, in paragraphs 11 and 12.

7.2 For there to have been one major inconsistency would clearly not, in itself, have been evidence of Simon's innocence. However, there are so many, and of such a fundamental and important nature, that they combine, in my opinion, to indicate his innocence, rather than guilt.

7.3 Ironically, and in my view, totally absurdly, a number of these aspects were in fact put forward by the prosecution as somehow evidence of guilt.

7.4 To appreciate many of the major inconsistencies, it is necessary to first have an understanding of what experience has identified as being the profile and role of the drugs courier, and the objectives of the gang's leaders.

8. PROFILE OF A KNOWING DRUGS COURIER

8.1 There have been cases where a principal, himself, has for some reason been forced to act as the courier and a member of his family, such as his wife, has accompanied him, usually as cover. There have also been instances where a member of the family has acted as the courier. However these instances are unusual and rare.

In the vast majority of cases the courier will not be a member of a principal's family. The reasons are logical. Firstly, even drug-smuggling principals have some morals, and are usually loathe to put their immediate family in such jeopardy. Secondly, there is no need to do so, as suitable non-family couriers are normally easy to recruit. Thirdly, and most importantly, for reasons of self-preservation, principals will avoid using a person who can readily identify them, and who has such an obvious, and direct, link to themselves.

8.2   Couriers, unfortunately, are easy to recruit. They will not be paid on a percentage of the value/profit basis. He/she will be paid an agreed fixed sum for the trip, with money for expenses being provided, or re-imbursed. Normal commercial considerations apply, which result in the courier being paid as little as possible, thus maximising the profit to the principals. As such, given that he is in the immediate firing line, the courier is the person who takes the most risk, for the least reward. Usually they will receive 'peanuts' in comparison to the profits of the principals. A courier will invariably have one, and usually more, of the following characteristics:

- one of life's failures, or a person who has suddenly fallen on hard times.

- either no, or no regular, employment, or menial employment with no prospects.

- as a result of the above, has few, if any, assets, and is desperate for money.

- a weak character who, for the above reasons, can be persuaded to take the enormous risks, for little reward.

9.   THE COURIER'S ROLE

9.1   A courier's role is exactly what the title means – a person who merely transports something, safely, from place A to place B, usually for a set fee.

In total contradiction to the assertions of the prosecution during the trial, and to the evidence of Mitchell, one of the convicted principals, a courier will:

- not be responsible for packing the drugs into the vehicle, nor for their subsequent unloading.

- not normally even be present during the loading and unloading.

- not know the actual quantity of drugs being transported.

- not necessarily know the exact place of concealment.

9.2   The reasons are simple. Any half-professional smuggling operation will operate on a compartmentalised, 'need to know' basis. So far as the principals are concerned, the less the courier knows, the better. The less he knows, the less damage he can do should he be caught, and talk. The principals will therefore seek to ensure that he knows as little as possible about either their identities, or the links of the whole operation Therefore, he is equally unlikely to know the identities of either the suppliers or distributors. He will meet only the person(s) who have recruited and briefed him. He may also meet the person(s) from whom he collects the vehicle, and to whom he delivers it, unless there have been prearranged locations for collection and delivery.

In practice, the whole operation will rarely involve him in having to meet more than one or two different persons, i.e. one principal will frequently recruit and brief him, and deliver and subsequently receive the vehicle.

10.   THE SMUGGLING 'RUN' AND THE COURIER'S BRIEFING

10.1   For many years now, few countries have had the Customs/police resources to effectively combat even amateur, let alone professional, smuggling – certainly in Europe. Therefore, disregarding intelligence operations, the practical danger to the professional smuggling operation is if the courier in some way attracts the attention of the authorities (or is stopped at random), either in transit through a country or at a border control, and subsequent questioning/search provides some reason for a full, in-depth, search.

10.2   All this is, of course, known to the professional smugglers. The principal(s) will therefore seek to minimise the likelihood of the courier being initially stopped, and, if he is stopped, to ensure that the authorities are provided with no reason to probe deeper. The principals will therefore ensure that the courier:

- has been provided with a suitably low key vehicle, unlikely to attract attention, and consistent with the driver and the supposed trip.

and, with a knowing courier, that:

- he has been extensively briefed with a sound cover story, appropriate to the trip, e.g. holiday, business, etc.

- his itinerary, since originally leaving home, is not suspicious or unusual, and is consistent with the purported purpose of the trip.

- he has nothing incriminating, or suspicious, either in the car, in his baggage, or on his person. He will also be instructed not to acquire any such items en route.

- he has ample time to complete the journey, and that the time taken should be consistent with the supposed nature of the trip. What the principals would wish to avoid would be for the car to be involved in an accident, or for the courier to be stopped by police for traffic offences. The courier will therefore be firmly instructed to drive carefully and to 'take things easy' – to avoid alcohol, to observe traffic laws, and to take regular breaks to ensure that he does not become overtired.

10.3   As a practical safeguard, in case the drugs are detected, the principals will also seek to ensure that their own involvement, and identities, cannot readily be established. Therefore, they will ensure that the car cannot easily be traced back to them, and that the courier does not have anything on his person, or in the car, that directly links them. It would be expected that telephone numbers, if necessary to the courier, would be coded.

11.   MAJOR INCONSISTENCIES – GENERAL

11.1   There is *prima facie* evidence to suggest that Christopher Hayward was involved in this and perhaps previous drug runs to Sweden. However, there are a number of major inconsistencies concerning the general organisation of Simon's trip. Their fundamental nature clearly indicates to me that whoever was responsible for it was for some reason it was forced to 'cut corners' and act in an 'unprofessional' manner. The evidence suggests that the reason may well have been financial. My enquiries in Ibiza established that by the time of Simon's trip, Christopher was apparently short of money, and was also under some kind of pressure from the shadowy Irishman, 'Dook'.

11.2 However, whatever the reason, the organisation of the trip was conducted in such an 'unprofessional' manner that it clearly indicates that whoever initiated it was desperate. In my opinion, if Christopher was that desperate, he would equally have been desperate enough to dupe Simon into unwittingly acting as courier.

The only other logical explanation is that Christopher himself was not involved on that occasion, and some third party took advantage of the known trip to Sweden.

11.3 *Choice of Simon, and availability of couriers.*
For the reasons detailed in paragraph 8, it is clearly inconsistent that the brother of one of the apparent principals should be recruited as the courier.

Furthermore it was totally unnecessary. My enquiries in Ibiza indicated that Christopher had ready access to a large pool of suitable couriers there, ready and eager to be recruited. In my experience, and supported by other recent cases, the going rate in England for such a courier would have been in the region of £5,000. In Ibiza, I believe that for £5,000 Christopher would have been besieged by suitable willing recruits. Even were Christopher short of funds, that would not have altered the situation. The courier'is always paid after the trip (to prevent them backing out and disappearing with the money).

Therefore, under normal circumstances, it was inconsistent for Christopher to have recruited his brother as the courier, and a totally unnecessary risk to Christopher given that cheap, suitable, couriers were freely available.

11.4 *Simon's Intinerary*
Simon's whole prior travel pattern was inconsistent with that of a drugs courier. It would have aroused automatic suspicion, had only a preliminary examination been conducted by any of the border authorities during his drive to Sweden. It was therefore exactly what the principals, under normal circumstances, would have avoided at all costs.

The reasons are basic. For an Englishman, resident in England,

to have flown from England to Gibraltar, then to Ibiza, then to
have driven someone else's car, on his own, from Ibiza to Sweden
would have been highly unusual. To hard-pressed border
authorities, things that are unusual are naturally suspicious, and
merit further attention. Therefore, under normal circumstances,
the principals would have recruited someone whose itinerary
appeared reasonable and consistent, such as they had done on
previous runs to Sweden i.e. someone who had clearly had the car
throughout their travels – certainly not a person such as Simon,
who apparently hopped suddenly from planes to cars.

11.5   *Use of the Jaguar*
The Jaguar was, of course, of suitable size for the quantity of
drugs – so too would have been a Volvo. However, I understand
that Jaguars, unlike Volvos, are unusual in Sweden and, as such,
it was likely to have attracted attention from the border
authorities, if only from a curiosity point of view. If, as was
planned, it was to be then parked at a quiet railway station in
Sweden, and driven to a small country village in the middle of the
night, it would have stood out like a sore thumb. Again, therefore,
on the basis that anything unusual is likely to draw unwanted
attention, it was a totally unsuitable make of car for a 'run' there.
    All this would, of course, have been known to one of the
self-confessed principals, Mitchell, who looked after the Swedish
end of the operation, and had previously recruited the couriers.
    Therefore, it was entirely inconsistent for the Jaguar to have
been used, especially as other suitable cars could easily have been
obtained either in Sweden, Ibiza or elsewhere.

11.6   *Ownership of the Jaguar*
Perhaps the greatest inconsistency of all, was the fact that the car
was actually registered to Christopher Hayward. I consider this to
be extraordinary. As detailed earlier the fundamental objective of
the principals is to distance themselves from the vehicle, as well
as the courier, in order to prevent their involvement being readily
identified. However, if the car that the drugs are concealed in is
actually registered to you, this is clearly ridiculously self-defeating!!

11.7   *General Organisation – Conclusions*
Why then, did the principals organise the 'run' in such a totally
incompetent fashion – breaking vitually every 'rule' known to
them? On the face of it, Christopher Hayward might just as well
have driven the car himself.

The logical explanation, in my opinion, is that Christopher was for some reason so desperate that he decided to dupe Simon into unwittingly acting as courier. As stated earlier, in my opinion, the only other logical explanation is that Christopher himself was not involved in the 'run' and that some knowledgeable third party took advantage of the trip to Sweden.

Only with Simon being an innocent courier do the apparently gross inconsistencies, and incompetence, surrounding the organisation of the 'run' become logically explained. Quite simply, it would have had to have been organised like that in order to avoid Simon 'smelling a rat':

– there would have been little opportunity to dictate Simon's itinerary, and certainly no plausible reason for requesting him to drive a car from England to Gibraltar, then on to Ibiza, and then to Sweden.

– the Jaguar was effectively the only vehicle that Christopher could plausibly ask Simon to drive to Sweden, without arousing Simon's suspicions. Firstly, Simon knew that it was his brother's car. Secondly, Simon could see with his own eyes that it was totally unsuitable for the rock track leading to Christopher's new home, and most other Ibizan roads. Thirdly, Simon would also have known that Christopher had therefore recently acquired a suitable vehicle, a Lada Jeep, and that the Jaguar was now clearly surplus to requirements.

In summary, therefore, although the Jaguar was unsuitable for the 'run' to Sweden, and easily traced to him, Christopher effectively would have had no option other than to use it. Neither would he have been able to engineer a more plausible travel itinerary for Simon.

Conversely, if Simon was a knowing courier, then a suitably inconspicuous vehicle, untraceable to Christopher, could easily have been obtained, preferably driven by Simon from England to provide a more plausible itinerary.

12.   MAJOR INCONSISTENCIES – SPECIFIC TO SIMON

12.1   There are numerous significant matters concerning Simon's background and character which, together with his actions and behaviour from the time that he left England, are totally inconsistent with those to be expected of a knowing courier, employed by what we know was a professional drug ring. In fact, virtually everything that he did was the wrong thing to do had he been a knowing courier.

12.2 *His Background and Character*

For the reasons detailed earlier in paragraph 8, his background and circumstances are just not those of a knowing drugs courier.

He held a highly responsible position, and was highly thought of in terms of both character and ability. In short, he had a secure career with considerable prospects.

In addition, he enjoyed a good salary and, to my knowledge, had no financial problems.

Lastly, and of considerable significance, his anti-drug stance had already been established.

12.3 *The Money found on Simon/His expenses*

There are a number of major inconsistencies relating to the £7,500 in cash that he obtained from his bank prior to his departure from England. He stated that the money was to purchase a car in Germany on his way back to England. This explanation (confirmed by his Bankers when granting the facility) was both plausible and was not rebutted by the prosecution, who made little of the fact. However, in my opinion, the money is highly relevant for a number of reasons:

– it is further clear evidence of Simon's credit worthiness. Had he been temporarily short of funds for some reason, he could clearly have borrowed it.

– it demonstrates an apparently nonsensical situation whereby a courier – who has agreed to do the 'run' because of financial difficulties – actually has, and takes with him on the trip, more money than he would normally be expected to have been paid.

– when Simon was arrested in Sweden he had some £6,800 remaining. He had spent the balance of £700 on living expenses. As detailed earlier, a courier would be provided with funds for expenses, or have them paid for him. He would certainly not be expected, or be prepared, to disburse/expend that sort of money out of his own pocket.

– my enquiries established that the airline ticket that Simon purchased for his flight from England to Gibraltar was, in fact, effectively a cheap standby ticket. In my experience, drugs couriers simply do not travel on such tickets; it provides further evidence that Simon was paying his own way, as would be expected were he simply going on holiday.

12.4 *Theft of the Jaguar in Ibiza*

By way of explanation as to how the drugs may have got into the car, Simon stated that the car had been stolen in Ibiza City, and later recovered by the police, shortly prior to his departure from Ibiza. This provided an opportunity for the drugs to have been concealed by Christopher, or some third party with knowledge of Simon's intended trip.

The prosecution in Sweden attempted to suggest that there had been no actual theft, and that the situation had been 'set up', with Simon's knowledge, to provide a 'get out' for Simon if he were subsequently caught.

This initially appears plausible, until the apparent facts are examined further.

During my enquiries, I interviewed the police inspector on Ibiza who was in charge of the Hayward case, concerning the circumstances surrounding the car's theft, and subsequent recovery. These enquiries confirmed that:

– the theft had indeed been reported to the police by Simon on the evening of 9 March.

– the car's details had then been circulated to the police traffic division, and that it had been found by a normal traffic patrol, with no 'tip off', at 2pm the following morning, 10 March. Simon had reclaimed it, as stated, at about 11.30am that day, after visiting the police station to enquire whether there was any news about the car.

– one of the windows was smashed, and Simon had reported the theft of various items from inside the car.

– theft of, and from, cars was not uncommon in Ibiza.

– Simon had left Ibiza on the 12.30 ferry that day, and that therefore there would have been insufficient time for the drugs to have been concealed after he had reclaimed the car.

Simon stated that he had, in fact, parked the car in Ibiza City on the evening of 8 March 1987. This was not disputed by the Swedish prosecution. Simon had driven into town for a social evening and, having got drunk, had left the car there, and returned home by taxi. On returning to collect the car the following evening, the 9th, he found it missing and had then reported its loss to the police.

It is clear that the drugs had already been concealed in the car by the time he reclaimed it on the 10th. Therefore, the drugs must either have been concealed in the car prior to the evening of the 8th, or subsequent to it having been left in Ibiza.

If the theft was genuine, and Simon was a knowing courier, I consider it inconceivable that he would have driven it (or been allowed by the principals to have driven it) into Ibiza and left it unattended for some 24 hours, given the value of the drugs.

However, if he were innocent, then there was no reason why he should not have done so, given that Christopher, for example, may not have anticipated that he would do so, or had considered that it would be suspicious to Simon if he had instructed Simon not to use the Jaguar and not to leave it unattended.

Alternatively. if the theft was a charade, I consider it to have been equally inconceivable that the principals would have allowed the vehicle to have been left unattended for that length of time, in furtherence of their ploy. It may well then have been genuinely stolen, or seriously damaged. For them to have sat watching the car for that length of time (including two nights) would clearly have been totally impractical, as well as highly suspicious.

12.5 *The Trip to Sweden*

As detailed in paragraphs 9 and 10, the sole function of the courier, and the primary objective of the principals, is to ensure that the drugs are safely transported to their destination, without detection. Therefore, anything that may jeopardize that would be avoided at all costs, by both the principals (who stand to make substantial profits) and the courier (who doesn't want to get caught).

That is why, as detailed earlier, the courier will always be extensively briefed on the do's and don't's of drug transportation. He will be told (in addition to it being commonsense) that he must do nothing, nor have anything in the car that may be dangerous or draw attention to either himself or the vehicle. It is also well known that the primary thing likely to draw the attention of the border authorities is anything unusual.

In this respect, virtually everything that Simon could have done wrong during the trip to Sweden, he did. The number, and nature, of these basic errors, is totally inconsistent with him having been a knowing courier, especially in the light of his particular professional background. However, if he was an innocent courier, who could not be so briefed because it would have aroused his suspicion, then everything would have been entirely consistent, given his known character.

(a) *The route via Andorra*

The prosecution made great play of the fact that he drove from Spain to France via Andorra, rather than by the direct route. They argued that this was because the border controls via Andorra were less vigilant, and that therefore this was evidence of Simon's guilt.

However, during the hearing, I, and another witness, gave evidence to the contrary. Not only was Simon's explanation – that he hoped to buy some low cost ski equipment – perfectly plausible, but it was established that both border controls were lax and, if anything, the Andorran controls were more stringent.

It was further established that because of the snow and road conditions at that time of year, to have driven via Andorra was positively dangerous and could have resulted in an accident. Furthermore it was a longer route. Even the principal, Mitchell, stated that couriers would be told to keep to the main roads i.e. to have travelled on the direct route.

The court, on this point, for once appears to have agreed with the defence, and stated that it attached no weight to the matter. However, in my opinion, it was a significant inconsistency that in fact supported Simon's claim to have been an innocent courier, and should actually have been viewed in his favour.

In my opinion, it was a typical example of the nature of much of the prosecution evidence – biased inferences, capable of innocent explanation. The court adopted the wrong test. Having discarded it as a feature of the prosecution case, it became a factor in the defence case, indicating innocence.

(b) *Journey time to Sweden*

Again, the prosecution made great capital of the fact that Simon drove virtually non-stop, without sleep, from France to Sweden, and that this was indicative of his guilt.

However, it can be equally, and in fact better, interpreted, as the reverse. As detailed earlier, a courier would be told to 'take it easy' – to take regular breaks, in order not to become overtired and careless, and not to get stopped by traffic police for speeding etc. Through lack of sleep, Simon's high speed dash across Europe, in contrast, could well have resulted in a serious accident which would have jeopardized the entire operation. His behaviour was therefore far more consistent with that of an innocent courier. I, myself, for example, once drove non-stop from Spain to England – and I was not a drugs courier!

(c) *Articles carried in the car*
As detailed earlier, anything unusual would be potentially suspicious to a border officer, and likely to lead to a closer examination. Therefore, the principals, and courier, would allow nothing unusual in the car. It was therefore entirely inconsistent, were Simon a knowing courier, and asking for trouble, for him to have had with him:

– a highly unusual, and expensive, nightsight.

– nearly £7,000 in cash.

12.6   *The Screwdriver*

The prosecution also attached great significance to a screwdriver that Simon had purchased after arriving in Sweden, in order to tighten loose screws on the car's driving seat. The screwdriver was, alleged the prosecution, to be used by Simon to remove the seats and gain accesss to the drugs. The convicted principal, Mitchell, added considerable credibility to this theory by stating that it was normal drug-smuggling practice for couriers to unload the vehicle. There is only one comment that sums up this aspect of Mitchell's testimony – it was pure invention, and further evidence that he lied to the court.

As detailed earlier in this report at paragraph 9, the courier is not responsible for either loading, or unloading, the car, and usually will not even be present. He may not even know exactly where the drugs are concealed, or the method of access. One of the principals, in this case clearly Mitchell, would always have been responsible for the unloading of the vehicle – to avoid any later disputes as to quantity, for example.

Neither would it be the responsibility of the courier to buy any items of equipment, along the route, necessary to later extract the drugs from the vehicle. Mitchell would clearly have known where the concealment was, and it would have been his responsibility to have obtained, if necessary, any relevant tools. As evidenced by Simon's purchase, the screwdriver was freely available in Sweden. Furthermore, the evidence clearly demonstrates that the car, on Mitchell's instructions, was actually being taken to a garage belonging to a friend of his. The police, however, negligently failed to record what tools were found at the garage, and had disposed of them prior to Simon's trial.

12.7   *The Jaguar's Broken Window*

As an extention of their 'theory' concerning the theft of the car in Ibiza, the prosecution also alleged, again supported by the testimony of Mitchell, that it was a common practice for a window to be deliberately broken, to provide the courier with an excuse that the drugs must have been planted. Personally, I have never heard of that – neither, I understand, had the Swedish police – and I consider it a nonsense. If it were common practice it would be expected that the authorities would know of it. Therefore, if Simon had turned up at the border with the broken window, that would have been as sensible as hanging sign out saying 'I'm probably transporting drugs, come and search me'.

Therefore, in my opinion, it would have been more consistent, if Simon was a knowing courier, for him to have been told to get the window repaired, so as not to attract attention.

12.8   *The Meeting with Mitchell on Ibiza*

According to Mitchell, he was told by Christopher that Simon was to be the courier, whilst Mitchell was on Ibiza. It was suggested by Christopher, according to Mitchell, that he should bring Simon to Mitchell's house in order for them to meet. Mitchell said that he later thought this to be a bad idea, as it would involve Mitchell's family. He therefore called round one day to where Simon was staying in order to be able to later recognise him in Sweden. Both Mitchell and Simon agree that this was a brief meeting at which Mitchell introduced himself as a friend of Christopher's, and merely exchanged pleasantries in the doorway. The meeting was so brief that Mitchell's girlfriend stayed in the car. According to Simon, he was not even aware at that time that Mitchell was the person to whom he would be delivering the Jaguar in Sweden. Mitchell admits that nothing was said during this brief meeting, by either party, that intimated that Simon was a knowing courier. Neither did Mitchell even mention that he was the person who would be meeting Simon in Sweden. Mitchell further admits that he had no further contact with Simon until he met him in Sweden.

I consider this meeting, and the lack of any others, to have been crucial, and totally inconsistent with Simon having been a knowing courier:

– why was Mitchell not prepared at that meeting to discuss, or even chat about, Simon's forthcoming trip, given that it was Mitchell that he would be meeting there? Why the reticence on Mitchell's part?

– according to Mitchell, he already knew from Christopher that Simon was a knowing courier. Mitchell would also have known, or assumed, that Simon would know that it was Mitchell whom he would be meeting in Sweden.

– whilst I can understand his reluctance to have Simon come to his home, the same clearly would not apply to meetings and discussions elsewhere.

– it was, after all, Mitchell who would be meeting Simon, Mitchell who had been in charge of previous couriers, and their briefing, and it was only Mitchell who had detailed knowledge and experience of such important aspects as the Swedish border system and controls, and routes.

In normal circumstances, therefore, I consider it both inconceivable, and illogical, that Mitchell would not, in fact, have insisted on getting together with Simon, in order to brief him fully. Especially as Simon was not some Tom, Dick or Harry, but clearly the trusted brother of Mitchell's supposed co-principal. Similarly, I believe that Simon would have insisted on such a meeting in order to be fully briefed concerning Swedish border controls, and favoured routes.

In my opinion, I believe that Mitchell's attitude and behaviour was, in fact, totally consistent with him having believed that Simon was NOT a knowing courier, or that he was unsure.

12.9 *Simon's Professional Background*

Simon is clearly an unusual animal - certainly not a run of the mill type of low level courier. His career and background have given him the talents and experience that would have enabled him to plan and execute a drug running operation with military efficiency and precision.

I therefore consider it inconceivable that he would knowingly have allowed himself to have been a minor cog in a 'run' that was so unprofessionally organised. I believe that he would have insisted on having a major input into the operation, and ensured that it was suitably well organised before putting himself into the firing line. Similarly, I consider it inconceivable that he would, himself, have later committed so many basic errors.

The facts are therefore far more consistent with him having been an innocent courier, albeit with the benefit of hindsight, naive, rather than having been an unprofessional incompetent.

13.   OTHER MATTERS OF SIGNIFICANCE

13.1   *Testimony of Mitchell*
Mitchell was a leading principal in the drug ring and had been already sentenced to seven years imprisonment at an earlier hearing.

In my opinion, the court was duped by Mitchell, and as a result was heavily influenced by his testimony, to the detriment of Simon.

I have analysed his police interviews, his testimony at his own trial and his evidence at the District Court. I was also present during his testimony at the Appeal court. This analysis reveals to me a considerable number of major contradictions and inaccuracies. It appears clear to me that he is a man of considerable cunning, and an accomplished liar, and that he lied during the Appeal. In terms of motivation, the defence clearly established that there were major personal reasons why he had had everything to gain, and little to lose, by false or misleading testimony.

In addition, Mitchell's personal feelings against Simon were shown in their true colours during an interview with *The Sunday Times* on the 18 September 1987, shortly before the Appeal hearing. When asked about Simon's brother, Christopher, Mitchell said:

'He's a better man than his brother I can tell you . . . He wasn't in Ireland popping out paddies'.

However, one of the most damaging aspects of his testimony – concerning what Christopher had allegedly told him on Ibiza – was pure hearsay, which would, quite rightly, never have been admissable in a British court.

In addition, experience has shown that the evidence of co-conspirators should always be treated with considerable caution. That is why, again quite rightly, it is unlikely that a British court would have attached much weight to Mitchell's general testimony, unless sufficient independent corroboration was available. In Mitchell's case, not only was there essentially no independent corroboration, but the opposite was demonstrated in that on various important points his testimony was clearly, and deliberately, inaccurate.

13.2   *The mystery 'Informant' and the Scotland Yard Memo*
The court also clearly placed considerable weight on a memo prepared at an earlier date by two British police officers attached

to the National Drugs and Intelligence Unit at Scotland Yard, and their interview with an unidentified Scotland Yard 'informant' – attended by a Norwegian Interpol officer.

However, Scotland Yard subsequently refused to permit the two officers to attend either the District Court or Appeal hearings to give evidence, essentially on the grounds that the information contained in their memo was both unsubstantiated and would not be admissable in an English court.

Nevertheless, the Appeal court still allowed the memo to be entered as evidence, and allowed the Norwegian officer to give totally hearsay evidence originating from the meeting with the informant, at which he had been present.

I need say little concerning the memo. The subsequent view, and attitude, of Scotland Yard speaks for itself. In relation to the 'evidence' of the informant, even were he/she to have given evidence personally at the Appeal, informants are notoriously unreliable and therefore are to be treated with extreme caution. Their motives can be highly suspect. Even when they provide information in good faith, it may be inaccurate and may, in turn, have been obtained from some other person – a whole chain of hearsay may be involved, as appears likely in this case. Independent and admissable corroboration of an informant's testimony is therefore normally considered essential.

That the Appeal court nevertheless allowed, let alone gave credence to, damaging testimony from an informant, whose identity, motive, veracity and credibility could not be tested by the defence, was nothing short of iniquitous.

In relation to the sum of £20,000 that Simon was 'allegedly' to be paid as courier, I have detailed earlier in this report that such a sum would have been ridiculously excessive, given the going-rate and availability of couriers. It was therefore totally inconsistent that Simon would have been offered £20,000 when there was such a plentiful pool of suitable, and willing, potential couriers on Ibiza who could have been recruited for about £5,000. The principals would have simply been 'throwing away' some £15,000 – a considerable sum.

13.3 *Simon's alleged inconsistent testimony*

The prosecution, and court, clearly attached considerable significance to the fact that Simon had subsequently changed his story during the various police interviews. To the prosecution, and the court, these apparent lies were evidence of Simon's guilt.

However, as I told the court, in my experience such behaviour was not necessarily proof of guilt. In situations where their relatives or friends appear to them to be involved, it is not uncommon for innocent suspects, and witnesses, to lie, or be evasive – in an (often mistaken) attempt to protect those near and dear to them – when questioned by the police. Given the circumstances, it was therefore not necessarily evidence of guilt that Simon should initially have sought (mistakenly) to protect his brother.

13.4 *Simon's alleged counter-surveillance driving*

The prosecution, and Appeal court, also attached considerable importance, and concluded guilt, to the manner in which Simon allegedly drove, during the physical surveillance operation conducted by the Swedish police. Although I, myself, have been trained to the highest standards in the techniques of physical surveillance, I am not familiar with the detail of the police evidence on this point, and therefore I am unable to offer a professional opinion. However, I understand that the defence provided other expert rebuttal evidence. In addition, although the police evidence was available at the Trial stage, for some reason the prosecutor did not call it, and it was first heard at the Appeal.

What I can say is that it can be extremely difficult, especially for the less experienced, to differentiate between suspect behaviour caused by the target knowing, or suspecting, that he is under surveillance, and equally apparent suspect behaviour caused, in fact, by innocent factors unknown to those conducting the surveillance. Many a surveillance operation has resulted in a premature 'bust' or has been abandoned, for the latter reason.

It is also important to detail Mitchell's testimony on this matter. Mitchell was the passenger in the car driving in front of Simon, leading the way. The Judgement records that Mitchell told the Appeal Court that:

'Judging from Simon Hayward's driving behaviour, Mitchell was convinced that Simon understood that they were being followed.'

However, during the interview with *The Sunday Times* on 18 September 1987, shortly before the Appeal hearing, Mitchell stated:

'. . . I mean those guys were good (the Swedish police). I'm a pro and I had no idea that they were tailing me. They were following me around Stockholm for a week before I was arrested. I spend my life checking for things like that and I had no idea'.

and later, on being asked what it was like when he was arrested:

> 'I was really calm, I mean I knew they were coming for us, there were just too many cars on the road. We were travelling along this narrow country lane late at night and there were just too many cars on the road. You can just tell. I said to the guy that was driving that we were being followed, but he didn't believe me.
>
> We slowed down to let them pass and they came alongside and swerved in front of us . . .'

This would appear to be in total contradiction to Mitchell's testimony at the Appeal hearing. In the interview with *The Sunday Times*, Mitchell made no reference whatsoever to Simon having driven in a manner that convinced Mitchell that Simon believed that they were being followed.

Mitchell made it quite clear that, although even his driver did not believe that they were being followed, Mitchell suspected that to be the case, purely because of the number of cars on the road at that time of night, and nothing to do with Simon's driving behaviour.

14. CONCLUSIONS

Given the known facts in this case, and my considrable experience and knowledge of drug-smuggling operations, it is my professional opinion that the prosecution failed to prove its case, and that there existed considerable, genuine, doubt that Simon Hayward was knowingly involved.

In my opinion, much of the prosecution's 'evidence' was based more on 'theories' than on relevant facts, and was established by the defence to be either inaccurate, unreliable, and would not have been deemed admissable by an English court.

As such, it is my opinion that Simon Hayward should have been acquitted by the Appeal Court, and I consider that that would have been the outcome had he been tried before an English court.